AF182951

From Economic Dependency and Stagnation to Democratic Developmental State

From Economic Dependency and Stagnation
- to -
Democratic Developmental State

Essays on the Socio-Political and Economic Perspectives of Ethiopia

Asayehgn Desta

THE RED SEA PRESS
TRENTON | LONDON | NEW DELHI | CAPE TOWN | NAIROBI | ADDIS ABABA | ASMARA | IBADAN

THE RED SEA PRESS
541 West Ingham Avenue | Suite B
Trenton, New Jersey 08638

Copyright © 2014 Asayehgn Desta
First Printing 2014

All rights reserved. No part of this publication may be reproduced, stored in a retrieval system or transmitted in any form or by any means electronic, mechanical, photocopying, recording or otherwise without the prior written permission of the publisher.

Book and cover design: Saverance Publishing Services

Library of Congress Cataloging-in-Publication Data

Desta Asayehgn, author.

From economic dependency and stagnation to democratic developmental state : essays on the socio-political and economic perspectives of Ethiopia / Asayehgn Desta.

pages cm

Includes bibliographical references and index.

ISBN 978-1-56902-396-9 (hard cover) -- ISBN 978-1-56902-397-6 (pbk.) 1. Ethiopia--Economic conditions. 2. Ethiopia--Social conditions. 3. Ethiopia--Politics and government. 4. Ethiopia--Foreign economic relations. I. Title.

HC845.D47 2014

330.963--dc23

2013044936

This book is dedicated to the memory of my:

friends and classmates, **Sebhatu Wubneh** and **Giday Gebrewahed**, who gaveup their young life to further radicalize the Ethiopian Student Movement todesign effective strategies to dismantle the oppressive regimes in Ethiopia;

insightful brother, **Yemane Asayehgn**, who was butchered by the fascist Derge for not following its hollow promises and for being suspected as an underground agent of the Tigrai People's Liberation Front that eventually liberated the Ethiopian masses from the Derge's tyrannical rule;

nationalistic sister-in-law, **Saba Berhe**, who disappeared in 1998 from the streets of Asmara, Eritrea. Dear Saba, as you face this hard time, please know that your family members and all your friends are praying day and night for your safety;

and Alumus, **Ato Bekele Berhane**, a man of great dignity, touched the lives of so many graduates of the Queen Sheba School. While he was the Chair of the Queen Sheba Alumni Association, Ato Bekele Berhane worked day and night to establish alumni associations in various parts of Ethiopia and in the United States. He raised a substantial amount of money to overhaul the torn and ramshackle class rooms at the Queen Sheba School.

Table of Contents

List of Appendices

List of Tables

Acknowledgments

I would like to thank several friends and colleagues who provided helpful comments on drafts of this book. This book represents the culmination of nearly 40 years of directed thinking and practical experience. The seeds of my ideas for the four chapters of book came from my professors Martin Carnoy and Henry Levin, Stanford University of California. While I was a graduate student at Stanford University, they constantly challenged and offered me thought-provoking, stimulating and challenging feedback when I was developing the theoretical framework for the first four chapters of this book. Their ideas have become so entangled with mine that it is no longer possible to sort out ownership. Also, I would like to thank the eminent researchers at the International Institute for Educational Planning (UNESCO), who have recognized promise in an early draft of the book and unanimously endorsed it to be published by the **International Institute of Educational Planning** as a working paper entitled "Socio-economic and Educational Change in Ethiopia (1900-1974): Correspondence and Contradiction" (see IIEP/Prg/Bs/79.56, 12 February 1979).

In addition, chapters 5 to 14 of this book would have not been possible without the feedback I got from the anonymous reviewers of the articles that were presented in a number of conferences. Thus, I would like to acknowledge that I have benefitted greatly from the insightful comments of the various seminar participants. Most of the articles I wrote have appeared previously in different journals. Therefore, I would like to take this opportunity to express my appreciation and gratefully acknowledge to the publishers for granting me permissions to reprint the following articles originally authored by me. The reprinted articles include:

- the second part of chapter five entitled "Reversing Ethiopia's Intellectual Capital Flight", which originally appeared in the **Journal of International Management Studies**, Vol. 11, No. 1, 2011, pp. 11-20;

- the first portion of Chapter 6 entitled "Economic Growth and Income Convergence in Ethiopia: A critique," originally appeared in the **International Journal of Business and Social Sciences.** Vol. 2, No. 2. February 2011. The second section "The emergence of a Dual-System of Primary Schooling in Ethiopia and its Impact" originally appeared in the **International Journal of Academic Research in Business and Social Sciences (IJARBSS***),* Vol. 2, No.10, October 2012;
- Chapter 7, "Microcredit for Poverty Alleviation and Fostering Environmentally sustainable Development: A review of African Case Studies," originally appeared in the **International Journal of Business Research (IJBR),** Vol. 10, No. 2, 2010, pp. 1-26;
- As part of Chapter 8, "kaizen management techniques to manufacturing plants in Ethiopia" appeared originally in the **Asian Journal of Business and Management Sciences,** Vol.1, No. 6 (09-19), 2011;
- Chapter 9, was originally published as "China's South - South Cooperative Investments and co-development Modalities in Africa" in the **International Journal of Business Research (IJBR),** Vol. 9, No. 6, 2009;
- Chapter 10, originally appeared as "Chinese Investment in Ethiopia: Developmental Opportunity or Deepening China's New Mercantilism? in the **Journal of Academy of Business Strategy (IJBS),** Vol. 9, No. 6, 2009;
- Chapter 11, originally appeared as "Economic Growth for Inflation: The Ethiopian Dilemma" in the **International Journal of Global Business and Economics (IJGBE),** Vol. 2, No. 1, 2009;
- Chapter 12, originally was published as "The Viability of Malaysian Development State for Africa in an Area Economic Globalization," in the **International Journal of Business and Behavioral Sciences (IJBBS),** Vol. 2, No. 12, December 2012;
- Chapter 13, originally appeared as "The Continuing Saga of Globalism: Comparing Ethiopia's Development State Strategies to those of Malaysia." in the **International Journal of Management Sciences and Business."** Vol. 1, 1-Issue 11, 2013.
- A section of Chapter 14, "The Attributes of Rent-Seeking Behavior" was originally published in "The Effects of Rent-seeking in Dissipating Developmental Efforts: The Ethiopian Experience" in the **International Journal of Business and Management Tomorrow.** Vol. 2, No.1, January 2012.

I would like to thank Dr. Dan Moshavi, the ex-Dean of the School of Business and Leadership, Dominican University of California, for the financial support that he rendered me to present my papers at a number of conferences and seminars. Special thanks go to Ms. Katherine Erickson and Jason Frazier for proof reading, editing, and indexing the manuscript. In particular, Kassahun Checole, Publisher of the Africa World Press Inc. provided insights concerning the structure and organization of the book were exceptional. I am indebted to Damola Ifaturoti, Senior Editor and Editorial Coordinator of the Africa World Press, and the Red Sea Press for his comments and suggestions. A minute never goes by without thanking my wife, Elsa Berhe, my daughter, Elda, and my son Adeda Desta for their cheerful support and for being the driving force in motivating me to write this book. In particular, Dr. Tesfay Teklu, Yetbarek Desta, and Getachew Belay need very special thanks because without their invaluable comments and feedback, I would have not been able to convert my previously published articles into this book.

Desta, Asayehgn, Ph.D.
Sarlo Distinguished Professor of Sustainable Economic Development
Dominican University of California

Introduction

The idea to write this book arose in 1977, when I was working at the International Institute of Educational Planning, the United Nations Scientific and Cultural Organization (UNESCO). Based on the theoretical framework, "Correspondence and Contradiction", developed by two of my professors at Stanford University, Martin Carnoy, and Henry Levin, I documented a historical account of the nature of the socio-economic formation and the dependent and subordinate relations of Ethiopia to the hegemony of the United States up to the early part of the 1970s. Further, attempts were made to examine dialectically how some unintended schooling outcomes contradict the stagnant economic situation in Ethiopia. That is, in order to analyze the development of modern education in Ethiopia, an analytical framework based on the principles of correspondence and contradiction was adopted.

Briefly stated, the principles of correspondence refer to how the means of production determine the conditions and practices in the superstructure and how the superstructure in return reacts back on the economic base, creating unexpected antagonism between the two (See Carnoy, 1974; Carnoy and Levin, 1976; Carter, 1976; Bowles and Gintis, 1976; Lange, 1962). Stated in simple words, the means of production include: a) productive forces such as technology, skills, materials resources, and source of power (water power, electricity, and the like) and b) the productive relations, that is, the relationship between people engaged in producing material goods. The relations refer to the relationship between the owner of capital and wage earners or, in a feudal mode of production, the relationship between landlords and serfs or tenants. In short, the principles of correspondence are based on the assumption that the superstructure adjusts itself to the needs of the economic base. When the economic base changes, factors within the superstructure change to adopt with the requirements of the new economic base (See Lange, 1962).

However, even though there might be a relative conformity between the economic base and the superstructure, and institutions located at the superstructure can facilitate the tasks initiated from the economic base, it would lead to a mechanistic formulation to totally assume that it is the economic base which determines whatever happens at the superstructure. In fact, it could be argued that the superstructure can act independently and can have its own autonomy and at times contradict the economic base. For instance in Ethiopia, as it would be shown later, the Orthodox Church and Quranic Schools functioned side by side with the Western-oriented schools, even though their teachings were dysfunctional to the internally generated and imported economic forces. Even in centralized school system, it is very difficult and challenging to make teachers and learners strictly adhere to the message given by the new mode of production. For example in China, before the Cultural Revolution was launched to purge the institutions whose practices were in conflict with the socialist mode of production, higher institutions kept on producing experts and taught elite values which were not consonant with the predominant mode of production (Grossman, 1975).

To safeguard ourselves from over-determinism and from a mechanistic outlook, especially when analyzing a transitional society such as Ethiopia, we will include remnants of the superstructures of former social formations in addition to looking at changes in the educational system which correspond to changes in the socioeconomic structure. In short, to analyze the development of modern schooling in Ethiopia, the analytical framework used in Chapter 4 is based on the principles of correspondence and contradictions. By applying the principle of correspondence, we will try to examine changes in the educational systems which correspond to the changes in the socio-economic systems. On the other hand, applying the perspectives of the principle of contradictions, using the socio-economic changes pinpointed in Chapter 1 and 3, Chapter 4 examines how the Ethiopian educational system, albeit unintended, brought about both latent and manifest contradiction in the socio-economic structure.

Chapter 1 surveys the political and socio-economic structure of Ethiopia. During the period 1900-1935, Ethiopia went through the: a) establishment of politico-economic hegemony over autonomous nationalities whose socio-economic organizations were diametrically opposed to the Shoan military feudal colonists; b) expropriation and alienation of land from the masses and the formation of absentee landlords in the incorporated areas; and c) dislocation of the evicted tenants into the incipient urban areas and the predominantly foreign-owned agricultural estates. Though the Ethiopian empire expanded to encompass various nationalities, the existing feudal mode of production was not in consonance with the surrounding colonial capitalist mode of production and thus could not generate and facilitate a viable "modern" state as envisaged by Menelik II. At this time the neighboring colonial powers, Great Britain, France and Italy, were attempting to out maneuver each other to gain a foothold in

Ethiopia. To withstand this external threat and to safeguard Ethiopia's independence, Menelik II, on his own initiative, invited and employed agents of foreign capitalists in several key posts. Once the agents of the European capitalist countries got the ear of Emperor Menelik II, they used their influence to control the state apparatus, thereby controlling the economy and exposing Ethiopia to markets in the metropolis. Indeed, Menelik II encouraged the agents of the metropolitan countries to have a free hand in investment in the country. He granted concessions to the European capitalists and their agents from India, Syria, Yemen, Greece, etc. The surplus he got from the export of coffee, skins and hides, etc., was not accumulated in the country, but went to the metropolitan counties in order to buy fire-arms and luxury items for the ruling class.

Chapter 2 reviews the nature of Ethiopia's occupation period, 1935-1941. It was documented to show that Italy's annexation of Ethiopia in 1935 was primarily motivated by the lust for raw materials and the creation of markets for Italian manufactured goods. Concomitant with Italy's "divide and rule," it is shown in chapter 4 that separate schools were created for the different ethnic groups of Ethiopia. The fascist educational system was specifically designed, by and large, with two main purposes, a) to train young Ethiopians in basic technical skills in order to supply the demand for cheap labor and b) to inculcate in them a sense of loyalty to the fascist regime through political indoctrination.

After the restoration of Ethiopia's independence in 1941, Chapter 3 assesses the conditioning of Ethiopia to dependence and economic stagnation from 1941 to 1974. It is shown that after independence from Italy, Ethiopia was dominated by a) the appointment of foreigners as advisors in key government posts; and b) the influx of foreign capital and the gradual insertion of the economy into the capitalist economic order. Initially, the politico-economic sphere of Ethiopia was dominated by the British. However, after the decline of British imperialism around 1952, through the economic and military assistance, investments and the establishment of U.S, military bases, Ethiopia was made a satellite state and integrated into the sphere of U.S. imperialism. That is, the Ethiopian economy was restructured to mirror U.S. interest and to fulfill the international division of labor.

Chapter 4 assesses the development of human capital and economic development in Ethiopia. Based on the survey of Ethiopian educational development, it was shown that Ethiopian schooling was geared to mirror the existing class structure and foreign domination of the exchange economy. Side by side with the indigenous schools, western-oriented schools were set up, to serve opposing social classes. The urban laborers and rural landless peasants (serfs) on the one hand, and the emerging middle class and the ruling class, on the other hand. In order to develop local cadres who could facilitate a harmonious relationship between the metropolitan and the Ethiopian masses, the school curriculum stressed mastery of foreign languages to perpetuate social differentiation. Though the education system in Ethiopia was developed in line with the development and through the advice of the American experts and nationals trained in the United States and Western Europe, it demonstrates that the numerous educational initiatives introduced to Ethiopia by the U.S. experts were largely ineffective in either providing equal educational opportunity for the school age children or in creating productive employment opportunities for graduates.

Thus from 1941 to 1974, the economic dependence and the heavy reliance on foreign loans of Ethiopia contributed to two antagonistic forces. On the one hand, they contributed to Ethiopia's under development due to draughts, famine, wars and escalating oil prices. On the other hand, though modest, there was an over-supply of credentialed students relative to the requirements of the existing job structure, thus resulting in a contradiction between the sluggish performance of the economy and the output of schools. In contradistinction to the oversimplified, dogmatic, and mechanistic view that the educational institutions fulfill a conservative role and serve in the reproduction of the existing social relations and production, Chapter 4 further demonstrates that starting in 1965, there was a breakdown of correspondence between the economic base and the educational institutions located in the superstructure. Though unintended, schools in Ethiopia produced politically conscious and highly militant students. By reaching back on the socio-economic structures, the output of schooling contributed to dismantling of the corrupt and decaying system of the old.

Chapter 5 recounts the 1974 to 1991 period of economic crises during the socialist military rule in Ethiopia (Derge). The first part of the chapter reviews the myth of Ethiopia's Military Socialism instituted by the Derge to restructure the existing outmoded socio-economic order. The internal and external economic conditions of Ethiopia during this time clearly indicate that the country regressed as the 'bread basket' of the Middle East. It did not grow enough food to feed its own people. With the decline in per capita income, food consumption declined rapidly. While the economy was in shambles, preoccupied with its own existence, the Derge heavily borrowed funds from Western private lending institutions and multilateral organizations in order to buy armaments. By 1989, Ethiopia's external debt amounted to 51 percent of its Gross National Product (GNP). Based on the amount of external debt which Ethiopia accumulated during the Derge period, if Ethiopia was not a sovereign nation, it would have been forced to declare bankruptcy. Stated differently, during the Derge period, Ethiopia was mortgaged to foreign creditors because by 1989 Ethiopia's external debt amounted to 51 percent of its GNP.

During the Derge regime's era of Red Terror, a number of Ethiopian intellectuals were either assassinated or were forced to leave the country. Thus the second part of chapter 5 proposes how the current regime in Ethiopia could attempt to reversing the Ethiopian intellectuals who predominantly left the country during the Derge period. Therefore, the cycles and economic crises which beset the Ethiopian economy under the Derge regime could be partly attributed to the exodus of intellectuals that occurred during the Derge period. Therefore, using the New Growth Theory, the second part of Chapter 5 proposes that the current Ethiopian Government must establish a well-developed infrastructure base and have a reserve of highly talented human capital in order to grow in global knowledge. In addition, it is suggested that to innovate effectively, Ethiopia needs to form links with well-known global universities, international consultants, and other friendly overseas organizations. If these types of friendly environmental factors are integrated systematically and harmoniously with pertinent human policies, there is no doubt that Ethiopia can entice the Ethiopian Diaspora to return to their motherland. The ability to harness the intellectual capital of the returnees with their contacts from the outside world would bring about very competitive ventures. Ethiopia therefore would achieve its Medium Growth and Transformation Plan but also, in the long run, endure sustainable development.

As discussed in Chapter 5, when Ethiopia was ruled by a military regime from 1974-1991, its economic system was conditioned to reflect the socialist mode of production, and the commanding heights of the economy were nationalized, run by the state apparatus and managed by a military cliques. However, as a result of the Derge's repression using the Red Terror Campaign to liquidate the progressive Ethiopian intellectuals and the failed economic policy that ensued, the military junta was dismantled by the Ethiopian People's Revolutionary Democratic Front (EPRDF) in 1991. To bring about a "renaissance for Ethiopia," the EPRDF initiated a number of developmental plans such the Growth and Transformation Plan (GTP) of 2011-2015. Chapter 6 therefore presents a reflection on Ethiopia's Federalism in an Era of Globalization. In short, it is argued that given that effective federalism is a license to self rule and also an effective structure for shared rule with the assurance of checks and balances, it is suggested that a predictable and transparent democracy needs to be widely entertained at the local level. Given that Ethiopia can effectively implement at the local level a working democracy that empowers local citizens, the first part of Chapter 6 questions the relevance of Article 39 of the Ethiopian Constitution.

The first portion of Chapter 6 seriously questions the effects of ethnic federalism on economic growth and income distribution. Over the last twenty years, Ethiopia has gone through various structural changes which included reforms in land redistribution, investment in quantitative educational programs, limited privatization schemes, some types of outward-oriented economic reform, reforms in the composition and compensation of the labor market, etc. The reforms in many sectors have changed the allocation of resources and payment structure which affected income distribution in Ethiopia. However, the economic literature does not seem to support Ethiopia's Gini coefficient of 0.29, which is far below the Gini coefficient of newly industrialized countries.

The second portion outlines the emergence of a dual-system of primary schooling in Ethiopia and assesses its impact. It is argued that over the last twenty years, in quantitative terms, Ethiopia has expanded and universalized the enrollment of school aged children. In addition, in Ethiopian primary schools, in line the International Covenant of Economic, Social, and Cultural rights, the Government has wished to minimize the irregularities that have existed over the years. However, when the existing primary schooling in Ethiopia is visualized in terms of quality and equity, it is sad to observe that privately-run ultra-modern primary schools seem to be mushrooming in Ethiopia in order to serve the sons and daughters of a newly emerging privileged class. On the other hand, the sons and daughters of the poor and disadvantaged are confined to over crowded classes manned by semi-qualified teachers and equipped with inadequate teaching materials. Stated differently, it is unbelievable to observe that primary schools in Federal Ethiopia are sliding into a class-based education. Thus, it is suggested that if the government believes in equity and fairness, it needs to completely redesign and better equip the public primary schools.

With the hastening of the global poverty crisis and the absence of an adequate social safety net for those marginalized, vulnerable sections of society in the less developed countries, a number of researchers have moved beyond the relentless pursuit of short-term anti-poverty toward long-term, environmentally sustainable paradigms to assist chronically poor sectors of society. It is also assumed that the disadvantaged groups will become productive members of society if they involve themselves in small businesses that may contribute to powerful changes within their lives. However, Chapter 7, "Microcredit for Poverty Alleviation and Fostering Environmentally Sustainable Development: A Review of African Case Studies," depicts that the existing literature, which has burgeoned over the past decades, indicates that it would be an over exaggeration to claim that microcredit programs have significantly helped to lift the poor out of poverty. The existing microcredit programs seem to be focusing on borrowers living above the poverty line rather than on the hard core poor. Given this, microcredit policies may not be effective in achieving sustainable development unless the projects in the developing countries: 1) systematically address the cause of poverty 2) identify the poverty segments of the population 3) pay special attention to raising the awareness of the chronically poor, and 4) train the participants to specialize in particular skills so that they could compete with other self-employed workers in entry-level types of ventures.

Fully convinced that the Japanese kaizen management model would be an effective strategy for latecomers like Ethiopia to industrialization and realizing that the contribution of the manufacturing sector to GDP is only about 5%, employees of thirty pilot companies from Ethiopia were sent to Japan. Chapter 8 therefore reviews the literature and develops a conceptual framework for assessing the transferability of the Japanese "kaizen" management techniques to manufacturing plants in Ethiopia.

Contrary to Western debt and assistance marked by various forms of economic and political overtones, China, using the South-South Cooperation, is in the process of bestowing a mix of loans with generous terms, debt forgiveness, infrastructure development, and other assistance to African nations so that they could be relieved from Western cultural, political, and economic hegemony. African governments have appreciated and responded enthusiastically to this new source of bottom-up, multiple, bilateral investment, trade, and aid because China has professed a willingness to ignore the political, conditional terms that characterize Western assistance. Based the review of the literature, Chapter 9 reviews the socio-economic impacts of some of the Chinese cooperative investment in Africa which are summarized using the following dimensions: a) local employment, b) human management skills (control of decision making process), c) technological transfer, d) local content requirements, e) efficiency, and f) the terms of trade. Though the findings of the chapter are anecdotally focused, the modest contributions upon which we hope other researchers will build is that longitudinal studies need to be undertaken to determine if Chinese investments in Africa are politically motivated or are meant to fulfill the agenda of the South-South Cooperative goals. Nonetheless, being engaged in constructive exchange, Chapter 9 suggests that African policy makers need to redefine Chinese investments to undertake their environmental guidelines so that Africa could use them as a means to achieve self-sufficiency and sustainable development in the long-run.

China's deepening involvement across Africa can be viewed from two perspectives. The protagonists of political warfare theory argue that China's policy in Africa is a nonviolent instrument of grand strategy. It involves coordinated activities that could precipitate intangible effects on intended targets such as economic aid and development assistance, as well as training, equipping, and arming military and security forces to achieve political and economic influence. The South-South development cooperation school of thought, on the other hand, views China's increased aid, trade, and investment in Africa as a means to foster Africa's self-sufficiency and sustainable development in the 21st century. Chapter 10 attempts to advance the understanding and rationalization of the various Chinese investments in Ethiopia. The four case studies given in Chapter 10 seriously challenge the argument of political warfare theorists that

China's investment in Ethiopia would perpetuate underdevelopment through exploitation, extraction, and destruction of Ethiopia's resources and industrial capacity. Except for the negative environmental externalities caused by the Sino-Ethiopian investments, the case studies seem to demonstrate that Ethiopia has substantially benefited from the Chinese cooperative investments. The Chinese investments in Ethiopia are not complementary but appear to be aligned very closely with the South-South cooperative strategies and goals.

In Chapter 11, it is argued that moderate inflation is an inevitable consequence of sustained economic growth. Moderate inflation can enhance economic growth by mobilizing the resources of a country. For the last eight years, Ethiopia has recorded sustained economic growth. However, inflation in Ethiopia is beyond the break-even point. Instead of stimulating economic growth, inflationary pressure in Ethiopia seems to be on the verge of distorting the allocation of resources and is likely to be a deterrent to undertaking productive investments. Based on the multiple regression analysis results, it has become quite clear that the main determinants of inflation in Ethiopia are imports, mainly oil prices, depreciation of the Ethiopian currency, the *birr*, and a decline in the domestic lending interest rates or an increase in broad money supply. Thus, the lesson to be ascertained from the analysis given in Chapter 11 is that to jump out of the inflationary trap successfully, the Ethiopian monetary authorities need to tighten the stock of money in the country. A tight monetary policy could serve as an anchor for inflationary pressure in Ethiopia. Thus, it is absolutely vital that economic policymakers design strategies for Ethiopia that could curtail the on-going erosion of purchasing power—to curb inflation before it deepens the economic crisis and contributes to political instability.

Despite the implementation of several economic development blueprints in Africa for the last 60 years, the poverty rate of Sub Saharan Africa (SSA) has increased from two hundred million in 1981 to almost three hundred eighty million in 2005. Entrepreneurial creativity and ingenuity were stifled and a number of African states became unstable when ruled by despotic rulers. To revitalize Africa's development process in the 21st century, the Economic Commission for Africa (ECA) has challenged the African states to refute the intolerable conditions required by the Neo-liberal policies of the Washington Consensus to borrow capital from the International Monetary Fund, which over the years has submerged African countries into a deep chasm of economic crises. Instead, the Economic Commission for Africa has encouraged the African countries to emulate the Malaysia developmental state (i.e., also referred to the Post-Washington Consensus that advocates greater roles for the government sector with embedded private sector to stimulate the economy) and along with addressing and practicing democracy and good governance. Therefore Chapter 12 maps out briefly the various economic development blue prints that have been attempted in Africa since its political independence in the late 1950s. The second part of the chapter explores the trajectory of the Malaysian Developmental state model.

Based on the conceptual framework forwarded by the Economic Commission for Africa, Chapter 13 states that Ethiopia's developmental state is unique and is operating differently from the Malaysian developmental state model. Economically, Malaysia has recorded staggering economic growth since it has adopted the developmental state. From 2005-2011, Malaysia's GDP grew at 5.23 percent. As targeted by the Malaysian Developmental target, the incidence of poverty in Malaysia declined from 49% in 1970 to less than 5% in 2000. On the other hand, without speeding the direction of industrialization and mainly being plan-oriented rather than being a full market-oriented state, Ethiopia achieved an average of 9.9 percent growth rate in its GDP from 2005 to 2011. With the recorded economic growth, the poverty reduction measured by poverty head count in Ethiopia has declined from 41.9 in 2005 to 29.6 percent in 2011. However, even though Ethiopia's Human Development Index (HDI) has increased by 16% from 2005 to 2011, it HDI score is about 22% less than the average score of the sub-Saharan countries. The poverty ratio of people living below $1.25 a day in Ethiopia is very close to about 30 percent. The bureaucratic elites in Ethiopia who designed and managed the short and long term plans are not politically neutral and do not get the necessary feedback from the public. Based on this, it is suggested that if Ethiopia desires to use the state as a very important vehicle to tackle the deep-rooted developmental problems, it needs to create constant improvement in its public administration sector that could allow the employees of various institutions be politically neutral and professionally competent.

Chapter 14 summarizes the main findings of the book and charts possible environmentally sustainable development for Ethiopia at the grassroots level. That is, the book: 1) proposes food for democracy as an alternative development strategy, and 2) outlines how a democratic development-oriented state could foster full employment at stable prices for rural and urban Ethiopia.

Chapter 1

THE POLITICAL AND SOCIO-ECONOMIC STRUCTURE OF ETHIOPIA FROM 1900 TO 1935

The last half of the nineteenth century was marked by the Scramble for Africa. At the Berlin Congress of 1885, Africa was partitioned by the colonialists. Great Britain acquired more than half of the continent. France captured one-third of Africa. Germany took Tanganyika, Togoland, the Cameroons, and Southwest Africa. Belgium got the Congo. Spain annexed the Spanish Sahara. The Portuguese colonialists acquired "Portuguese" Guinea, Angola and Mozambique. In addition to what it acquired in Somalia and Libya, Italy was formally given Eritrea by Menelik II, who was then the king of Ethiopia, in a treaty signed in Addis Ababa in October, 1896 (Brockway, 1963, p. 7). During the same period Ethiopia underwent a different socio-economic process. The Italians were defeated by Ethiopian forces at the Battle of Adwa. The Ethiopian empire expanded southward and the Ethiopian economy was inserted into the capitalist economic system.

Emperor Menelik II expanded his empire to the southwest, south, and south-east. In 1875 he annexed part of Gurage. In 1881 Jimma, Limmu, Gera, and Gura became tributary states. In 1886 Wollega and Arsi (Arusi) were captured. In 1887, Harar and Illubabor were annexed. In 1889 the rest of Gurage, Konta and Kulo were taken over. In 1891 Ogaden, Bali, and Sidamo were captured. In 1889, Kambata was subdued. In 1894, Gofa and Walamo were captured. In 1897, Konso and the heart of Oromo land, Borona, were taken over (Pankhurst, 1968; Addis 1975). In all, in a little over twenty years, Menelik II increased the territory of his empire by approximately two-thirds.

In general, the new territories in the south, southeast, and southwest received from the conqueror (from to use Addis's term, the Amhara "military-feudal colonialists") the treatment accorded to the vanquished. The natives expropriated from their lands and were forced to work for the "strangers." The alienated land was distributed among the Shoan feudal empire builders and their followers, the Orthodox church, the royal family, and the indigenous chiefs who proclaimed their loyalty to Menelik's government. Moreover, the Amhara feudal empire builders and some of the indigenous elites were appointed as governors of the newly acquired territories. The Amhara military conquest and its accomplishments are discussed by Markakis *(1974, p. 106)* as follows:

> Most of the conquered provinces were "given" to victorious generals or other nobles of Menelik's entourage to rule. The governors subdivided their domain among their principal lieutenants, who in turn assigned portions of the territory under their control to officers in their command, until a complete hierarchy was established. Some areas were treated as the personal fiefs of powerful nobles who enjoyed absolute authority within their jurisdiction. Other areas were assigned to imperial madbet (kitchen) were administered by lower officials appointed by the emperor. Still others were granted to members of the imperial family of high nobility, who exercised absentee governorship from Addis Ababa through their deputies. And some remained under the rule of their traditional rulers, as in Wollega, Jimma, Aussa, Ogaden and briefly in Walamo.

Though the Ethiopian empire expanded to encompass various nationalities, the existing feudal mode of production was not in consonance with the surrounding colonial capitalist mode of production and thus could not generate and facilitate a viable "modern" state as envisaged by Menelik II. At this time the neighboring colonial powers, Great Britain, France, and Italy, were attempting to out maneuver each other to gain a foothold in Ethiopia. To withstand this external threat and to safeguard Ethiopia's independence, Menelik II, on his own initiative, invited and employed agents of foreign capitalists in several key posts. For instance, Alfred Ilg, a Swiss technician, was appointed as the Emperor's key adviser for foreign affairs. In 1897 he was promoted to rank of Chancellor of State. Among his duties were interviewing foreign representatives and conducting diplomatic correspondence on Menelik's behalf. Mac Gillivary, the British governor of the Bank of Abyssinia, an affiliate of the Bank of Egypt, was consulted on foreign trade; however, the Emperor's chief commercial adviser was a Frenchman—Michel Chefneux, the director of Posts, Telephone and Telegraph, was the Emperor's chief adviser for communications. With other Italian engineers he supervised the telephone line between Addis Ababa and Djibouti.

A German agronomist was also appointed as the Emperor's adviser for forestry. Last but not least, some French and German military experts advised Menelik II in military affairs (Pankhurst, 1965/66 and 1968).

Once the agents of the European capitalist countries got the ear of the Emperor, they used their influence to control the state apparatus, thereby controlling the economy and exposing Ethiopia to markets in the metropolis. Indeed, Menelik II encouraged the agents of the metropolitan countries to have a free hand in investment in the country. He granted concessions to the European capitalist and their agents from India, Syria, Yemen, Greece, etc. The surplus he got from the export of coffee, skins and hides, etc., was not accumulated in the country, but went to the metropolitan counties in order to buy fire-arms and luxury items for the ruling class.

As early as 1898, Ilg, was sent to Europe to investigate the possibilities of importing mint to Ethiopia. Ilg and his company were also involved in the importation of fire-arms, and in 1899 he was granted mining rights to Wollega (Pankhurst, 1965/66). In 1894 the country's national currency and postage stamps were ordered from France. As stated by Pankhurst (1965/66, p. 10), "Chefneux ...is said to have been the first person to have put forward the plan of producing postage stamps and was instrumental in arranging for their printing in France, as well as for the striking in France of Ethiopia's first currency which appeared in 1894." To expose Ethiopia to the outside world, France was granted a ninety-nine year contract to construct a railway line from Addis Ababa to the French post of Djibouti. Edouard Camboul, a French engineer, also received a concession for minerals. Among other things he identified the existence of gold and coal in the country. The French activities were not limited only to administrative tasks and the exploration of minerals; they were also heavily involved in road construction and owned many big restaurants and shops in the capital and other major towns, namely, Dire Dawa and Harar. They were also given large estates where they grew cotton, bananas, papayas, vegetables, coffee, and citrus fruits.

Though not allowed to exploit the country as much as they would have wished, some Italian capitalists also were involved in road construction, café ownership, and mineral exploitation. Two Italian companies were granted concessions for minerals in the northwest and southwest of the country. The Italian government, through its Prime Minister, was involved in fire-arms trafficking. For instance, on January 13, 1888, the Italian Prime Minister, Francesco Crispi, in order to win Menelik's support against Emperor Yohannes IV, dispatched a gift of 1000 Remington rifles to Shoa (Pankhurst, 1965/66, p. 13).

Some British capitalists, directly or indirectly through their agents, were also involved in importing capital, or, in effect "milking the country dry." By establishing a private bank—the Bank of Abyssinia in 1905—they gained control of the finance capital of the country. They appointed their own representatives and exercised a great influence on the financial policies of the country. As discussed by Bondestam *(1975, p. 126)*:

> The material Bank of Egypt obtained a 50-year concession in Ethiopia. Shares of the new bank were offered for public subscription in New York, in major capitals in Europe and in Addis Ababa. No other bank was allowed to establish in Ethiopia; the Bank was the sole issuer of bank notes; all government funds were to be deposited with the Bank; it was given preference in the issue of the loans, etc. Ethiopian representation in the Board of Governors was limited to two persons only, and of more than 7% of the share capital was subscribed by Ethiopians.

Being the major financiers, the British capitalists held large rubber plantations, grew tobacco, received concession for minerals, and built an ammunition factory in Addis Ababa. Pankhurst *(1965/6, p. 37),* illustrates the British capitalist's direct and indirect involvement in the exploitation of Ethiopia's resources as follows

> The right to exploit the country's rubber resources was entrusted to a British company, the Ethiopian Rain Proof Monopoly Company in 1905 founded by the Syrian merchant, Yedlbi. An even more important monopoly, the Tobacco monopoly, Ragie Co,--interesse des Tobacco del' Empire Ethiopia, was given in 1905 to a Lesghian, M. Hanefi, a Greek, M. Kekatar, and an Ethiopian nobleman, but it was transferred in 1908 to the Indian merchant, Mohamedally, and in 1909 to the Armenian trader, Matig Kevorkof.

A concession for gold exploitation was also extended to German capitalists. The United States of America through its multinational corporations got involved in importing American cotton goods and exporting coffee and hides and skins from Ethiopia to the United States. American involvement in Ethiopia trade grew rapidly. In 1903, Robert Skinner was commissioned by President Theodore Roosevelt to negotiate a commercial treaty with Menelik II and procure exact information for American exporters and manufacturers. With a group of experts, Skinner toured the country to collect and assess the investment climate in Ethiopia. In 1904 alone, Ethiopia's trade with the United States amounted to 58% of the total of Ethiopian trade (Pankhurst, 1968, p. 407).

Syrians, Lebanese, Afghans, Greeks, Armenians, and Indians were also heavily involved in exploiting all sectors of the Ethiopian economy. Syrian and Lebanese merchants were engaged in import-export activities. The Afghans were mainly retailers. The Greeks were major concession holders, tailors, distillers, and bankers, bar, and café and grocery proprietors. They operated in Addis Ababa, Harar, Dire Dawa, Mekale, Adwa and in the western provinces. The Arabs were engaged as shopkeepers in the capital and in other large and small urban centers. Most of them were representatives of the British companies located in Aden. The Armenians were photographers, upholsters, tailors, saddlers, goldsmiths, and ironmongers. The Indians, who came as brokers of the British firms in Aden and India, infested the virgin market of the country by flooding it with cheap quality Manchester and Indian cotton goods, which undermined the indigenous cottage industries. The Indians established themselves in Addis Ababa, Jimma, Nekemte, Debre Marcos (see Addis, 1975; Pankhurst, 1965/66). Pankhurst *(1965/6, p. 23)* drawing from Michel's writings described how the Indian traders were brought into the country by their British colonialists and what their activities inside Ethiopia were

> The opening up of Anglo-Ethiopian relations in 1897 led to a remarkable influx of Indian traders, the first of who arrived in the capital in December 1899. Operating, Michel Says, on the invitation and with the encouragement of the British envoy Harrington, they flooded the market with cotton cloths of all kinds, spices, perfumes, etc. They found no difficulty in competing against longer established firms. Firstly, they were accustomed to a very low standard of living and were willing to operate on a small profit margin. Secondly, they obtained their supplies from relatively nearby, mainly from Aden or Bombay, and therefore had fairly small transport costs. Thirdly, many of them had some experience of Africa or Middle Eastern trade and an understanding therefore, of the potential demand of the indigenous population. Their lower prices and greater attention to consumer wants were well rewarded for the bulk of the population, Michel says, soon preferred their shops to those of the Frenchmen and other Europeans.

Whatever was brought to the Ethiopian market by the Indian traders was not what the masses wanted. There were enough cottage industries and, in fact, the local products were even cheaper than what the Indian merchants brought. The imported commodities, namely, perfumes and spices, which were not biologically necessary, were made essential because the masses were induced to feel they needed them through market mechanisms and because they were endorsed by the ruling class, who had a stake in the imported goods.

The influx of foreign capitalists and their agents was not curtailed during Haile Selassie's period. Enough evidence in available to show that what was started by Menelik was expanded by Haile Selassie. The interests of metropolitan capitalists were perpetuated. Foreign capital deeply penetrated and maintained control over the major economic sectors of the county. As stated by Pankhurst *(1968:64)*

> At the governmental level the Emperor Haile Selassie developed and extended Menelik's practice of making use of foreign advisers of man nationalities. Probably the most important of his foreign aides were an American financial expert, Everett Colson; a Swiss expert, Maitre Auberson; a Swedish military expert General Virgin; an English anti-slavery adviser Frank de Halpert; a Swedish expert on international affairs, J. Kolmodin; an American educational expert, Ernest Work; the Swedish director of the Bet Sayda hospital, Dr. Kurt Hanner; the British governor of the Bank of Ethiopia, C.S. Collier; and Dr. K. Ewert, and Austrian attached to the Ministry of Commerce and the Bureau of Public Health.

After his visit to European and Middle Eastern countries in 1924, Haile Selassie was convinced that contact with European progress would expedite Ethiopia's progress. Forbes quotes Haile Selassie as saying, "We need European progress because we are surrounded by it ... That is, at once a benefit and a misfortune. It will expedite our development ..." Of course, what Haile Selassie completely forgot was that the European capitalists were not coming to Ethiopia to help her development but to suck its capital and "expedite" its underdevelopment. Like his predecessor Menelik II, Haile Selassie kept on inviting foreign capitalists to the country. As shown in *Appendix 1.1*, the number of foreign capabilities and merchants increased from 205 in 1906 to 1096 in 1910 and increased to 14460 in 1935.

With the increase of foreign capitalist activities in the major sectors of the economy, Ethiopia's dependence on the metropolitan countries became quite obvious. Ethiopia specialized in the production of agricultural products destined for export. Some of the major primary products exported to the metropolitan countries include coffee, hides and skins, wax, ivory and civet. After the close of World War II, however, Ethiopia's export was primarily limited to coffee and hides and skins. Furthermore, these commodities were primarily sold in one market, that is the United States of America.

Similarly, the major imports of the country came from the metro poles located in Europe, the United States and Japan. For instance, Great Britain, British firms located in India, the United States and Japan became the major suppliers of textiles. Wine was imported from France and Italy. Silk was under the monopoly of Germany and France. Pankhurst cites that "French unbleached silk yield a profit of more than 300%." (1968: 383). Woolen materials for the aristocratic class were imported from Great Britain. France had a monopoly of importing ammunitions to Ethiopia.

Trade relations with the metropolitan countries also reveals that Ethiopia's primary goods were sold at a cheap price and the goods processed at the center were sold at an exploitative price. As shown in Appendix 1. 2, import-export via the port of Djibouti had been rising since 1900. However, Ethiopia was faced with a large balance of payments deficit. (An exception to this trend was observed in 1925 where the value of exported commodities was higher than the value of imported goods). In 1930, export earnings declined by 1.62 million Maria Theresa dollars. On the other hand, the value of imported commodities increased by 16.69 million Maria Theresa dollars. In 1935 alone imports were 121% higher than exports.

So far our discussion has focused mainly on how the Ethiopian economy, due to both the Ethiopian ruling class and the capitalist lusting for profit, got integrated into the metropolitan economy. We have also demonstrated how unequal exchange reduced the country to a state of economic dependency. To complete the picture of socio-economic changes in Ethiopia in 1900-1935, the impact of the country's economic dependency on the living standard of the Ethiopian masses is considered essential.

It was mentioned earlier that in the new territories acquired by Menelik II, the predominate means of production, land, was alienated from the masses. The peasantry was reduced to an inferior position. Moreover, classes which cut across ethnicity emerged. A new social stratification based on ownership of land, which already existed in the central and north-western part of the country, was transplanted to the newly acquired territories. The majority of the natives in these areas became tenants on their own land. Some of the indigenous elites (balabatas) were accorded status and power. They enjoyed the wide immunities which wholly or in part exempted them from taxation. As time passed, the indigenous elites and the Shoan empire builders became one. The Christianized and acculturated indigenous elites were accepted into the Shoan Amhara group. Intermarriage between the two groups became quite common. Status symbols of the conquerors were gradually internalized by the vanquished.

At the same time, the economic and personal status of the peasantry was encroached upon in the newly acquired territories. Through the destruction of the existing communal type of organizations and the extension of land-grants to new retainers and the indigenous elites, a compromise of interest was effected. Upon this basis there was gradually built up a centralized state machinery and a standing army raised and equipped with modern light weapons powerful enough to defend the created empire.

For example, in 1907 the country's first cabinet was set-up. In 1922, the Department of Commerce and Public works, which in 1931 became the Ministry of Commerce and Public works, was expanded. In 1931, with practically no change in its function, the Bank of Abyssinia was replaced by the National Bank of Ethiopia. To man the already expanding state machinery and repressive state apparatus about two hundred Ethiopians were sent for study abroad. Infused with the imported capital from France (i.e., the Addis-Ababa – Djibouti railway line) in the hinterland many towns mushroomed. River communications between south-western Ethiopia and the Sudan started. Through the Port of Gambelia, located on the mouth of Baro River, coffee and wax were exported to Sudan. On the other hand, through the same port textiles, Maria Theresa dollars, liquors sacks, salt, soap, wines and spirits, furniture and machinery were imported (Pankhurst, 1968, p. 451).

With the expansion of the state apparatus and the appearance of nascent urban areas as commercial and administrative centers, one might have expected productive employment opportunities for the Ethiopian masses. However, the empire created by Menelik II and maintained by Haile Selassie was not autonomous enough to determine its own affairs and enhance the welfare of its people. Just as the masses were in subordinate positions to the ruling class, the ruling class had little guiding functions; rather, it was subservient to foreign capitalist and served the interest of the metropolis.

As stated earlier, the Ethiopian government gave concessions for the exploitation of mineral resources. Plantations and major financial capital (banks) were under the control of foreign capitalists. It imported a railroad have access to the outside world. In order to buy ammunition and unproductive consumption items for the aristocracy and to pay the salaries of its functionaries. That is, the army and government bureaucrats started levying taxes in cash where before they had been paid in kind. The monetization of taxes induced further exploitation of peasants who had no ready cash at hand to pay. Instead they had "to sell their cattle to get money and were in consequence forced to cultivate their land without their animals" (Pankhurst, 1968:510). For instance, the peasants around Harar were forced by Dejazmach Balcha to sell their cattle and pay taxes in cash. The peasants of Jimma were also obliged to pay an annual tax of five dollars per head instead of a bar of salt a year which they were accustomed to. When Menelik II needed revenue to finance the Addis Ababa-Djibouti railroad, he ordered his representatives to levy an annual tax of twenty-five dollars per 1000 beasts on the Oromos of Borena. By 1930 all local chiefs, even in remote areas, were to collect taxes in cash rather than in kind (see Pankhurst, 1968 and Addis 1975).

The introduction of a money economy, the establishment of monetary taxed by the central administration, and the existing complicated tenancy arrangements in the country forced an increasing number of peasants to leave their families behind and seek wage labor in the capitalist sector; that is, on plantations, in mines and in the nascent urban centers. A case in point is that many Gurages, Oromos and Derzes, etc., left their families behind and migrated to the urban areas to sell their labor and raise enough cash in order to pay taxes. This constituted proletarization (or perhaps even a process of lumpen-proletarization).

The migration from rural areas to urban areas had three social consequences. Firstly, most of the villages became dependent upon the cash income of some of their members in order to pay their tax obligations to the government. Secondly, the rural areas served the foreign capitalists providing cheap labor, thereby keeping labor and social cost at its minimum and thus making the rural areas complement wage work in the capitalist sector. Last by not least, the specialization of rural and urban areas in specific commodities and services resulted in a division of labor and a cleavage between the two.

In the mines and plantations granted to foreign capitalists, the invaders, and the indigenous elites, transformed the laborers into proletariat. Moreover, the rural peasants were integrated into the capitalist system though the foreign comprador class (i.e., Indians, Syrians, Lebanese, Greeks, etc.). Practically no stone was left unturned.

The situation in the central, north, and north-western part was little different from that in the acquired territories except that here some of the communal mode of production was partially maintained. The land was in the hands of the kinship groups and most of the peasants had their plots of land. However, indigenous industries were undermined by the importation of cheap quality products from the capitalist-owned industries. On the other hand, weavers, blacksmiths, potters, and masons were relegated to separate places as subhumans and were looked down upon. The previous communal mode of production for use value was transformed to exchange value for profit. The traditional market based on bartering was exposed to the money economy. With the introduction of monetary taxes, many Amharas and Tigreans left their villages to work in Italian-owned plantations and factories in Eritrea. Pankhurst quotes Wylde as saying that the Italians in Eritrea "...who were in need of labor, encouraged Ethiopians to cross the frontier...The result was a steady influx of immigrants in the colony" (Wylde as quoted in Pankhurst, 1968, p. 50).

Hence, what we observe in Ethiopia during the period 1900-1935, is partly preservation and partly a transformation of some elements of the pre-capitalist mode of production in the north, center, and north-west, and a complete devastation in the south, south-west and south-east. Whatever was not directly disturbed was indirectly integrated into the capitalist economic system. In general, the socio-economic changes in Ethiopia were characterized by the integration of the country into the capitalist economic system, foreign dominance of the economy, the expansion of the state apparatus, and the mushrooming of urban areas with dislocation of peasants from rural to the nascent urban centers.

Appendix 1.1
An Estimate of the Number of Foreigners Residing in Ethiopia (1906-1935)

Nationality	1906	Number in 1910	1935
Afghansh Baluchis	--	8	N/A
Americans	--	5	103
Arabs	N/A	227	4000
Armenians	449	146	2800
Austrians	--	3	50
Belgians	5	2	28
British	6	14	75
Caucasians	--	6	N/A
Czechs	--	--	50
Chinese	--	--	2
Danes	1	--	--
Dutch	--	--	2
Egyptians	N/A	11	60
French	35	63	350
Germans	12	20	N/A
Greeks	65	334	3140
Indians	--	149	3000
Italians	21	42	350
Japanese	--	--	4
Jews	--	--	125
Portuguese, goons	--	7	-
Russians and other East Europeans	9	20	66
Swedes	7	1	55
Swiss	--	13	30
Syrians and Lebanese	--	10	40
Turks	--	15	20
Totals	205	1096	14460

Source: Compiled from Pankhurst: *Economic History of Ethiopia 1800-1935*

Appendix 1.2

Ethiopia: Exports and Imports through the Port of Djibouti 1900-1935 (in millions of Maria Theresa Dollars)

Year	Exports	Imports	Balance of Trades
1900	--	2.1	
1905	3.37	4.45	-1.18
1916	9.01	14.57	-5.56
1920	11.2	21.36	-10.16
1925	26.57	25.47	1.1
1930	24.95	4216	-17.21
1935	28.5	63.11	-34.61

Source: Compiled from Pankhurst, Richard. *Economic History of Ethiopia 1800-1935*, 1968:430.

Chapter 2

THE NATURE OF THE OCCUPATION PERIOD, 1935-1941

Italy defied the Tripartite Agreement of 1906 signed by Britain, France, and Italy to keep Ethiopian Sovereignty intact. They also violated the Treaty of Perpetual Friendship of 1928 signed by Italy and Ethiopia, which stated they would together "not to take any action that may prejudice or damage the independence of the other" (Schwab, 1972, p. 19). In this way, Fascist Italy annexed Ethiopia on October 3, 1935. Historians have forwarded many explanations for Italy's annexation, among the most important of which are a) Italy's revenge for the annihilation suffered at the Battle of Adwa in 1896 and b) Mussolini's colonial appetite and lust for raw materials.

As mentioned before, in 1896 the Ethiopian soldiers crushed the Italian force at the Battle of Adwa. As stated in this encounter:

> *261 Italian officers, 2918 non-commissioned officers and men, and about 2000 askaris, or native troops were killed; 954 Italian soldiers were permanently missing; 470 Italians and 958 askaris were wounded. Total Italian causalities thus amounted to over 7560, or nearly 43 percent of the original fighting forces (*Pankhurst, 1968, p. 23*).*

The Italians also lost all their cannons (i.e. 58), as well as about 11,000 rifles (Pankhurst, 1968:23). In that same year, the peace treaty of Addis Ababa was signed between Italy and Ethiopia; whereby Italy recognized Ethiopia's independence. As will be shown below, however, the Italian dictator, Benito Mussolini, was bitter about humiliation suffered by Italy; he wanted to prove to the world that Adwa could be avenged. Thus he revived the "Adwa Complex" as a scapegoat in order to mobilize the Italian people. The Wal Wal incident, which occurred in 1934 between a handful of Italian and Ethiopian soldiers inside Ethiopian territory in the Ogaden Region, was also disproportionally exaggerated as reasonable cause for embarking on a policy of conquest in Ethiopia. Though it was not clear who started the clash, the Italian government demanded an apology, a salute to the Italian flag and reparation. The Ethiopian government, on the other hand, applied to the League of Nations to investigate the matter. When the Ethiopian government failed to fulfill the Italian's demands, Mussolini, in this address to the Italian people, announced that "we have been patient with Ethiopia for forty years, now our patience is exhausted." The fascist-controlled press was also ordered to exaggerate the Wal Wal incident "as a deliberate act of aggression on the part of Ethiopia, an act of so grave a nature that it could not be condoned" (see in Del Boca, 1969, p. 19).

Even though Mussolini only proclaimed his intent to annex Ethiopia after the Wal Wal incident, evidence seems to indicate the plan had been formed for a long time. The testimony given by Tulles Pastori, an Italian geologist and owner of a mineral concession in Ethiopia, is a clear indication that Italy had been making internal plans since 1924. As he stated it:

> *I can vouch for the fact that shortly after the Fascist regime had established itself, the Italians in Eritrea began to think of the reconquest of Ethiopia. In 1924, I was approached by Captain Malladra....who asked me if I would undertake a delicate mission. During the course of my annual explorations for minerals, he wished me to make an exhaustive study of the rivers that form the defensive system of the Ethiopian highlands. I was to measure the water level in the dry and rainy seasons, indicate where these rivers could be forded, and so on. I agree to do so and for years sent notebooks crammed with figures to Malladra (pastori as quoted in Del Boca, 1969, p. 16).*

This testimony is revealing in many ways. First of all, it shows that Fascist Italy had been making preparation to conquer Ethiopia for about eleven years. Secondly, the quotation reflects that the foreign capitalists in Ethiopia were not individual adventurers mainly interested in profit making, but were agents of the metropolitan countries.

True, the Wal Wal incident might have reinforced Italy's long range plans of avenging the defeat suffered at Adwa. However, the Wal Wal affair and the "Adwa Complex" cannot by any means be taken as sufficient causes for precipitating the Italo-Ethiopian War of 1935. Other crucial explanatory factors are Italy's economic conditions and the economic gains which Mussolini was expecting to get from the Ethiopian conquest. Thus, in order to have better grasp of the Italian conquest, a brief look into the economic conditions in Italy prior to 1935 is crucial.

As stated in section two of this paper, when compared with the French and British capitalists, the few Italians living in Ethiopia proper did not gain much in controlling the major sectors of the Ethiopian economy. For instance the French-controlled the Addis Ababa-Djibouti railway line and were also involved in mineral exploitation. The British capitalists were the major financiers. They controlled the Bank of Ethiopia and were, directly or indirectly, engaged in major commercial enterprises through their agents (i.e., Indian, Syrian, and Lebanese merchants). With the exception of the two major companies which granted concessions for minerals in northwestern of southwestern part of the country, the Italians were either working as road engineers or were the employees of the Ethiopian government in the French-controlled telephone and postal system.

A clear indication of Italy's ambition to have predominance in the Ethiopian economy can be seen from a statement by Agusto Rosso, Italy's Ambassador to the United States. When asked by Secretary Cordell Hull of the United States "why Italy had not invested $100,000,000 in Ethiopia instead of waging a war which would cost it a great deal more, Rosso retorted that for forty years his country had attempted to carry out a policy of economic development and agricultural settlement in Ethiopia but with no practical result" (Villari, 1956, p. 153).

Internally, when the Fascist government assumed power it promised economic development and devised "comparative principles" for organizing the country's economy, but evidence seems to indicate that the fascist regime did not live up to its promise. The economic situation of Italy during the Fascist era was worse than the pre-Fascist period. The rural and urban proletariat were hard hit. Since the wealthy land owners, the industrialists, and the middle class were among the principal creators and early defenders of the regime, they benefitted from the fascist land-reclamation policy and duties on wheat. The rural proletariat, which amounted to two-thirds of those employed on the land, had been promised better housing and other social services, but their lot did not improve under fascism. There was considerable agricultural unemployment. (see Fines, 1965).

In the urban areas, the Fascist regime's economic policy favored the capitalists. The industrial firms and banks were given greater financial assistance. The working class suffered at the expense of the big industrialists. Unemployment in the urban areas was rampant. For instance, during the period of 1930 to 1934, the total unemployment was understated because "many potential unemployed were sent back from the towns to their families in the country to live miserably there" (Fines, 1965: 531). To silence potential urban unrest, the regime concentrated almost all its energy on stifling internal political power and destroying every vestige of organized opposition. Labor suffered both from unemployment and a decline in real wages. Real wages were 10 to 20 percent less when compared with the pre-Fascist period (see Fines, 1965).

Italy's problem was further complicated because its colonies in Africa, that is, Libya and Italian Somaliland were not naturally endowed with adequate economic resources to solve Italy's internal economic crises and productively accommodate the unemployed Italians. As stated by Del Boca, Libya and the Italian Somaliland "were wretchedly poor colonies and could never have solved the peninsula's critical demographic problems, as Mussolini realized when he visited Tripoli in 1926" (1969, p. 9).

To cope with the demographic and unemployment situations in Italy, Mussolini exaggerated the Wal Wal incident as a deliberate act of aggression on the part of Ethiopia. There is no doubt that his tactic worked. He was able to recruit many of his Italian soldiers from the rural and urban proletariat. Of course they promised a lot. For instance those who wanted to join in this venture were promised they would be paid 45 lire a day which was equivalent to a week's wage in Italy. Members of the Fascist bureaucracy also rushed off to Ethiopia to fatten their pockets. The industrialists at home "gave the campaign their full support, for in wartime prices rocket" (Del Boca, 1969, p. 27).

Intoxicated by Mussolini's demagoguery and fully convinced that they could improve their lot, the Italian soldiers left Italy for Ethiopia singing:

> *Hardworking, warrior people who*
> *follow your leader, Mussolini.*
> *We'll open up the way for you;*
> *you shall have bread for your bambini (children)*
>
> (Del Boca, 1969, p. 5).

On October 3, 1935, the Fascist forces started a two-pronged invasion on Ethiopia. General de Bono launched his attacks from Eritrea. General Rodolfo Graziani advanced from the Italian Somaliland and launched his offensive against the Ethiopian people living in the Harargh, Bali, and Sidamo provinces. With the limited ammunition they had, the Ethiopian troops tried to curtail the advancement of the Italian troops. They fought major decisive battles at Tambien, Maichew, Dessie, Negelli, Kalafo, Gorahai, etc. However, the Ethiopian troops were overpowered by Italy's use of mustard gas and aerial bombs. After the defeat of the Ethiopian forces at Ashenge, Emperor Haile Selassie fled to Djibouti and thence to Palestine and the city of Bath in England, where he was kept by the British authorities in "cold storage for future use" (Villari, 1956, p. 156).

The capture of Addis Ababa on May 5, 1936, culminated in Italy's victory in the war and the Ethiopian forces resorted to tactics of guerrilla warfare tactics. On May 9, Mussolini, in his state address to the Nation, proclaimed that Ethiopia was an Italian colony with King Victor Emmanuel III as emperor.

Interestingly enough, Britain and France, who had a stake in the Ethiopian economy, did not come to the help of Ethiopia. They also did not use the organization of the League of Nations to resist Italy's aggression on a member country. France did not come to the side of Ethiopia because the Italo-Ethiopian war did not directly affect its economic interest in Ethiopia. The Italians left the Addis Ababa—Djibouti railway under the administration of the French authorities, although Italy did take some shares in the railway line. Moreover, after the German rearmament, France's interest in Ethiopia was given secondary importance. She sought to secure Italy's friendship against a potential enemy (i.e., Germany) at the expense of sacrificing Ethiopia to Italy. Britain, like France, did not fully try to implement the League's decision of economic and military sanctions of November 18, 1935, against Italy; nor did it pursue upholding the League's international obligations by force. In fact, from the beginning Britain was tilted in favor of Italy. Her main interest was to secure access to the source of the Blue Nile and to win Italy's friendship in its dispute with Turkey over the ownership of Mosul. Moreover, Britain was very much interested in avoiding an Italo-German agreement on Austria and a possible confrontation with Italy in the Mediterranean Sea. Thus instead of implementing the League's decision of sanctions against Italy, Britain tried to work out a conciliatory settlement. She proposed that territorial concessions from the Ethiopian territories annexed by Menelik II be granted to Italy, in exchange for an Ethiopian outlet to the sea via Port of Asseb in Eritrea. Though the proposal was very favorable to Italy, it was rejected by Mussolini as inadequate. On May 22, 1939, Italy concluded a political and military alliance with Germany. A year later, Italy declared a war on Britain. After Italy's declaration of war, Britain came to the support of the Ethiopian liberation fighters. Before we discuss the role played by the British in the Ethiopian resistance movement, a brief look into the socio-economic consequences of the occupation period is in order.

It was argued before that Italy's annexation of Ethiopia was influenced by economic factors—the desire for raw materials, the settlement of unemployed Italians and the creation of an additional market for Italian manufactured goods. As stated by Hess, "Mussolini had great hopes for developing Ethiopia as a granary for Italy, a source of raw materials and a colony of settlement" (Hess, 1970:68, see also Lipsky, 1962:30). Indeed, during the five years of the occupation period, Italy concentrated on the construction of roads as a base for exploring the natural resources of the new colony. To connect the urban centers with the hinterland, about 5000 kilometers of all weather and dry weather roads were built (for details on public works, see Appendix 2.1). To construct the new roads and other public works, capital and skilled labor were brought from Italy; however, unskilled labor was procured locally through coercion. Against their will, able-bodied natives were recruited from their communities and forced to work in the construction of roads and plantations and in urban-based factories. As stated by Lipsky, "During the Italian occupation the use of forced labor was increased. Although Italy signed the 1930 Convention, thousands of Ethiopian workers were forcibly employed on public work projects and on Italian plantation for nominal remuneration (1962, p. 279). In addition to the 300,000 Italian soldiers and construction workers, 986 professional men, 540 agricultural concessionaires, 4,007 industrialists, and 4,785 business men settled in Ethiopia. According to Del Boca's estimation, the Italian colonialists invested a total of 3 million and 800 million lire (1967, p. 237). Out of these, 180 million lire was invested on the exploration of metallic, nonmetallic, and other materials for construction purposes. (see Appendix 2.2 and Appendix 2.3). During the occupation period alone, the import of capital goods increased by 3000% (Lipsky, 1969, p. 309). The Italian invaders were given the land which belonged to the imperial family, the church, and the liberation fighters. Whenever needed, they took over the richest land for the benefit of the colonists and they propagated all the seeds of racial evil apparent today in apartheid (Del Boca, 1969, p. 229).

Due to the influx of settlers from Italy and the forced native labor migration from rural to urban areas, the population growth in some urban areas was tremendous. From 1938 to 1939 the population in Addis Ababa, Jimma and Gondar grew by 76.7%, 73.7%, and 15% respectively. In 1939 alone there were 38,882, 4,265, 5,282, 3,542, and 2,000 Italian residents in Addis Ababa, Harar, Jimma, Dire Dawa, and Gondar, respectively (see Mesfin, 1966 and Del Boca, 1969).

In the urban areas strict zoning based on racial background was enforced. Italian and native residential areas were separated. The natives were prohibited from attending cinemas, visiting parks, or having access to other European-oriented social amenities. Since the Fascist policy both at home and in the colonies was to preserve the "purity" of the Aryan race, it prohibited marriage between Italians and Ethiopians. To create disharmony among various ethnic groups, and strengthen Italian central ethnic groups, ethnic rivalry and religious animosity was purposely exploited and encouraged. Some groups especially non-Amharas were favored by providing them with high-paying and high status jobs. The newly-converted Catholics and Muslims were favored more than the adherents of the Orthodox faith (see for example, Del Boca, 1969).

Appendix 2.1
Fascist Italy's Expense for Public Works in Ethiopia (1937-1948)

Types of public work	Cost in Lire
1. Main roads and secondary roads	4,258,425,140
2. Telegraph and Telephone plants	48,045,000
3. Streets, Squares and Urban parks	59,507,094
4. Hydraulic works	16,292,288
5. Sanitation works	54,678,656
6. Building works	475,970,000
7. Track roads	71,311,305
Total	**4,984,230,083**

Source: Compiled from Instituto Agricolo Coloniale-Firenze: *Main Features of Italy's Action in Ethiopia 1936-1941*

Appendix 2.2
Public and Private Investments in Metallic, Non-Metallic Minerals and Materials for Construction

Type of investment	Investor	Locality
Metallic Minerals		
Gold	AMAO (East Africa Mining Estate)	Beni & Sciangul
Gold	COMINA (Ethiopian Mining Co)	Western Galls & Sidamo
Gold	PRASSO (Prasso Co)	Jubdo (Wollega)
Gold	SAPIE (Ethiopian Undertakings Co)	Beni Sciangul
Gold	SMIT (Italo-German Mining Co)	Ondonoc (Beni Sciangul)
Platin	PRASSO (Prasso Co)	Jubdo
Iron	Mine Office of Jimma	Dombova
Copper	SAMAOI (Italian East Africa Mining Co)	Chercher
Molibden	SAPIE (Ethiopia Undertakings Co)	Chillu Valley (Wollega)
Non Metallic Minerals		

Petroleum	AGIP (General Italian Petroleum Co)	Dolo & Ogaden
Mica	MICA Company	Carrara & Fiambrio (Harar)
Lignite	Italian Military Engineer Corps	Uccialli (Wollega)
Lignite	SAPIE Ethiopian Undertaking Co	Neggio (Wollega)
Lignite	Mines Office - Gondar	Chelga
Materials for Construction		
Cement	Cement Factories of Ethiopia Co	Dire Dawa
Lime & Brick	Brink Industry Co	All over the country
Marble, Stones & Granite	Private & Public Undertakings	All over the country

Source: Compiled from *Instituto Agricolo Coloniale-Firenze*, 1946.

Appendix 2.3
Public and Private Investments in the Mining Industry in Ethiopia

Investing Organization	Value in million lire
Mine Corps	30
Mines & Kilns	20
Minor Grantees	5
Cement Factories of Ethiopia	20
COMINA (Ethiopian Mining Co)	25
AGIP (General Italian Petroleum Co)	2
PRASSO (Prasso Co)	10
MICA (Mica Co)	3
SMIT (Italo-German Mining Co)	10
SAMAOI (Italian East African Mining Co)	15
AMAO (East African Mining Estate)	10
SAPIE (Ethiopian Undertaking Co)	30
Total	**180**

Source: Compiled from *Instituto Agricolo Coloniale-Firenze*, 1946.

Chapter 3

THE POST-WAR CONDITION OF DEPENDENCE AND ECONOMIC STAGNATION

With the restoration of Haile Selassie to the throne on May 5, 1941, Ethiopia regained its political independence from the fascist colonists. However, it was de facto controlled by the British. This independent country, for all practical purposes, became a British semi-protectorate, and took shelter under the protective shield of British imperialism. British officials were appointed advisers in the government to ensure that Haile Selassie could not counter British interests. Upon the decline of British imperialism after the Second World War, however, British predominance in the Ethiopian politic-economic sphere faded out and was replaced by the United States of America and other capitalist countries. We will now consider these points in detail.

The British Predominance in Ethiopian Politics

As mentioned above, considering themselves as liberators of the country, the British imperialist replaced the Italian colonists as the occupying power. In return for their military assistance during the Ethiopian resistance movement against fascist Italy and the 3¼ million pound economic aid given during the restoration period on January 31, 1942, the British asked for and were conceded enormous privileges in the internal affairs and international relations of the country. Some of the privileges accorded to the British were (1) the precedence of the British Ambassador over other foreign representatives, (2) the levying of taxes and allocation of expenditures in Ethiopia with the prior approval of the

British government, (3) the handling of the Ethiopian administrator by British advisers, (4) the trial of all enemy war-crime suspects by British military tribunals, (5) the prohibition of Ethiopia from establishing trade relations with the Axis Powers (i.e., Germany, Italy and Japan), (6) Allowing only British airlines to fly throughout the country, and (7) putting the area of the Addis Ababa-Djibouti railway, the Haud, the Ogaden, and the Reserved area (i.e., a stretch of Ethiopian territory adjacent to the French Somaliland) under the British administration. Given all these privileges, "liberated" Ethiopia

> *...remained essentially under British control. British military units as part of the BMME (British Military Mission to Ethiopia) were present everywhere, as were British advisers. All communications, including the Emperor's personal correspondence and air and surface transport were controlled by them. Foreign airlines other than British were excluded... The East Africa shilling replaced the Italian lire and the traditional Ethiopian currency. Ethiopia was part of the sterling area. Goodyear, Goodrich or Firestone tires could be purchased only if they had been manufactured by their branches in England. All dollar exchange earned by exports had to be converted into pounds sterling... (Spencer, 1977, p. 9. See also Schwab, 1972, 35).*

Ravaged by economic dislocation wrought by the Second World War, and in order to pacify those progressive Ethiopians who were opposed to the British presence in Ethiopia, Britain after three years of predominance in the Ethiopian politico-economic sphere modified the Treaty of 1942 by an Anglo-Ethiopian Agreement of December 9, 1944. As discussed by Schwab, under the 1944 Agreement

> *Ethiopia was permitted to appoint British advisers as the Ethiopian government sees fit. The direction was transferred to the Ethiopian government from the British. In addition, jurisdiction over British subjects was to be exercised by Ethiopian courts, and the British government relinquished control of the Franco-Ethiopian railway running from Addis Ababa to Djibouti. The agreement provided for the establishment of a British military mission to Ethiopia and until the termination of the agreement, the British military was permitted to administer the Ogaden region of Harar province (1972, p. 35).*

In 1948 Britain withdrew from the Ogaden. With the return of the Haud and the reserved area in 1954 to the Ethiopian government, British privileges in the country were reduced.

US Monopoly on Foreign Direct Investments in Ethiopia

Taking advantage of the deterioration of relations between Ethiopia and Britain, the United States started establishing economic and military relations with Ethiopia. Presented below is a brief review of how the Ethiopian economy became involved in dependent and subordinate relations with the United States through commercial ties, investments, economic assistance, and the establishment of U.S. military base and military advisory group.

After the American Economic Commission visited the country in 1944, Haile Selassie was promised a U.S. loan of Eth $7.5 million at 3 percent interest rate per year. A year later, Haile Selassie "briefly conferred with President Franklin Roosevelt on an American warship near Suez" (Lipsky, 1962:220). In 1946, an American, Mr. Blowers, was appointed as the Governor of the State Bank of Ethiopia. As stated by John Spencer, Haile Selassie's chief adviser:

> *In that year the East African Shilling was replace by a new currency, the Ethiopian dollar. While that action did not free Ethiopia from the pound sterling; it laid the ground work for eventually detaching it and basing it on the U.S. dollar (1977, p.14).*

The minting of the divisional coinage as well as the printing of the new paper currency was done at the U.S. mint in Philadelphia (Spencer, 1977, p.14).

With the implementation of President Truman's Point Four Program of technical assistance to less developed countries, on June 16, 1951, the United States government signed an agreement with Ethiopia whereby the U.S. gained full access to the exploitation of natural resources in the country. Initially, the basic aim of the Point Four Program in Ethiopia was to give economic assistance, scholarships, and training to Ethiopian personnel in the fields of education, agriculture, and public health. However, later Ethiopia's potential in the realm of other economic resources attracted U.S. dollars with the force of a huge magnet, and the program was expanded to include:

> *An investigation of the economic potential of the land and water resources of the Blue Nile River Basin and the development of the Surveys and Water Resources Department for the Imperial Ethiopian Government. The Imperial Ethiopian Mapping and geography Institute (was) established to develop and train an organization which will produce maps utilizing photogrammetric techniques, collect economic, political and physical geography data and compile the necessary maps to depict these data (*Ethiopia Observer, December 1958, p. 5*).*

As indicated in Appendix 3.1, in the six years from 1952 to 1958 the U.S. Government spent Eth $51 million through the Point Four Program.

In 1969, U.S. economic assistance to Ethiopia totaled about Eth $571.8 million. By 1970 Ethiopia was the foremost recipient of U.S. assistance among all African counties. She accounted for 65% of all United States assistance to African countries. That is, out of total of U.S. $18 million allotted to African countries in 1970, Ethiopia received U.S. $12 million compared to $1.08 million for Zaire, $100,000 for Ghana, $580,000 for Nigeria and $3 million for Tunisia (Committee on Foreign Relations, 1970: 1953). (See Appendix 3.2 for the amounts and purposes of credits from IBRD, IDA, USA, US-Export-Import Bank, and other U.S. agencies).

U.S. interest in Ethiopia was not limited to economic assistance and the feasibility for future U.S. investments but also involved military ties and the establishment of U.S. bases in the country. In 1950 and 1960, Ethiopia sent its troops to Korea and the Congo. In his testimony to the U.S. Senate Committee on Foreign Relations, Mr. David Newsom, the former Undersecretary for African affairs, revealed that Ethiopia got huge economic assistance from the United States because (it) "has on two occasions sent its force to participate in actions which are parallel with our own objectives at the time, once in Korea and once in the United Nations' efforts in the Congo" (1970, p. 1903).

The exchange for economic aid which trained and equipped three Ethiopian divisions of 6000 each on May 1954, U.S. asked for and was granted the right to build and maintain military bases in Ethiopia for twenty-five years. In 1954 the U.S. government opened a U.S. Army strategic communication base at Kagnew Station in Asmara, Eritrea. As stated by Spencer, the United States wanted the communications base at Amhara because

> *It was located in the tropics far from the north and south magnetic poles, the aurora borealis and magnetic storms, in a zone where the limited degree of seasonal variations between sunrise and sunset reduced the need for numerous frequency changes. It was an important addition to the worldwide network of U.S. communications including the Philippines, Ethiopia, Morocco and Arlington, Virginia and could also serve the NATO area within Western Europe whenever electrical and magnetic disturbances upset communication in those higher latitudes (1977, p. 22-23).*

On June 1, 1970, more than three thousand U.S. military personnel and their dependents were stationed at Kagnew (Committee on Foreign Relations, 1970, p. 1913).

Following Haile Selassie's visit to the United States in May, 1954, and Vice President Richard Nixon's visit to Ethiopia in 1956, military assistance started flowing to Ethiopia. A brief summary of the main contents of the Ethio-U.S. military agreements of the 1960's is presented below.

In 1960, the United States agreed to equip and train the Fourth Division of the Ethiopian Army, gave the Ethiopian Navy a seaplane tender (AUP) and also "reaffirmed its continuing interest in the security of Ethiopia and the opposition to any activities threatening the territorial integrity of Ethiopia" (Committee on Foreign Relations, 1970, p. 1905).

In 1962, the U.S. Government provided ammunition and armored personnel carriers to the Ethiopian army. The Air Force portion of the agreement was to provide T-28D, T-86, and T-33 aircraft and to continue support of the T-28A and F-86 squadrons. The Navy portion of the commitment was to provide one LCM (Committee on Foreign Relations, 1970, p. 1907).

In 1963, the U.S. agreed to reorganize the Ethiopian Air Force; the Ethiopian Navy was provided with 40-foot Coast Guard Utility Boats. In 1964, the Ethiopian Air Force was promised a squadron of 12 F-s aircraft (Committee on Foreign Relations, 1970, p. 1907).

As shown in Appendix 3.3, between the years 1953 and 1970, U.S. military assistance to Ethiopia amounted to Eth $397.5 million. U.S. counter-insurgency training teams instructed the Ethiopian army; between 1953-70 a total of 2,813 Ethiopian officers were trained in the United States at a total cost of approximately Eth $17 million (United States Senate, Committee on Foreign Relations, 1970, p. 1915).

It is worth noting that U.S. economic and military aid to Ethiopia was not a gesture of good will, to enhance the development of Ethiopia, but was precisely geared to facilitate capitalist expansion—i.e., to protect markets and investments and to secure cheap raw materials. For instance, after the U.S. government, through the Point Four Program and other economic assistance, paved the way for investment and assured the safety of American investors, many American firms which were desperately looking for investment outlets rushed to Ethiopia. Of course, it should be added that American firms were also encouraged to flock to Ethiopia after Haile Selassie promulgated a protectionist policy which favored the private investors.

As the passage quoted below clearly indicates, Haile Selassie welcomed foreign investors with open arms, in a speech on Addis Ababa Radio on 11 October, 1962:

> *It has for long been a part of the tradition of Ethiopia to welcome foreigners and safeguard their rights and interests during their stay here. In the case especially of these foreigners who have invested capital in development projects in their country, apart from working in cooperation on the part of both Our Government officials and Our people,*

> *there has never been a case in Ethiopia's history when the property of a foreigner has been unlawfully confiscated. This is a source of pride for Ethiopia. Ethiopia will at times welcome foreign investors who may be willing to employ their money for development works, either in partnership with Ethiopians or as private entrepreneurs (*Ethiopia Observer, 1966: 286*).*

In the Investment Guarantee Agreement signed by the U.S. and Ethiopia in August 1962, every American investor was further assured by the U.S. government that "he will be protected up to the amount specified in the guarantee from loss through expropriation, inconvertibility, or from loss by reason of war" (Ethiopia Observer, 1966:291).

To a startling extent in an investment protectionist policy known as the "Investment Decree, 1963." the Ethiopian government promised five major types of benefits to investors. The policy was put into effect in September 1963. Included in this were exemptions from income tax, for a period of five years, for enterprises whose capital was Eth $200,000 or more; import duty relief for capital goods; export duty relief for capital goods; export duty relief for manufactured finished goods in order to enable them to compete in the international market; the remittance of profits of foreign investors to their countries of origin; acquisition of land required for the establishment of industrial, agricultural, mining, transport, and touristic enterprises (Ethiopian Economic Review, 1963: 94-96).

Blaug, who is at times less than critical of foreign investments in developing countries, thought of the Investment Decree as excessive and detrimental to Ethiopian economy. As he puts it, "although a certain degree of protection is useful to foster infant industries, the level of protection in Ethiopia seems excessive. Thirty percent protection has been found to be sufficient for many infant industries in UC's (underdeveloped countries) and a 50 percent protection is high by international standards—protection in Ethiopia exceeds 50 percent" (1973:7).

Appendix 3.4 shows, while industrial and agricultural machinery for foreign investors and the comprador class were exempted from duty tax, most of the tools commonly used by laborers, artisans, and small firms were heavily taxed.

As expected with the full implementation of Haile Selassie's liberal protectionist policy, many Americans and other capitalist investors came to the country and were granted concessions in the industrial, agricultural, and mining sectors of the economy. To mention only a few of the major investors, a 50-year monopoly concession was granted to Sinclair Oil Corporation to explore for oil in the country. Both Tenneco and Whitestone and the Louisiana Land and Exploration Company (American) were granted concessions to exploit oil and gas, the former in the South-eastern and the latter in the eastern part of the country. The exploitation of potash and saline deposits in the Danakil Depression fell under the domain of two U.S. companies, the Parsons Corporation, run by Ralph M. Parsons, and Seatankers. However, since Parsons Corporation had potash mines at Saskatchew in Canada, Ethiopia's potash deposits were not fully exploited. In this explanation of why Parsons and company never mixed Ethiopia's potash deposit, Bondestam (1975) makes the following observations,

> *By extending their activities and producing potash in Ethiopia, they would cause the world market price of potash to fall, thereby affecting the profitability of the mines in Canada. Ethiopians who studied the matter are of the opinion that it is for this very reason that Parsons had a high price for imported potash. The Indian Government has therefore asked the Ethiopian official in the Ministry of Mines for a deal. The Indian Government is willing to pay any price to start potash production in Ethiopia to be exported to India; but the arm of the Ethiopian Government is being twisted: breaking contract with Parsons and Company might threaten Ethiopian trade with the U.S.A. (to which 50% of all exports go).*

In the 1960's many American companies "invested large sums of money in three other areas of the Ethiopian economy; the production of coffee, construction of hotels and forestry" (Ahooja, 1966:287). For example, about seventy percent of the shares the Ethiopian-American Coffee Company were owned by American companies. In Ahorja's words the coffee estate owned by the Ethiopian-American Coffee Company "spread over 10,000 acres of land with some two million coffee trees and a nursery containing over half a million seedlings. This is one of the largest coffee plantations in Ethiopia and is the only one with all-weather airstrips capable of handling DC-3's" (1966:287). The largest hotel in the country, which was constructed with the loan procured from the U.S. Export-Import Bank, is by and large owned by Hilton Hotels International. Fifty percent of the paper industry in the country was owned by two U.S. companies, Parsons and Whittemore. An American company, International Industrial Development Consultants, Inc. (INDEVCO) was granted concessions to start a lumbering project for te logging of a large number of acres of forestland for timber export (Ahooja, 196:287).

From its inception in 1946, Ethiopian Airlines was a dumping ground for surplus DC-47's parked at the edge of Payne Field outside Cairo and has been under the monopoly of Trans World Airlines. As stated by Geiger "Ethiopians regard EAL as an Ethiopian company even though most of its top officials are from the United States and TWA is responsible for its operation" (1959:62; see also Spencer, 1977:15).

Since 1967 many American companies have been receiving regular financial support from USAID and IBRD to explore investment opportunities in Ethiopia. Bondestam makes the following observations:

> *Actually, it is hardly possible to distinguish American companies from assistance agencies such as USAID and IBRD. Their interests are closely linked and these two agencies, probably together with the few others, should therefore logically be included in an enumeration of foreign commercial interest in Ethiopia. They do not invest directly, but the impression they give is that their task is to prepare the ground for a penetration of American business capital. Moreover, they tie more local capital into so-called development projects than pure companies do. This means that given the dependence of foreign capital through "aid", local capital, which would otherwise have been available for investing in improvements for the Ethiopian people, is often "lost" in development-alienated projects* (Bondestam, 1975:133).

Though the hegemony of U.S capital over other investments in Ethiopia was substantial, starting in the 1960's a few British, Japanese, Indian, Italian, Dutch, and Israeli investors were granted permission to start investments in the country.

Being unsure of their situation in Kenya and the Sudan after these two countries won their independence from Britain, and using Haile Selassie's liberal foreign investment protectionist policy, a few British firms began feasibility studies for future investment and eventually got involved in three major activities: cotton, meat production, and pharmaceutical factory. For instance, the Mitchell Cotts, Ltd. was given a land lease to grow cotton in Tendaho. As stated by Ahooja:

> *In 1960, almost hesitantly, a few British investors bought shares in Tendaho. With the improvement of conditions of cotton crops and investment in agriculture research, the cotton yield rose from 200 pounds per acre to 800 pounds within a few years. As a result, the capital of Tendaho was increased from an initial Eth $14 million* (1966: 287).

After the full implementation of Haile Selassie's Investment Decree in 1964, the International Packers (Chicago and London) started a slaughter-house, the National Meat Corporation of Ethiopia, in which the Ethiopian government owned only 24% of the share capital. Smith and Nephew Associated Companies, London (SANACO) was given 50% of the share capital in the Ethiopian Drugs Manufacturing Company (Ahooja, 1966: 280).

The Japanese capitalists were given major concessions in the textile and metal processing factories. Three Japanese companies, Toyo Rayon Co., Sakai

Textile Manufacturing Co., and Mitsuisui Shoji Kaisha Ltd., owned half of the share capital in the Ethio-Japanese Synthetic Textiles, S.C. (Bondestam, 1975:135). The largest cotton company, the Cotton Company of Ethiopia, was 50% owned by a group of Japanese firms—The Sabean Utility Corporation (SUC), "which also has a share in the Fibre Company of Ethiopia" (Bondestam, 1975:135). The Sabean Utility Corporation was given the metal factory at Akaki. Similarly, another Japanese mining firm, the Nippon Mining Company, was given copper concessions at Debaroa in Eritrea. As stated by Bondestam

> *Nippon has 49% of the shares and the Ethiopian government the remaining 51%. A condition for the Japanese investment was that the Ethiopian government arranges the loans and stand as the sole guarantor. In practice this means that Nippon brings the technology to Ethiopia and returns to Japan with the copper—at a rate considerably below the world market price (1975:134).*

Since 1954 a Dutch Company HVA (Handels Vereniging Amsterdam) has been involved in the plantation and production of sugar at Wonji and Shoa, and later it extended its operations to Metahara. Though the project initially started as a joint venture between the Dutch firm and the Ethiopian government, there is some evidence that HVA was the exclusive owner of the sugar plantation and sugar factory. For example, until 1974 only 10% of the shares were owned by the Ethiopian Government, and HVA was allowed to remit 10 percent of the invested capital yearly and 15 percent of its annual profits (Bondestam, 1974: 432).

Other major foreign investments in the country were represented by the French, Indian, Swiss, Israelis, and Italians. More than 50% of the Addis Ababa-Djibouti railway is owned by and operated by the Compaignie du Chemin' de Fer Franco-Ethiopian de Djibouti a' Addis Ababa. The Indian capitalists own the Indian Ethiopian Textile at Akaki (Shoa). The director of Birla Brokers Ltd. Company (BBLC) "is simultaneously both responsible for the operation of the state-owned Bahr Dar Textile Mills and the director of one of the largest distribution firms in textile, namely the Indian Shantial and Company Ethiopian Ltd. Moreover, BBLC is partly associated with the Indian firm, Messrs Duncan Brothers and Co., Ltd., which has 50% of the shares in National Textiles" (Bondestam 1975: 136). The Swiss and Israelis invested in meat packing and canning and owned a large plantation of about 2,000 hectares at Abadir. The Italians owned textile factories and enumerable large plantations in Eritrea and had a plantation at Nura Era in the Awash Valley.

Against this background of the establishment of transnational companies, let us now review the impact of economic assistance, loans (in 1974 alone Ethiopia received a loan of Eth $472.7 million from the United States, the World Bank, the European Community, Germany, and other European countries. For details, see U.S. Senate, Committee on Foreign Affairs, 1967:128), and foreign investments in the country on the economic development (stagnation) and the improvement (deterioration) in the standard of living of the Ethiopian masses.

Taking account of the amount of economic assistance and the massive dosage of loans which Ethiopia has been getting from various sources during the last two and a half decades, one might have expected enhancement in the country's economic development and improvements in the living conditions of the Ethiopian masses. Similarly, with the huge amount of foreign investment in the country one might have assumed that these investments would have created productive employment opportunities for the Ethiopian people and improved the productive capacities of the country's economic resources. However, contrary to one's expectations, we note the following:

- A chronic, unfavorable balance of trade,
- A stagnation in the Ethiopian economy and an increasing penetration and dependence on the international financial institutions, particularly the United States, and
- An increasing deterioration of the standard of living of the Ethiopian working class and the peasantry. The following section will briefly discuss the problems outlined.

Ethiopia's Foreign Trade

Ethiopia's trade patterns, with its major capitalist partners, have been based primarily on an exploitative relationship. Appendix 3.5 indicates that the country had a persistent trade deficit in 23 out of the last 28 years. It had a minor, visible, favorable balance of trade in 1951, 1953, 1954, and 1957; and after 15 years of chronic deficit, we observe that in 1973 there was a surplus of Eth $53 million because of an increase in world market prices of raw products and food. The irony of the matter, however, was that with the 1973/74 famine over 500,000 persons are said to have died in Wollo and Tigrai provinces, whereas the "official trade statistics show a net export surplus for cereals, oil seeds, and pulses of 203,900 MT in 1973, the largest export surplus in any year since 1962" (Holmberg, 1977:9).

It is also interesting to note that after the full implementation of the Investment Decree of 1963, the value of both imports and exports has increased substantially. However, a careful examination of the commodities imported indicates that in 1972 alone about 38 percent of the imports were duty free—capital goods such as machinery, industrial inputs, and manufactured goods. About 32 percent of imports were consumer goods, such as private cars, whiskey, and cream butter, deemed so important for the foreign capitalists and the national bourgeoisie (see Appendix 3.6). As indicated in Appendix 3.7, for the last eight-year period about 76% of the imported goods came from Italy, Japan, West Germany, United Kingdom, and the U.S.A.

Ethiopia's export trade is largely dependent upon agricultural products. As shown in Appendix 3.8, during the eight-year period, coffee accounted for over 60% of Ethiopia's total exports, followed by hides and skins, oil seeds, live animals and meat, fruits and vegetables. However, in 1970, 1971 and 1972, 79%, 75% and 70%, respectively, of exported coffee was sold in the United States (See statistical Abstract, 1972: 108). As accurately observed by Assefa and Eshetu, "Ethiopia's dependence on the United States for its coffee market" can cause serious damage to the economy if for some reasons, political or otherwise, the United States stops or cuts down on its coffee imports from Ethiopia. The whole economy lies at the mercy of a single unreliable market." (1969: 61).

As shown in Appendix 3.9, over 80% of Ethiopia's total export value goes to seven countries. However, for the last eight years the U.S. had been Ethiopia's biggest trading partner. Over 40% of Ethiopian yearly export goods have been sold in the United States followed by West Germany and Italy. It is worth noting at this juncture that Ethiopia's import-export firms were dominated by foreigners. For instance, in 1964 about 77% of the foreign capitalists were engaged in import-export activities compared to 23% Ethiopians (Economic Review, 1966:39).

To summarize, Ethiopia's foreign trade is characterized by an unfavorable balance of trade. In order to cover the deficits, the Ethiopian economy has depended too much on foreign loans, and economic assistance; foreign investors were invited to do business in the country under generous conditions. An analysis of the major components of Ethiopia's foreign trade reveals that in line with the existing international division of labor, Ethiopia has specialized in the production of primary goods. For its imports it is largely dependent on Italy (this might reflect Italy's trade with Eritrea rather than with Ethiopia proper, since being a former colony of Italy, there are a large number of Italians living in Eritrea); for its exports it is highly dependent on the United States.

Ethiopia's chronic commercial dependence, particularly on the U.S., has become increasingly obvious because over 70 percent of the total coffee export, the sole source of Ethiopia's foreign exchange is sold in the United States. Moreover, the following discussion will show that despite the massive dosage of foreign aid and grants and the establishment of transnational companies, what we observe in the Ethiopian economy during the 1968-73 period was a chronic stagnation.

Ethiopia's Economic stagnation

In addition to the unfavorable balance of trade, we observe that for the last seven years (that is, from 1966/7 to 1972/3 over 24 percent of the Ethiopian yearly budgetary revenue, on the average had been derived from technical assistance and foreign loans. The coverage of the budget deficit with economic assistance and loans clearly manifested that the economy had been dependent on aid donors. Moreover, Appendix 3.10 clearly shows that the country had serious problems with repayments to foreign creditors. For instance, in 1973 Ethiopia's outstanding foreign debt amounted to Eth $585-9 million, of which 44 percent was to IBRD and IDA and 31 percent was to the United States. Moreover this was an increase of 81 percent over that of 1967.

An analysis of the Gross Domestic product (GDP) for the last ten years also reveals that the rate of output growth in Ethiopia declined from 4.8 percent in 1963-68 to 3.6 percent in 1968-73. The rate of growth per capita gross national product was 1.0 in 1968-73 compared to 2.3 in 1963-68 (United Nations, 1975:60). Economic stagnation in Ethiopia during the period 1968-73 reflects in part the worsening terms of trade of Ethiopia with its trading partners and the reduction of agricultural outputs. For instance, agriculture, which is supposed to engage about 90 percent of the population, grew at the rate of 2.1 percent per annum over the past ten years; on the other hand, the population is believed to have increased at the rate of 2.4 to 2.6 percent per year (See Blaug, 1973). Furthermore, it can be argued that the relations that were established through foreign assistance, foreign investments, and international trade contributed to Ethiopia's subordination and dependence:

1. Ethiopia was inserted into the imperialist chain through the establishment of U.S. bases, loans and economic assistance grants and military training programs.
2. This politico-economic and military dependence on the imperialist countries, championed by the United States, was accelerated and consolidated in the 1960's after Haile Selassie pronounced an open door policy for foreign investments.
3. Ethiopia's economic dependence is manifested by an unfavorable balance of trade and the nature of its imports and exports. In conformity with the international division of labor it has specialized in agricultural products of which over 70 percent of its coffee, the single export crop is sold in the United States. For its technological imports it has heavily depended on the Western European countries and the United States.

4. In order to cover the chronic trade and budget deficit, Ethiopia's development has been oriented to the external world-economic assistance, loans and capital inflow from abroad. For instance, for the last seven years on the average 24 percent of the public revenue was procured from external loans. This helped Haile Selassie's corrupt government to stay afloat.
5. Finally, dependence on trade and foreign investment has resulted not only in technological dependence but also has produced cultural dependence. For the welfare and comfort of the national bourgeoisie the country was forced to adopt modes of consumption and behavior characteristic of the imperialist countries. As discussed above, for the last seven years over 30 percent of the imports (on the average) were consumer goods such as private cars, whisky and brandy, cream butter, etc. for the comprador class while the peasants starved to death. (see Admassu, 1978 and Addis, 1975).

With the existing economic stagnation in the country the hardest hit were the peasants and the workers.

The Conditions of the Peasants and Workers

It was demonstrated above that the massive dosage of economic assistance, foreign loans and Haile Selassie's liberal Investment Decree of 1963 neither contributed to Ethiopia's economic development nor counteracted the chronic imbalance of trade which the country was faced with for the last 16 years. We also saw that during the period 1967-73 Ethiopia's indebtedness to foreign creditors increased substantially because the foreign investors were overpricing the imported capital goods in order to maximize their profits.

In this dependent economic system there was hardly any improvement in the living conditions of the urban and rural proletariat. The investments did not generate productive employment of the Ethiopian masses. The urban proletariat was hard hit due to high unemployment in the cities. For instance, in 1970 open unemployment in the towns was around 5 to 10 percent of the labor force (Blaug; 1973:11). Similarly, the effects of the investments in the rural areas did not trickle down to the peasantry. Most of the tenants were forced to leave the farmlands with the establishment of large scale commercial farms. Moreover, despite the introduction of commercial farms, for the last ten years the agriculture sector grew at only 2.1 percent while the population is estimated to have increased at the rate of 2.4 to 2.6 percent per annum. As stated by Blaug, "...the recent growth of agricultural output below the growth of population implies a progressively worsening situation of the great majority of the population, and particularly for the poorest members of society" (1973:5). Rightly so, in 1972, the average income obtained from agriculture, estimated on the basis of sector G.D.P. and population was about Eth $75 per year (see Blaug, 1973:23).

It was only the foreign investors, the national bourgeoisie (that is, the landed autocracy, those who hold offices in the administrative apparatus who received land grants from Haile Selassie, the rich merchants and the capital-owning agriculturally skilled persons who contracted land from the absentee landlords), who benefitted from the investments and the free duties on fuel, income tax, and capital goods.

With the introduction of mechanized farming by the foreign capitalists, the national bourgeoisie prospered. (For example, in 1970, the feudal autocrat, Sultan Ali Mirah, had a commercial farm on 14,200 hectares of land). The peasants and the pastoralists who lived in the Awash Valley were either pushed aside into the arid areas or evicted from their land and forced to migrate to face unemployment, starvation and possibly death in the urban areas.

After the Dutch, British, Italian and Israelis gained access to the Awash Valley through concessions (i.e., in 1970, the Dutch, British, Italian and Israelis owned 10,840, 8,200, 2,000 and 2,800 hectares respectively of cultivated land). Many of the Afars, a group of pastoralists who lived in the area for centuries, were pushed aside to the periphery or totally evicted from the land. For instance, after HVA was granted a concession to plant and process sugar at Wonji and Shoa and later at Metahara, many of the Afars were forced to leave their river-watered pastures without any compensation. Similarly, with the development and preservation of wild animals in the upper portions of the Awash Valley for tourists, the Kereyn and Ittu Oromos were driven away from their land. To make matters worse, those Afars who lived within the proximity of the Sugar plantation lost many of their cattle because HVA was discharging chemicals into the river and was indiscriminately spraying various insecticides (i.e., Endrin or D.D.T. compounds) on the pastures (Bondestam, 1974: 428-29).

Experience from CADU, (Chilalo Agricultural Development Unit, initiated in 1967 in Chilalo, Arusi Province with the assistance of the Swedish government) WADU (Welamo Agricultural Development Unit started in 1970 with the assistance of I.D.A.), the Bako Minimum Package Project (in Wollega) and the Setit Humera (Begemdit, both financed by the World Bank, clearly shows that the peasants who lived in these areas were evicted from their land. For example, CADU was established with the sole purpose of improving the standard living conditions of small farmers at Chilalo; however, with the establishment of mechanized farming the price of land skyrocketed, the credit system unilaterally favored the rich farmers and in 1969 and 1970 alone more than 500 tenants were evicted. As stated by Stahl, it is believed that some of the evicted tenants had moved to nearby areas while the majority had left Arussi Province for southern Shoa, Bale, and Hararge Provinces in the "belief and hope that in these places there was land available for cultivation" (1973: 7-8).

At Bako, with the establishment of comprehensive package projects, many tenants were evicted without any compensation. As stated by Stahl,

> *when I visited Bako in May 1972, 107 tenant families (approximately 500 individuals) had been informed by the entrepreneurs that their tenancy relationship was to be terminated. They were threatened with immediate eviction. Within a year, land which had been producing food crops for local consumption (maize and sorghum) was made to grow haricot beans in response to the high world market price (1973:31, see also* Abdul Mejid, 1976:19).

Alienation of land from the peasantry was not only limited to the commercial farms but it was also quite prevalent in most of the regions incorporated by Menelik II. As mentioned in Section II of this paper, with the expansion of the Ethiopian Empire at the close of the nineteenth century to the south, southwest and southeast, the natives were expropriated from their land and were forced to work for the settlers. The alienated land was distributed among the conquerors, the Orthodox Church, the royal family and those indigenous elites who proclaimed their loyalty to the central government. As described by Ellis

> *Armed with rifles obtained from the Italians and French, Menelik's armies rapidly defeated a host of kingdoms which had fought the Empire to a standstill for centuries. The conquered lands were split up into gash units of from 80 to 100 acres. Generally, one-third was set aside for local leaders and two thirds were divided between soldiers, governors and the church. Peasants in these lands were allocated to officials in accordance with rank, soldiers receiving from two to five families each, while governors were given hundreds* (1976: 282-283).

Since 1941 several proclamations relating to land taxation and ownership were issued by Haile Selassie's government and for the main contents of the 1941, 1942, 1944, 1947, and 1967 land proclamation, (see Markakis, 1974: 118-129). Being aware of deleterious effects of the outmoded tenure system, the government established in 1961 the Special Land Reform Authority to implement some of the measures suggested by the Land Reform Committee. In 1966 the Land Reform Authority was elevated to the rank of Ministry of Land Reform and Administration. However, a national sample survey, 1966-68, conducted by the Central Statistical Office, clearly shows that there was a continuous expropriation of the peasants and ownership of land was concentrating in the hands of a few landowners. For instance, in 1968 it was found that about 75 percent of the total areas in Hararge Province alone belonged to 0.2 percent of the landowners (Blaug, 1973:125).

Interestingly enough, not only did the landowners defy the government's proclamations and block legislative actions by parliament, they also continued exacting a special fee before a new tenant could move onto a rented holding. In addition to rental payments (i.e., about 40 percent of the produce of the land), in order to maintain his tenancy and win the favor of his landlord the tenant had to provide his landlord with firewood, maintain the landlord's fence and present a gift on religious holidays and other social occasions. Moreover, the entire tax burden, wrote Markakis

> *Fell entirely on the shoulders of the peasant cultivator, where it has been since time immemorial, while the landholders not only escaped taxation but also continued to appropriate part of the taxes they collected for the state (*1974: 121-22; see also Abdul Mejod, 1976:14*).*

The rist system of landholding, in principle, ensured that "everyone holds land by virtue of membership in the kinship groups" (Markakis, 1974:80). Even though the land in the northwestern part of Ethiopia was supposed to be communally owned, eviction of peasants was common. For instance, in 1972, it was estimated that because of leasing, litigation, and confiscation by the state for failing to pay tribute, more than 20 percent of the households were landless (see Blaug, 1973:126 and Markakis, 1974:82). In addition, there is ample evidence to show that since 1958 many peasants migrated to the other parts of Ethiopia to become beggars or, if lucky enough, to take up jobs as porters in the urban areas and as seasonal laborers at the commercial farms. The following factors were predominant: (1) Heavy taxation (i.e., agricultural income tax, tax for development projects, health, and education; (2) surcharge for the maintenance of churches. For instance, Lundstrom notes that in Wodjirate (Tigrai Province) with a population of about 25,000 each peasant on average paid some Eth $20 a year for the construction and maintenance of the 39 churches (1976:40); (3) soil erosion and fragmentation of holdings in order to accommodate new members who have established a family. A report by the Ministry of Land Reform and Administration in 1970 reveals that about 50 percent of the holdings in Tigrai and Begemder were smaller than half a hectare. About 68 percent of the holdings in Tigrai (on the average about seven persons per hectare) and 69 percent in Begemdir were smaller than one hectare (Ministry of Land Reform and Administration as quoted in Markakis, 1974:81). Last but not least, the famines which occurred in 1958, 1965, and 1971-74 are believed to have driven hundreds of thousands of peasants off their land. In 1971-74 alone, it is estimated that over 500,000 people died in Wollo and Tigrai provinces. Brian Aris, a noted journalist, has this to say about the famine in Wollo:

> *I have visited refugee camps in the Middle East, photographed starving babies in India and children injured by war in Vietnam, but I have never seen anything so horrifying and distressing as the situation in the Wollo province of Ethiopia* (Aris as quoted in Addis, 1975:103).

Like the peasants, the workers were equally repressed and exploited in the hands of the local and foreign investors. Following Haile Selassie's Investment Decree of 1963 (according to 1963 decree investors with a capital over Eth $200,000 were exempted from income tax, tax on fuel, and most important, capital goods), most of the production in agriculture and industry became capital-intensive and labor-displacing. The technology employed in many industrial processes became capital-intensive because the means of production were geared to the needs of the industrial countries where the inputs were imported.

As indicated in Appendix 3.11, there was virtually stagnant employment in the ten industrial sectors in the face of continued population growth and rural-urban migration. In 1968/69 and 1970/71 there was a decrease of workers by 0.9%, 0.1%, 0.3%, 0.6% and 0.3% in the beverage, tobacco, textile, non-metallic mines, and printing press industry respectively. Moreover, there was no appreciable increase of workers in the food, wood, chemical, steel and electrical industries.

According to Blaug's estimation, in Addis Ababa, where most of the major industries are concentrated, between 1964-69 "manufacturing only increased by 2 percent while output increased 100 percent" and urban population grew at 7 percent per annum, consisting of 2.4 percent natural growth and 4.6 percent immigration (1974:73-82).

Two cases in point where the use of capital-intensive technology by employers have reduced the ability of industries to offer adequate number of jobs are well demonstrated by HVA, a sugar industry, and Tendaho, a cotton plantation. Despite a substantial increase in the production of sugar by HVA, evidence seems to show that there was no appreciable increase in the number of employees. Furthermore, native wages remained perfectly constant for more than a decade. Bondestam describes the situation at HVA as follows:

> *The capital-intensive investments have only befitted the industrialists in Europe (who exported the machinery and technology) and have contributed to the outflow of capital at the expense of increased employment opportunities in Ethiopia.*
>
> *Thus huge reserves of manpower remain underutilized, and this has made the minimization of wages possible—so long as the supply of manpower exceeds the demand; the wages are alive, and not on their contribution to production. Although a doubling of wages of low-paid labourers could mean a reduction of profits by not more than 20*

> *percent, wages are kept down [to] the minimum level, which is Eth $1-2 per day. In 1971, 90 percent of the wage-earners received 33 percent ... while the 2 percent who are highly paid earned 37 percent. A small group, mostly foreigners, live a comfortable isolated life in big villas with access to all possible entertainments. Their contact with the common workers are via educated or semi-educated groups of Ethiopians, usually foremen, technicians, mechanics, and clerks, of whom most (but not all) have little or no interest in the socio-economic conditions of the exploited masses. Rather they compare their own situation to the ruling upper class (*1974:434*).*

Moreover, Bondestam states that in 1967 and 1971 workers' strikes were aborted by the company because of the abundance of a "reserve army," the absence of a workers' union, and the presence of troops which used force to dispense the strikers (1974).

Similarly, the cotton plantation at Tendaho, mostly owned and managed by Mitchell Cotts, a British firm, the production of cotton had increased substantially because of the company's use of capital-intensive technology and cheap seasonal labor. In 1973 alone, the net profits of the company constituted about "67 percent of the value of production." The daily wage of the native cotton-pickers was Eth $1, whereas the "unproductive labor," the technical supervisory staff, who were mostly foreigners were getting about Eth $80 a day (Bondestam, 1974:436). The abysmally low wages and the working environment were insufficient to reproduce the labor; hence some of the cotton pickers had to go back to the highlands (that is to the capitalist substance economy after they collected enough cash to pay their taxes).

To conclude, the most notable socio-economic changes we witness in Ethiopia during the 1942-74 periods are:

1. The insertion of the Ethiopian economy into the ensemble of international financial institutions through economic assistance, loans, investments and international trade.
2. A stagnation in the economy as manifested in a chronic budget deficit and heavy indebtedness to foreign creditors.
3. The emergence of capital-intensive and labor-displacing large-scale commercial farms and manufacturing industries, mainly dominated by foreigners.
4. The deterioration in living standards of the rural and urban proletariat.

Appendix 3.1
Point Four Expenditures in Ethiopia 1952-1959

Year	Expenditure (in Eth S)*
1952	1,985
1953	1,552
1954	3,892
1955	6,707
1956	8,195
1957	9,052
1958	12,410
1959	13,342
Total	57,342

*Average exchange rate U.S. $1.00 = Eth $2.50

Source: The International Cooperation Administration as quoted in Getachew, 1971, p. 133.

Appendix 3.2
IBRN, IDA, AID, EXIM-Bank and Other U.S. Loans to Ethiopia up to June 30, 1964

Creditor	Maturity Period	Interest Rate	Purpose of Credit	Amount (in millions Eth$)
International Bank for Reconstruction and Development (IBRD)				
	1950-1971	4%	Highways	12.5
	1951-1971	4%	Development Bank	5.0
	1951-1971	4%	Telecommunications	3.75
	1957-1977	4%	Highways (2nd project)	37.5
	1961-1971	variable	Development Bank	5.0
	1962-1982	5%	Telecommunications	7.25
	1964-1989	5 ½	Electric Power	58.75
International Development Association (IDA)				
	1963-2013	N/A	Highways (3rd project)	33.75
United States Agency for International Development (USAID)				
	1961-1981	3 ½%	Airports	50.625

	1961-1982	3 ½%	Jet Aviation	7.75
	1961-1974	3 ½%	Highways (maintenance)	9.0
	1961-1976	4%	Development Bank	5.0
U.S. Export-Import Bank				
	1956-1977	5%	Civil Aviation	24.75
U.S. Bank	1962-1969	5%	Jet Aircraft	29.4
U.S. Government	1949-1954	none	----	0.5
U.S. Government	1962-1978	3%	Raw cotton for textile companies	3.39

Source: *Ethiopian Observer*, as quoted in Ahorja; 1966, p. 317.

Appendix 3.3
U.S. Military Assistance to Ethiopia 1953-1970

Year	Eth $ (million)
1953-61	101.25
1962	26.25
1963	26.25
1964	25.75
1965	20.75
1966	26.75
1967	22.50
1968	43.50
1969-1970	104.50
	397.50

Source: Compiled from the Agency for International Development as quoted in Getachew, 1971:136 and U.S. Committee on Foreign Relations, 1970.

Appendix 3.4
Custom Tariffs in Ethiopia for Some Capital Goods

Item		Tariff
Agricultural machinery and parts thereof		Free
Electrical machinery for power generated		Free
Machine tools		Free
Tools: commonly used by labourers, artisans and mechanics		
	Hammer	\$3.20 per piece
	Axe	2.50 per piece
	Pieke	2.50 per piece
	Chisel	1.60 per piece
	Pliers	1.60 per piece
	Pincettee	1.50 per piece
	Screw drivers 4-7 & 10	1.00 per piece
	Shovel	2.50 per piece
	Mason's spoon	1.20 per piece
	Sickel	1.50 per piece
Prime movers, i.e., gas engines, oil engines, steam engines, hydraulic steam turbine, etc.		Free
Road and farm tractors and trailers		Free
Bonds & betting of all kinds for driving machinery		Free

Source: Ministry of Finance, as quoted in Blaug, "Report of the Exploratory Employment Policy Mission in Ethiopia", 1973:87.

Appendix 3.5
Ethiopian Imports, Exports and Balance of Trade 1946- 1973 (in millions of Ethiopian dollars)

Year	Imports	Exports	Balance of Trade
1946	94.9	76.2	-18.7
1947	121.2	98.7	-22.5
1948	124.0	96.6	-27.4
1949	119.1	94.0	-25.1
1950	105.5	91.3	-14.2
1951	147.4	151.9	+4.5

1952	161.9	131.4	-30.5
1953	137.9	169.4	+31.5
1954	160.1	160.3	+0.2
1955	168.0	162.2	-5.8
1956	157.1	151.4	-5.7
1957	178.4	192.0	+13.6
1958	193.6	156.8	-36.8
1959	208.9	179.2	-29.7
1960	219.3	192.6	-26.7
1961	235.6	188.7	-46.9
1962	257.3	199.5	-57.8
1963	276.4	223.4	-52.7
1964	307.6	262.5	-45.1
1965	375.7	289.8	-85.9
1966	404.3	277.0	-127.3
1967	357.4	252.7	-104.7
1968	432.5	266.0	-166.5
1969	388.3	298.1	-90.2
1970	429.1	305.9	-123.2
1971	469.5	314.1	-155.4
1972	435.6	387.3	-48.3
1973	501.2	448.2	+53.0

Source: Central Statistical Office, *Ethiopia Statistical Abstract* 1960-1972

Appendix 3.6
Ethiopian Major Imports 1966-1972

Commodity	Percentage						
	1966	1967	1968	1969	1970	1971	1972
Capital Goods	42.6	40.1	47.3	33.3	31.1	34.1	38.4
Consumer Goods	30.6	28.9	22.7	34.6	36.4	32.5	31.6
Fuel	6.8	8.8	6.2	8.0	8.0	9.4	8.3
Other	20.0	22.2	23.8	24.0	25.5	24.1	21.7

Source: Compiled from Economic Commission for Africa: *Economic Summaries of Economic Data*, Ethiopia, 1969 & 1973

Appendix 3.7
Ethiopia's Imports by Country of Origin 1966-1972

Country of Origin	Percentage						
	1966	1967	1968	1969	1970	1971	1972
Italy	24.2	24.5	22.1	19.3	20.1	19.6	18.5
Japan	16.3	17.6	11.6	13.6	18.2	18.2	16.7
West Germany	13.9	18.1	13.9	18.0	16.9	12.8	14.4
United Kingdom	11.4	10.0	11.6	12.6	9.2	11.3	11.6
U.S.A	10.3	12.2	22.9	12.6	10.5	11.0	10.6
All other countries	23.9	17.6	17.9	23.9	25.1	27.1	28.7

Source: Compiled from Economic Commission for Africa: *Economic Summaries of Economic* Data, Ethiopia, 1969 & 1973

Appendix 3.8
Ethiopia's Major Exports 1966-1973

Commodity	Percentage							
	1966	1967	1968	1969	1970	1971	1972	1973
Coffee	62.0	60.8	64.8	66.2	68.7	62.8	51.9	42.3
Hides & Skins	14.2	13.0	10.6	11.1	9.3	9.2	13.5	15.3
Oil seeds, etc.	8.6	10.0	9.1	8.8	10.8	10.3	13.7	11.6
Live animals and meat	3.7	4.0	3.4	2.9	3.1	4.1	5.5	5.7
Fruits and nuts	2.1	2.6	2.1	1.8	1.3	1.1	1.5	0.7
Vegetables	9.5	9.6	1.0	9.2	6.8	8.9	8.5	18.1
Sugar	-	-	-	-	-	1.5	2.6	3.7
Oil seeds cake	-	-	-	-	-	2.0	1.8	2.5

Source: Compiled from Economic Commission for Africa, Summaries of Economic Data, Ethiopia 1969 & 1973

Appendix 3.9
Ethiopia's Exports by Country of Origin 1966-1973

Country of Origin	Percentage							
	1966	1967	1968	1969	1970	1971	1972	1973
U.S.A.	49.1	49.2	47.3	46.7	54.8	49.1	41.5	36.2
West Germany	6.3	6.1	9.2	10.7	8.2	8.6	8.2	10.6
Italy	10.2	9.5	7.0	7.9	7.0	5.8	9.6	9.4
Affan & Tssar	3.9	3.5	4.3	7.1	5.7	6.9	6.9	8.4
Saudi Arabia	6.0	6.3	7.3	6.4	6.1	7.0	6.9	7.5
Japan	4.7	4.9	4.9	5.3	6.1	6.7	8.2	6.7
Netherlands	2.7	2.3	2.1	1.7	1.5	3.1	2.7	4.9
All others	17.1	18.2	17.9	14.2	10.3	12.8	16.	16.3

Source: Compiled from Economic Commission for Africa, Summaries of Economic Data, Ethiopia 1969 & 1973

Appendix 3.10
Ethiopia's External Debt 1967-1973 (in million Eth $)

Agency or country	Dec 1967	Dec 1968	Dec 1969	June 1970	Dec 1972	Dec 1973
IBRD & IDA	122.9	140.56	145.28	166.56	225.4	256.9
U.S.A	108.7	145.36	149.10	156.89	177.8	180.0
U.S.S.R.	35.15	37.19	37.59	34.03	24.2	20.5
Netherlands	23.37	18.48	16.62	12.71	3.0	-
Yugoslavia	18.04	15.75	13.42	10.95	3.8	2.3
Italy	2.66	13.30	23.60	55.38	63.8	51.7
West Germany	9.08	8.17	9.37	10.44	26.2	33.5
All others	5.01	4.20	21.68	32.91	44.9	41.0
Total	323.92	383.04	417.06	479.87	56.91	585.9

Source: Economic Commission for Africa, Summaries of Economic Data, Ethiopia 1969 & 1973

Appendix 3.11
Percentage of Employees by Industrial Branches

Industrial Branch	1962/69	1970/71
Food Manufacturing	15.3	16.7
Beverages	6.7	5.8
Tobacco	1.2	1.1
Textile	45.8	43.5
Leather & Shoes	4.2	4.2
Wood	6.6	7.8
Non-Metallic Mines	8.1	7.5
Printing	3.3	3.0
Chemical	5.4	6.1
Steel, Metal & Electrical	3.4	4.3

Source: Compiled from Statistical Abstract, 1972, p. 51

Chapter 4

HUMAN CAPITAL AND ECONOMIC CHANGES IN ETHIOPIA

A historical account of the nature of the socio-economic formation and the expansion of the Ethiopian Empire southwards reveals that for approximately six decades Ethiopia was dependent and subordinate to the hegemony of the United Kingdom and the United States. During the period 1900-1935 we witnessed: (1) the establishment of politico-economic hegemony over autonomous nationalities whose socio-economic organizations were diametrically opposed to the Shoan military feudal colonists; (2) the expropriation and alienation of land from the masses and the formation of new classes in the incorporated areas; (3) the mass exodus of the evicted tenants into the incipient urban areas and the predominantly foreign-owned agricultural estates; (4) the appointment of foreigners as advisers in key government posts and (5) the influx of foreign capital and the gradual insertion of the economy in to the capitalist economic order.

In terms of the schooling, the Ethiopian schooling was geared to mirror the existing class structure and foreign domination of the exchange economy. Side by side with the indigenous schools, western-oriented schools were set up to serve opposing social classes: the urban laborers and rural peasants on the one hand, and the emerging middle class and the ruling class, on the other hand. In order to develop local cadres who could facilitate a harmonious relationship between the metropolitan and the Ethiopian masses, the school curriculum stressed mastery of foreign languages to perpetuate social differentiation.

In early Ethiopian history the sole agency responsible for education in the Christian areas was the Orthodox Church. The exact date when the Orthodox Church started offering formal schooling to children is not known, but the general assumption is that it started around the fourth century when Christianity was introduced into the country. At that time, schools were found attached to church and monasteries. The main aim of church education was to prepare youngsters for service in church as deacons, priests, and cantors. Yet church schools also served the state machinery in providing scribes who served as chroniclers in the court of kings and nobles and did correspondence for the feudal lords (Girma, 1967; Paulos, 1976; Haile Gabriel, 1974).

In conjunction with the Orthodox Church Schools, starting in the 7th century, the Mosques in Muslim areas were also engaged in the teaching of morals and religious matters in the Arabic Languages to young Muslims. Unlike those who graduated from church schools, however, graduates from the advanced level of the Quranic schools were not recruited to the state machinery. As observed by Markakis, "these schools received no attention or assistance from the Christian Kings. Such schools were maintained by the local communities themselves and received no State assistance of any kind" (1974, p. 156).

With the opening of the Suez Canal and the scramble for Africa, many missionary societies established themselves in Eritrea. From there they expanded their religious and educational activities in Ethiopia. More particularly, during the time of Emperor Menelik II, many missionaries were encouraged to settle in the country and were granted permission to set up mission houses. For example, Evangeliska Fosterlands-Stiftelsen and Capuchin missionaries established schools in Harar in 1895 and 1897, respectively. In 1898, the Lazist Brothers opened schools in Gouala and Altena. In 1905, the Evangeliska Fosterlands-Stiftelsen and Ecole desSoeurs de S. Vincent set up schools in Addis Ababa, as did Alliance Française in 1912 (Haile Gabriel, 1976, p. 365).

With the importation of skilled foreign labor, however, Menelik's interest in missionaries waned. He discovered that when compared with the imported Indians, Greeks, Armenians, Syrians, Arabs, etc, the missionaries were less competent in commercial ventures and had no skills in repairing the imported ammunitions. Menelik's lack of interest in missionary activities is stated by Wylde as follows:

> *The chief reason why Menelik at first welcomed some of the foreign missionaries was that they knew trades and they were useful in teaching his subjects to become good blacksmiths, carpenters, masons, and bricklayers. Now that he can procure as many Indians as he likes from Bombay via Aden, or Arabs from that port, he does not want the missionaries as they are more trouble than they are worth; and what with the French merchants who will supply him everything he requires, as long as he has the money to purchase it; or concessions to give, he has no more need of other foreigners* (Wylde as quoted in Pankhurst, 1965/66, p. 21).

However, since the missionaries and the metropolitan capitalists worked hand in hand and most of the "Christian missionaries were a major lobby in Europe urging continued imperialism" (Mazui, 1975, p. 193), expulsion of the missionaries would have been to the distaste of the metropolitan advisers; hence few efforts were made by Menelik II to limit their activities. In fact, in order to have a smooth relationship with the metropolis and their representatives in Ethiopia, Menelik II allowed the missionaries to stay in the country and set up mission houses in the capital and in the incorporated areas.

In order to man the expanding state apparatus, Menelik II decided to introduce Western-oriented schooling to the country. However, the introduction of western schooling was not smooth. Abuna Mateos, the Egyptian head of the Ethiopian Orthodox church, and some conservative elements from the nobility, for fear of being overwhelmed by western values, showed some resistance. Due to this opposition, Menelik II could not make use of the German experts sent to him in 1906. The English teachers ordered from Great Britain had also returned home from Aden before reaching the country (Haile Gabriel, 1974).

Menelik II did not want to alienate the Orthodox Church because it gave him its blessings when he annexed the south-east, south, and south-western parts of the country. In the annexed areas the Orthodox Church also institutionalized Menelik's legitimacy by establishing churches and converting to the Orthodox faith. Moreover, Menelik II did not want to repeat the mistakes committed by King Susneyos and Emperor Tewdros. "The downfall of Emperor Susneyos in 1632 and the defeat of (Emperor) Tewdros by the British in 1868 were strongly influenced by the opposition of the Church" (Paulos, 1975, p. 86). Hence Menelik II reached a compromise with the head of the Orthodox Church – the Orthodox schools were allowed to function and were partly subsidized while Menelik II opened the first western-type school. As stated by Girma:

> *Emperor Menelik II had to employ all kinds of conciliatory techniques to soothe the Church in his efforts to launch Ethiopia into modern world. To avoid a sudden break with the traditional system of education he allowed the church to have a hand in the running of the new educational system that he introduced in 1908. He ensured that the foreign teachers engaged were of the Coptic faith. He also allowed the church complete freedom to run its own schools (1967, p. 10).*

The opening of Ecole Imperiale Menelik II in 1908 marked the creation of a dual-system of education in Ethiopia. The Orthodox Church, Quranic, and missionary schools were allowed to function side by side with a government-operated, western-oriented school. To staff the new school, ten teachers were recruited from Egypt because of their compatible religious background. The school was housed at the house of Alfred Ilg, the Swiss technician, and Menelik's key advisor for foreign affairs. In accordance with their practice in Egypt the language of instruction was French, which was also a popular subject with the students, who nevertheless also studied English, Italian, and Amharic (Bowen 1976, p. 315).

It is worth noting here that even though Menelik's intention in introducing western schooling to the country was mainly to produce local masons, blacksmiths, carpenters, etc., the school did not offer full-fledged vocational subjects but concentrated on the teaching of foreign languages in order to facilitate a harmonious relationship between the metropolis and the Ethiopian masses. Whatever vocational subjects were offered, they were only given in the urban areas. Given the foreign capitalists' economic interest in the country and the class background of the early clientele of the school, one can argue that even if vocationally-oriented subjects were offered they would not have been successful because: 1) The foreign capitalists controlled the administrative and commercial enterprises and had already imported skilled labor from their colonies and sphere of influence. Hence, offering vocational skills to Ethiopians would have eventually led to the replacement of the imported foreign labor which the capitalists would oppose. Moreover, at this juncture, what the foreign capitalists wanted was acculturated Ethiopian intermediaries who supported what the capitalists wanted and who would carry out their instructions and act as brokers between the metropolis and the Ethiopian masses. In commenting about the attitude of the foreign teachers Haile Gabriel makes the following observation: "At the time Europeans were interested to advance their national language and culture, if not national colonial interest. As such those Europeans imported to teach or lead schools that were not interested to advance science and technology but European culture, languages and some academic subject" (1974, p. 142). 2) The early clientele of the school were mainly the sons of the nobility. Among the first students were the future emperor, Lij Eyassu who succeeded Menelik, and Dejazmatch Tafari Makonnen who later became Emperor Haile Selassie (Markakis, 1974). As mentioned before, the Ethiopian aristocratic class had a prejudice against manual labor in general and looked down upon the artisan class in particular. So learning vocational subjects was totally unacceptable to these groups. 3) Finally, the reason students at the Menelik II school did not want to learn vocational skills could be explained as a direct function of the opportunity structure in the European dominated urban areas. Students saw high status and reward in joining the bureaucracy and doing European type of work and not in vocational professions (For further discussion on how European type of work affected students' perceptions, see Foster, 1966; and Carnoy, 1974).

Following the Menelik II school, other schools were opened in Harar, Dessie, and Ankober. Several private schools operated by Ethiopian priests also mushroomed in the capital. As stated by Bowen:

> *During this period about a hundred private schools sprang up in the capital, Addis Ababa, where large numbers of children were taught to read and write; most schools were usually held in the open air with the students sitting on sheepskins which they brought every morning and took away in the evening (*1976, p. 316*).*

Other schools owned by foreigners were operating in Addis Ababa. Included in these schools were a Greek school, founded in 1915, and Armenian schools, established in 1918 (Pankhurst, 1968, p. 66).

Following Menelik's footsteps, Ras Tafari (later Haile Selassie) set up a few modern schools in the country. In conjunction with the promise he made to the League of Nations in 1923 that he would abolish slavery and modernize his administration and place Ethiopia among the "civilized nations," Ras Tafari opened about 29 modern schools. These include vocational-oriented schools but the student's enrollment in these schools was very low. Being himself tutored by missionaries, he encouraged the missionary societies to expand their educational activities. As stated by Haile Gabriel, "the missionaries were at this point a very welcome source of expertise and the Government helped them to expand by guaranteeing safe conduct and by grants of sites and sometimes money" (1976, p. 366). By 1935, there were about 100 mission schools with an enrollment of nearly 2,000 students. The Regent also heavily recruited his advisors from those Ethiopians educated in mission schools. He allowed them to publish a weekly newspaper called "Berhane Salem" and propagate western values and glorify western development.

During his European tour in 1924, the Regent purchased books and equipment which were used in the first days of operation of the Tafari Makonen school in 1925. The school was French-oriented and the students were required to sit for the French government's examination of competence in primary studies. The headmaster and the faculty were French and French-speaking Lebanese; however, in another stream, English was used as a medium of instruction (see for example, Abebe and Mohammed, 1970, p. 85; and Bowen, 1975, p.315).

From 1908 to 1935, more than 35 government schools were set up in Addis Ababa and some provinces. A careful analysis of the distribution of the schools, however, shows that there was a close correspondence between urbanization and the establishment of western schooling. Most of the schools were set up in urban areas. In rural areas where foreign contact was less conspicuous, schools were hardly established. Schools were set up in the urban areas because foreign-dominated commercial enterprises and other government employment opportunities were heavily concentrated in the mushrooming urban centers and they were educating future employees. For instance, thirteen of the thirty-four western-oriented schools were situated within the catchment area of the imported capital from France, i.e., the Addis Ababa–Djibouti railway line. Ten of the schools were located within the proximity of foreign-owned coffee plantations.

A particularly interesting feature of the curriculum in most of the schools was that it was geared toward instruction in the mastery of the French and English languages. In some schools, history, geography, and other subjects were offered, but the emphasis was not on local history or geography, it was on European history and geography. Foreign languages were given undue emphasis in schools because mastery of foreign languages was considered the key to modernization and a means of maintaining political, economic, and cultural relations with the metropolitan countries. However, the country's dependency on foreign teachers and textbooks not only resulted in the socialization of young Ethiopians into western values, but also produced indigenous manpower thoroughly socialized to accept the status quo and work as trade partners, interpreters, clerks, etc. in European-dominated commercial enterprises. For instance, in 1823/24, most of the 800 students who graduated from the Menelik II schools were working as interpreters, accountants, secretaries, etc. in private and public establishments (See African Education Commission, 1925, p. 326). Hence, to use Foster's words, what was taught in the schools was consonant with the prevailing "exchange economy and the continued succession of European enterprises" (1966, p. 60). Furthermore, it is worth stressing that mastery of either French or English was not only a means of acquiring prestigious positions within the foreign dominated enterprises, but also an effective instrument in gaining access to political power and a means of reinforcing the existing culture. However, the envisaged "harmonious relationship" based on an unequal exchange between the metropolis (mainly France and Britain) and Ethiopia did not last long; it was interrupted by Italy's annexation of Ethiopia in 1935. The socio-economic and educational change in Ethiopia during the five years period of Italian occupation is given below.

The Italian Fascist Educational Policy for Ethiopia

The Fascist educational policy for Ethiopia was designed to produce semi-skilled natives to fill the demand for cheap labor and to socialize young Ethiopians with a sense of loyalty to the fascist regime. In order to destroy the power base of the previous regime, its practices and remnants were totally suppressed. For example, the few schools that were established before 1935 were either closed or appropriated and given Italian names. The Tafari Makonnen School was renamed Liceo Victorio Emmaual and streamed into academic and technical departments to be used by the sons and daughters of the settlers (see Miaza, 1966 and Bowen, 1976:322). The few Ethiopians who were educated prior to the annexation of the country were either lost in action against the invaders or were liquidated as dangerous elements (Haile, 1976:324). To minimize the influence of the Orthodox Church and prevent its ability to teach against fascism, hundreds of monks were liquidated and many churches throughout the country were burned. Except for the Italian and German missionaries who gave Mussolini their blessing when he annexed Ethiopia and later, in their teachings, sanctified the legitimacy of the Fascist regime, the other missionary societies were barred from teaching and consequently expelled from the country.

In consonance with the segregation policy of fascism, separate schools for Italian and native children were set up. As stated by Pankhurst:

> *The (Italians) were provided with schooling similar to that of their brothers and sisters in Italy, while the natives were restricted to more meager fare, education for Africans being designed to prepare them for a life of subordination in a fascist colony (1967, p. 327).*

Schooling for the natives was limited to grade four and was geared as an instrument of social control. The main objectives of the curriculum was to teach a) the 3R's b) to give some training in vocational skills and c) to instill obedience and socialize the young Ethiopians to Fascist values.

The teaching of reading, writing, and arithmetic was accomplished by the use of the vernaculars. The governors were instructed to see that local languages were implemented as media of instruction in the schools. In accordance with this, Amharic was used in the Amhara areas, Tigrigna in Tigrai and Eritrea; Galligna (now Oromigna) in the Oromos areas; Harari and Alligna in Harar; Amharic and Gallinga in Addis Ababa; Somali in the Somalia area; and Arabic in the Muslim areas. It should be noted, however, that the central goal of using vernaculars in schools was not only to strengthen local cultures and familiarize the learners with their local environments, but also to accentuate feuds among the various nationalities, in order to restrict the movement of the natives. Hence the school curriculum through the use of the media of instruction was made to correspond to the fascist policy of "divide and rule".

The technical skills offered to the natives were in line with the division of labor. That is, natives were trained to supply the existing division of labor. Natives supplied cheap labor thereby helping the capitalists keep labor and social cost to a minimum. In his discussion about the technical subjects offered to the natives, Pankhurst states the major objectives of the technical course as follows:

> *To train the pupils in the cultivation of the soil or to become qualified workers (not specialized) in order to create gradually native-skilled craftsmanship for all fields of labour where, for reasons of climate, surroundings, or race prestige, the use of Italian labour is not admissible*

> *or convenient and for the purpose of reducing the cost of labour and production in general by making use of native labour...*(Pankhurst as quoted in Haile Gabriel, 1974, p. 148).

Italianization of the natives was to be accomplished by the use of classroom rituals and exposing the learners to such symbols of fascism as the Italian flag and photographs of the leaders of the fascist state. In order to establish an emotional orientation toward the symbol of fascism and the Italian flag, the following passages were recited daily by the students:

> *O children of Ethiopia, love the three colors of the Italian flag, because it is your flag, salute it, raising your right hand to it and promise to serve it with faithfulness and honour...*
>
> *(the Italian flag) is the symbol, the sacred and inviolable sign that unites all the wishes and hearts of the Italians under the leadership of the king for the greatness of the fatherland.*
>
> *...This glorious flag is always victorious, because it represents 54 million people. We salute every morning and every evening, the tricolour which represents our dear fatherland....*(Pankhurst, 1967, pp. 330-331).

The textbooks also dealt mainly with the glorification of the Italian empire, life histories of Emperor Victtorio Emthe, the Queen of Italy, and Mussolini. Obedience and respect to authority was inculcated through injunctions – "love your teachers, who teach you to love Italy, the common mother." To accomplish the socialization of the natives into the fascist mainstream, native teachers who knew the local languages were employed; however, they were carefully supervised by Italian priests or nuns (Bowen, 1976. p. 322).

Despite the fascist effort to Italianize the young Ethiopians, however, the indoctrination programs had little impact. Due to the counter-socialization effort of the liberation fighters, school attendance was very poor and the dropout rate was quite high. As stated by Miaza "...it was considered unpatriotic to attend such schools as did admit Ethiopians since they were merely organs of Fascist propaganda and were largely used as a means for stirring up disunity among the peoples of the Empire" (1966, p. 68). Moreover, after the Ethiopian independence fighters launched a full-scale war against the Italian invaders, all the schools were closed down.

As mentioned before, upon Italy's declaration of war against Britain in 1940, the British feared an Italian invasion of the Sudan from Ethiopia; hence the British came to the support of the Ethiopian patriots. Carrying a message of support from General Sir William Platt, chief of the British force I the Sudan, many British intelligence officers left Khartoum to contact the Ethiopian liberation fighters in Gojjam and Begemder. Included in General Sir William Platt's message to the Ethiopian patriots was

> *Peace with you, England and Italy are now at war. We have decided to help you in every way to destroy the common enemy. If you are in need of rifles, ammunition, food or clothing, send as many men and animals as you can spare to the place where our messengers will tell you* (Platt as quoted in Del Boca, 1969, p. 251).

Daniel Sandford, the British Consul during the First World War and Haile Selassie's adviser from 1920-1935, was sent to Ethiopia to organize the full-scale revolt of the population. With the help of the British, the Ethiopian patriots launched a full-scale war against the fascist invaders and the war was over on May 1, 1941. After the restoration of Ethiopia's constitutional independence in 1941, similar to the politico-economic sphere, the Ethiopian education system from 1942 to 1952 was under the domain of the British. With the decline of British influence in the Ethiopian political economic sphere in 1953, however, the educational reforms implemented in the country were by and large U.S. imports. In the following section, the major educational reforms by the British will be reviewed. This will be followed by a brief discussion of some of the salient educational reforms implemented by the American experts. Finally, how some of the contradictions stemming from the educational system resulted in the politicization of high school and university students and ultimately contributed to the down fall of the Haile Selassie's regime is discussed.

The Major Educational Reforms in Ethiopian Schools, 1942-74

A year after Ethiopia got its constitutional independence from the fascist colonists, the Ethiopian Government started to rebuild the education system. The Ministry of Education was reestablished and some schools were opened (namely the Menelik II and the Tafari Makonnen school for boys and the Itegue Menen school for girls). As in the other ministers, however, the British maintained a great influence in the organization of the education system and closely supervised the day to day activities of the schools. A British representative at the Ministry of Education, Mr. E. R. J. Hussy, ensured that the curricula, textbooks, some of the teachers, and the school principals were imported either from England, Canada, or from one of the British colonies and protectorates, such as, India, Sudan, or the Middle East. For instance, the Inspector General, the coordinator of the curricula, and the head of buildings and grounds were all British. Many of the elementary school posts and almost all the secondary school posts were held by British or Indians (Perham, 1947, p. 256). Since the primary objective of education was to make the students proficient in the English languages, English was used as a medium of instruction. To accomplish this objective, all the academic subjects were taught in the English language, starting from grade four; also, the textbooks were primarily designed for schools in the colonies and were imported from England.

Little effort was made to adopt the school curriculum to the needs of the learners. For example, in the arithmetic lessons given at the elementary schools, a British series of the 'High Way" was used which involved problem solving in pound sterling, shillings, and the metric units and had little or no relevance to the day to day activities of the students. Similarly, the flora and fauna of the British Isles, the history of Western Civilization, and the story of the British Knights formed the core of the social sciences and literature. The science courses were highly theoretical. Lessons in health, personal hygiene, sanitation, and agriculture, which could have been relevant to the needs of the students and the community at large, were completely neglected.

Since the content of what was taught was foreign to students, and English was by and large their third language, the students had no choice but to memorize the textbook by heart in order to pass their examination. In his discussion about the teaching and learning process of the period, Lipsky, has this observation:

> *Teaching in the primary and middle school is still largely by rote. The student is rewarded for knowing extensive, recondite texts by heart and for memorization of impressive arrays of facts. Skills in reading and recitation are rewarded but reading comprehension is practically ignored (1962, p. 97).*

As one would expect, learning based on rote memorization and accumulation of unrelated facts did not enable the students to be 'proficient' in English. Students, particularly those from the provincial schools, had very poor results in the national examination given at the end of the elementary school year. Consequently, they could not gain admission to the secondary schools in the capital city. To counteract this deficiency, elementary schools in the provinces were extended by more years to include grades seven *and eight.* As stated by Miaza, the training however,

> *...was little more than a rehash of the requirements for grades V and VI, with a few textbooks added, notably two volumes of "School Science" and the Old World Past and Present" a volume of more than six hundred pages for the teaching of geography and history (1966, p. 84).*

In the secondary schools, the curriculum was based on the London Matriculation Examination. As far as the headmaster and teachers were mostly supplied by the British Council, the main objectives of the curriculum were to make the students proficient in the English language. For example, in the two elite schools in Addis Ababa, the Haile Selassie I Secondary School (opened in 1943 for the sons of the ruling class who completed their primary education in Kenya, the Sudan, and the Middle East, where their parents had been in exile during the Italian occupation), and the General Wingate secondary school (established in 1946 in memory of Orde-Wingate, a British general who served as a commander-in-chief of the Ethiopian Liberation Army in 1941), the students were prepared for the London Matriculation Examination and the General Certificate of Education. Students who passed their examination were sent for further teaching to England or Canada. Indeed, some of the future leaders of the country and particularly those who were at the Haile Selaasie Secondary School became proficient in English. Perham quotes the headmaster of one of schools saying that "the boys had worked with tremendous zeal and enthusiasm and had shown progress even in subjects which were quite new to them. Some of them had written essays in English which were on a level with those written by English boys in corresponding forms" (1947, p. 251).

The University College of Addis Ababa, established in 1950 as a two-year liberal arts college by a group of Canadian *Jesuits was originally a branch of the University of London. To ensure that the college had met the necessary standards an approach was made to the British inter-University Council to evaluate the program and the educational qualification of the faculty members.* In line with the program offered at the University of London, being a liberal arts college, to use Mazrui's words, "it was designed and reserved for the study of high culture and the pursuit of high scholarship" (1975).

After the implementation of President Truman's Point Four Program of Technical Assistance to Ethiopia in 1953, the British predominance in the Ethiopian educational system dwindled. Like the economy, the education system was inserted into the American System. The British experts in the Ministry of Education were replaced by members of the Ethiopian United States Cooperative Education Program. Experts from Oklahoma State University came as advisers under contract with the United States Operations Mission in Ethiopia. Upon the recommendation of Dr. William Winkle, Director, Ethiopian United States Cooperative Education Program, "...a consultant of the Public Administration Service of Chicago, Illinois, was invited in 1953 to study the Ministry's organization and make suggestions for appropriate change" (Miaza, 1966, p. 100). Based on the consultant's recommendation, the Ministry of Education was reorganized to reflect the educational set up in the United States. For example, departments such as Teacher Education, Tests & Measurement, Arts and Crafts, Audio-Visual, Research, and Higher Education, etc, were created.

From 1952 to 1958, alone, more than 3,500 professional textbooks for teachers, over 495,000 copies of textbooks and 292,550 copies of periodicals for students were either imported from the United States or produced by the Point Four establishments in Ethiopia (Ethiopian Observer, 1958, p. 7). Upon the advice of the American experts, a system of eight years of elementary and four years of secondary education was effected throughout the country. As stated by Andargatchew, the main arguments in favor of the 8-4 structures was that "... students would be better prepared, in terms of their knowledge of English, both for secondary and higher institutions of learning where English would remain as the medium of instruction." Another argument, put forward by experts was that "many students dropped out of school after the elementary cycle. If they were to remain in school for more than two years, they would not only acquire additional education but would also be more mature and suitable for employment" (Andargatchew, 1975, p. 1973, p. 62).

In addition, as mentioned before, the University College of Addis Ababa was re-oriented to look like one of the liberal arts colleges in the United States. It had two faculties – one arts and the other in science. The College of Agriculture was established in 1953 as a branch of Oklahoma State University (Trudeau, p. 1968). In collaboration with a handful of Ethiopian educators, the American experts prepared a ten-year development plan (1955-1965), which was subsequently incorporated into the country's First Five Development Plan. The major objective of the plan included 1) the inauguration of a new type of community school, grades 1-4, for basic education, 2) the completion of the then existing primary schools with less than four grades, 3) the limitations of class size at the primary level to a maximum of 40 students, 4) the admission of selected students into the middle school (grades 5-8) and further selection at the end of grade eight, 5) the establishment of at least one middle school in each district (awraja), and 6) the preparation within the ten year period of more than 2,000 and 950 teachers for the community schools and middle schools respectively (Ministry of Education, 1935, pp. XVII –XXII).

With a change of leadership in the United States Government in 1960, the Point Four Program was transformed and renamed Agency for International Development (A.I.D.). The major objectives of the A.I.D. were:

> *...to assist Ethiopia to mobilize its own resources and expand the monetary economy by a) increasing commercial agricultural and industrial production; b) developing manpower, training, and education; and c) improving organizational and administrative skills. By helping Ethiopian economic effort, in order to safeguard important U.S. strategic interests, the U.S. A.I.D. attempted to promote economic and political development (emphasis added, the A.I.D., as quoted in Getachew, 1971, p. 157).*

We have shown above how the United States military's agriculture and economic interests were fulfilled after the A.I.D. and other U.S. connected programs were launched in Ethiopia. In the education sector, most of the U.S. staff that came under the Point Four Program were replaced by A.I.D. staff. As one would expect, the new A.I.D. advisors had different approaches as to how the Ethiopian educational system should be organized. Based on their advice, the education structure at the school level was re-organized to include six years of elementary and six years of comprehensive secondary education (that is, two years of junior and four years of senior secondary program).

In the elementary schools, multiple classes were introduced in which students were grouped according to ability and with a self-contained pattern of organization in "which one teacher teaches all subjects" (see Handbook for Elementary Schools, 1964, p. 6). In order to implement the new programs, one-year and summer in-service training programs for elementary school directors and supervisors were established at the Haile Selassie I University, Faculty of Education, beginning in the 1962-63 academic year.

Upon the advice of the USAID staff experts and financial assistance procured from the World Bank and the United States, comprehensive secondary schools were imported to Ethiopia in the beginning of 1961 in order to man the expanding administrative machinery, to export capital labor goods to the country in the form of teaching equipment and construction materials, and of course to supply the cheap semi-skilled labor needed in the foreign owned enterprises, since it is cheaper for the foreign investors to have the work force trained for them at public expense. For example, like the junior high school program in the United States the junior secondary schools in Ethiopia were designed to differentiate students into separate streams according to abilities and vocational goals. With proper guidance, it was hoped that the two years would serve as a stage for channeling the students into the various streams in the senior comprehensive secondary schools and subsequently into the university or other junior colleges and the labor market.

In the senior secondary schools, a dual system of education-vocational along-side academic streams was opened with the same compound. After brief experimentation with the Woizero Sihen School in Dessie and the Tafari Makonnen School in Addis Ababa, many of the existing academic secondary schools (with the exception of the prestigious schools such as the Wingate School, which were exclusively reserved for the children of the wealthy Ethiopians and foreigners) were converted into comprehensive secondary schools. Starting in 1962, "USAID assisted in equipping of the vocational and technical stream of sixteen comprehensive secondary schools, and the IDA agreed to provide Eth. Birr 18,000,000 in a loan for the expansion of facilities (Abebe and

Mohammed, 1970, p. 95). In 1972 alone about forty of the sixty-one secondary schools in the country had some form of comprehensive secondary school program (see Desta, 1977).

To teach in these comprehensive secondary schools, 177, 326, 490, and 350 American Peace Corps Volunteers were recruited in 1962, 1963-64, 1965, and 1966 respectively (see Tickaher, 1975, p. 132). Starting in 1968, however, the number of Peace Corps Volunteers teaching in the comprehensive secondary schools has been decreasing because of the prevalence of anti-American feeling among students.

Contrary to what was envisaged, the graduates for the comprehensive secondary schools did not get productive employment opportunities in their area of specialization. Quite to the contrary, as will be demonstrated later, unemployment among high school graduates was quite rampant starting in 1968. Furthermore, it can be argued that since the construction of the comprehensive secondary schools was expensive and was mainly used as a means of exporting capital goods to Ethiopia (under the pretext that the construction of class rooms had to meet international specifications at a cost a number of times higher than that of classrooms built to some suitable local standards), they left the country dependent on foreign assistance and loans. For instance, foreign sources provided 28 percent of the financial impact to education in Ethiopia, compared with 10 percent in the case of Kenya and three percent in the case of Tanzania (ter Weele, 1973).

Moreover, since those active in the economy where big foreign finance capital has wielded great influence, the gentry and other functionaries in the Ethiopian administrative machinery sent their children to attend schools in the United States of America, or registered their children in foreign-operated elitist secondary schools such as the Nazareth, American, or English schools, which were well equipped, staffed with highly-qualified faculty members, and focused on academic subjects which lead to the university. Those in the academic streams got special encouragement from their teachers and were given special help sessions. On the other hand, those in the vocational streams did not get adequate attention from their teachers. In fact, in most cases they were discouraged from taking the Ethiopian School Leaving Certificate Examination (ESLCE). However, since students paid to sit for the ESLCE, they were not prevented from taking the examination. But since they were bound to fail, most of them did fail. The few who somehow managed to pass at least three subjects were relegated to lower status diploma-oriented training institutions in order to block their ambition for higher degrees. In short, streaming served the interest of the well-to-do parents and has subsequently contributed to educational and socio-economic inequalities. Students in vocational streams, by the virtue of being assigned to these tracks on the basis of performance in the Grade Eight

National Examination, are substantially disadvantaged in their future educational careers and in the acquisition of social benefits which go with the credentials. Hence, we argue that the dual system of schooling in Ethiopian secondary schools not only reflected the hierarchical social structure, but acted to sharpen and perpetuate class differences.

The USAID influence was not limited to the first and second level of the Ethiopian education, it extended to the university. Like the comprehensive secondary school, the university was reorganized to serve U.S. interests or, to use Mazrui's words, "produce appropriate manpower and redefine the market through acculturation" (1975, p. 198). Upon the recommendations of the University of Utah team headed by Dr. Bentley, the various colleges in the country were integrated into one centrally located financial and administrative unit. Administrators and financial experts from U.S. universities were assigned to the administrative hierarchy of the university (See Getachew, 1971, pp. 182-183 and Markakis, 1974, p. 152; and United States Committee on Foreign Relations, 1970, p. 1905). For instance, until the early part of the 1970s, the Vice President of the Haile Selassie I University, the Dean of the Business College, the Dean of the Law School, the Associate Dean of the Faculty of Education and most of the faculty members were Americans. Teaching materials and other equipment were bought from U.S. markets or from American firms located in other countries. Potential graduates who were expected to promote U.S. interests in Ethiopia were carefully screened and sent to the United States for further training under the USAID scholarship program. To meet U.S. academic standards, the curricula was modeled on college programs in the United States (an exception to this was that a few courses on education studies were offered). As adequately described by Markakis, "the organizational structure of the University, its curriculum design, the materials and methods of instruction are copies of the American undergraduate model" (1974, p. 188).

To summarize, from 1942-1974, the Ethiopian educational system, like the society at large, reflected inequality. As nicely put by one educator, the education system in Ethiopia had not only opened the door to some sections of the population and closed its doors to others and had left many unaware that such doors existed. The few sons and daughters of the working class and peasantry who managed to go to schools attended second rate public institutions. The few fortunate ones who managed to get admissions to these schools were systematically screened through a series of nationally administered examination (see Desta, 1977). As the Ethiopian educational system passed through various profound changes, like the economy, in the 40's and the first quarter of the 50's, the major educational reforms introduced into the country were British–oriented. For the last three decades, the curricula and the teaching materials were basically U.S. imports. Depending on the economic interest of the country and their educational exposure, the American advisers imposed enumerable educational packages upon the Ethiopian scene. Yet despite the educational reforms introduced into the country and a token proclamation by the Ethiopian Government in 1955 that "all boys and girls between the ages of seven and eighteen" are entitled to receive equal educational opportunity (The voice of Ethiopia as quoted in Miaza, 1966, p. 114), one cannot help but notice that in 1974 the Ethiopian educational system was characterized by; 1) low participation rate of primary and secondary school age children, 2) disparity in educational opportunity between the different regions, between the sexes, and between rural and urban areas, 3) a high dropout rate in both elementary and secondary schools, 4) a high pupil-teacher ratio and inadequate operational budget, 5) a high dropout rate of unemployment among high school graduates due to the stagnation of the economy, thereby contributing to student politicization and open confrontation of the corrupt and decaying system of the old in 1974. In the Ethiopian economy, the supply of manpower at the secondary level outstripped demand, contributing to around 25 percent of high school graduates unemployed and actively seeking jobs. The students felt cheated by the schools, which raised their sights, and the society, which failed to fulfill their employment aspirations. Thus, under this socialization process for failure, the students had no choice but to reject the political and economic order and to feel that they had nothing to lose and everything to gain by shaking up the reproduction of the existing social relations of production. Indeed they did shake up the system by exposing its inherent contradictions to the public, and thus in part contributed to the downfall of Haile Selassie's government.

Student Politicization and Activism in Ethiopia

Except for occasional minor strikes concerning their conditions as students, before the 1960's, student agitation against the political system was a rare phenomenon. For instance, "in 1956 the editorial in the first issue of the student paper of the University College invited students to write articles on any topic except politics and religion" (Markakis, 1974, p. 358). This does not by any means, however, imply that students of that period had no dissatisfaction with the socio-economic and political order. In fact, there is ample evidence that many students were caught in a dilemma. On the one hand, they wanted to see the system reformed, but on the other hand, they wanted to get into it and share its privileges. However, there was no opportunity for the students to express their opinions. They were forbidden from participating in school activities such as debates and literary contests (see Addis, p. 1975).

To the surprise of the regime, the year 1960 marked the birth of the Ethiopian student movement when university students, particularly those at the University College of Addis Ababa, demonstrated in support of the coup *d'état* of December 1960. Even though the demands of the students mainly focused on a peaceful transition to a bourgeois-oriented democratic government, modeled on the American pattern, the fact that the students were able to demonstrate and openly confront the regime set an unprecedented stage for their radicalization, which involved demonstrations on social-oriented issues and the publication of militant pamphlets.

It is worth nothing here that after the loyalist army crushed the so-called "rebels", the regime turned against those students who took part in the demonstration. In order to humiliate them, the students were ordered to "write letters of apology to the Emperor as a condition of being readmitted to study. They did so and returned to school (Levine, 1965, p. 139). However, the attempt by the regime to cow the students into submission, did not deter them from exposing the glaring contradiction in the system to the public. In their annual oratory and poem contest they continued attacking the socioeconomic and political order. Indeed, they were able to politicize and win public support against the regime. They also drew support from the prospect-less high school students who were looking for leadership. As stated by Hess, "as in Europe and America, dissenting University students in Ethiopia became the model for protest by secondary students. Ironically, the government itself established the link between the two groups of students—through the establishment of University program." (1970, p. 169).

Starting in 1965, that is, a year after University Services students were assigned to teach in the provincial secondary schools as part of their degree or diploma requirements, student "demonstrations became annual events, and a pattern of confrontation was set, with university students taking the lead, followed by secondary school students in the capital and some of the larger towns" (Markakis, 1974, p. 359). Thus, starting in 1965, secondary school students in Ethiopia had either joined demonstrations led by university students or organized their own demonstrations and class boycotts.

In 1965 university and high school students in and around Addis Ababa demanded land reform. In 1966 they protested against governmental rounding up of jobless and destitute in concentration camps. As described by Addis:

> *...a group of militant students surreptitiously entered these concentrations in Shola, and at great personal risk took photographs of the horrifying scenes of life in the concentration camps. Dead bodies unburied and littered all over the place, mothers emaciated in agonizing childbirth, and other unable to survive it, the living unfed and unclad. These pictures more than any other evidence clearly showed the exact nature of the ruling class, whose solution to unemployment and peasant eviction was the rounding up of the destitute in concentration camps. The*

> *forces of the student movement were then fully mobilized for a massive demonstration calling for the dismantlement of the Shola camp, proper medical treatment for the victims, security of employment, and the trail of those who were directly responsible for such a policy* (1975, p. 97).

In 1967, the university students demanded the affirmation of the right to public demonstration and assembly.

Between 1968 and 1969 secondary school students throughout the country voiced their grievances on a number of cases. In Debreberhane, students went on strike after the director of Hailemariam Mamo secondary school transferred two popular Ethiopian teachers. The confrontation between the security force and the students resulted in the killing of one student.

At Nazareth, students of Atse Gelawdos comprehensive secondary school demonstrated against the Twelfth Grade National Examination fee. They stoned the provincial governor, the local military commander, and the town elders who tried to persuade them to pay the fees for taking the 12th national examination (Hess, 1970, p. 170).

At Welamo Soddo, the expulsion of a student leader led to a student strike. In support of Debre Berhane, Nazareth, and other secondary school students' demands, secondary school and university students in Addis Ababa presented a comprehensive list of student demands to the government. Their demands included:

- Compensation for the parents of the dead student in Debre Berhane and the trial of the Debre Berhane police chief;
- Abolition of national examination fees;
- Automatic entrance into university for all secondary school graduates;
- A more just allotment of scholarships given by foreign countries;
- An increase in the budget for education;
- Dismissal of the Minister of Education, Akale Work Habte Wolde;
- Faster economic growth;
- An end to unemployment;
- Cuts in money spent on embassies, banquets, ministers' salaries, and visits abroad; and
- The expulsion of "immoral Indian" and American Peace Corps teachers (see Hess, 1970, p. 170).

After presenting these demands, university and high school students in Addis continued boycotting classes. Emperor Haile Selassie, in his broadcast to the nation of March 7, 1969, warned the students that the university and high schools in Addis Ababa would be closed if students did not resume classes within three days. The Ministry of Education also appealed to parents of secondary school students to ensure that they take their children to school. This did not seem to frighten the students; in fact, these warnings made them take a determined stand not to return to classes and to continue their agitation. They "circulated pamphlets attacking the king as corrupt and senile and urged peasants, workers, and soldiers to revolt (Hess, 1970, p. 171).

> *Convinced that the matter was getting out of hand, on March 25, 1969, the then king asked to meet with a delegation of students' councils and asked them to explain to him the reasons for their boycott of classes. The students representatives openly told the king that they would not go to class unless and until the following demands were met: free and equal education for all Ethiopians; a fair examination system; the replacement of foreign teachers whose moral standards were "bad" for Ethiopians; reform of the educational system; an increased educational budget that would provide allowances for poor students; and the release of all students who had been detained in the current disorders" (Schwab, 1972, p. 134).*

After listening to the student demands, Emperor Haile Selassie then promised that "students who could not afford to pay tuition would not have to. He said that the cabinet was studying school reforms, but that it would be difficult to provide universal free education and that Ethiopia depended on foreign teachers to staff its schools. He said that the arrested students would be tried through the normal legal channels" (Schwab, 1972, p. 134). The Emperor however, on September 8, 1969, pardoned all students jailed in the spring demonstration and those who were suspended from schools for inciting strikes. The Minister of Education, Akale Work Habte Wolde, was transferred from the Ministry of Education to the Ministry of Justice.

In September 1969, classes were started, but agitation against the government and strikes against school authorities and teachers whom students perceived as "unfair" or severe disciplinarians continued. As a result of the student strikes a number of principals were transferred and some were even beaten to death. As chronicled by Grey, "Some of strikes that occurred were not trivial incidents. The Ministry of Education frequently must settle the strikes" (1970, p. 190). University students also changed their strategies, instead of openly confronting the government they started circulating pamphlets attacking the government. For instance, in the student paper *Struggle* they called for the various people of the Empire to be allowed the right to self-determination. A few days after an article "on the question of nationalities" was published, the president of the University Student Union of Addis Ababa (USUAA), Tilahun Gizaw "was killed by two bullets fired from a passing car without license plate number" (Youth Action, 1970, p. 11).

As a result of this, tension mounted, all work came to a halt at the university and all secondary schools throughout the country. University and high school students from Addis Ababa schools marched to the university administration office chanting "we want to know how he died" (Youth Action, 1970, p. 11). Then a group of demonstrators broke into the Haile Sellasie I Hospital and forcefully took the remains of the Tilahun Gizaw to the University Faculty of Medicine building for a post mortem examination. At that point, the imperial bodyguards arrived, blocked off all approaches to the campus, and started shooting students. The resulting causality was the death of a militant student, Sebhatu Wubneh, along with more than ten who were wounded (Gilkes, 1975, p. 250). The government then shut down the university for most of January 1970, but high school students throughout the country boycotted classes until the end of March, 1970.

Generally speaking, the year 1971 was quiet. There were no major demonstrations against the government. But demands for replacement of teachers, reforms in school policies and programs continued as very important issues in many secondary schools. Due to the endless student unrest in many secondary schools, many highly qualified high school principals either resigned from their posts or applied to the Ministry of Education for a transfer to the central offices. Fresh graduates from the university even declined appointments as high school principals. These factors forced the Ministry of Education to call a general meeting of all high school principals to discuss the problem and find solutions to the existing student unrest. As pinpointed by the secondary school directors who attended the meeting, the internal causes of student unrest were inadequate facilities, absence of communication between students and administrators, fear of failure in examinations, dislike of some subjects and certain teachers. The main external cause of student unrest was political agitation against government programs and policies, manifested in refusal and reluctance to attend flag ceremonies and other ceremonies at the schools (see Ministry of Education, 1971, pp. 44-45). Though the committee on student unrest was aware of the external causes of student dissent in Ethiopian schools, the political situation of the time did not allow the committee to recommend changes in government policies. However, with regard to internal causes, it was decided that schools should make the maximum use of available supplies, and recruit and train better teachers. It was also recommended that cordial relations between students and administrators be established.

It is very difficult to determine whether the above recommendations were implemented, but evidence suggests that student unrest in Ethiopian high schools did not decrease. In the spring of 1972, high school students in Addis

Ababa implemented an urban-based plan of action designed to accomplish revolutionary objectives. They attacked high bus fares and had considerable effect in getting price control in Addis Ababa. When students boycotted classes for more than a month, those students who failed to show up for classes were arrested under Ethiopia's ninety-day detention order. As described by Glikes "altogether about 1,000 were sent to a number of isolated work camps for three-month periods. Most of them were freed by a Liberation Day Amnesty (5 May), but the Government announced that they could not expect automatic reinstatement" (1975, p. 250).

In 1973, agitation over the famine in Wello and Tigrai was the main cause for student agitation but the year was over without major disturbances. In 1974, student unrest was revived with great intensity. In February 1974, high school students in Addis Ababa staged a demonstration in support of teachers' demands and practically in opposition to the proposed education reform (Education Sector Review). They attacked city buses and with the university students they participated in every demonstration of workers, and the demonstrating Muslims called for equality of all religions and the establishment of a secular state (See Addis, 1975, p. 98). In March 1974, many high school and university students in Addis Ababa burned the effigy of then Prime Minister Endalchacew Makonnen. The students also demanded the arrest and trail of the former cabinet Ministers. On September 11, 1974, the Emperor was arrested and the Derge (the Provisional Military Administrative Committee) formally assumed power, but students started attacking the Military government and demanded a provisional civilian government; distribution of land to tenants; formation of political parties; freedom of the press, assembly, speech, and demonstration, separation of religion and politics, etc. They also warned the Military Government that until and unless the above and other popular demands of the masses were immediately met they would continue to struggle. The Military promised to fulfill their demands; however, university and high school students from grades eleven and twelve were assigned to work in rural areas in a program called "Development through Cooperation."

To conclude, the preceding analysis of student activism, reveals that over the last ten years Ethiopian students have been significantly alienated and have increasingly turned to militancy. This was observable from demands for land reform, better treatment of beggars, the right to public assembly and demonstration, price control, demands for educational reform, and assistance during famine conditions. Finally, after a decade of struggle, in 1974, the Ethiopian student movement emerged as a mass movement embracing the peasantry, urban proletariat, and the rank and file of the army and was instrumental in bringing about the downfall of Haile Selassie's government. Therefore, contradicting the oversimplified dogmatic mechanistic view that educational institutions fulfill a conservative role and serve in the perpetuation of the existing social relations of production, we witnessed in the Ethiopian scene, starting in 1965, a breakdown of correspondence between the economic base and the educational institution located in the superstructure. Though unintended, schools produced alienated, politically conscious, and highly militant students, (see for example, Carnoy and Levin, 1976, and Weiler, 1972). By looking back to the socio-economic structure, the outputs of schooling contributed to the dismantling of the corrupt and decaying system of the old.

Chapter 5

MILITARY SOCIALISM AND ITS IMPACT ON HUMAN CAPITAL FLIGHT FROM ETHIOPIA

As shown in Chapter 4, it was student protest in addition to the official cover-up of the catastrophic drought and famine in Wollo and Tigrai and the widespread of corruption accompanied by economic recession that contributed to the down fall of the Haile Selassie's regime in 1974. That is, as the government was raising fuel prices, in January of 1974, army units in the southern part of the region mutinied in protest of the inadequacy of food and water rations. By the end of June 1974, a military Coordinating Committee from the 40 units (i.e., representatives of privates, non-commissioned officers, and junior officers up to the rank of major) from the Ethiopian Army, Air Force, Imperial Guard, Territorial Army Police force and Navy was formed. On September 12th 1974, the Military Committee of the Derge (the Amharic word for committee) transformed itself as the Provisional Military Administration Council (PMAC) and took over the state and government power, know as the Provisional Military Administration Council (see Balsvik, 1985).

To eliminate student arrest, the Military Government (Derge) in the name of "Development Through Cooperation Campaign (Zamacha)" dispatched all university and junior and senior high school students and their teachers to rural areas. Furthermore, to control student unrest, the Derge that replaced the *ancient regime*, issued on December 20th, 1974, a proclamation of Ethiopian Socialism (Hibrettesebawinet) as an ideology to restructure the outmoded socio-economic order. In the economic structure, it partially nationalized the commanding heights of the economy in 1975. To mention only a few, banks, insurance companies, financial intermediaries, and industrial enterprises were brought on short leash under the control of the state. It abolished private ownership of rural and urban land. According to Ottaway's observation "the nationalization of urban land and rented houses in August 1975, had profound impact on the society. They effectively destroyed the social basis of the growth of entrepreneurial bourgeoisie, although private investments in commerce and small industries were still permitted" (1976, p. 80). Stated differently, on March 4, 1975, the Derge declared: a) the nationalization of all rural land; b) the abolition of tenancy; c) the maximum family farm was to be ten hectares (25 acres); d) no one could employ farm labor; e) peasant cooperatives of 800 hectares would be organized; f) the peasants would be in charge of enforcement of the land reform, and the urban land was nationalized in July of 1975 (See Ottawy, 1976 and Balsvik, 1985).

Though it was an empty promise, in 1976, the Derge issued major policy directives on the "nationalities question". In a document entitled "National Democratic Revolution" (NDR), the Derge declared that the rights to self-determination of all nationalities will be recognized and fully respected. It went farther and suggested that regional autonomy was viable solution to the existing political problems in Ethiopia. Following this, the Derge was able to bring together the five left-oriented rival groups MEISON, Waz League, Malerid, Abyotawi Seded, and Ichat and worked with them to create, the Provisional Office for Organization Affairs (POMOA), which was later transformed into EMALD or Ethiopian Marxist-Leninist Organization (see Gadaa.com). In 1976, however, EMALD was divided on the issue of the nationalities question. "One group favored the implementation of the principle of self-determination up to independence while those opposing opted for regional autonomy. This led to the disbandment of the EMALD, and many of its members and a few Derge members who supported self-determination in its true sense for nationalities were either shot, imprisoned, or exiled (see Gadaa.com, 2012).

Actually, as the Derge consolidated its power and successfully fought off the invasion from Somalia in 1977, it turned against the very forces and groups who brought about the revolution by unleashing the "Red Terror". "The streets of Addis Ababa and other cities and towns were littered with the dead bodies of youth, workers, and intellectuals, and victims of the Derge 'Red Terror' campaign" (see Gadaa.com, 2012).

Subscribing to the socialist model of centralized planning, in October 1978, the Derge announced the national Revolutionary Development Campaign to mobilize human and material resources to transform the economy. For instance, in line with the commitments of the National Democratic Revolution, in 1978, the then Ministry of Agriculture and Settlement prepared an annual development plans for its sector which was mainly designed to ensure: a) sufficient agricultural products for the growing population, b) produce various exportable crops for foreign exchange, c) to produce the supply of primary goods for local industries, and d) provide employment opportunities (as quoted by Getachew. D. 2010).

Until 1984, local plans called "Zemetchas" were formed that focused on the spatial and economic reorganization of the peasantry into producers and service cooperatives. In addition, Cooperatives and Peasant Association and Agricultural Marketing Corporation were also formed, to control prices of agricultural products, by the regime as instruments of regimentation and political control over the peasant mass (see Tadesse, K. 1995). As illustrated by Tadesse the

> *Collectivization restricted the democratic rights of the peasantry, both in political and economic terms. Party agents were purposely planted among the collectivized peasantry and Peasant Association, not to help them politically in the rigid principles of a socialist ideology and to curb their freedom* (1975, p. 113).

Realizing that industrialization was the engine for achieving rapid economic development, the Derge also initiated the Ten Year Perspective Plan (1884/5 to 1993/4), an agricultural plan to generate the financial surplus for the country's long term industrialization program. More specifically, in line with its socialistic plan to promote industrialization, the Derge introduced a new agricultural development program known as the Peasant Agricultural Development and Extension Program (PADEP).

Scholars in the area have mixed feelings about the content and implementation of the declared socialist policy. Its supporters see the change from the existing remnants of feudalism and capitalism to the path of socialist orientation as a positive strategy for Ethiopia's development. The critics saw it as an ideology forged purposely to promote petty bourgeois class interest. For example Markakis argues that

> *Nationalization created a large number of executive posts for the educated petty bourgeoisie, whose members replaced the former owners, managers, and higher level administrators of the nationalized enterprises. In the state administration, the purge of the bureaucratic bourgeoisie created a vacuum at the upper levels of the apparatus, which was quickly filled with promotion from below and appointments from outside ... The self-employed sector of the petty bourgeoisie also gained through the forceful elimination of foreign capital competition* (1977, p. 23; and see also Addis, 1975, p. 55).

The opponents inside Ethiopia seriously doubt if the measure taken in the name of Ethiopian socialism amounted to socialist revolution. They argue that the workers and peasants have been promised much but given little. Each of these designations might contain an element of truth. During the seventeen years the military government was operating under many strenuous conditions, the fruits of the socialist experiment have not materialized. Some of the initiatives taken by the military government in the implementation of socialism, for instance, the workers and peasants were promised much but given little. In a very cynical and telling way, the masses referred to the Derge's propaganda as *diabo be radio* (bread by radio). Stated differently, from the beginning, the Derge's socialist rhetoric was perceived by the Ethiopian masses as pure demagoguery amounting to nothing. Eshatu describes the Derge's socialism in Ethiopia "...as a half-hearted exercise that fell far short of addressing the serious policy failures of the past" (1992, p. 4). In addition, Getachew (2010) feels that the "Cooperative and Peasant Associations formed by the Derge in 1984-85, served as repositories for surplus extraction by the government. They functioned more as instruments of state control and regimentation than as the lowest tiers of local administration.

Given that the Derge or military junta was in power for seventeen years, potion of the chapter given below will assess: 1) the lessons that could be learned from the process of development or the lack of it in Ethiopia? and 2) the impact of the military junta on human capital flight from Ethiopia. Since assessing the impact of development process requires a multi-dimensional approach, more specifically, the purpose of the chapter given below is limited to a brief analysis of the socio-economic strategies and outcomes of the Derge – as an organ holding the reins of state power in Ethiopia for seventeen years.

Socio- Economic Conditions in the Era of Military Rule

As shown in Table 5.1, during the 1976-86 period, Ethiopia's nominal gross national product (GNP), rose on the average by 2.5 per year. At 1984/85 constant price, however, Ethiopia's GDP per capita decreased by the rate of 1.6 percent per year during the 1989 because the official cost of living index increased from 4.4 percent in 1973/83 to 5.2 percent in 1990. Similarly, with the decline in gross domestic investment from 2.6 per annum (1973/83) to 2.0 percent during 1980/88 period, gross domestic product declined from 2.3 percent during 1973/83 to 1.4 percent during the 1980/88 period, and to -0.4 in 1990. In general, the GDP increased by 1.9 percent per year during the Derge's period (1974-1990), while population increased at a rate of 2.9 per year.

In contradiction to the Derge's lofty ten year plan (1984/85 -1993/94) of building a socialist Ethiopia on an expanded agricultural base and making it self-sufficient in food production, the growth in the agricultural sector, the most dominant sector in the country, was disappointingly low. That is, agricultural productivity declined sharply from 1.2 percent during 1973/83 to a negative growth rate of 1.1 percent during the 1980/88 period. As described by Makonnen and Eshatu, the,

> *... economic record of the seventeen years of military rule was to prove an unmitigated disaster. By almost every major index of economic growth, the country retreated rather than advancing forward. Wrong-headed policies, war, environmental degradation, a rapidly growing population, adverse external development, and a number of other factors combined to drive the economy to the edge of the precipice* (1992, p. 3).

TABLE 5.1: ETHIOPIA'S DOMESTIC ECONOMIC CONDITION, 1974-1990

INDICATOR	1963/73	1973/80	1976/86	1980/88	1989	1990
Nominal GNP Growth rate/year (%)			2.5			
Real GDP Growth rate (%)	4.1	2.3		1.4	-1.6	-0.4
Population Growth rate (%)		2.7		2.9		
Annual rate of Inflation (%)		4.4		2.1	7.8	5.2
Domestic Savings (%) of GDP					8.7	7.6
GDP per capita, purchasing power parity (PPP$)					392	369
Gross Domestic Investment	1.5	2.6		2.0		
Agriculture	2.1	1.2		-1.1		
Health	5.7	5.7		3.6		
Education	14.4			10.6		
Human Development Index					0.237	0.249
Budget Deficit		4.1 (1975)				14.5
Defense/Administration		7.3 (1980/81)		8.6 (84/85)		

Source: The World Bank, *World Development Report 1985;* the *Economist Intelligence Unit,* 1986-87, 1997; and IMF, Investment Financial Statistics

The government budget deficit, which increased from 4.1 percent in 1975 to 14.5 percent in 1990, clearly indicates that government expenditure has grown. However, in line with the Derge's militaristic attitude, the budgetary process also clearly exhibits a built-in bias toward defense and internal security matters to the neglect of agriculture, health, and education. For instance, while military expenditure increased approximately at the rate of 8 percent per year for the last 15 years, expenditure on education for the period 1976-86 declined from 14 percent to 11 percent.

The peasants were not allowed to participate in the process of production. While land reform abolished the existing feudal serfdom and redistributed land to the farmers, subsequent collectivized agriculture were not meant to increase productivity but were meant to subjugate and control the farmers. As pinpointed by Getachew (2010), the military junta that dressed itself in socialist garb used the instruments of the state to control and regiment the masses. "... efforts to consolidate and expand mechanized state farms...faced a number of technical, financial and managerial difficulties. Famine and the insidious civil war also ravaged the country's economy." For example, with the establishment of the "Villagization Program" in 1985, though 12 million peasants were relocated and collectivized, the famine of 1984/85 contributed to a mass exodus of Ethiopian refugees to neighboring countries.

As shown in Table 5.1, in terms of the Human Development Index, Ethiopia ranked below 160 out of 173 countries. More particularly, during the Derge's period the educational system was not thoroughly designed and articulated with the economic structure to create productive employment opportunities for school leavers. That is, the centrally-controlled economic structure of the Derge was not tailored to meet the manpower requirements. The dual system of education (that is, private vs. government, vocational vs. academic streams) perpetuated class differentiations. The national curriculum was not designed to produce well-rounded people. With a total restructuring of the existing organization and of social relations in schools, students were not allowed to participate in decision-making that affects their lives in school. As done in other socialist countries, schools in Ethiopia were not catered to produce students integrated with productive labor. That is, schools were not established with their own factories, farms, and agricultural cooperatives (see for example, Lu Ting-Yi, 1962, p. 124).

Having analyzed the military era of Ethiopia's internal economic conditions, in order to get a comprehensive picture, a brief look into the external economic relations as measured in terms of current account balance, export composition, export destination concentration, foreign aid, external debt, and debt service ratio is in order.

As shown in Table 5.2, Ethiopia's current account deficit (excluding official transfers), increased from three percent of the GDP in 1970, to eight percent of GDP in 1988. During the 1980-88 periods, while exports declined at the rate of 0.7 percent, imports, which included food products, crude petroleum, and machinery, increased at the rate of 7.2 percent. Until 1983, the US was the major market for Ethiopia's exports. Starting in 1985, however, the Federal Republic of Germany became Ethiopia's largest single export market. Following Ethiopia's dependency on the Soviet Union for armaments during the Ethio-Somalia border dispute of 1977, the Soviet Union provided a bulk of Ethiopia's imports. But the existing trade relations seem to be in favor of the Soviet Union. For instance, during the 1985-87 period, Ethiopia's trade deficit with the Soviet Union reached about US $438 million.

TABLE 5.2; THE STATUS OF ETHIOPIA'S EXTERNAL ECONOMIC RELATIONS

Current account/GDP	3% (1970)	8% (1988)
Annual Growth of Exports	-0.5% (1965-80	-0.7% (1980-88)
Annual Growth of Imports	-.0.7% (1965-80	7.22 (1980-88)
Trade with the Soviet Union (US$M)	-739 (1980-84)	-438(1985-87)
Official Dev. Assistance/GDP	5% (1982)	17.4% (1988)
External Debt/GNP	9.5% (1965-80)	50.6% (1980-88)
Debt Service Ratio	11.4% (1970)	37.4% (1988)
Soviet Military AID(US $M)	1500 (1975/79)	4200 (1983-87)
Soviet Economic Credits (US$M)	170 (1975-79)	770 (82-84) 158 (1985-87)
Growth in international reserves (months of Import Coverage)	1.1 (1989)	0.6 (1990)

Source: the World Bank, World Development Report, 1985/90 and David E. Albright, "Soviet Economic Development and the Third World" Soviet Studies, 43:1, (1991), pp. 27-60.

During the Military era, Ethiopia had a high concentration of commodity exports. On the average, the share of Ethiopia's two principal exports (i.e., coffee and hides and skins) accounted for 78 percent of the total exports in 1985. Among other factors, a high concentration of commodity exports had been the cause for foreign exchange earnings in Ethiopia in the event of price changes. Rightly so, the price of coffee declined between 1979 and 1982. Though a nation is supposed to have foreign exchange balance to cover imports at least for three months, Ethiopia's growth of international reserves coverage declined from 1.1 months in 1989 to 0.6 month in 1990 (See EIU, 1987/87).

Due to economic mismanagement (that is, maintaining an over-valued exchange rate, increasing the money supply, and maintaining a high government budgetary deficit), Ethiopia's external debt from leading western industrial institutions increased from 9.5 percent during the 1965/80 period to 51 percent during the 1980/88 period. Similarly, after Ethiopia signed a 20-year treaty with the Soviet Union in early 1978, Soviet economic credit and military-related assistance increased substantially. In addition, the Official Development Assistance as a percentage of the GDP increased from 5 percent to 17.4 percent in 1988.

To summarize, an analyses of the internal and external economic conditions of Ethiopia during the Derge's era clearly indicates that on the economic indicators, except population, the country had regressed as the "bread basket of the Middle East." That is, it could not grow enough food to feed its own people. With the decline in per capita income, food consumption declined rapidly.

Preoccupied with its own existence, the Derge heavily borrowed from western private lending institutions and multilateral organizations in order to buy armaments. By 1989, Ethiopia's external debt amounted to 51 percent of its GNP. Therefore, based on the amount of external debt Ethiopia had accumulated, if Ethiopia was not a sovereign nation, it would have been forced to declare bankruptcy. Thus the military junta had therefore mortgaged the nation to foreign creditors. The cycles and crises which beset the Ethiopian economy suggest that the Derge had practically no control over the economy.

For example, though an attempt was introduced by the Derge to liberalize the Ethiopian economy in November 1988, the measures announced did not contribute to improvement. The prescription was therefore more nationalization, more settlement, more villagization, etc, in brief, more of the same medicines (See Eshetu, 1992). By the time the head of the Drege, Mengistue, left the country, Ethiopia was characterized by economic crises. Various factors can be cited for the military regime's poor performance. In 1974-78, the growth rate was 0.4 percent because of instability and the war with Somalia. In 1979-83 growth rate was 4.2 percent because of good weather conditions. In 1984-84, the economy plummeted to -5.3 percent because of severe drought. In 1986-87, the economy grew up by 7.9 percent and declined to about -1 percent in the 1989-90 periods (see Eshetu, 1992).

The total blame, therefore, directly and squarely falls on the Derge's misdirected policy. For example, the misguided implementation of the Derge was curtailed because a) of the nationalization of farm land, b) of the villiagisation program, c) of the Agricultural Marketing Board pricing strategy, d) of the inadequate attention given to private sectors in the economic construction of the country, and e) the Derge could no longer get aid from the Socialist countries, due to the Soviet Union being mired in its internal turmoil because of Mikhail Gorbachev's *glasnost* and *perestroika*. Furthermore, the economy was in disarray when the Derge started persecuting and eliminating the intellectuals and imposing the Red terror. For example, as a result of the Red Terror, a number of intellectuals left the country. Due to the mass exodus of people from Ethiopia, the Mengistu regime outlawed departure from Ethiopia without government approval. Furthermore, the Derge started labeling those who left the country as traitors against the country and the people. Those who were caught agitating against the regime were made to receive a punishment of five to 25 years imprisonment or faced execution (Terrazas, 2007). In the section given below, some suggestions as to how the current regime could entice the Ethiopian Diaspora to return to their motherland are proposed.

Reversing Ethiopia's Intellectual Capital Flight

It is claimed by the current Ethiopian government that it has drafted a five-year program (2010/11 to 2014/15), a medium-term strategic framework in consultation with its citizens, private sector, civil society, etc., to achieve the country's growth and transformation plan (GTP). To accomplish the envisaged GTP, Ethiopian policy makers are determined to maintain at least an average real GDP growth rate of 11% to a) meet the Millennium Development Goals (MDGs), b) expand and ensure the quality of education and health services, c) achieve the MDGs in the social sectors, and d) establish favorable conditions for sustainable state-building through the creation of a stable, democratic, and developmental state (Ministry of Finance and Economic Development, September 2010).

If we analyze Ethiopia's GTP in light of the new growth model, or endogenous growth, or innovation economics theory, the driving force behind Ethiopia's anticipated economic growth seems to be based on the improvement in knowledge, technology, entrepreneurship, and innovation (see, Paul Romer, 1994, and Robert Lucas, 1988). Using the endogenous growth model, Hugue and Kim (1995) also argue that the emigration of people with high levels of human capital reduces the growth rate of effective human capital that remains in the country and generates a reduction in per capita growth in the source country (Hague and Kim, 1995). In addition, Grandy states that the new growth theory "places technological change and knowledge at the center of explanations for why high-income countries continue to grow (June 1999)." Stated in simple terms, "without enough trained agronomists, biologists, engineers, scientists, doctors, nurses, and information and communication technology professionals, it is impossible for the firms and farms to use technology to upgrade their products and efficiency – and that makes it difficult for them to face foreign competitors" (University World News, 2007). In addition to the new growth theory, government policy plays an important role in supporting the accumulation of knowledge that contributes to high standards of living. Economists, now more than ever, seem to be convinced that effective government policies contribute substantially to the economic growth of a nation (Grandy, June 1999).

Therefore, to ensure a long-term, sustainable, macroeconomic growth pattern, the Ethiopian government needs to establish a well-developed infrastructure base and have a reserve of highly-talented human capital, both of which are so vital for growth in global knowledge. In addition, to be involved in an effective and innovative system, Ethiopia needs to form links with well-known global universities, international consultants, and other friendly overseas organizations. If these types of friendly environmental factors are integrated systematically and harmoniously, with pertinent human rights policies, there is no doubt that Ethiopia can entice the Ethiopian Diaspora to return to their motherland. The ability to harness the intellectual capital of the returnees with their contacts from the outside world would bring about very competitive ventures.

The acute lack of intellectual capital is a core problem not only in Ethiopia but also in other parts of Africa. As stated by Idehen (2010), the United Nations has reported that the failure of the postcolonial state in Africa in the 1970s and 1980s is due to the exodus of highly-skilled Africans as the result of low morale, lack of academic freedom, and collapse of tertiary education, as well as the rise of authoritarian regimes, and hardship and paralysis ushered in by Structural Adjustment Programs (SAP). For example, the United Nations Economic Commissions for Africa estimated that between 1960 and 1990, an estimated 67,000 highly-qualified Africans left the continent for the West. Between 1985 and 1990, Africa has been losing an average of 20,000 skilled human resources annually. Similarly, the World Bank reported that some 70,000 highly-qualified African professionals, experts, scholars, and managers with internationally marketable skills leave the continent every year (World Bank, 2002). For example, "...the continuous outflow of skilled personnel from Africa has widened the gap in science and technology between Africa and other continents. Africa's share of global scientific output has fallen from 0.5 in the mid-1980s to 0.3 in the mid-1990s" (Woldetensae, 2007).

To offset the serious skill shortage created by lost human capital, Atanga, et al. estimate that African countries have been recruiting about 100,000 skilled non-African expatriates at an exorbitant cost, estimated at US $4 billion annually (2006). What is disturbing is, "...the outflow of the best and the brightest qualified personnel makes it impossible for Africa to train either enough or enough qualified persons to the high standards desired, nor is it able to do so in numbers sufficient to offset and replace those who migrated from the continent" (Mohamoud, 2005). Put in simple terms, the flight of intellectual capital from Africa has crippled African economies and imposed huge strains on the African continent. Although the data is incomplete and not wholly reliable, if the net potential benefit (i.e., benefits minus costs) is computed by subtracting productivity of labor supply acquired by the receiving countries from remittance benefits sent to the source countries, the problem of the "brain drain" has affected Africa more severely than any other region. As Mohamoud narrates it, the problem is now a matter of especially great concern "...because Africa is losing the research and innovative capacity needed to participate in the development and exploitation of global knowledge–knowledge required to find solutions to the eradication of hunger and abject poverty and degradation of the natural environment" (2005). Similarly, as succinctly narrated by Sachs, Africa now actually lacks the capacity to design good policies and deliver services in all sectors and at all levels. Among other factors, to be competitive in the globalization era, Africa will need far more scientists, engineers, accountants, health professionals, managers, teachers, economists, and agricultural instructors than are currently available on the continent (January 17, 2005).

It is reasonable to argue that African countries are funding the education of their nationals only to see them end up contributing to the growth of developed countries with little or no return on their investment. As stated in one of the editions of *African Journal*,

> ...African universities are actually training one third of their graduates for export to the developed nations. We are operating one third of African universities to satisfy the manpower needs of Great Britain and the United States. The African education budget is nothing but a supplement to the American education budget. In essence, Africa is giving developmental assistance to the wealthier western nations which make the rich nations richer and the poor nations poorer" (Emeagwal, 2010). When we look at the impact of human capital at a country level, between 1980 and 1991, Ethiopia alone lost about 74.6% of its human intellectual capital. Currently, Ethiopia ranks first in the continent in terms of the rate of loss of human capital, followed by Nigeria and Ghana.

To galvanize the intellectual capital of the African Diaspora, in recent years a number of African countries have either changed their rules to allow dual citizenship or are considering such changes. Among those countries that have changed the rules in the last 15 years are Angola, Burundi, Republic of Congo, Djibouti, Gabon, Gambia, Ghana, Kenya, Mozambique, Rwanda, Sao Tome, Principe, Sierra Leone, Sudan, and Uganda. Others, including Egypt, Eritrea, and South Africa, allow dual citizenship but only with official permission of the government. Still other countries like Tanzania and Liberia introduced a Citizenship Retention Act. For example, December 14, 2010, the Liberian President, Ellen J. Sirleaf introduced to the Liberian parliament a proposal that Liberians who had left during the civil war and had become naturalized as citizens in other countries could be allowed to reclaim their Liberian nationality (Manby, 2010, p. 58).

As mentioned above, during the Derge regime, Ethiopia has lost enumerable human capital. The current regime has therefore created an intermediate status for over 2 million of the Ethiopian Diaspora who have settled abroad. In 2002, according to a government proclamation, No. 270/2002, foreign nationals of Ethiopian origin were issued special identity cards, called "Ethiopian Origin Identity Cards." Though the Ethiopian diaspora may not vote or be elected to any office at any level of government, or be employed on a regular basis in the armed forces or diplomatic corps, holders of such cards do enjoy rights and privileges that other foreigners do not, including visa-free-entry, residence, employment, the right to own immovable property in Ethiopia, and the right to access public services (Manby, 2010, p. 76).

With the unleashed forces of globalization, the problems of brain drain and capacity building have become pertinent to the ongoing discourse on development among conscientious Ethiopians. Ethiopia at this moment in time is in dire need of massive capacity building projects and has planned to achieve the medium-term Growth and Transformation Plan by 2015. If the assets of the Ethiopian Diaspora are purposefully tapped, there is no doubt that this would enable Ethiopia to accomplish its growth and transformation goals.

The focus of this section of the chapter is to trace briefly the push and pull factors that contribute to the brain drain of skilled Ethiopians who move to more advanced countries. In addition, the paper examines the policy options available to the Ethiopian government and to host countries for ways to restrain and manage the brain drain. By drawing on some policy initiatives undertaken elsewhere, options include reversing the brain drain so that highly skilled personnel can return to their homelands, and/or establish some kind of brain circulation between those of the diaspora and those still residing in less developed countries (Mohamud, 2005).

The Push and Pull Factors of the Migration of Highly Skilled Ethiopians

The term "brain drain" was coined to describe the outflow of scientists and engineers to the United States and Canada that took place in the 50s and 60s (see Grozard and Llull, November 2004). Before the 1960s, the brain drain was from developing countries in the South to industrialized countries in the North, and it "...involved mainly manual workers and poorly qualified service personnel...the migration of professional and academically-qualified staff, by contrast, occurred primarily between industrialized countries and reached its peak (immediately after) the two world wars...when a large number of well-trained workers and academic and professional specialists emigrated to North America from the economically weak countries of Europe" (Korner, 1996). Currently, the impact of the brain drain on the developing economies has been assessed by the divergent and convergent schools of thought. The divergent and dependency school of thought argues that brain drain from the developing countries to the developed countries drains the sending countries of their best and most talented human capital and is regarded as the most important cause of underachievement in the developing countries.

On the other hand, looking at brain drain from the functionalist perspective, adherents of the convergence school argue that remittances from the receiving countries promote development by improving income distribution and quality of life. The value of migrant remittances can significantly exceed that of national export earnings. Expanding this perspective, the "brain gain" hypothesis argues that the brain drain is not a dead end that intensifies economic and social crises of the sending countries. Instead, the brain gain hypothesis deduces that through a remigration of elites the human capital stock increases and contributes to the potential growth of the developing country (Rena, 2007). Furthermore, the brain gain hypothesis assumes that "returned migrants will probably invest (i.e., make better investments than foreigners) their capital with advanced economic know-how that they gained in the industrialized country" (Hunger, January 2002).

Placing the brain drain argument within a very sound theoretical framework, Zimmerman (1996), analyses the migration of skilled professionals from developing to developed countries and concludes that it is a result of internal home "push" factors that dislodge skilled personnel from their home countries, or "pull" factors that attract the highly-skilled to more advanced countries. Despite that globalization is leading to further marginalization of developing countries and to a deepening of inequality, in spite of global interdependence of production, consumption, knowledge creation, and sharing, Zimmerman implicitly assumes that, by default or design, the newly industrialized and developed countries have become magnets for the migration of highly-skilled workers from the developing countries.

The Push Factors

The push reasons for emigration are: adverse domestic conditions such as the inability to advance professionally, the lack of educational opportunities to undertake more research and training, lower living standards, inadequate coordination between the education and labor market, internal political instability, and uncertainty about the future. For example, of those 20,000 Ethiopians who left the country from 1941-74 for higher education and diplomatic missions, Levine (1965) indicates only 63 Ethiopians were granted asylum in the United States. A vast majority returned, not because the economic prospects in Ethiopia were so attractive, but because a number of the returnees felt that they had an obligation to serve their country and at the same time politicize high school and college students, labor, and members of the military to stand against the ruling class. In fact, it was the student, labor, and military demonstrations that aggravated the conflict that eventually brought the collapse of the Haile Selassie regime in Ethiopia in 1974.

However, the greatest push factor of migration in the history of Ethiopia arose after the council of soldiers known as the Derge seized power in 1974 and proclaimed socialist order in Ethiopia. For example, during the Carter administration, "Volunteer Departure status" was accorded to a number of Ethiopians in the United States. In 1977-82, the Derg imposed the Red Terror to persecute and eliminate those opposed to the Derg rule. During the Ogaden War of 1978, and the establishment the "Villagization Program" in 1985, about 12 million peasants were relocated and collectivized. Then there was the famine of 1984-85. All of these events contributed to the mass exodus of Ethiopian refugees to neighboring countries.

The number of Ethiopians who emigrated to the periphery such as the Sudan, Djibouti, Somalia, and Kenya were urged to settle in the United States, Canada, Australia, New Zealand, United Kingdom, Sweden, Federal Republic of Germany, Denmark, Holland, Netherlands, Israel, Switzerland, Greece, Italy, and France via Sudan or Kenya, etc., either because of the family reunification policy in the West, or they were given refugee status to establish permanence in European and Western countries. Facing a "massive flight of people from Ethiopia, as discussed before, the Mengistu regime outlawed departure from Ethiopia without government approval." Anyone who fled was labeled a traitor "against the country and the people, and could receive a punishment of five to 25 years in prison or in extreme cases, life imprisonment or execution" (Terrazas, 2007).

The Pull Factors

The pull reasons for migration from less developed countries to advanced countries are generally related to self-selection for those seeking better personal and professional opportunities in the host country, international wage differentials, differences in the quality of life, educational opportunities for children, interaction with other professionals, and political stability (see for example, Dzvimbo, 2003). According to the factor price equalization theory (FPE) that originated out of the Heckscher-Ohlin (H-O) model, when the prices of the output of goods are equalized between countries as they move to free trade, then the prices of the factors (capital and labor) will also be equalized between countries (Suranovic, 2006). Therefore, using the factor price equalization theory, Solow (1956) developed the income convergence model or the inequality-decreasing effects across economies in a perfectly competitive market. That is, once free trade is allowed to set the prices of factors, capital and labor are likely to be relatively equal between countries that follow free competition.

The brain drain rates are well above 40 percent, particularly for Sub-Saharan African countries, and Central American countries (Marhiori et al, June 2009). The rationalization given by economists for the migration of highly-skilled workers from the developing countries to the developed countries is that in an integrated international labor market migration will eventually equalize oversupply (the brain overflow) and demand in different locations and that both economies benefit (Korner, 1996). It is generally assumed that "emigration serves as a vent for surplus labor, alleviating the pressure to remove the structural rigidities which exist in many Third World countries and causes labor market inflexibility (Korner, 1996).

At the same time, many industrialized countries introduced favorable immigration policies with active recruitment opportunities to fill gaps in their labor force from the developing countries. Such gaps are caused by aging population and by shortages in rapidly growing fields that are mentioned above. For instance, in 1967, Canada adopted the point system that favors highly-educated and highly-skilled, young individuals. Australia followed suit in 1989, then New Zealand in 1991. In 2006, a detailed plan was presented in the British Parliament on how to implement a points-based immigration system. In 2007, the European Commission announced a "Blue Card" system in the hope of luring more qualified migrants for specific technology fields (Marhiori et al, June 2009, p.3).

According to Shinn, putting aside the traditional emphasis on family reunion, the United States has implemented a number of immigration bills to attract skilled labor, such as a selective, temporary immigration policy to select the best and brightest skilled workers during the 1990s. It also offered the diversity immigrant visa program, better known as the DV program, to encourage the immigration of underrepresented nationalities to the United States. The E-category visa of the Immigration and Nationality Act for about 140,000 employment-based immigrants was divided into five preference categories. The three categories generally applicable to Ethiopians are: 1) persons of extraordinary ability in the sciences, arts, education, business, or athletics; 2) professionals with advanced academic degrees, and 3) investors who can invest at least half million dollars (November 23, 2002).

After 1991, a number of Ethiopians migrated to some of the more advanced countries because in Ethiopia every citizen is allowed free access to the Ethiopian passport and also, unlike the Derge period, the country does not require an exit visa for Ethiopian visitors leaving the country. As a result, a number of Ethiopians in the diaspora have been accorded lawful immigrant status and permanent residency, or have eventually been allowed to become naturalized citizens in the United States of America because they have claimed that Ethiopia is ravaged by ethnic violence and various types of human rights violations endangering their return (see for example, Terrazas, 2007).

With globalization trends, over the years the emigration wave of highly-skilled persons from Ethiopia has significantly increased to the West, especially starting in 1974. Given that there are no reliable global estimates on brain drain from Ethiopia, it is very difficult to estimate precisely the amount of foreign currency repatriated to Ethiopia. As defined by Mishra, workers remittances are "... the value of monetary transfers sent to the source countries by workers who have been abroad for more than one year. These are recorded under "current transfers" in the current account of the IMF's Balance of Payments Statistics Yearbook" (Mishra, January 2006).

A broad measurement of remittance includes compensation of employees (i.e., is the value of gross earnings of foreigners residing abroad for less than 12 months, including the value of in-kind benefits such as housing and payroll taxes), migrant transfers which include the net worth of migrants who move from one country to another, and from informal transfer systems that operate outside the formal banking or financial channels, also know as hawala (January 2006). Today, workers' remittances are becoming increasingly important as a source of external funding for many developing countries. Though unstable due to business cycles, the World Bank estimated that diaspora remittances to Ethiopia "grew from US$18 million in 2001 to US$174 million in 2005, an increase of over 300 percent" (cited by Terrazas, June 2007). Though the official report of the National Bank of Ethiopia indicates that the amount of money Ethiopia gets from remittance inflow has never surpassed the one billion dollar mark, the World Bank on the other hand states that the country gets at least 3.2 billion of dollars yearly (Tamene, 2010).

Those who came from wealthy families may not have the incentive to remit and remittance tends to decline with the length of migrants' stay, the Ethiopians of the diaspora are very involved in many activities which benefit their home country. For example, they have been sending money to family members to build houses and to start and expand businesses. As social networks, they mobilize through hometown associations and groups for community development, serving as cultural ambassadors, maintaining and extending public infrastructure (schools, hospitals, health centers, and roads), and donating clinical equipment. However, other than inflow of remittances which have been affected by business cycles, emigration from Ethiopia has decreased human capital stock and there is a very limited transfer of venture capital such as investment in green technology. Currently, it has become obvious that the underdeveloped countries are in the process of being stripped of their skilled human capital leaving them ill prepared to face globalization and survive in the new global economic order. Given this information, what possible strategies can be proposed to policy makers in developing countries that will assist underdeveloped countries to become included instead of excluded from the emerging technological path?

Policy Implications for Dual Citizenship

There are three possible objectives developing countries could target to improve and reverse the flow of knowledge: a) minimize losses by trying to retain the highly-skilled, b) seek to increase the benefits of emigration by adopting the brain-circulation approach, and c) offering dual citizenship to the diaspora.

a) Retaining highly-skilled. The loss of high-skill labor from migration is very substantial in developing countries. Though reliable data is not available, it is assumed that more than 80 percent of Ethiopia's GDP (i.e., calculated in terms of income) is composed of labor wages. The negative externalities of migration from Ethiopia's GDP is likely to outweigh the remittances sent by Ethiopians living abroad. Due to human rights, Ethiopian graduates cannot be prevented from migrating to countries where their skills are needed. Therefore, a civilized way to retain the skilled labor force in Ethiopia is to reorganize the education system and provide higher skills in agro-business and medical technology, both of which dominate the economy. It has become axiomatic that a large number of developed countries are moving away from agriculture. Therefore, by changing the present system of land ownership, Ethiopia can add value to its endowed resources by re-orienting the curriculum of its educational system toward sustainable and environmentally-oriented agri-business and medical technology. Making clear the value of environmentally-oriented agri-business to the local communities can make them aware of the pressing the need to conserve local resources for future generations. Thus, Ethiopia's comparative advantage is in its resources, the government might reap higher returns in the long run by investing in agri-business, medical education, infrastructure, and better employment and career opportunities, leading to greater retention of the highly-skilled (see for example, Mishra, 2006). Due to globalization, even if the education system in Ethiopia is restructured, it may be difficult to prevent emigration, therefore, the real policy challenge is how Ethiopia, while respecting human rights, can maximize the benefits of its high-skilled labor by retaining them.

b) Brain-circulation. In the early 1990s, in a number of developed countries the idea of brain-circulation emerged. The "brain gain" hypothesis encourages those of the Diaspora to undertake collaborative research projects in the countries of their birth without requiring them to relocate back to their home countries. This approach is based on the premise that the home country would thrive from such vibrant intellectual networks by gaining from the added value of human capital in the Diaspora who reside in host countries. From this perspective, the brain drain was viewed as a potential asset rather than a liability. Therefore, it became a challenge to devise ways to tap into the pool of nationals abroad (Tettey, W., 1 May, 2003). It is argued by Hunger, that two basic social trends support the idea that emigrated elites represent a resource for developing countries that can be used for the development process, "Firstly the trend towards transnationalization due to globalization which makes it possible to live in two countries simultaneously, and secondly the trend towards a 'knowledge society', in which the importance of human beings – who carry the knowledge –in the development process is increasing (2002). Therefore, the "brain gain hypothesis" highly encourages the sending countries to motivate and induce their Diaspora to return home and/or to build up a transnational network. To justify this argument, Hunger mentions that the Taiwanese boom in its technology sector in the 1990s was influenced by non-resident Taiwanese returning from the United States of America. Similarly, the positive economic development in China is related to the remigration of the so called Overseas Chinese. Like India, the South-Korean state government has installed a government office, which is supposed to motivate emigrated elites to return to their home country (Hunger, 2002).

c) **Dual citizenship.** This chapter goes one step further and argues that if Ethiopia is to achieve its medium term Growth and Transformation Plan in 2015, it needs to welcome and offer dual citizenship to the Ethiopians scattered throughout the world. Yes, it was quite innovative in 2002 to offer the "Dual Origin Identity Card" to all Ethiopians in the Diaspora. Now, since we are in the period of highly interconnected global economies involving diverse human interactions, Ethiopia need not left behind but instead must offer dual citizenship to the Ethiopians scattered throughout the world. As stated by Raghuvanshi, dual citizenship is becoming more common in our increasingly interconnected global economy. Many countries are now seeing the advantages of dual citizenship and are liberalizing their citizenship laws. They see that dual citizenship has the advantage of broadening a country's economic base by promoting trade and investment between citizens and their two respective countries (2010).

As dual citizenship has become a hot button topic, almost all African countries are vigorously pursuing it. Ensuring the continental trend, "the countries of the East Africa Community (EAC) - Burundi, Rwanda, Kenya, Tanzania, and Uganda,...have taken steps in recent years toward the legalization of dual citizenship" (Manby, B.(2010, p. 60). Therefore, it will be advantageous for Ethiopia also to pursue the legalization of dual citizenship for its original citizens, now in the Diaspora. For example, the UNDP cites of the Philippines, whose 2003 restoration of dual citizens resulted in increased economic and governing participation by the country's citizens in the Diaspora (Mpofu, May, 2010). However, since a favorable political and business environment is perquisite to bear fruit for dual citizenship, the necessary human rights need to be practiced in Ethiopia. It will encourage not only those planning to leave the country to remain in Ethiopia but also it will entice those Ethiopians in the Diaspora to return to their revered motherland.

To mitigate the "reverse technology transfer" or the indirect transfer of prosperity (or the subsidization of the North by the poor South) or the intellectual migration of skilled labor force from the developing countries to developed countries, Jaddish Bhagwai issued a pioneering proposal in the 1970s. Bhagwati's tax plan was designed to compensate the developing countries for the loss incurred by the outflow of intellectual knowledge. Put differently, the basic idea of the migration tax initiated by Bhagwati proposes that migration tax would either be paid by qualified migrants themselves to their home countries or levied by the governments of the destination countries and transferred to the originating developing countries through the United Nations to compensate developing countries for the losses experienced by those natives left behind (See Korner, 1996, Wilson, 2006 and Marchiori, 2009). A different line of argument by Groizard and Llull, suggests that if developed countries establish specific programs to attract skilled workers from developing countries, "one useful way of reducing the impact of brain drain in sending economies is to subsidize education through foreign aid. Investing in local education becomes a necessary condition to replace human capital flight" (November 2004). But, it is worth emphasizing that to apply Groizard and Llull's proposal there needs to be a synergy between the design and implementation of human capital that originates in the sending countries in collaboration with the returnees, and the development packages that are given by the sending countries.

On the other hand, if a country transforms brain drain into brain gain through the re-integration process so that the returnees are gainfully employed and they begin to participate in the social and economic development of their home country, it is likely that the returnees might face double taxation. That is, the returnees might be levied taxes on their income from their original home and also from the countries where they have become naturalized citizens. Under international law a country can tax the income of its expatriates abroad as long as they retain its citizenship. For instance, the US regularly taxes its citizens abroad (see for example, Lowell, 2001). However, it should be left up to the original home country to negotiate with the host country to make the returnees only pay taxes to each country based on the incomes obtained in each country. The host countries, as their developmental aid, could be generous enough to give a tax write-off of income generated abroad to those who have returned to their original home country. Then, the returnees could give the amount of tax write-off to the home government so that it could be spent on productive environmentally sustainable projects.

Through the now out-of-date "Origin Identity Card," the current government attempted to lure Ethiopians in the Diaspora to return home and invest.

Similarly, the Ethiopian government attempted to use a minimally opportunistic mechanism to explore the potential of the Diaspora, such as remittances, bank deposits, investment in government bonds, etc. Though controversial and with the possibility of creating dissension between those who stayed home and the Diaspora, the government has gradually attempted to employ professionals and scholars by offering to pay their relocation expenses, giving free or subsidized housing, and tax relief for the first few years (see Shinn November 23, 2003). To reiterate, the Ethiopian Diaspora need to be offered dual citizenship status rather than the outdated status, known as the "Origin Identity Cards" so that the returnees may collaboratively design with policy makers to implement a new socio-economic developmental plan for their beloved country.

In order to effectively tap the developmental potential of the Ethiopian Diaspora, existing laws need to be amended to allow for dual citizenship so that the attachment of the emigrants to their home country becomes a permanent one. In addition, offering the Ethiopian Diaspora a dual citizenship would make up for the shortfalls of highly qualified human capital which the country lacks. The returnees would bring back the necessary entrepreneurship skills, offer academic talents, engineering, medical, and scientific research skills, and other professional resources. In addition, instead of the current status of brain drain, by offering dual citizenship, Ethiopians are likely to play a major role in influencing the economic and political decisions in their host countries to favor their countries of birth and descent. As argued by Emerson, Naturalized US citizens are not legally obligated to give up their citizenship of their country. The United States has never ordered newly naturalized citizens to present themselves to their native country's embassy in order to formally renounce their original citizenship. Legally, there is nothing in the constitution and there are none from the United States Supreme Court preventing in the constitution (via the State Department) from requiring all naturalized citizens to officially renounce their citizenship to their native country as condition for naturalization (April, 2009).

By effectively recruiting the Ethiopian Diaspora back to their respective homes, Ethiopia could serve as a magnet for attracting competitive investments by galvanizing capital knowledge from a number of higher educational institutions. But foreign diplomatic missions which Ethiopia is now pursuing need to be reformed. For example, the United States could be divided into four regions—North, South, East and West. The existing Diaspora residing in those four regions could nominate three representatives from each region to the council of Ethiopia's Foreign Affairs to serve as "Attachés of Intellectual Capital" for their region. Then, the Council of Ethiopia's Foreign Ministry, could select four attachés from the twelve candidates to represent the four regions in the United States as "Attachés for Intellectual Capital." Of course, these selected representatives though autonomous in their decision process are supposed to work under the guidance of the Ethiopian Foreign Affairs Ministry. In addition, it is worth mentioning that the person elected to represent a region, say in the United States should never be asked to be involved in issuing visas. Issuing visas to foreign visitors who are intending to visit Ethiopia can be handled efficiently by diplomatic missions either in Washington or New York.

In short, the "Attaché for Intellectual Capital," selected by the Council of Foreign Affairs upon the recommendation of residents of the four regions in the United States needs to be highly skilled in marketing and disseminating the most current and valuable information about Ethiopia. In addition, to be credible any "Attaché for Intellectual Capital" needs to be endowed with research capabilities and communication skills. If these innovative strategies are carefully integrated into its developmental strategies, it is axiomatic that Ethiopia could achieve not only its Medium Growth and Transformation plan but Ethiopia in the long run will likely endure sustainable development.

Chapter 6

FROM A TURBULENT COMMAND ECONOMY TO ETHNIC FEDERALISM AND TRANSITIONAL DEMOCRACY

Over the last five decades, by design or default, the Ethiopian political environment has been pursuing various externally designed economic paradigms. For example, from the 1930s to 1974, Ethiopia was ruled by a highly centralized and semi feudal authoritarian regime. When Ethiopia was ruled by a military regime from 1974-1991, its economic system was conditioned to reflect the socialist mode of production, and the commanding heights of the economy were nationalized and run by the state. In short, from 1974 to 1990, the military government created a command economy, managed by cliques and run by the state apparatus. As a possible panacea to its constant hiccoughs, one year before it was laid to rest in 1991, the military attempted to diversify the Ethiopian economy into a mixed economy instead of one that was entirely run by the state. (see Eshetu, 1992).

However, in 1989, a coalition that included the Ethiopian People's Democratic movement (EPDM), the Oromo People's Democratic Organization, (OPDO), the Southern Ethiopian People's Democratic Front (SEPDF), and the Tigray People's Liberation Front (TPLF) formed an umbrella of Ethio-national front, known as the Ethiopian People's Revolutionary Democratic Front (EPRDF) to dismantle the Military Junta and its functionaries from the Ethiopian power structure. With an oversimplified dogma and the mechanistic view of Ethiopian socialism, and then an attempt to form a mixed economy, a civil war broke out in Ethiopia and in 1991. The EPRDF replaced the military junta and "...adopted a provisional national charter, created an 87-member

Council of Representatives and formed the transitional Government of Ethiopia" (Crisis Group, September 2009). Though the Oromo Liberation Front withdrew from the transitional government in 1992 and some members of the Southern Ethiopian Peoples' Democratic Coalition also abandoned the coalition government; the remaining members of the coalition started implementing its new constitution in 1994. Finally, On August 21, 1995, the Federal Democratic Republic of Ethiopia formulated the creation of a federal structure of government, and organized the country's first multiparty elections in 1995 (World Bank, 2005, p. xxi).

Over many decades, African scholars have attributed Africa's poverty and underdevelopment to its economic dependence on the values of Western nations. Given this argument, a number of states in Africa have been endeavoring to transform the indigenous structure of communal organization by recasting it into a new and modern mould which fits the present African situation. As a negation to the Western political and economic models, Kofi and Desta, for example, have formulated economic development theories for the indigenous African. According to Kofi and Desta: 1) Africa's development programs need to be built on existing local knowledge and capacities, or have to be adapted and agreed upon by the people in order for them to be beneficiaries of the development process; 2) If Africa is to achieve legitimate and sustainable development, local Africans need to be drivers of the change; 3) The African countries should examine critically Western capitalist economic theories, since they were developed for a different social order, and modify them, if need be, before using them; 4) African countries should critically study and examine the socialist models, adapt them and use the more relevant aspects; 5) African governments have to relinquish their direct control over many community organizations; and 6) Africa's rural and urban poor must be helped to organize so that their needs are met. The poor cannot depend on benevolent rulers or non-government organizations. The poor people and the strengths of their numbers in organizations could truly help them to represent themselves in pressing their demands and subsequently becoming masters of their own destiny (2008, p.320).

Given the fact that the Ethiopian regime has openly declared in Article 39 of the constitution that it is transforming its political system to bring about a "renaissance for Ethiopia" under autonomous regional federalism states and achieve a democratic developmental system. The major purpose of this chapter is therefore to assess 1) the effects of federalism in Ethiopian politics, economic growth and income distribution in an era of globalization, and 2) impact of autonomous regional federalism states on primary schooling in Ethiopia.

Ethiopia's Ethnic Federalism in an Era of Globalization

The cardinal principles of the 1995 constitution were to establish a federal governance based on unity and diversity, and to achieve stability in the remaining Ethiopian polity. The Ethiopian polity was predominantly divided into nine ethnic regional states (i.e., Tigray, Afar, Amhara, Oromia, Somali, Benishangual-Gumuz, Gamebella, and Harar); the Southern Nations, Nationalities and Peoples (SNNP—a voluntary merger of 5 regions); and the cities of Addis Ababa and Dire Dawa (see Habtu, 2003; Serra-Horguelin, A. 1999). To achieve this, in line with Article 39 of the constitution, each Nation, Nationality and Peoples in Ethiopia were assured the unconditional right to self-determination, including the rights to secession. As stated in the constitution the rights of self-determination could only come into effect:

- when a demand for secession has been approved by a two-thirds majority of the members of the Legislative Council of the Nation, Nationality and Peoples concerned;
- when the federal government has organized a referendum to take place
- within three years from the time it receives the concerned council's decision for secession;
- when the demand for secession is supported by a majority vote in the referendum;
- when the federal government will have transferred its powers to the Council of the Nation, Nationality or People who voted to secede; and
- when the division of assets is effected in a manner prescribed by law (Selamata, December, 2013).

For the implementation of the 1995 constitution, a brief review of the literature indicates that three outstanding perspectives seem to have been advanced over a period of fifteen years as possible explanations of Ethiopia's current federal status. The first perspective argues that the federal state is moving in the right direction to render its people self- and shared rule. Opposing the first view, the second perspective strongly argues that the ethnic federalism designed by the Ethiopian Peoples' Revolutionary Democratic Front (EPRDF) and in particular Article 39 of the Constitution is a threat to the unity and territorial integrity of Ethiopia. The third perspective, highly endorsed by the writer of this article, holds the opinion that the type of ethnic and regional federalism created in Ethiopia in 1995 was not carefully worked out and is too cumbersome to facilitate adequate communication among the constituents in the New

Age. The 1995 Constitution was too haphazardly designed to appeal to some of the disgruntled and powerful Oromio groups at that time. This third perspectives further argues that confining the various Nations, Nationality and Peoples of Ethiopia into watertight compartments was not wisely strategized because times are changing and the world known then is not the same today in the era of globalization (Tabor and Manlam, 2010). It is not too late for the existing Ethiopian federal structure to be altered and amended to cope with the challenges of the emerging era of globalization. Among other things, since globalization is no longer an idea but an imperative strategy that institutions and regional groups must incorporate into their framework for long –term growth and prosperity, the various constituents within the Ethiopian federation need to be interdependent and have effective communication among themselves to serve in today's global environment (see for example, Tabor and Manlam, 2010).

Government officials who played a major role in designing the 1995 federal constitution and who have been busy implementing it, expressed their opinion on Ethiopian Television that the *modus operendi* of the Ethiopian federal structure is more democratic when compared with the oppressive, centrist-oriented, feudal monarchy, and unitary military dictatorship that subsequently ruled Ethiopia. Moreover, they argue that by giving assurance to the Ethiopian people as stated in Article 39 of the constitution, that the Ethiopian people will understand that they have been given shared rule and may live in relatively stable political environment that guarantees their inalienable rights of enjoying divers life-styles. After reviewing the literature on federalism and articulating the lessons that can be learned, Ambassador Habisso almost agreed with the position of the government officials. In his words, "Today, the gradual and incremental growth and development as well as practice and management of the (Ethiopian) federal model (federation) is deepening and progressing in the right direction" (December 06, 2010).

People of the second perspective complain that the current federalism in Ethiopia is exclusively dominated by the Tigrai Peoples Liberation Front (TPLF) and EPRDF. They strongly argue that it will inevitably threaten the unity and territorial integrity of Ethiopia. In addition, unlike those who wholeheartedly support the existing federalism in Ethiopia, the second group argues that instead of giving assurance to the Ethiopian Nations, Nationalities and Peoples, Article 39 of the Ethiopian Constitution would cause political turmoil. Though not as extreme as those who categorize the current government in Ethiopia as nihilist and an enemy of the Ethiopian people, Hirbe (August 13, 2010), for example, argues that "the current government in power has at least recognized in principle the rights of nationalities to self-rule. People of different nationalities in Ethiopia are no longer ashamed of their identities and are not afraid to speak their native language. They can develop, promote, and preserve their language and culture. They have achieved cultural autonomy. Since diversity (ethnic, linguistic, religious, etc.) is a very important human rights issue, Hirbe argues that "this is a huge step forward and there will be no way of turning back. ...the TPLF/EPRDF should be commended for this achievement. But on the other hand, Hirbe argues that the same people are denied to exercise their political and economic rights" (August 13, 2010).

There are more than enough reasons to demonstrate that the centralism of the past in Ethiopia led to atrocities that created grave consequences in Ethiopia. But, unlike the first and second perspective, the third group based on historical materialism, offers constructive criticism by suggesting pragmatic imperatives to Ethiopia's policy makers to improve federal governance in Ethiopia. The third perspective, however is taking into consideration how the federal systems in the Soviet Socialist System (USSR) and Yugoslavia (which according to their communist constitutions gave each republic a right to self-determination and secession) have eventually disintegrated. Thus, it can be argued that Ethiopia's structure for federalism was not only ahistorical but was implemented without pondering its relevance to the Ethiopian society.

Considering the aim of Ethiopian federal administrators in line with Africa's communal deliberation *modus operandi*, in order to achieve internal harmony among distinct and irreconcilable ethnic and various groups as beneficiaries, policy makers should have attempted to include the various stakeholders in designing the nation's federal development process. Participation by the local stakeholders would have given a deeper understanding of local conditions and concerns of each resident, which is so vital for decision making. In short, since the process lacked any systematic studies or discussions by the various stakeholders there were hardly constructive initiatives to reconcile cultural diversity that could lead to equal power- sharing necessary for forming a cohesive Ethiopian nation. In retrospect, the third perspective argues that it was the politicians running for office, who were socializing with the various local constituents in order to be elected. Thus, the local people were hardly involved in the creation of the federal system. Because the Ethiopian Federal constitution was hurriedly accepted without adequate deliberations that would appease some disgruntled ethnic groups, whom the EPRDF perceived to be very important actors in the then very volatile political environment, the federal system was imposed on various regional states.

Therefore, to use Hirbe's phrase now, Ethiopia "can not go back." Instead, Ethiopia has to march on realizing that the federal model is a challenging work in progress and that the federal structure has to be constantly altered and amended to cope with the challenges that are likely to arise in an Age of Globalization (see for example, Forum of Federation, October, 1999; August, 2002; March, 2005). If the inhabitants in a federal state have more than one identity, every individual should have the right to travel and settle within any region of Ethiopia not as second class citizens as is overtly and covertly practiced today. Each citizen of Ethiopia should be regarded as a primary citizen of the Ethiopian federal system. That is to say, every Ethiopian citizen has the same opportunity to enjoy the same social conditions and the same ability to establish business in every part of the federation. To achieve this, the educational framework in Ethiopia needs to be restructured so that the curriculum is created with one language system that could be taught starting in the primary grades, in addition to vernaculars designed for each region. Moreover, as discussed below, the teaching of English should begin in the first grade in order to broaden the minds of students so that they are aware and ready to encounter the emerging global environment.

Since the current federal system is cumbersome and regional states feel threatened by ever-growing federal institutions, instead of basing them solely on ethnicity, for efficiency purposes each region could be demarcated into a number of manageable units and then incorporated into the federal system. To reduce inequity, for example, the Oromia region, Amhara regions, Benishangual-Gumuz, and the Tigrai regions could be subdivided into smaller, more manageable regions. However, since sub-national units can not be equal in resources, to reduce disparity among constituent units, the federal government could design an equalizing income support for inter-unit transfer of resources so essential for social services. These infrastructure basics such as health, education, etc., are effective drivers of growth (see Sen, 1999).

Finally, a more effective way to carry out the above briefly suggested solutions and the right way to mend the existing federal system in Ethiopia is to create a democracy. Of course, the cornerstone of a democratic federal polity is based on diversity. Among other things, the most viable and necessary condition for an Ethiopian federal government is to encourage and require each community to choose its own representatives in government. In short, in addition to power-sharing, an effectively designed federal system of government can not be a panacea for solving some of the economic problems that Ethiopia is facing today. If we subscribe to Laurate Sen's hypothesis that large scale famines have never happened in a democracy, instead they can only happen in authoritarian systems that lack openness of information and transparency. Then when Ethiopia redesigns its federalism and practices a sound democratic system (based on mutual checks and balances and gives power-sharing that empowers the local people), it is very likely that hunger is likely to be a thing of the past. Therefore, given that effective federalism is a license to self rule and also an effective structure for shared rule with the assurance of checks and balances, it is suggested that a predictable and transparent democracy needs to be widely entertained at the local level. Participation often results in a multiplier effect since it promotes the empowerment of stakeholders (see for example, Rogers, et al., 2009). If Ethiopia can effectively implement at the local level a working democracy that empowers local citizens, the relevance of the alien Article 39 of the Ethiopian constitution seems to be unnecessary. In fact, it is our opinion that if Article 39 of the constitution is eliminated by the Ethiopian Parliament, the invigorating federal system suggested above will most likely be the basis for enticing the silent majority at home as well as rallying a number of disgruntled Ethiopians in diaspora to be designers and vibrant actors in the global economic order. In the section given below, an analysis of the impact of economic growth and income distribution is in order.

Economic Growth and Income Redistribution

The argument about the relationship between economic growth and per capita Gross National Product (GNP) was heavily influenced by the Kuznets inverse –U hypothesis. In his Presidential Address to the American Economic Association, Kuznets argued that changes in inequality are associated with structural change in the economy (Atkinson & Brandolini, 2009). That is, in the early stages of economic growth, the distribution of income tends to worsen and only during later stages of economic growth does equality begin to improve. Kuznets' inverse-U hypothesis was based on five observations from the US, five for the United Kingdom, and two each for Prussia, Saxony, and United Germany. The data was, he admitted, unreliable being mostly from urban areas in developed countries. The implication of Kuznets' hypothesis is that income inequality in Western nations seemed to support Kuznets' inverse-U hypothesis. In simple terms, inequality initially increases, but eventually declines, as per capita income increases (Atkinson and Brandolini, 2009). Also, there was an income gap between the urban and rural areas in developed countries. That is inequality in the expanding urban areas was much greater than inequality in the rural sector. As stated by Todaro, output growth in any country is accompanied in the early stages of development by a widening wage differential between skilled and unskilled labor, whereas in a later stage this wage differential declines due to the income convergence theory (1994).

Briefly stated, the Gini coefficient of inequality was crudely formulated by an Italian statistician, Corrodo Gini, in 1912. It was refined in the 1970's to provide a useful figure that reveals the degree of income inequality in any given country. Family percentages are recorded on the horizontal axis and the percentage of income is recorded on the vertical axis. The theoretical possibility of a completely equal distribution of income is represented by the diagonal line known as the 45-degree line or reference line. The farther the Lorenz bends away from the 45-degree line, the greater the inequality of income distribution.

As a gauge for measuring income distribution, the Gini coefficient lies between 0, which indicates that everyone has exactly the same income, and 1 corresponds to absolute inequality. Thus the Gini-coefficients are always greater than 0 and less than 1. At times the Gini coefficient is expressed in percentage terms, and is equal to the Gini coefficient multiplied by 100 (Dixion, 1987, and see Word IQ, 2010).

The Gini-coefficient satisfies *anonymity* (does not matter who the high and low earners are); *scale interdependence* (does not consider the size of the economy); *population interdependence* (does not matter how large the population of the country under consideration is); *transfer principle* (if we take 1 percent of the total income from the richest group and give it to the lowest group, it would raise the income of the poor, but the decrease in the Gini coefficient could be insignificant).

The Gini coefficient can be used to indicate how the distribution of income has changed within a country over a period of time. Comparing income distributions among different countries may be difficult because some countries give benefits in the form of money, food stamps etc, which may not be counted in the Gini coefficient. Also, the Gini coefficient may be unreliable because the data collected for a country could be affected by systematic and random errors. Even if the data collected does not suffer from questionable validity and a lack of reliability, it has to be understood that the Gini coefficient is much more sensitive to changes in income of the middle classes but is less sensitive to changes in incomes of the lower and upper classes (WOLRDIQ, 2010).

Poor countries with low per-capita GDP have coefficients that span the whole range from low (0.25) to high (0.71), while rich countries have generally intermediate Gini coefficients (under 0.40). The lowest Gini-coefficients can be found in Scandinavian countries and in the recently ex-socialist countries of Eastern Europe and in Japan. The Gini-coefficient of Sub-Saharan countries is generally 0.50, indicating that the Sub-Saharan countries have greater inequality in income distribution.

In reality, neither perfect equality, nor perfect inequality is possible. Excessive equality in income distribution can be bad for economic efficiency. For example, in the former socialist countries of Eastern Europe and North Korea, deliberately instituted low inequality with minimal differences in wages and salaries, deprived people of the incentives needed for dynamic activities and vigorous entrepreneurship. Excessive inequality can affect people's quality of life and may result in political instability (World Bank Group, 2010).

In the early part of the 1990s, in Taiwan, Yugoslavia, Korea, Israel, and Singapore, economic growth has been rapid and fairly equitably distributed (Ahluwalia et al. 1977). However, the policies underlying this successful performance vary between the countries, from reliance on market forces in Taiwan, Korea, and Singapore to substantial income transfers and other forms of government intervention programs or poverty-reducing public expenditures in Yugoslavia and Israel (Meier, G, 1989).

The long-run data for Western nations do seem to support the Kuznets inverse-U hypothesis, but studies of the phenomenon in Less Developed Countries (LDCS) produced conflicting results because of methodological problems. Because of the "...absence of time-series information for most LDC, researchers have to test a *longitudinal* phenomenon with *cross-sectional* data. ...Drawing conclusions from cross-sectional data for a time-series phenomenon is fraught with hazards" (Tadaro, 1994, p. 155). Using longitudinal data from 1960 to 1988, Park and Bratt examined the relationship between global inequality and global economic development. The outcome of these studies supported Kuznets' inverted U-hypothesis. Similarly, studies by such authors as Randolph and Lott (1993), Ram (1995), Jha (1996), and Fielding and Torres (2005), examined the relationship for a group of developed and developing countries worldwide and the results conformed to Kuznets' hypothesis. Chang and Ram (2000) found that high economic growth is associated with low income inequality at all levels of income. Examined in the globalization era, Bhatta's (2002) study examined the relationship of 120 countries by using a time series approach. The result of his empirical study showed that there was a downward trend of global income inequality for the period of 1960 to 1989. On the other hand, Deininger and Squire (1998) have found that unlike the Kuznets hypothesis, they found that there is no significant relationship between growth and changes in income inequality.

Factor price equalization (FPE) is an economic theory that originated out of the Heckscher-Ohlin (H-O) model. Simply stated "when the prices of the output goods are equalized between countries as they move to free trade, then the prices of the factors (capital and labor) will also be equalized between countries" (Suranovic, 2006). Therefore, using the factor price equalization theorem, Solow (1956) developed the income convergence model or the inequality-decreasing effects across economies in a perfectly competitive market. That is, once free trade is allowed to set the prices of factors, capital and labor are likely to be relatively equal between countries that follow free competition. However, Jeong's study of Thailand supports Kuznets' hypothesis that income gaps had divergence then convergence trending over the 1976 to 1996 period (2008). There is a wage differential between unskilled and skilled workers. Wage inequality between workers with higher education and those with primary and secondary education for 18 Latin American countries for the period of 1980 to 1998 shows that there is wide wage inequality in terms of returns to human capital. On the other hand, the privatization of state enterprises and peasant's access to factor endowments such as land and capital narrows wage differentials (see for example, Behrman, 2000, Lu, 2008).

The lesson that can be learned from the literature survey is that empirical studies confirm Kuznets' inverted U-curve hypothesis. That is, in the short run with the increase of per capita income, income inequality will diverge. A number of intra-national studies also show that trade is associated with increased income inequality in the industrial sector (see for example Beyer et al. 1999). Contrary to Kuznets' hypothesis, while the results of income convergence is nebulous, on the surface a substantial reform of land ownership, the privatization of state enterprises, and improvement of human capital seem to result in a decrease in income equality. Given Barro's (2000) argument that higher inequality tends to obstruct economic growth in poor countries but encourages growth in developed countries, the next section of the chapter will review briefly the literature and investigate the possibility for a developing country, such as Ethiopia, to register if economic growth could achieve income equity at the same time. In short, the study focuses on determining if it is universally possible for a developing country to achieve income redistribution with an economic growth-oriented pattern. The key policy question then is: to what extent does economic growth in developing countries contribute to a reduction of income inequality?

Ethnic Federalism on Economic Growth

In its review of Ethiopia's economy, the International Monetary Fund (IMF) has indicated that Ethiopia has been attaining economic growth for the past seven years. In addition, the IMF highlights that the lifestyle of the Ethiopian people has been getting better for the last two decades. In the same vein, the *Economist* indicated that Ethiopia has become the fifth fastest growing economy in the world (for a review see, Desta, 2010). The International Food Policy Research Institute (IFPRI) also states that Ethiopia has shown significant improvements on the Global Hunger Index. The Global Hunger Index is based on the proportion of people in a country who are malnourished, the proportion of children under five who are underweight, and the child mortality rate (see Aiga Forum, 2010). Going one step further, in his presentation at Columbia University on September 22, 2010, Ethiopia's Ex Prime Minister Meles Zenawi brought to the attention of the audience that the Gini coefficient of inequality of Ethiopia is about 0.29. In simple words, according to the late Prime Minister Meles Zenawi's statement, in recent years Ethiopia has not only registered rapid economic growth but the income from economic growth has been redistributed equitably.

As stated by Prime Minister Zenawi, while the Gini-coefficient of Ethiopia is 0.29, the Gini coefficient of South Africa, Singapore, China, Mauritius, South Korea is 0.65, 0.63, 0.48, 0.42, and 0.39 respectively (CIA-The World Factbook; see also, Wikipedia and Love.iciba.com, 2010). As pointed out by the World

Bank however, the Gini coefficient is not strictly comparable between countries because the underlying household surveys differ in terms of methods and type of data collected. Also, while an increase in the Gini coefficient implies the rising of income disparity, it does not necessarily indicate worsening of poverty, because the absolute income of the rich and the poor may increase simultaneously (United Nations, 2010).

Ethiopia's Gini coefficient of 0.29 as reported by Prime Minister Meles Zenawi at Columbia University, New York, appears to negate the accepted underlying theories that have been established in economic literature. For instance, it was pointed out by Chenery et al, in its early stages economic growth in developing countries generally increases rather than reduces poverty, nor does it bring about income equality (1974). Similarly, it has been argued by Frank and Webb that the middle-income and upper-income groups rise more rapidly than those of the poor in early stages of growth. They assert that development involves a shift of population from the slow-growing agricultural sector to the higher-income growing modern sector. This process inequality is first accentuated by more rapid population growth in rural areas and ultimately reduced by rising wages produced by more rapid absorption of labor in the modern sector (1977). Todaro states, "disregarding the merits of the methodological debate, few development economists would argue that the Kuznets' sequence of increasing then declining inequality is inevitable" (1994, p.155).

Over the last twenty years, Ethiopia has gone through various structural changes which included reforms in land redistribution, investment in quantitative educational programs, limited privatization schemes, some types of outward-oriented economic reform, reforms in the composition and compensation of the labor market, etc. The reforms in many sectors have changed the allocation of resources and payment structure which affected income distribution in Ethiopia. For example, as indicated above, over the last decade, absolute poverty in Ethiopia has been reduced. Unless the Ethiopian population is experiencing extreme poverty that is undetected, or measuring only the income distribution in rural areas or the economy is completely controlled and managed by the state inducing minimal differences in wages and salaries, or instituting poverty-reducing public programs, though inconclusive, the economic literature does not seem to support Ethiopia's Gini coefficient of 0.29 which is far below the Gini coefficient of newly industrialized countries. If the Gini coefficient of countries where there is substantial economic reform such South Africa (0.65), Singapore (0.63), China (0.48), Mauritius (0.42), and South Korea (0.39) respectively, to say with certainty that Ethiopia's Gini coefficient is 0.29 seems to be based on some type of methodological error, even though Ethiopia has shown an increase in economic growth for the last seven years. Therefore, the policy implication of this study is that the study that gave the entire world an impression that Ethiopia's Gini coefficient is 0.29 needs to be replicated by other economists in order to confirm or invalidate the study and determine if it was based on sound methodology and reliable data.

The Emergence of a Dual-System of Primary Schooling in Federal Ethiopia and Its Impact

Based on the manpower planning process where schooling is considered an important tool for the training of a workforce, an essential prerequisite for economic growth, and an effective instrument of citizenship training, the central goals of schooling in Ethiopia during Haile Selassie's reign were to build a limited number of trained human resources, instill obedience to the established authority, and to develop respect for the then existing political institutions. Stated differently, the few schools that existed in Ethiopia during Haile Selassie's reign were not only elitist but were designed to maintain respect for the existing order. In short, the school system during the ancient regime was not open to everyone but was predominantly geared to the elite, reinforcing consensus values for regime norm acceptance and trust in the system, thereby producing obedient citizens.

As discussed in Chapter 4 and 5, with the rampant student activism that brought the collapse of the Haile Selassie regime in 1974, the Military Junta or Derge (1974-91) replaced the Haile Selassie regime and embarked on socialism to restructure the outmoded socio-economic order. Furthermore, to inculcate a sense of loyalty to the Military Junta, and to establish a new Ethiopian society, the Derge closed all higher educational institutions and senior secondary schools and forced the remaining junior and elementary schools to go through a massive indoctrination of Marxism and Leninism. In short, the Military Junta overwhelmingly urged all schools to instill in their students the socialist ideology. To create the "new socialist Ethiopian man," over the seventeen years of its rule, the Military Junta committed not only to reduce mass illiteracy, but to emphasize the indoctrination of the young and the adult Ethiopians to unquestionable discipline by terrorizing them so that they would accept socialist ideological commitments and values.

The Derge's oversimplified dogma, the mechanistic view of Ethiopian socialism, and economic stagnation induced a civil war in Ethiopia in 1991. The then transitional government that replaced the communist Military Junta introduced a new constitution in 1994 and also formulated the creation of a federal structure of government, and organized the country's first multiparty elections in 1995 (World Bank, 2005, p. xxi).

Whatever the vagaries in practices, in line with "the International Covenant on Economic, Social, and Cultural Rights" (Article 13.2(a), and UNESCO and UNICEF, 2007), the Ethiopian People's Revolutionary Democratic Front (EPRDF) was based on the Sustainable Development and Poverty Reduction Program (SDPRP). Also it announced that every citizen would have universal entitlement to education as a human right and the education sector was expected to help reduce poverty by offering universal primary education in order to produce a workforce capable of fulfilling jobs that required skilled labor. The 2004 World Bank Poverty Assessment for Ethiopia estimated that if all of adults in the country had at least four years of primary education, the share of households living in poverty would drop by 8 percent (World Bank, 2005, xviii).

Given that the goal of the EPRDF led government of the Federal Democratic Republic of Ethiopia is to render universal education at the primary level, this prompts a number of questions at this juncture: 1) has the current government in Ethiopia for the last twenty years rendered the rights to quality and quantity of educational services to all school age children at the primary level? 2) If so, what resources have been allocated to achieve the stated goals? and 3) Is there equity in the delivery of primary schooling among the different social classes in Ethiopia?

The Universalizing of Primary Schooling in Ethiopia

Since 1991, a casual observation of primary school age children in Ethiopian schools reveals that in quantitative terms, it is remarkable that Ethiopia has almost achieved universal primary education. For almost all households in the country there is at least one primary school available within a distance of less than 10 kilometers (World Bank, 2005). The gross enrollment ratio for females and males enrolled in grades 1-8 has increased from 37 percent in 1996 to 91 percent in 2011. Also, there is an equitable representation of males and females in the Ethiopian primary schools (Lisane Masie (March 2012).

In addition, unlike the patterns of stagnation, reversal, and uneven growth of the past regimes (World Bank, 2005) and the fact that the education system was urban biased, and the rural areas were sparsely covered, today Ethiopia has almost fulfilled its goal to educate in both rural and urban areas. It has been shown that student enrollments in urban areas are almost 100 percent, and about 86 percent of school aged children are enrolled in rural areas.

Also, the rate of attrition, or the dropout rate at the primary level has declined from 13.3 percent in 1996 to 4.2 percent in 2011, though the problem of school dropouts due to the need for work and sickness seems to be more serious in rural (i.e., 4.7%) than in urban areas (i.e., 2.2 %) areas (See for example, Lisane Masie, March 2012, pp. 50-53). Thus, in quantitative terms, it is possible to assert that the Ethiopian primary school system seems to be in the process of universalizing primary education by providing basic education for all school aged children.

Quality and Equity of Primary Schooling

In terms of quality and equity, Ethiopia has the highest student-teacher ratio in the world. It was reported by the World Bank that since 1993-94, the pupil-teacher ratio is 65:1 and the number of pupils per section is 75 to 82 in government primary schools compared with about 30 in privately operated schools in non-governmental organizations, religious bodies, business enterprises, etc. (2005, p. xxiv). Also, for public schools, the government spends only 3 percent of the country's gross domestic product on administrative overhead and post-secondary levels of instruction, though the Ethiopian government is supposed to spend 4.5 percent of GDP just to attain the Millennium Development Goal of 100 percent primary school completion by 2015 (World Bank, 2005, p. 172). Moreover, while the teachers of private primary schools are well paid and better equipped, a sizable number of teachers in public schools don't meet the certification standards. Because of the shortage, administrative regions have hired para-professional (uncertified) teachers for relief (World Bank, 2005, p. 172).

In addition, given the dual system of primary schooling in the country, the existence of well-furnished private primary schools that "...house the children of the emerging upper class against the ill-equipped public schools that harbor the children of the down-trodden classes may not only perpetuate class differentiation but also are likely to deter the government's initiated plans for growth and transformation" (Desta, 2012, p.18).

Summary and Policy Implications

Over the last twenty years, in quantitative terms, Ethiopia has expanded and universalized the enrolment of school aged children in primary schools in order to minimize the irregularities that have existed over the years. However, when the existing primary schooling is visualized in terms of quality and equity, it is sad to observe that privately run ultra-modern primary schools mushroomed from 6 percent in 2009 to 11 percent in 2010 (See world Bank, 2012) in order to serve the sons and daughters of a newly emerging privileged class. On the other hand, the sons and daughters of the poor and disadvantaged are confined to over-crowded classes manned by semi-qualified teachers and equipped with a dearth of instructional materials. While the sons and daughters of the down trodden masses are "harbored" to study up to grade eight in local languages that could lead them nowhere, the sons and daughters of the rich are prepared for the globalized world by having access to well-qualified teachers and entertained by the latest pedagogical innovations using the world's lingua as a medium of instruction.

Stated differently, it is sad to observe that primary schools in Ethiopia are sliding into a class-based education system that strongly encourages emerging social classes in Ethiopia to tighten their grip on selected positions in society. While the new elites can afford to send their children to distinguished private schools, the boys and girls of the poor, who might overcome the challenges in public primary schools and score marks to enter the emerging universities may find road-blocks when competing with the sons of the well-to-do because they are inadequately prepared in the English language used in instruction at the universities.

Thus, given that a dual-system of primary education is perpetuating class differentiation in Ethiopia, if the government believes in equity and fairness, it needs to completely redesign and better equip the public primary schools by upgrading their services to be in line with private schools. Furthermore, if concerned about the emerging class structure, the government should charge higher taxes to private schools and redistribute the revenues to subsidize public primary schools in order to improve their services. Otherwise, it is immoral to pretend that the government in Ethiopia is universalizing primary education while the dynamics on the ground reveal that primary public schools in Ethiopia are malnourished and are mainly tailored to the down-trodden poor.

In addition, the practice of appointing school administrators should be based on professional qualification instead of on the appointment of political cadres to run schools. The present system encourages cronyism and corruption. Given the inadequacy of the public primary schools in Ethiopia, the probability of their graduates ever becoming able to compete successfully in a globalized world seems to be very slim. Thus, it is time for the government to think seriously about dismantling an education system that has developed a public primary school system that continues to hold back children from poor backgrounds and prevents them from competing with those from private schools.

The current dual schooling system in Ethiopia is challenging and highly disturbing. Rather than allow the present structure to be prolonged, policy makers need to listen to all stakeholders in the school system within the Ethiopian polity and then redesign a new coherent, transparent, and accountable program for both the haves and the have-nots. However, it entails courage to restructure the existing organization in order to dismantle the emerging social divisions in schools.

Chapter 7

MICRO CREDIT FOR POVERTY ALLEVIATIONY

In an era of unprecedented world-wide economic growth, it is interesting to note that the richest fifth of the world's people consume 86 percent of all goods and services while about a fifth of the world's poor population (1.2 billion people) still live on less than US $1 a day and almost half of the world's population live on less than US $2 a day (UNDP 2002, Gibson, 2009). Poverty is not simply having a very low income. It is a multifaceted phenomenon. In addition to low income, poor people also suffer from illiteracy, unsafe drinking water, and lack of access to basic health services. They live in remote, resource-poor areas, and atrocious slums. Frequently encountered with their vulnerability, the "chronically poor are unable to develop their personal capabilities or provide a good start in life for their children, and often die prematurely of preventable causes" (Alston and Shepherd, 2008-09).

With the hastening of the global poverty crisis and the absence of an adequate social safety net for those marginalized and vulnerable sections of society in the less developed countries, a number of researchers have moved beyond the relentless pursuit of short-term toward long-term anti-poverty, environmentally sustainable paradigms to assist chronically poor sectors of society. Though a remarkably polarizing issue, in the last three decades microcredit programs has been made available to the chronically poor as a viable option to involve them in the formal economic sector. It is assumed that the disadvantaged groups will become productive members of society if they involve themselves in small businesses that may contribute to powerful changes within their lives. (See Microcredit Summit, 1997, Fisher and Sriram, 2002).

In formal financial markets, the poor are excluded from establishing their own small businesses because they are not recognized as being credit-worthy, i.e. unable to save, lacking verifiable credit history, and with no goods to offer as collateral to secure loans. This forces them to turn to traditional money lenders. (See for example, Zamperetti and Franca Dalla Costa, 2008.) Recognizing the needs, capacity, and the talents of the poor to repay the loans, micro lending programs are loans extended to group members rather than to individuals. In view of the contingent group loan approach, it is generally assumed that group members would have an incentive to monitor their progress and that this would lead to a greater rate of repayment of their loans since each borrower's creditworthiness would be a factor in the overall credit-worthiness of the group (Fisher and Sriram, 2002; Stiglitz, 1990; Varian, 1990; and Becker, 1991). In short, the success of group lending creates positive incentives for members to repay because in case of default, no member of the group will receive future loans. For prompt repayment, there is repeat lending to the group. In group lending, the probability of moral hazard is largely reduced because all borrowers are members of the group and subject to peer pressure, group dynamics, cohesiveness, and the ultimate success of every other member of the group (Ajit, A; Sunil, R; and Raman k. R, 2006).

In simple terms, microcredit refers to the process of lending small amounts of seed money to groups of jointly liable borrowers rather than to one person, without collateral, to help poor people to establish their own business. Microcredit, especially designed for eco-entrepreneurship, encourages innovation in rural and urban areas to produce environmentally friendly products for the marketplace. Thus, the philosophy of demand-led microcredit finance visualizes the poor not as objects of charity but as socially productive persons. The rationale and objective of advancing micro-loans to the ultra poor is to diminish their liquidity constraints, create employment opportunities, and induce sustainable incomes by engaging the poor in the reinvention of everything from the bottom-up, with limited top-down directives. Therefore, the loans accorded to the poor are not only bankable but it is assumed that micro-enterprise activities will eradicate poverty and foster sustainable development. As argued by Doocy et al., (2005), "Microfinance is a logical approach to development because it functions at the grassroots level, can be sustainable, is capable of involving large segments of the population, and builds both human and productive capacity." Stated differently, microcredit is an investment in people, the poor and their abilities, which sharpens entrepreneurial initiatives, and strengthens developing countries' economies. Microcredit is a grass-rots instrument, a tool for economic development because it enables the poor to build assets, increase income, and reach self-sufficiency. Thus, microcredit not only delivers macro benefits but creates a silent revolution in poverty-stricken rural areas (Sharma, 2005).

As a result, in the 1990s the commercialization of microcredit continued to gain force as one of the key tools of development. The World Bank, the U.N. Capital Development Fund, and the European Bank for Reconstruction and Development have created full-scale movements to promote the availability of microcredit programs to a number of developing countries. Based on anecdotal assessment of the impact of microcredit as a financial instrument, the United Nations declared 2005 as the International Year of Microcredit. Realizing that chronically poor people merit the greatest international attention, using the year 1990 as a baseline, the United Nations has advocated the reduction of both extreme poverty and hunger by half or more by the year 2015 of those whose income is below US $1 per person/day.

The Millennium Development Goals (MDGs) are seen by many as being overly modest. However, it needs to be mentioned in passing that this assessment omits or glosses over some of the greatest challenges to lowering the poverty rate. For example, one of the most serious issues omitted in the report is the fact that it failed to establish that it is the lack of access to land ownership (micro-landowning program) that has caused many people to remain in poverty, and that microcredit loans have accomplished very little in solving the land ownership systems in developing countries (Prosterman, R. April 2005). Instead, the promotion of microcredit ventures in developing countries have the potential to create private groups (cutthroat money-lenders), which have vested interests in perpetuating the prevailing poverty situation (Elahi, K.Q. and Danopoulos, C. P., 2004). Microcredit participants end up borrowing more from other non-institutional sources (double-dipping) to reduce their indebtedness, which is a paradox. As it stands now, instead of reaching the core poor, microcredit improves incomes of the better-off poor. It is more beneficial to borrowers living above the poverty line than to borrowers living below the poverty (Hume and Mosley, 1996). As succinctly argued by Kamani (2007), "...although microcredit yields some noneconomic benefits, it does not significantly alleviate poverty. Indeed, in some instances microcredit makes life at the bottom of the pyramid worse."

Contrary to the hype about microcredit being the best way to create jobs, increase workers' productivity, and eradicate poverty, Banerjee and Duflo (2006) argue that, "Although some microcredit clients have created visionary businesses, the vast majority are caught in subsistence activities. Participants have no specialized skills and so must compete with all the other self-employed poor in entry-level activities." In his critique of the newest financial technology of the Washington Consensus, Flynn (2007) argues that while the technologies are new, the rhetoric is familiar and suggests that we may be seeing a new form of green washing or "charity washing" in the making. The risk is that new microfinance technologies targeting people with low incomes will be mistaken as benevolence. Bankers are not in the business of charity. They galvanize their activities to the bottom line generating sufficient priorities to stay in business. In addition, Neff (1996) argues that microcredit models have been judged disproportionately from a lender's perspective (repayment rates, financial liability) and not from the borrower's. Therefore, according to Neff, microcredits have privatized public safety-net programs and stimulated governments to cut their budgets on education, public health, and the early livelihood needs of the poor.

Despite the provocative criticisms enumerated above, the idea of microcredit as a key to socio-economic transformation has taken a prominent place in the international sphere. A number of voluntary associations, non-government organizations, friendly societies, savings-and-credit cooperatives, national and regional government organizations, and commercial banking institutions have joined hands in providing financial services to the marginalized sectors of the world's developing countries for community growth and socioeconomic development. Since microcredit loans are focused on building a foundation for individual or small groups to develop products and services that will both enrich and increase the wellbeing of those involved as well as the surrounding community, it seems evident that these specialized loans integrate sustainability into the dynamics of the structure. (See for example, Gehlich-Shillabeer, 2008).

Therefore the central questions of the study include: a) are the participants of micro credit loans chronically poor, b) do microcredit programs alleviate poverty? c) do the beneficiaries of microcredit loans participate in environmentally sensitive projects? The purpose of this paper is therefore to review the existing literature which has burgeoned over the past decades and investigate the methodological issues. Specifically, the article is organized as follows: Section I examines the different methods used by microcredit ventures to measure poverty and target the beneficiaries. Section II presents an operational definition of environmentally sustainable development. Using case studies from Ethiopia and other African countries, section *III* attempts to examine whether or not the extended microloans contributed to environmentally sustainable development. Finally, results and conclusions are presented and policy implications are drawn for further research. Before we review how various studies target their clientele and assess the impact of microcredit programs on the lives of clients, a brief historical background of the Grameen (derived from a *Banglai* word for village) Bank in Bangladesh is in order.

The Grameen Bank of Bangladesh: A Brief Review

A number of waves of micro-enterprise lending were initiated in the United States of America in the 1950s to subsidize developmental credit programs in the rural areas. However, the incarnation of micro-financing actually started in

1974 after Bangladesh experienced drought and famine that contributed to the deaths of about 1.5 million people (Macfarlane, 2002). The program was conceived when Professor Mohammad Yunus noted that a number of poor women living near his university were trying to earn a living constructing bamboo stools, but they had no money to purchase materials. Realizing and being conscious of the problem, Professor Yunus and his students strategically designed an experimental credit program to assist the needy women. He provided the needy women with a small amount of credit (about $69 each) without normal bank collateral and at a reasonable rate, from his pocket for self-employment. (see Desta, 1998.) To his pleasant surprise, all the borrowers repaid the loans, in the process convincing him that this success could be replicated across Bangladesh (Mainsah, Heur, and Zhang, 2004). Following this, the Grameen Bank was initiated to be a full-fledged lending institution in Bangladesh. In 1983 the Grameen lending institutions were incorporated as a bank after the government had passed legislation allowing Grameen Bank to accept deposits.

The unique operating procedures of the Grameen Bank had four features that distinguished it from conventional banking practices. The Grammen bank started: a) offering collateral-free loans or seed money of less than one hundred dollars to rural-based poor women; b) creating income-generating activities through self-employment in particular ventures; c) requiring internal local savings (capital) as a pre-requisite for getting loans from Grameen financial enterprises; and d) converting borrowers into depositors and shareholders. The Grameen Bank system united all interested parties with its managers behind the common goal of creating sustainable poverty-alleviation programs (Elahi and Danopoulos, 2004; Mainsah, Heur, and Zhang, 2004).

Through self-selected lending groups of five to forty members, the women whose family's assets fell below the bank's threshold were navigated through the microcredit system. As stated by Mainsah, Heur, and Zhang (2004), Yunus devised a typically unorthodox solution for the issue of the poorest of the poor. He decided to prove that Grameen was indeed a banker to the poor by requiring that the bank make every effort to lend to those whom it considered the poorest.

In the beginning, the poverty status of the women who borrowed funds from the Grammen Bank were subjectively determined. That is, poor women who lacked the funds to begin their own businesses were considered eligible to borrow funds from the Grammen Bank. However, as Grammen Bank developed over the years, women whose family assets fell below the bank's threshold were also selected to participate in the program. After the clientele were selected they were required to: a) recite the Grameen's guiding principles that included, discipline, unity, courage, and hard work through the building of family prosperity every day; b) indulge in repairing and improving houses; c) drink water from wells; d) participate in growing vegetables year-round; e) plant seedlings each year; f) build, repair, and use pit-latrines; g) introduce physical exercise in centers; h) stand against the practice of accepting or giving a dowry; i) insist on self-reliance; j) liberate themselves from victim mentality; and k) take responsibility so that the whole community (of 8 -10) not to fall behind (Mainsah, Heur, and Zhang, 2004). To assess whether or not the borrowers passed the poverty line, each year, each borrower was required to pass tests that included: a) having a roof overhead; b) sleeping in a bed; c) having access to safe drinking water; d) having access to warm clothing; and e) enrolling all children of school-age in schools (Yunus, M. 2003).

Over the years, the microcredit programs in Bangladesh have championed a paradigm shift in lending. To be effective, nonetheless, micro financing policies need to: a) systematically address the causes of poverty; b) identify segments of the population living in poverty; c) pay special attention to raising the awareness of the chronically poor; and d) train the poor to specialize in particular skills so that they may compete with other self-employed people in entry-level of ventures.

Operational Definition of Poverty and Targeting the Poor for Microfinance Programs

As referred to earlier, microcredit programs generally refer to the process of lending small amounts of money, without collateral, to help the chronically poor people and the most vulnerable segment of the population, to enable them to be very productive business entrepreneurs. However, since poverty is a complex socio-economic problem, the above statement seems to prescribe the medicine for poverty before the malady is known (Oyen, 1996). Since poverty is an international social problem, to effectively conquer and assess its remedies, the concept of poverty needs to be operationally defined and the chronically poor people need to be targeted in order for micro finance programs to be viable. To help decision-makers to efficiently target poverty and use microcredit programs as remedial strategies, analysts need to operationally define poverty and identify the marginalized segments of the population. Effectively targeting the poor for microcredit projects necessitates careful consideration of the following factors: a) determining the types of participants and how chronically poor they are; b) identifying the sectors in which the participants are going to be engaged; c) researching the availability of resources needed for the implementation of the micro-enterprises; d) verifying the availability of infrastructures needed for the implementation of the micro-enterprises; and e) exploring the impact of the enterprises on the sustainable poverty alleviation programs. More specifically, before providing micro loans for micro enterprises, the concept of poverty needs to be operationalized. As the foregoing review shows (see also Table 7.1), most researchers have developed the following indicators to measure the dimensions of poverty. They a) have low income, b) lack skills, c) Human Development Index d) lack socially perceived necessities, e) subjectively feel need because of the status of poverty, and f) suffer from a combination or cumulative aspects of poverty.

Income-based Approach

The income approach method of measuring poverty has been dominant for a number of years in most countries and internationally (Bradshaw and Finch 2003). From a conventional economist's standpoint, the measurement of poverty depends upon the median level of national income and the degree of income distribution. Economists typically measure poverty by income or consumption levels at the aggregate level. Being relative to the norm in a particular country, a person is considered poor if either income or spending falls below the median poverty line that represents basic needs. When measuring poverty, economists generally make a distinction between absolute and relative poverty. Absolute poverty measures set a poverty line at a certain income amount or consumption amount per year, based on the estimated value of a 'basket of goods' (food, shelter, water, etc) necessary for proper living. Using absolute poverty, the World Bank defines extreme poverty as living on less than $1 per day US (adjusted for Purchasing Power Parity). "Those with incomes below the poverty line are the poor. Poverty begins below and ends above the poverty line in question" (Njeru, 2004). Though there are variations of diets, shelter, etc., depending on the diversity of cultures and modes of production, the major weakness of the concept of absolute poverty as identified by the World Bank is based on the assumption that there are minimum basic needs uniformly applicable to all social and economic categories in all societies (Njeru, 2004).

In contrast to absolute poverty, relative poverty makes a distinction of the standards in both time and place in the assessment of poverty. More precisely, relative poverty measurements would compare the bottom 20% of the poorest population with the total wealth of the richest 10% of the population in individual countries. Thus, the notion of relative poverty is elastic and receptive to rapid changes (Njeru 2004).

Historically, in the 1970s, developmental economists took a major step to distinguish the poor from the non-poor by establishing an international poverty line which is sufficient to provide a minimum acceptable level of consumption. "In theory, a consumption-based poverty line can be thought of as comprising two elements: firstly, an objective measure of expenditure necessary to buy a minimum level of nutrition, and secondly, a subjective additional amount that varies from country to country reflecting the cost of individuals participating in the everyday life of society" (Thirlwall, 1995). More specifically, the income or consumption based measure of poverty was generally based on: a) headcount ratio b) poverty gap, and c) the severity of poverty index.

The headcount ratio of poverty measures the prevalence of poverty and captures the number of people who fall below the poverty line in any population. Compared to the total population, the headcount estimates the ratio of people living below the poverty line. Though the headcount gives a quick and simple way of assessing the incidence of poverty, it fails to ascertain the location of the poor and the distribution of income of those situated below the poverty line. Therefore when analyzed at a conceptual level, it would have made sense to focus on the household as the unit of account instead of adopting an individual methodological perspective to assess the incidence of poverty in developing countries. (See for example, Shimeles and Thoenen, 2005.)

The poverty gap index as the magnitude of poverty is generally expressed as a measure of "...the transfer of income required to bring the income of every poor person up to the poverty line" (Thirlwall, 1995). In simple terms, the poverty index assesses the characteristic of the poor and the average deprivation of poverty in society. Nonetheless, it needs to be underlined that the poverty index is insensitive to assessing the extent of inequality amongst the poor. "For example, if income is transferred from a poor person to someone who is even poorer, neither of the measures changes, but poverty will be more evenly spread..." (Thirlwall, 1995).

Unlike the head count index and poverty index, the severity of poverty index seems to be very comprehensive. It measures the incidence of poverty, the depth of poverty, and income distributional effects of the group of people living below the poverty line. As pointed out by Shimeles and Thoenen (2005), if income is redistributed from the poorer to the less poor (without anybody being lifted above the poverty line), neither the headcount index nor the poverty gap index will reflect this change. The severity of the poverty index, on the other hand will show an increase of poverty indicating that the poorest have become more severely impoverished. Though very instructive, the severity poverty index masks poverty dynamics – changes in wellbeing experienced by individuals and households over time. For example, many chronically poor (those who are below the poverty line) households may experience improvements and declines in their poverty status without exiting poverty. Thus, panel data that track the same households at multiple points in time need to be used to measure dynamics. To understand poverty, therefore, a longitudinal (panel), of qualitative (semi-structured interviews, direct or participatory observation and so on) and quantitative data seems to be very fruitful. (See, Alston and Shepherd, 2008-09).

To develop efficient methods to fight poverty, a number of researchers have focused on analyzing poverty in terms of vulnerability rather than on the problem of levels of income. Vulnerability or the movement in and out of poverty is related to differential capacities to access to resources necessary for survival (Sen, 1981, 1992). Vulnerability, a more dynamic concept reflects the risk of exposure of people below the poverty line due to a combination of political, natural, or health-related disasters. The three different levels of vulnerability are: a) transiently poor, usually above the poverty line, but sometimes fallen under it; b) chronically impoverished, persisting for a lifetime, or for generations below the poverty line; and c) persistently poor who are always below the poverty line (Thinkquest.org). According to Sen (1983), however, any poverty index worthy of consideration should be able to provide three basic details of information on poverty: a) identify who the poor are, b) capture the average deprivation of poverty, and c) estimate the relative deprivation among the poor. The three types of poverty index discussed above, however, seem to be based on income and barely meet the basic needs.

As narrated by Hulme and McKay:

> Existing work on chronic poverty, and poverty dynamics in general, has been so far been conceptualized in very narrow terms, and this has created important limitations in our understanding. In particular, chronic poverty has been studied almost exclusively in relation to income or consumption poverty, and using household panel survey data. Further, much of the focus has been on the identification of chronic poverty and finding correlates, without developing an understanding of the underlying processes by which some people are trapped in persistent poverty while others escape (June 2005).

Based on the above analysis, there seem to be three important points to note about contemporary literature on chronic poverty: 1) it is dominated by economists and econometricians using panel data set to distinguish chronic poverty from transient or transitory poverty; 2) virtually all of the empirical data have been analyzed using income or consumption measures of poverty as its main variable; and 3) the variables were almost entirely quantitative and findings were, at best, only partially contextualized (Hulme and McKay, 2005).

Capability Deprivation

Unlike income or consumption which is the standard criterion of identification of poverty and the 'basic needs' approach which emphasizes on the poor to have access to basic needs and services, Sen (1983) succinctly argues that deprivation of individual choices or their capabilities needs to be taken into consideration while addressing poverty. According to Sen, unlike low income, which is only *instrumentally* significant, the capabilities approach concentrates on deprivations that are *intrinsically* important. In addition, Sen argues that though the instrumental relation between low income and low capability is *variable* between different communities and even between different families and different individuals, the impact of income on capabilities is contingent and conditional. Given that material goods are not an end in themselves, Sen (1983) suggests that the most essential components of the capability index for a good life include adequate nourishment, leading a long and healthy life, literacy, shelter and political and civil rights. Though Sen freshly looks at the whole concept of poverty from the perspective of the ability to produce an end use of goods and services, the measurement of the capability space is problematic (Harkness, 2004). Similarly, Shimeles and Thoenen (2005) also argue that serious theoretical and operational problems of the capabilities approach make it difficult for empirical research

Human Development Index

To capture capabilities, most researchers use an expanded set of indices representing well-being like UNDP's Human Development Index (2005). The HDI ranks countries according to their progress toward the maximum attainable values for life expectancy, literacy and weighted real GDP indicators. "These factors are combined to provide a composite of diverse data. It is assumed that nutritional status and child mortality are reflected in life expectancy, and employment rates are reflected in real income" (UNEP, 1995). Nonetheless, the HDI Index has been criticized as conceptually weak and the choice of components and weights attached to the components of the HDI Index are value laden. As questioned by Harkness (2004), "How for example should a change in the index be interpreted if it rises because one indicator has gone up and another down?" Therefore, if Sen's capabilities approach and the Human Development Index fail to fully address the nature of poverty in developing countries, it might be worth a look at an asset-based approach to assess the incidence of poverty.

Asset-based Approach

Assets capture longer term dynamics much better than a measure of income at one or two points in time. For this reason Hulme and McKay (2005) argue that "...having longitudinal data may be crucial. In addition, assets can in principle be considered in a range of different dimensions including social capital in developing countries." To analyze the status of poverty in developing countries, the asset-based approach uses assets extensively, such as natural capital, physical capital, human capital, social capital, and financial capital (Carney 1998;

Scoones 1998; Ellis 2000). However, since poverty is multidimensional, some researchers go one step further to gauge poverty by asking individuals whether or not they feel poor.

The Perception of Poverty

Subjectively the "felt need" approach to poverty entails asking people whether they feel poor or deprived. The purpose is to see, through the eyes of the poor themselves, how they perceive their situation. It is believed that through their participation, the poor are the ones most able to find adequate solutions to their poverty. Lamarre and Miller (2003, p. 11) argue that to listen to the poor "...is a demonstration of respect, because it takes into account their life experience instead of imposing on them an a priori definition of poverty." In their research for example, Bradshaw and Finch (2003) asked the respondents: "how many pounds a week,..., do you think are necessary to keep a household such as the one you live in, out of poverty?"

Because the poverty index incorporates subjective and objective deprivation and cannot meet all the desirable properties simultaneously, some researchers use a cumulative dimension to measure chronic poverty. For instance, Chowdhury, Gosh, and Wright (2005, p.303) used a combination of the objective poverty line (i.e., the cost associated with obtaining a minimum daily requirements of 2112 calories, including 58 grams of protein) and the subjective poverty line (i.e., defined as being poor if the household head answered 'yes' to the following question: Do you consider your family poor based on your current yearly income?

The Cumulative or Multi-dimensional Approach

This method of assessing poverty assumes that a person who is poor according to objective and normative dimensions is more likely to be poor than someone who is poor on only one of the dimensions (Bradshaw and Finch, 2003). On the other hand, others seem to be inclined to select the poverty index based on properties consistent with their policy objectives and ask the community or local government to identify the real poor people in their locality. Given this, "Future studies of poverty and the extent to which poverty is being relieved should present results using a combination of measures" (Bradshaw and Finch, 2003).

To summarize, based on a review of the literature, it can be ascertained that assessment of the chronic components of poverty is an unsettled issue. The tentative conclusion that can be reached from the above review of the definitions of poverty is that it depends upon the way someone or some group of people perceives it to be. Generally, poverty is defined in terms of the lack of income, power, capacities, freedoms, or deprivations of basic needs, and so on. As stated by Lamarre (2000, p.26), "So an individual; a research worker; a charity organization; the World Bank; the United Nations Development Program (UNDP); the various national governments, to give a few examples, do not tackle poverty in the same way. " Therefore, the effectiveness of any policy of poverty needs to be articulated around the definition of poverty which could allow an evaluation of the number of poor, and design an intervention program that could alleviate poverty and foster long run sustainable development.

Given that the operational definition of poverty is not systematically designed, it is very difficult to assess how borrowers would have succeeded without micro loans. It is fair to say that the microcredit programs in Bangladesh have shown respectable performance in terms of their impact on the performance of its clientele. Nonetheless, when Khandker (2003) looked at the impact of microcredit programs through the loan-issuing process, he asserted that it would be an over exaggeration to pronounce that it significantly helped to lift the poor out of poverty and he further asserted that microcredit institutions had minimum positive spillover effects on the local community. In fact Khandker criticized the microcredit institutions in Bangladesh for not being able to reach the very poorest members of their constituency because they are too costly to identify. Also, he found that microcredit institutions that reach the poorest are not financially self-sufficient because of higher program costs, and a number of the institutions rely on public funds and private donors. More specifically, after studying three leading microfinance institutions in Bangladesh, for the period 1990-2003, Khandker stated that the results are resounding:

> *Micro-finance matters a lot for very poor borrowers and also for the local economy. In particular, micro-finance programs matter a lot to the poor in raising per capita consumption, mainly on non-food, as well as household non-land assets. This increases the probability that the program participants may be able to lift themselves out of poverty. The welfare impact of micro-finance is also positive for all households, including non-participants, indicating that microfinance programs are helping the poor beyond income redistribution with contribution to local income growth. Programs have spillover effects to local economies, thereby increasing local village welfare. In particular, we find that micro-finance helps reduce extreme poverty more than moderate poverty at the village level. Yet the aggregate poverty reduction effects are not substantial enough to make a large dent in aggregate poverty at the national level. This concern brings to the fore the effectiveness of micro-finance as an instrument to solve the problem of poverty in Bangladesh (2003).*

TABLE 7.1: THE DIMENSIONS AND METHODS OF ESTIMATING POVERTY

INDEX	REFERENCE & CASE STUDY	SPECIFIC INDICATORS	COMMENT
Income-based: **Absolute Income** **Relative**	The World Bank Projects in Bangladesh	*Income below USS $1 per person/day *Basket goods and Services: * Food * Shelter * water Headcount ratio Poverty gap Severity of poverty index Vulnerability Index	Assumes that there are minimum basic needs applicable to all societies. Reflects the risk of exposure of people below the poverty line due to a combination of political, natural, or heath factors etc.
Capabilities Deprivation	Sen (1983)	*Adequate nourishment *Healthy life *Literacy *Shelter *Political and civic rights	Problematic to operational define and apply to empirical research
Human Development Index (HDI)	UNDP	*Life Expectancy *Literacy rate *Weighted Real GDP	It is conceptually weak in the choices of components and weights attached to the components of the HDI.

Assets-based Approach	* Carney (1998), Scoones (1998), Ellis (2005) * Projects in Kerala (India) Projects * WISDOM Projects (Ethiopia)	* Natural capital Physical capital Human capital Social capital *monthly household income, *per capita monthly household income * household asset *livestock value * household asset * livestock index score	Though useful as an indicator to measure poverty in specific regions or community, it can not be standardized and uniformly applied to measure poverty at a national or international level.
Perception of Poverty	Lamarre and Miller (2003)	*subjectively felt need *See poverty through the eyes of the poor themselves instead of imposing prior definition of poverty.	
Multi-dimensional	Bradshaw and Finch (2003)	*a combination of subjective and objective dimensions	It selects poverty index based on policy objective rather than standardized measures

The microcredit programs in Bangladesh have championed a paradigm shift in lending. The lending programs have shown respectable results in terms of their impact on the performance of their clientele. What is surprising is, the various programs operating in Bangladesh under the microcredit programs seem to be focusing on borrowers living above the poverty line (or moderately poor women with relatively more education and also bestowed with entrepreneurial spirits) rather than identifying the hard core poor. In places where micro-enterprises are established, the poorest participants may be "hit hard and quickly by common surprises like crop failures, illness or deaths in the family, or natural disasters. This vulnerability can make micro-enterprises, which are quite individualistic in character, unattractive to lenders" (Vargas, 2000, p. 19).

The Microcredit Summit Campaign (MSC) of 1997, astutely aligned its goals with the UN Millennium Development Goals (MDG), which has a microcredit initiative aimed at reducing absolute poverty in the world by half (600 million people) by 2015 (Mainsah et al., 2004, p. 17). Though innovative, the MCI conference adhered to using the World Bank's narrow terms of income deprivation of less than $1 a day adjusted for purchasing power parity as the operational definition of poverty. It should have been vital to consider identifying the chronic poor and democratically empowering them to have access to microcredit programs. As stated by Lamarre and Miller (2003), it is by collective deliberation on the causes of their own situation that the poor learn by practice, by doing, how to work together to fight it. For the poor people of a community, the task consists in identifying the principal characteristics of the typical poor person, and the assets to be exploited locally that will contribute to self-actualization and the acceleration of local economic development.

For example, unlike the micro-loan programs in Bangladesh, the women-centered microcredit centers in the Kudumbashree, Kerala, India, used a combination of indicators to identify the poor women for microcredit programs in Kudumbashree, Kerala state of India. Rather than judging poverty using income or the consumption level of a family, they used a multi-dimensional approach (under the pilot of the Urban Basic Services Program in Alleppey town) to isolate the participants. As described by Ajit, Sunil, and Raman (Ajit, D., Sunil, R., Raman, K.R. 2006, p. 18), the Alleppyey methodology is believed to be superior to the conventional head count ratio as it captures the multi-dimensional characteristics of poverty (beyond the simple income approach) and leads to the identification of the most vulnerable families. To identify the poor, Kudumbashree carried out a baseline survey with the help of local government. Women constrained to having access to credit, restricted from having access to the wage labor market, and being restrained from an equitable share of power in household decision making processes, were identified using four or more of the following nine non-monetary psychosocial indicators. The nine indicators included families with: a) no land; b) no house, or a dilapidated house; c) no access to sanitary latrines; d) no access to safe water (within 300 meters); e) a woman head of household, the presence of a widow, a divorced or abandoned woman, or unwed mother; f) no regularly employed person g) a physically, mentally, or chronically ill member, h) socially disadvantaged groups like Scheduled Cast or Scheduled Tribe or/and with an illiterate adult member.

In addition, using the 500 Self Help Group (SHG), with 15 persons per SHG (of whom the majority were women from the poorest castes and tribes), there was launched a pilot program in India in 1992, formed to represent the 'felt need' of group members. With minimum documentation and without any tangible security, a small number of micro-loans were extended to the members of SHG by Indian banks. The SHG program and its linkage with banks has been a significant instrument of microcredit promotion framed in India. In short, microcredit institutions in the rural areas of India have been acting as an intermediary between banks and rural borrowers. Infusing SHG with conventional bank funds has provided a means to provide services to landless and marginal rural farmers in India.

As stated by Sharma (2005), though less than 5 percent of India's rural poor as compared to 65 percent in Bangladesh have access to microcredit, "... the extraordinary success of the SHG Bank Linage is attributable to its alignment with Indian history and circumstances and capitalization on the country's elaborate network of rural bank branches; availability of good policy, committed leadership; implementation of a hands-off regulatory policy for SHG Bank Linkage and the emphasis on quality during the early phase of SHG Bank Linkage." To assess the outcome of the World Vision microfinance affiliates in Ethiopia (known as WISDOM), established in 1999, Shannon Doocy, et al., used a cross-sectional design based on the socioeconomic status of participants. The socioeconomic indicators included, monthly household income, per capita monthly household income, household asset and livestock value, and household asset and livestock index score.

The Effects of Microfinance Programs on Sustainable Development

In 1968, Garrett Hardin argued that a society that permits perfect freedom of action in activities that adversely influence common properties was eventually doomed to failure. Spurred by the Club of Rome's popular report on the projection of trends in resource use, the United Nations' 1972 Conference on the Human Environment in Stockholm somehow attempted to establish a comprehensive framework on environmental degradation.

In late 1983, the Norwegian Prime Minister Gro Harlem Brundtland was asked to chair "...an independent commission on how to deal with the tensions that had arisen in Stockholm. Her commission's mandate was to determine not just how to protect the environment but also how to eliminate poverty and promote general progress on a limited and already abused planet" (Gibson, et al., 2007, p.48).

In 1987, the concern for the environment shifted to sustainable development as a result of the United Nations World Commission on Environment and Development report entitled *Our Common Future* (also referred to as the Brundtland Report). Sustainable development was defined as "the development that meets the needs of the present generation without compromising the ability of future generations to meet their own needs" (United Nations World Commission on Environment and Development, 1987, p. 43). In addition, the prologue urges that the *changes* in attitudes, in social values, and in aspirations, depend on vast campaigns of education, debate, and public participation.

Since the definition of sustainable development addressed the environment and development together, it received a large boost and obtained a widely accepted agenda for capacity building in the 21st century. As stated by Gibson et al. (2007, p. 49), sustainability became the featured objective of government pronouncements on development initiatives, domestic program agendas, and international aid targets. Major corporations and business associations also claimed adherence. Shelves of academic treatises, consulting reports and policy documents were prepared. Sustainability became a household term.

The Brundtland Report paved the way for the UN's Earth Summit, held in Rio de Janeiro, Brazil, in 1992. Under the auspices of the United Nations Conference on Environment and Development (UNCED), also known as *the Earth Summit,* more than 180 nations, development agencies, non-government Organizations (NGOs), transnational corporations, educators, and the world media, met in Rio de Janeiro, Brazil and developed a program of action (known as Agenda 21) to chart future actions of sustainable development worldwide. After it was found that there was a wide gap between the rhetoric of the 1992 Summit and the reality observed over the following ten years, at the UN conference on sustainable development held in Johannesburg, the concept of sustainable development was specifically operationalized to simultaneously achieve sets of objectives of sustainable development in the areas of economic (growth, equity, and efficiency), social (empowerment, participation, social mobility, social cohesion, cultural identity and institutional development), and ecological well-being (ecosystem integrity, carrying capacity, biodiversity, and protection of global commons). (Vargas, Feb, 2008, p. 11.) In addition, the United Nations General Assembly declared 2005-2014 a Decade for Education for Sustainable Development (DESD). To reduce both extreme poverty and hunger by half or more by the year 2015 of those whose income is below US $1 per person/day, the United Nations has strongly advocated, micro finance as one of the tools that could be used to contribute to sustainable development in the 21st century. According to the World Bank, sustainability policies need to cover the simultaneous achievements of three separate sets of objectives: Economic growth (equity and efficiency); *social objectives* (empowerment, participation, social mobility, social cohesion, cultural identity, and institutional development); and *ecological objectives* (ecosystem integrity, carrying capacity, biodiversity, and protection of global commons). Though economic, social, and environmental objectives can to a certain degree develop synergies, by integrating the three dimensions, Pearce and Warford (1993) define sustainable development as development that secures increases in the welfare of the current generation provided that welfare does not decrease in the future.

As shown above, sustainable development has broad appeal because it is multi-dimensional (involves economic, ecological, human well being, and other social considerations). It also emphasizes ethics in relation to future generations (rather than mechanical calculation), and involves a precautionary principle. Though intuitively appealing, the concept of sustainable development can not easily be translated into practices, because it projects different meanings for different groups. For instance, it fails to address how intermediate and long-run decisions on resources management can affect equity between people of different generations or inter-generational equity. Moreover, it generates debate on a society's specific values and how those values can be transferred to future generations. For example, it is very difficult to predict how the capital stocks of today will be viewed as economically optimal for sustaining future generations. Unless the current distribution of resources is altered, it is difficult to maintain intra-generational equity between people of the same generation. Finally, unless different socialization strategies are implemented, it might not be possible to convince the present generation to leave the same amount of natural resources per capita for the future generation. Due to persistent ambiguities in definitions, and the plurality of purposes in characterization and measurement, there cannot be constant set indicators backed by universally acceptable theoretical framework associated with sustainable development. As stated by Parris and Kates (2003), the oxymoron-like character of sustainable development may help us to identify what is to be sustained, but cannot help us to reconcile the real conflicts between economy and environment and between the present and the future.

However, the idea of environmentally sustainable development "...is the persistence of certain necessary and desired characteristics of people, their communities and organization, and the surrounding ecosystem over a very long period of time." (Hardi and Zdan, 1997.) Therefore, if microcredit programs are supposed to integrate sustainability, the pertinent questions that could be posed at this juncture are: a) Are the chronically poor segment of the population involved in microcredit programs? b) If so, how are the beneficiaries affecting the ecosystem? c) Would the beneficiaries of microcredit contribute to environmental sustainability in their business activities?

Given the ambiguity of sustainable development as a concept, it is challenging to evaluate and map out the progress made by the beneficiaries of microcredit towards sustainability so that decision makers can be able to monitor and evaluate the effectiveness of the program and adjusting it as necessary. The central evaluating and monitoring requirements are to track systematically the key variables and processes over time to see how they change as a result of strategic activities (Hardi and Zdan, 1997). Therefore, to measure whether a developing country has achieved or is in the process of achieving sustainable development, it might be necessary to use the standardized 2015 Millennium Development goals that encompasses economic, social and environmental goals.

The Copenhagen Conference (1996) states that to achieve economic well-being the proportion of people living in extreme poverty in developing countries should be reduced by at least half by 2015. The social and human development goals enunciated in Cairo, Copenhagen and Beijing conclude: a) There should be universal primary education in all countries by 2015; b) progress towards gender equality and empowerment of women should be demonstrated by eliminating gender disparity in primary and secondary education by 2015; c) death rates for infants and children under 5 years should be reduced in each developing country by two-thirds of the 1990 level by 2015; d) rates of maternal mortality should be reduced by three-quarters between 1990 and 2015; e) access should be available through the primary health care system to reproductive health services for all individuals of appropriate ages no later than 2015; f) access to improved water sources; g) access to improved sanitation, and access to secure tenure. To ensure sustainability, reverse, and regenerate the loss of environmental resources, the following indicators were suggested: a) proportion of land area covered by forest; b) land area protected to maintain biological diversity; c) GDP per unit of energy (as a proxy for energy efficiency); and d) per capita carbon dioxide emission (International Institute of Environment and Development, 2002, pp. 24-25).

A Review of African Case Studies

The area of sustainability that appears to be receiving the most attention from microcredit lenders is the reduction in land degradation and the development of healthier, more permanent and less destructive farming practices in Rwanda's Eastern Province, Kigali city Northern Provinces, and Huye District in the Southern Province. According to the Rwandan Red Cross (RRC) (2009, p.1), "The Rwandan economy is based on the largely rain-fed agricultural production of small, semi subsistence and increasingly fragmented farms. It has few natural resources to exploit, and a small uncompetitive industrial sector. Food security is threatened by a decline in soil fertility and poor crop management, pests, diseases, poor storage, ..., scarcity of farm land, poor agricultural practices and population density." The RRC also indicates that over the past five years, chronic childhood malnutrition rates in the country have increased from 43 percent to 45 percent, and that "Rwandan households are exposed to some vulnerability in access to or consumption of food while 28 per cent of households suffer from malnutrition" (2009, p. 1).

The aim of the microcredit projects spearheaded by the RRC is to improve communities' livelihoods by contributing to effective poverty reduction and complimentary economic development activities for sustainable food security. As stated by RRC, the overall objectives is to provide a venue for income-generating activities through a rotating microcredit scheme which is aimed at a number of sectors including in-kind agricultural inputs, livestock, commerce, retail, and carpentry. As stated by RRC (2009, p. 1), Examples of projects developed from this microcredit program include preparing agro-forestry and forestry nurseries for cooperatives and associations involved in the program, and the distribution of proper tools, seeds, and fertilizers.

A snapshot of some of the benefits reaped from the microcredit initiatives in Rwanda include:

- Increased agricultural production and other incomes
- Improved household nutritional status
- Boosted communities'capacity to manage their rotating funds
- Provided the means for small shops and stock in the community
- Enhanced knowledge and skills in families to resolve problems, manage projects, and participate in cooperative organizations and group works
- Replicated new practices in other areas so that more associations and vulnerable communities are being served
- Improved RRC staff and volunteers' capacity to plan, monitor, and evaluate their projects

In short, the lessons learned from the microcredit projects in Rwanda are that, "...the fact that in order for projects activities to be sustained there must be a concordant level of understanding between all stakeholders. Additionally, it is imperative that vulnerable groups are encouraged to participate in the steering committees and working groups. It is imperative that assessments of the associations be conducted with all members and that the information is then disseminated to others involved in the same line of activities" (RRC, 2009, p. 2).

Another case study which shows an example of the association between sustainable development and microcredit took place in Machakos in east central Kenya. As stated by Duran (2002 , p. 1), "In the last decade alone, drought periods in 91/92, 95/96, and 98/200?, and the devastating floods in 1997/98, and again in 2002 in different parts of the country have been recorded. These phenomena have had the cumulative effects of reducing household food availability, purchasing power, and coping capacity, impoverishing the rural population."

In 2001, a year after a devastating drought that left 4 million people in dire need of food, the International Federation, in conjunction with the Kenya Red Cross Society (KRCS), developed a program in the Machakos district of Kenya that would deal with the impact of drought and famine before problems developed. As documented by Duran (2002, p. 1), more than 50 per cent of the residents of Machakos were categorized as the absolute poor (i.e. those who cannot afford to meet the basic minimum food requirement even after spending all their total incomes on food only).

The International Federation of Red Cross initiated a bilateral cooperation with the Kenya Red Cross Society, contributed microcredit funds and designed a Drought Preparedness program for the Machakos District. More specifically, the Machakos program focused on "...developing branch capacities through training to enable the Machakos branch to mobilize volunteers, and through training to work closely with and from within rural communities. The three-year project, implemented by the KRCS – Machakos branch with technical support from the International Federation , aims at strengthening the local and district capacities, through local and innovative mechanisms to predict , cope with and recover from recurrent drought impacts" (2002, 2).

In addition, the microcredit projects implemented in the Machakos District included agriculture that focused on farming drought-resistant crops, education on storing and developing seed banks on a community level, development of small-scale water systems that were built with community assistance, and the formation of water committees that would provide stable water management practices. Kenya experienced another drought in 2004. The Machakos district, which was most affected by the 2001 drought, was able to work with the conditions in 2004 and was ultimately unaffected by the drought. In Duran's words, "Developing all these activities through microcredits we were able to mobilize the community, to reinforce the social tissues, and support their initiatives for their own development" (2002, p. 4).

For the last five years, with microcredits disbursed for food production in Gambia, Mozambique, Nigeria, and Tanzania, farmers increased their output and attained food security (Tsogde, 2002). For example, in Tanzania, after the Tanzanian Government approved a national microfinance policy in May 2000, the International Fund for Agricultural Development (IFAD), a specialized agency of the United Nations dedicated to eradicating rural Poverty in developing countries, helped mobilize savings and disbursed funds as credits to the agricultural sector. As a result, the poor, including women as user-owners were empowered. And the country's substantially improved in food security and income. Thus microcredits have become a formidable economic tool? (sector) of the agricultural policy makers (2002). In Gambia, the IFAD contributed to a rapid increase of rice growers with increases in different villages ranging from 50% to 200%. In Nigeria, the Cassava multiplication Program increased cassava production in the country, from less than 14 million tons in 1987 to over 30 million tons in 1998, becoming the world's largest producer of cassava. In Mozambique, microcredits improved the level of income, employment, and food security of fishermen and their families, through the provision of fishing inputs and credit. As summarized by Tsogbe (2002, p. 22), the examples taken from the four case studies show that microcredit can be a catalyst for reaching the goal of increasing agricultural production by creating both backward and forward linkages.

To test their hypothesis that the success of micro-finance institutions is measured according to the extent of their outreach to the poor and their financial viability or sustainability, Adams et al. (2002) studied four case sites on microfinance initiatives in South Africa. The case studies included the following sites: Mathabatha village) Limpopo Province), Kgautswane village (Limpopo Province), Oudtshoorn (Western Cape) and Mtshabe (Eastern cape). The finding of the research indicates that the village banks do not charge interest rates to cover costs. But, the informal group (i.e., credit unions, moneylenders, money keepers, families, relatives and friends, etc) charged minimum interest rates. Since microcredit financial institutions in the studied regions depend on external funds, Adams et al, proposes that microfinancial institutions need to incorporate interest rates in order to enhance self-sustainability of village banks and other group-based credit arrangements. In their own words, Adams and his group (2002) suggest that "Micro-finance institutions in South Africa therefore need to encourage clients and support the pooling of material resources. Nonetheless, since the objective of moneylenders is based on interest-seeking activities and not on altruism, there is a need for appropriate regulation by government" (p.125).

The main findings of the South African case studies included :

1) In Oudtshoorn, most of microcredit lending operations deepen the poverty levels of the poor.
2) Among the microfinancing institutions' services and operations, there are common aims and objectives, to serve the poor and help them develop sustainability by achieving financial and food security.
3) The microfinancing institutions need to cover the costs they incur. For that, they should charge high interest rates to cover these costs and grow.
4) Except for the Mathabatha Bank the other three microfinancial institutions are highly dependent on outside funding. Thus, the other banks need to begin weaning themselves away from their dependence on external subsidies.
5) Since funding does not mean money only, the case study village banks need educational advice on how to follow their savings' progress to determine whether or not they are really valuable to the community

6) Since women are diligent savers at the village bank and are always members of the village savings club, the empowerment of women should receive a lot of attention in the process of development.
7) Since most rural areas are led by traditional chiefs and follow strict cultural rules and formalities, village banks need to work in cooperation with village authorities to ensure the smooth operation of development programs.
8) Incentives should be provided to community-based savings schemes to encourage saving and investment. For example, the model of savings used by the school in Oudtshoorn could be adapted for use by schools and communities.
9) Despite an adequate supply of consumer credit in Oudtshoorn, the research findings concluded that credit was needed for productive purposes in short supply for those with no conventional collateral.
10) The village banks need to improve their marketing/promotion/outreach activities and re-engineering delivery systems.

The South African case studies were very extensive. Although the analysis was based at the village level, the case studies fail to address the status of poverty level of the client or households. The focus of the case studies seem to be more on the sustainability of the microcredit village banks and their financiers rather than on the effect that the sustainability-focused microcredits can have on the participants, the community, and the environment.

Since the issuance of Proclamations No. 40/1996, a number of finance (MFI) institutions were established in Ethiopia as share companies in accordance with the Commercial Code of Ethiopia. The ownership of Ethiopia's MFIs is based on the country's administrative structure. For example, in 2002, six out of 20 MFIs were largely owned by regional governments and non-profit organizations in the regional states. In other MFIs, the equity structures were sponsored by foreign donors who have contributed the initial capital for required registration. Seventy eight percent of the clients are from rural households and 41 percent of the clients are women (Al-Bagdadi and Bruntrup, 2002).

To minimize recurring costs and improve operational efficiency, and in order for clients to effectively invest microcredit funds into productive income-generating initiatives, almost all microcredit institutions in Ethiopia have established training formats for their clients. Though a survey conducted by Amha et al., indicates that business development services (BDS) "had very limited vocational and technical training (before starting business), received few short-term training, *extension and counseling, and marketing services*" (2006), the African Village Academy's claims to provide the following seven step training methods. These are:

> Step one introduces various types of financial institutions and tools. Step two encourages participants to discuss and examine themselves and their markets to identify potential microenterprise activities, which they then research individuals. In step three, participants discuss in detail their market findings (i.e. materials, transportation, and market costs), and then re asked to form groups of typically four or five people. Step four elaborates the purpose of group formation in creating support and collateral for individuals, as well as developing specific business plans and budget planning. In step five, participants meet each other's groups in units of up to ten groups, and discuss specific credit arrangements and requirements of Savings and Credit for enterprise Development program. In step six, group members present their basic plans for final approval of the unit, and in step seven all steps are reviewed to reinforce understanding of the program. (Un/OSCAL Model, 2002, p. 80-81).

To assess the outcomes of an Ethiopian Microfinance program (which was established in Ethiopia, as an affiliate of the World Vision microfinance–WISDOM) on the livelihoods of poor populations , a survey studied 819 rural households in Southern Ethiopia (i.e., Adama, located in the East Shewa Zone of the Oromiya Regional State and Sodo branches, located in Wolayita, in the State of Southern Nations, Nationalities , and peoples region). The indicators used to asses the socioeconomic status of the respondents were a) monthly households income, b) per capita monthly household income, c) household assets and livestock value, d) household asset, and e) livestock index score. In addition to assess the food security status of the respondents were assessed using household diet, child nutrition status, and food aid receipt. As stated by Doocy et al., (2005) in its methodological design:

> The study compared two groups of clients that received loans (incoming clients who had completed one loan cycle or less and had been participating in the program for no more than ten months, and established clients who had completed two or more loan cycle) and one group of community controls who were eligible to participate in the WISDOM lending program but had not received a loan within the past year and were not seeking a loan. A total of 408 established clients, 205 incoming clients, and 206 community controls participated in the survey. The sample was stratified by survey site and clients sex, participants were systematically selected from client lists of the microfinance institutions. (p.82)

Since the two case studies are based on a cross-sectional design, it was very difficult for the researchers to ascertain whether the clients in the two regions have moved towards sustainability or away from it. However, the aggregate findings of the questionnaire-based interviews indicate that "While the majority of WISDOM clients reported an increase in asset value since enrolling in the lending program, differences in household asset data between clients and community controls were statically insignificant. Findings from this study also indicate that participation in the WISDOM microfinance program did not result in increased household wealth" (Doocy, 2005, p. 87). In terms of wealth, "No significant correlations were observed between length of program participation (*time in months or loan cycles)* and either measure of change in asset value suggesting that participation in the lending program is not associated with an increase in client wealth" (Doocy et al., 2005, p. 88). Similarly, it was ascertained that there was no association between participation in the program and monthly household income. Nonetheless, in their conclusion, Doocy (2005) and his group showed that the WISDOM microfinance programs (i.e. in Adam and Sodo, Ethiopia,) improved client retention, increased savings, and increased the active participation of women.

Another study conducted in the Wereda of Atsbi-wemberta in the Tigray Regional State, northern Ethiopia in 2002 analyzed the impact of formal and informal credit on households' livelihoods. As reported by Vilei and Chisholm (2002), the results of a survey in 97 households and 5 group discussions showed that the interviewed households perceived that having access to credit had a positive impact. It contributed to enhancing the self-esteem of the beneficiaries by becoming less dependent on food aid. However, several of the interviewed households indicated that the local microfinance institutions such as the Dedebit Saving and Credit Institution (DESCI) lent higher sums of money but they imposed inflexible repayment conditions and lacked the skills to monitor successfully the invested loans. Many clients used the credits for food consumption and eventually the beneficiaries were forced to sell their livestock in order to repay their loans on time. Also it was reported that though informal credit from money lenders at interest rates of up to 60 percent are generally very small sums when compared with formal microcredits, they are widely used to cover food consumption or pay for additional social events such as marriage and funeral services.

Table 7.2: Microcredit Programs for Sustainability in Selected African Countries

Case	Author	Purpose	Examples of projects	Findings	Observation
Rwanda's Eastern Province, Kigali city Northern Provinces and Huye District in the Southern Province.	Rwanda Red Cross (2009)	Reduce in land degradation and the development of less destructive farming practices	Preparing agro-forestry ; forestry nurseries for cooperatives; distribution of proper tools, seeds and fertilizers	Improved agricultural production; improved household nutrition ; small shops and stock available in the community	The study showed that for sustainability to be achieved stock holders need to participate in the planning and implementation process.
Machakos District of Kenya	Duran , International Federation of Red Cross (2001)	To tackle the impact of drought and famine before problems developed	Farming drought-resistant crops, education on storing and developing seed banks on a community level, development of small-scale water systems	Microcredit helped to mobilize the community and support the local initiatives	The case study identified that 50 percent of the district were absolute poor and could not afford to meet basic minimum food requirements.
Tanzania	International Fund for Agricultural Development (IFAD), 2002	Eradicate rural poverty	Mobilize savings and disbursed as credits to poor women and the poor	Microcredits resulted food security and empowerment of women as users	The study was not conducted to show how micro credit empowered the poor women
Gambia	IFAD (2002)	An increase in rice growing in different villages	Rice growing	Microcredits contributed to a rapid increase of rice growers with the increase in different villages ranging from 50% to 200%	The case study failed to demonstrate if the poor benefited from an Increase in rice production and did not ascertain the impact on resource utilization on the clients.
Nigeria	IFAD (2002)	To increase the production of Cassava	The cassava Multiplication Program	Cassava production in the country increased from 14 million tons in 1987 to over 30 million tons in 1998, as a result Nigeria became the world's largest producer of cassava	The case study might have contribute both backwards and forward linkages. But it has failed to show the beneficiaries of the increase in cassava production. In addition, an analysis of the impact of fertilizers on the environmental degradation was not attempted.

Case	Author	Purpose	Examples of projects	Findings	Observation
Mozambique	IFAD (2002)	Increase food security of fishermen and their families	Microcredits for fishing inputs and credit	Microcredits improved the level of income, employment and food security of fishermen and families	The fish project in Mozambique seems to be focused on mostly on those whose income is above the poverty line.
Mathabatha, Kgautswane, oudtshoorn and Mtshabe villages in South africa	Adams et al (2002)	Investigate the outreach of micro-finance institutions reach the poor	Most of Microcredit lending operation (Oudtshoorn village) deepen the poverty level of the poor. The women participants did not get enough attention. .		Though extensive, the study failed to demonstrate the extent of poverty level of the clients on the studied households. The focus of the case studies seems to be more on the sustainability of microcredit village banks rather the effects of sustainability-focused microcredit on the participants and the community.
Adama, Oromiya Regional state and Sodo , State of Southern nations..., Ethiopia	Doocy etal (2005)	To assess the outcome of an micro finance program on the livelihoods of poor population	The indicators used to assess the socio-economic status of the respondents in the sample were: 1)Monthly households income 2)per capita monthly household income 3) household assets and livestock value 4)household asset 5) livestock index score 6) household diet 7)child nutrition status 8) food aid receipt	As a result of the WIDOM micro credit: 1) the majority reported that their assets the market value of the participants increased. 2)No significant correlations was observed between length of program participation 3) No association was ascertained between participation in the microcredit program and monthly household income.	1) The Adama and Sodo case studies were well-designed and very instructive. As admitted by the researchers since the case studies are based on cross-sectional design , the researchers seem to have difficulty to ascertain whether the clients in the two regions have ever moved toward sustainability or away from it. 2) The case studies did not attempt to demonstrate if the participants were / or not pursuing environmentally-friendly approaches in their productive activities.

Case	Author	Purpose	Examples of projects	Findings	Observation
Atsbi-wemberta, Tigray Regional State	Sonja Vilei and Nick Chisholm February – March 2002	To assess the impact of formal and informal credit on households	65 male headed and 32 female-headed households whose age ranged from 18-65. . The survey covered about respondents' assets, livelihoods, size and use of credit.	The results of a survey in 97 households and 5 group discussions showed that the interviewed households perceived that having access to credit had positive impact. It contributed to enhancing the self-esteem of the beneficiaries to be less dependent on food aid.	The study identified the participants in the study based on household assets indicator. The study indicates that formal credits were used for the purchase of oxen, cows,, cereal trade , basket making and home-made beer. However, since the study was conducted in about six months, it failed to address the environmental impact of the various activities on the region.

As shown in Table 7.2, it is very important to note that the efforts made by the case studies presented above show that the various microcredit projects initiated in a number of African countries have attempted to minimize the degree of poverty of the participants. However, since the core concept of poverty and sustainability development are not fully operationally defined and the case studies were based on cross-sectional rather than on longitudinal designs, they lagged to help their readers realize how Microcredit be made to minimize poverty and foster sustainable development in the long run.

Conclusions, Policy and Research Implications

The United Nations declared 2005 the international Year of Microcredit. Microcredit is a provision for very small loans and deposit services to predominantly poor, under-served, rural borrowers, who are excluded from the financial system. It has achieved a preponderant place as a lending instrument in the sphere of international finance in the last three decades (Jain, 2003). Microcredit or microfinance programs have become a popular approach, especially to reach those with low income, who would normally be excluded from formal lending institutions because they lack the collateral and credit history, necessary to borrow and establish their own businesses and become innovative entrepreneurs.

Though microcredit is not seen as a panacea for poverty and development, but rather as an important tool in the mission of poverty eradication (UN/OSCAL MODEL, 2002), it has captured the imagination of policy-makers and development practitioners. In addition, Africa's policy-makers fully understand that there no blueprint for microcredit initiatives and each program must adjust to the specific socio-cultural and economic setting in which it operates. For instance, a number of African countries have introduced microcredit programs to replicate the delivery system of Grameen Bank of Bangladesh as a strategy for poverty alleviation in rural areas (where a large portion of Africa's population lives), and as a means for fostering environmentally sustainable development goals for the 21st Century.

Given the ambiguity of poverty and sustainable development as concepts, it is challenging to evaluate and map out the progress made by the beneficiaries of microcredit towards sustainability so that decision makers can be able to monitor and evaluate the effectiveness of the program and adjust it as necessary. In simple terms, the effectiveness of any policy of poverty needs to be articulated around the definition of poverty in order to evaluate the number of poor and design a microcredit program of intervention to alleviate poverty and foster sustainable development in the long run. To be effective, the idea of environmentally sustainable development "...is the persistence of certain necessary and desired characteristics of people, their communities and organization, and the surrounding ecosystem over a very long period of time" (Hardi and Zdan, 1997).

The central evaluating and monitoring requirements need to be seen as the association between microcredit programs as a strategy, and sustainability as an outcome, so that they can be tracked systematically over time (Hardi and Zdan, 1997). More specifically, if microcredit programs are to act as a foundation for the hard core poor to develop products and services to increase their wellbeing while integrating sustainability, the pertinent questions that need to be addressed for Africa should include: a) Are the chronically poor segments of the population involved in microcredit programs? If so, b) How are the beneficiaries affecting the ecosystem? and c) Do the activities of the microcredit beneficiaries contribute to environmental sustainability?

As shown in Table 7.3, the African case studies conducted by the microcredit researchers rightly show that the various microcredit projects were designed to tackle poverty in the rural setting of Africa (where majority of the Southern African population lives and subsistence farming is the main stay of the economy). With the exception of the Ethiopian case studies conducted by Doocy et al., (2005), and Vilel and Chisholm (2002), which operationally measured poverty income using the beneficiaries' income and assets of households, the other case studies did not specifically identify the poverty status of the microcredit clients. In general, based on the notion that the existence of a 'poverty-environment trap' in Africa could be minimized by the implementation of micro credit programs most researchers targeted their microcredit research to focus on all rural people regardless whether or not they were beneficiaries of micro credit programs. In other words, with their sampling techniques, the case studies failed to identify that the actual beneficiaries of the microcredit programs in Africa were indeed hard core poor.

In addition, as the Asian studies briefly mentioned before, the microcredit programs in Africa didn't seem to help significantly to lift the poor out of poverty. The case studies did not attempt to show whether or not the micro studies yielded an income effect or manifested positive/negative spillover effects on the local communities. That is, the researchers presented above seem to be focusing mainly on borrowers living above the poverty line rather than the hard core poor. In addition, most of the case studies conducted in Africa were based on cross-sectional rather than on longitudinal data. So the studies did not effectively demonstrate that the various microcredit activities of the participants could be environmentally sustainable. Household-level impacts in rural Africa should have been incorporated in their studies when new enterprises began, to determine if the identified microcredit programs ever increased the amounts spent on durable assets and if the beneficiaries ever used environmentally-sensitive inputs in their various activities.

TABLE 7.3: THE COMPOSITE CORE THEME AND INDICATORS OF HUMAN WELL-BEING, ECONOMIC, SOCIAL AND ENVIRONMENTAL WELL-BEING SUSTAINABILITY INDEX

CORE THEME	INDICATOR	ACHIEVEMENT IN YEARS	
		T1	T4
Human wellbeing Index*	Living below poverty line (earning US $1 per day)		
	Subjective assessment of felt need		
	Access to land		
	Nutritional status of children		
	Mortality rate under 5 years old		
	Access to housing facilities/ floor area per person		
	Access to sanitary latrine		
	Access to safe drinking water		
	Regularly employed person in the family		
	Children going to school		
	Access to primary health care facilities		
	Adult literacy rate		

Eco-system wellbeing**	Activities impact on land Activities impact on water quantity Activities on water quality Activities impact on Air quality Activities on energy use Activities on water use Activities impact on species Activities impact on genes Activities impact on Biodiversity Resource use		
Environmentally Sustainability Index**	**Environmental systems:** deforestation Carbon emissions Sulfur emissions Toxic waste **Reducing environmental stress:** Air pollution Water stresses Ecosystem stress Waste Consumption pressures Population growth **Reducing human vulnerability:** Basic human sustenance Environmental health **Social and institutional capacity:** Environmental governance Eco-efficiency Economic and Human loss due to natural disaster		

Source: *V.P. Raghavan, " Likelihoods and Empowerment: The Kudumbashree Projects in Kerala, India-A New Paradigm of Participatory Economy. International Association for the Economics of Participation, July 13-15, 2006.

Thomas M. Parris and Robert W. Kates, "Characterizing and Measuring Sustainable Development." **Annual Review of Economic Resources (2003).

Though worthwhile, the African case studies reviewed above should have tracked systematically the activities of the chronically poor people in the sample to determine if they had positively or negatively affected the ecosystem, and to ascertain if the various microcredit activities are environmentally beneficial. As stated by Armendariz and Morduch (2007), "...there is no study yet that has achieved wide consensus as to its reliability; and this reflects the inherent difficulty in evaluating programs in which participation is voluntary and different customers use the services with varying degree of intensity" (p. 222).

As shown in Table 7.3, to better serve policy decision-making needs in evaluating the impact of microcredit access and participation on sustainability, the three standardized core themes of a) the human-well being, b) eco-system well-being, and c) environmental index, incorporate the 2015 UN Development Goals suggested to evaluate microcredit programs in the long run in developing countries. More specifically, as suggested by Armendariz and Morduch (2007), to calculate the impacts of microcredit on poverty alleviation and sustainable development any study however, needs to have a *Treatment group*, poor individuals who get access to microcredit measured in T1 (year 0) and then measured in T2 (after 4 years) to measure the microcredit impact. For the *Control group*, hard core poor individuals from an area without access to microcredit, measured in time CT0 and CT2 could be used. The difference between T2 and T1 captures the microfinance impact. However, since it might reflect broader economic and social changes that occur between year 0 and year 4, that are independent of microfinance, it is worthwhile to compare T2 and CT2 to address biases due to the broadly felt economic and social changes. Thus, isolating the true microfinance impact requires comparing the difference between T2-T1 with the difference between CT2-CT1 which is a so-called difference-in-difference approach . "... the difference-in-difference approach is adequate to deliver accurate measures of microfinance impacts. But in reality, these characteristics may change over time (perhaps a borrower gets more education or strengthens his/her social networks, for reasons unrelated to microfinance" (Armendariz and Morduch, 2007, p. 205).

The conclusion that can be derived from an analysis of the African case studies presented above is that in order to be useful for policy makers, the core concept of poverty and sustainability development need to be operationally defined. In addition, if microcredit programs are expected to minimize poverty and foster sustainable development in the studied countries, to measure the impact of the microcredit programs, the participants need to be systematically sampled and the framework of the studies need to be based on longitudinal design.

Chapter 8

THE GLOBALIZATION OF THE JAPANESE MANAGEMENT PROCESS: REINVIGORATING ETHIOPIA'S INDUSTRIES THROUGH "*KAIZEN*"

In the 1950s, American industry entered the "Golden Age" of manufacturing. Earlier, during the Post WWII era, a number of American companies maximized enormous profits as the world stood in line to buy their products at a premium. At the same time, Japanese goods were generally assigned low market prices in the world market because Japanese products were perceived as being 'cheap' and of 'low quality.' (See Becker and Snow, 1997, and Ohno, I. Hhno, K. and Uesu, S., October 2009.)

To revitalize its economy and reinvigorate its industrial base in the 1950s and 60s, Japan started framing the basic infrastructure needed to catch-up with the United States in the global market place. Japan then galvanized the strong support of the Union of Japanese Scientists and Engineers (JUSE) and Japan Productivity Center (JPC). Finally, in conjunction with the Shewhart cycle taught by W. Edwards Deming, and other statistics-based methods taught by Joseph M. Juran and its organizational culture and structure, Japan developed the foundation for a Japanese Management System (Weldemariam, H. 2010, Sharri, Nariai, 2006). The originally American technique which was adopted and adjusted became a Japanese management system (JMS), better known as *kaizen* (*ky'zen*). According to Imai (1986) *kaizen* is defined as continuous improvement involving employees in all levels of an organization. As operationally defined by Brunet and New (2003, the three characteristics of the *kaizen* system generally require that it be:

Continuous, nature that is a never-ending journey for quality and efficiency;
Usually incremental in nature, always improving instead of reorganizing or reinstalling;
Participative, requiring workforce involvement and intelligence.

Unlike Western business concepts, generally epitomized by the terms innovation or drastic change in order to create fast results, the foundation of the Japanese *kaizen* management system was made popular because it was adapted to adhere to a continual process of improvement (Becker and Snow, 1997). More specifically, in business *kaizen* includes quality control, automation, workers suggestion systems, just-in-time delivery systems and the 5S process. *(i.e.,seiri* (sorting); *seiton* (setting straight); *seiso* (cleanliness); *seiketsu* (standardization in the workplace); and *shitsuke* (sustaining self-discipline and promoting a sense of pride in workers in their work and being owners of their responsibility (See Genobz, July 15, 2010).

Based on the assumption that the most important asset a company has is its work force, with the importance of the individual worker being the key asset, the *kaizen* philosophy is committed to better quality and improved productivity. Based on workers self-criticism and adherence to the constructive critique of the process, *kaizen* involves bottom-up decision-making and practices an employee-driven management style that heavily emphasizes teamwork. As narrated by Hhno, Hhno, and Uesu, teams are not only formed across various disciplines, but the teams are given training in the dynamics of teamwork. After 'team training' is completed, the team groups are given a problem to investigate and asked to submit recommendations for improvement. A unique aspect of this recommendation process is that the team is empowered by upper management to take action on these recommendations and see them through to completion" (2009). In addition, the Japanese management systems work as a unit because:

> *All the characteristics work effectively on the condition of lifetime employment. The seniority system is based on the assumption that employees' abilities will increase along with the length of service and experience. In-house education also depends on lifelong employment because the company gains the benefit of education only when employees work for a long time. Enterprises union is necessary when people work for only one company. One-time recruitment is the other side of lifetime employment. The importance of an employee welfare program is obvious if the employee works within a company for a longtime. The*

> *other characteristics such as the bottom-up decision making system and family-oriented management are the results of lifetime employment (Ihara, 2004).*

In the 1970s, as the *kaizen* Japanese management system revealed a potential for never-ending efforts for improvement in production values, it diffused its new management system throughout Japanese companies. With the globalization of Japanese businesses in the 1980s, *kaizen* became a global activity. *Kaizen* "...was originally developed in Toyota and spread among other Japanese manufacturers as they gained fame in the international market for higher quality products (Imai, 1986)." That is, as Japanese multinational manufacturing companies expanded abroad they tried to duplicate the quality management methods within their new factories. When Japanese firms endeavored to increase local procurement of intermediate inputs, local suppliers were requested to conform to Japan's quality standards. Thus, Japanese companies often assisted their local partners in learning the *kaizen* philosophy and practices. Similarly, the Japan International Cooperation Agency (JICA) began actively to use the *kaizen* management style to transform the industrial activities of a number of developing countries. For instance:

> The first JICA project for productivity management was extended to Singapore from 1983 to 1990. Building on the success of this cooperation, the Singapore Productivity and Standard Board has subsequently grown to become a major organization to external training programs to other countries and regions, including the Southern African Development Community (SADC) under partnership arrangements with JICA (Hhno, Hhno, and Uesu,, 2009, p.7).

Based on its competitive success in the 1990s, in its aid package to support growth for those countries coming late to industrialization, Japan included *kaizen* as an additional means for enhancing their human potential and industrial enterprise capability. Before the proliferation of *kaizen*, Japan however, made sure that the following four vital prerequisites were met by each company. As outlined by Hhno, Hhno, and Uesu, 2009), some of the conditions, Japan wants to see in Africa include:

- the prospective firm is medium to large scale and must be licensed by a private,
- international, *kaizen* consulting group (for example, the license-giving consultant groups in Africa are now located in Mauritius);

- the plans for each project are customized according to the needs and conditions of the recipient from the *kaizen* projects, assisted by JICA;
- the main purpose of the Japan International Cooperation Agency (JICA) assistance is to provide organizational capacity building to various productivity improvement centers; and
- the sustaining of competitive and responsible enterprise programs already in operation.

To justify Japanese commitments and to intensify their engagement to boost Africa's economic growth, in May 2008, at the Fourth Tokyo International Conference for African Development (TICAD IV) at the Yokohama Action Plan, the Japanese Government outlined the following specific plans:

- to expand training programs in Africa to improve productivity in promising industries by JITA;
- to facilitate trade investment by transferring Japanese manufacturing and marketing skills by the Association for Overseas Technical Scholarship (AOTS);
- to establish mechanisms for Official Development Assistance (ODA) that will complement private sector activities that contribute to African development;
- to set up the Japan Bank for International Cooperation (JIBC) Facility for African Investment by offering equity investment, guarantees, and local currency financing;
- to provide, on a regular basis, information about the African business climate to private Japanese companies by Japan External Trade Organization, JETRO (Hhno, Hhno, and Uesu, 2009).

The Japanese management system as practiced in a number of countries has been seen positively by many managers and practitioners because the system has helped a number of enterprises to become productive, competitive, and has largely increased customer satisfaction. In fact, Yokosuka, K., et.al.,(2010) argue that "...two national characteristics are critical for successful *kaizen* transfer. One is the disciplined people who follow what they are asked to do i.e. keeping the deadline, quality control, and following standard operating procedure. The other is a hungry mentality, eager to do work which is above and beyond their responsibility."

Based on his theoretical contributions and experience, that Recht (1998) reviewed, he has come to the conclusion that "*kaizen*-oriented suggestion systems are transferable to non-Japanese cultural environments." But he asserts that to increase the chances of a successful transfer, six organization-culture conditions are necessary: a) a clear employee orientation, supported by a (contractually or verbally assured) non-lay-off policy; b) employees who are committed to the company's long-term viability; c) a free flow of information, both along the vertical axis and between units that belong to the same hierarchical level; d) empowered employees, i.e., employees that have the information and skills needed to take decisions on a wide range of issues concerning their own working environment; e) a so-called 'pragmative' orientation; and finally employees who are both process- and results-oriented (Recht. 1998).

On the other hand, some authors have concluded that *kaizen* has been dysfunctional in a number of foreign companies because it is insensitive to domestic cultures, urges foreign-owned companies to emulate the Japanese way of management, and is based on the assumption that what works in Japan has to be uniformly implemented in other countries (Shaari, 2010). Drawing on insights from the cybernetics of Beer (1966), it is possible to argue that *kaizen* categorizes the management of complexity in the management of target-oriented operations. In line with Beer's observation, a number of researchers argue since Japanese management practices are embedded in the Japanese culture it is difficult to transfer *kaizen systems* abroad. Many Japanese management systems are not easily adopted by an overseas counterpart due to environmental factors such as differences in national culture and work ethics. Transferred management systems are more likely to be hybridized with locally practiced systems (Yokozama, K. 2010). To use Lillrank's (1995) conclusion, the direct transfers of Japanese management practices often fail not because of geographical distance but rather due to the mental distance, i.e., culture, history, and strategic paradigms. Moreover, Hayashi (1994) argues that a *kaizen* management system works effectively in Japan because the Japanese organizations tend to have organic structures with decentralized decision-making, low degree of specialization and formalization, and above all the culture of horizontal communication.

Despite the above mentioned challenges with *kaizen* management systems, and because Sonobe's (2009) advice that under *kaizen* workers feel that they are really essential, integral parts of the enterprise, and can feel ownership, Ethiopia has decided to implement the Japanese management philosophy. Ethiopian manufacturers have been at a disadvantage, not only because of the lack of highly skilled human resources and a large technological gap but also because of a lack of differentiated managerial tools. As demonstrated by Berihu Assefa (2010), for the last six years, Ethiopia has recorded fast economic growth, but the ratio of its manufacturing sector is less than 5.0 % of its Gross Domestic Product. (See also, Hhno, Hhno, and Uesu,, 2009, p 19.)

It is worth mentioning at this juncture that in recent years, Japan's competitive condition does not seem to be worth imitating because Japan's position in the *World Competitiveness Yearbook* has dropped from 3rd position in 1993 to 27th in 2010 *(IMD, World Competitiveness Year book, 2011)*. Actually, due to its recent poor economic performance, a number of Japanese business managers have questioned pursuing the *kaizen* management approach in their business practices and some have started designing post-*kaizen* strategies that might prove very viable for the 21st century.

Despite the substantial economic slow down that Japan is manifesting today, policy makers in Ethiopia seem to view the *kaizen* system in a positive way because of its earlier success in Japanese firms. Fully convinced that the Japanese *kaizen* management model could be used as an effective strategy for latecomers like Ethiopia to industrialization, they seem to view the Japanese management system as an exemplary method for achieving the Growth and Transformation Plan of the 2010/11 to 2014/15. As stated by Weldemariam (2010), a number of Ethiopian firms have been instructed to launch a pilot project using the *kaizen* management system in order to accomplish the following three objectives: "first, to formulate a national plan to enhance both quality and productivity in the industrial sector; second, to produce a manual for explaining and guiding these activities; third, to transfer relevant skills and techniques to the staff members of the *kaizen* Unit in the Ministry of Trade and Industry (MoTI)."

Stated in simple terms, it became imperative for Ethiopian policy makers to endorse the institution of *kaizen* in Ethiopia's public and private enterprises in order to overcome the abysmal industrial situation. For late starters like Ethiopia, the Japanese tools of hands-on technical cooperation was expected to improve organizational capacity, empower and continuously improve the quality of workers, and add value to their products so that they would become productive and produce internationally competitive products that could meet the needs of a global market.

Given these assumptions, in July 2008, "PM Meles Zenawi requested two-part cooperation from Japan, 1) *kaizen* (factory improvement) by Japanese International Cooperation Agency (JICA); and 2) policy dialogue with National Graduate Institute for Policy Studies (GRIPS). The two components were implemented by GRIPS and JICA. (Ohno, 2010). On November 26, 2009, a seminar was given by the Ethiopian Ministry of Trade and the Ambassador of Japan to Ethiopia for about 300 attendees in Addis Ababa. As narrated by Weldemariam, the *kaizen* project in Ethiopia had three phases: the first phase which started in August, 2009 was involved in reviewing the quality and productivity of 63 companies. After preliminary diagnosis of these factories, 30 pilot companies were selected based on the following criteria: 1) proximity to Addis Ababa, within 100km distance, 2) contributions to exports and /or imports, 3) scale of capital, and 4) number of employees. The 30 companies included 10 from Metal, 6 from Agro processing, 6 from Chemicals, 4 from Leather, and 4 from Textiles (2010)..

Based on Sonobe's (2009) suggestion that for *kaizen* to work well for workers, they needed to have good skills and basic experiential training. From January 12 to January 15, 2010, four *kaizen* Unit members and JICA staff were sent to visit Egyptian *kaizen* centers and three *kaizen* Units were sent to Tunisia to have practical training and learn from the experience of the Egyptian and Tunisian *kaizen workers*. Finally, from May 8-23, 2010, the Ethiopian *kaizen* Unit members and participants from the 30 pilot companies were divided into two groups and were sent to kaizen training centers in Osaka and Nagoya, Japan, to acquire first hand experience and learn more about work place management, teamwork, and other kaizen management techniques (for details see, Weldemariam, 2010 and Hhno, Hhno, and Uesu,, 2009).

Given that kaizen pilot programs have already been launched in Ethiopia, some of the key issues that need to be addressed at this juncture are:

1. Are the Ethiopian value system and culture compatible with Japan's *kaizen* system of lean production and total quality management?
2. Is the transferred *kaizen* management system modified and appropriately designed to suit the diversity of practical circumstances and conditions of the Ethiopian manufacturing enterprises?
3. Were the organizational culture and structure of the pilot *kaizen* carefully analyzed before the transfer of *kaizen* to Ethiopia?
4. Is there synergy between the Japanese *kaizen* quality initiatives and the business environment of the pilot firms chosen in Ethiopia that will be embarking on a quality journey with Japan's experience as the guideline?
5. Will Japan's *kaizen* management system be adaptable enough to fit the Ethiopians' working culture?
6. Are factory workers in Ethiopia disciplined and motivated enough to share the underlying *kaizen* philosophy and go beyond formal job requirements to effectively participate in process improvement, i.e., to 1) identify opportunities, 2) make improvements, 3) challenge the status quo, 4) create favorable conditions to become self-starting and proactive?
7. Are enterprises in Ethiopia thinking of ways to improve continuously their products and services to meet customers' demands?
8. Are Ethiopian employees ready to utilize the *kaizen* process tools and methods to make the problems of their firms visible, and then use formal root analysis to identify and correct problems at the source?

To understand the transferability of the *kaizen* strategies to Ethiopia, the second section of the chapter summarizes studies related to the transferability of *kaizen* to overseas. The third section develops the conceptual framework needed to study the *kaizen* institutes in Ethiopia. Finally section four presents the conclusion of the study.

Literature Review

> *"Training will neither make a fish fly nor a bird swim; but training will certainly help a fish to swim faster and a bird fly higher" (Yong, AKB, 1996.)*

As mentioned above, Japan being the flagship of economic growth has been offering assistance through private channels such as intra-company technology transfer and support for local suppliers, and through public channels such as official development assistance (ODA) to public organizations in the form of the *kaizen* business strategy to a number of countries of East Asia, South Asia, Latin America, Eastern Europe, and more recently to Africa. (See for example, Ohno et al., 1997). Since the Japanese *kaizen* calls for continuous improvement that involves everyone in the organization from top management to the workers on the shop floor, its operating system allows employee participation and the delegation of responsibility. As described by Ohno, et al (1997), "*Kaizen* focuses on the way people approach work. It shows how management and workers can change their mindset together to improve their productivity." (See also, Imai, 1986). In addition, Lee et al (1987) argue that the Japanese management system is based on a philosophy and organizational culture that stresses: hard work for common goals; consultative decision-making; a two-way communication system; long-term planning; sharing of overall objectives of the organization by the employees at all levels; establishing harmony and loyalty; and showing a high degree of concern for people and their values. (See also, Tasie, G. 2009). Given these characteristics, the question that needs to be addressed is: Is the *kaizen* organizational structure that is embedded in the Japanese culture transferrable to other nations with different organizational structures; i.e., can it produce in the host country's manufacturing plants quality products that can compete in the global market?

As mentioned above, based on Recht's (1998) theoretical contributions and experience, he has come to the conclusion that "*kaizen*-oriented suggestion systems are transferable to non-Japanese cultural environments." But he asserts that to increase the chances of a successful *kaizen* transfer could be based on: a) clear employee orientation (supported by a contractually or verbally assured non-lay-off policy); b) employees commitment to the viability of their company; c) a transparent and free flow of information with the organization; d) well informed and fully empowered employees; e) practical workforce; and finally, process and results-oriented employees (Recht, 1998). The first JICA project was extended to Singapore, from 1983 to 1990. From productivity management and it was very successful. Building on the success of this cooperative effort, the Singapore Productivity and Standard Board has subsequently grown to become a major organization with external training programs in other countries and regions, including the Southern African Development Community (SADC) under partnership arrangements with JICA (Hhno, Hhno, and Uesu, 2009, p.7).

Similarly, when we look at *kaizen* companies operating in transitional countries such as those in Eastern Europe, the *kaizen* organizational structure seems to be easily transferable because the employees of these organizations have a 'hungry mentality" at work and "...are eager to learn advanced technologies and management systems imported from abroad in order to survive in the international competition. At the individual level, due to the lower standards of living, people are striving to earn better lives. Thus, people are motivated to work following the rules and standard operating procedures and also they tend to go above and beyond their job responsibility" (Yokozawa, Steenhuis and Bruijin, 2010). Also, it is persuasively argued by Yokozawa, Steenhuis and Bruijin that "...openness, creativeness, and the challenging mentality can positively influence the transfer of *kaizen* because people can easily accept the foreign idea and suggest for improvement using their creativity and challenging mentality" (2010). As a result, the *kaizen* mode of production has improved company productivity through "...Quality Improvement, Cost Reduction, shortened delivery, reduced lead time, inventory control improvement, safety improvement" (Dobi, 2006).

After studying Japanese management techniques and their transferability in India, Brazil, the Dominican Republic, Mexico and Zimbabwe, Kaplinsky and Posthuma (1988) argue that Japanese management techniques were adopted in these countries because of the fact that they are late starters and were seeking to be innovative. Hosono also endorses the view that *kaizen* as well as Japanese types of Total Quality Circles (TQC) and Total Quality Management (TQM) can be introduced to countries where the culture is very different from that of Japan. To illustrate his argument he gives three Japan International Cooperation Agency (JICA) projects, one in Brazil and two in Central America, where *kaizen* were introduced. "In the first case, JICA's Brazilian counterpart established its own concept of quality and productivity, adjusted to promote a new movement for productivity improvement in Brazil and meet the current requirements of the country" (October 2009). Though the management system in Central America is different from that of Japan, *kaizen* had various positive impacts on productivity because it brought about: 1) positive changes in attitude among workers; 2) introduced 5S and participation of management and not just workers; 3) simplification and standardization of the production processes; 4) improvements in team work; and 5) better awareness of international competition (Hosono, October 2009).

For example, a case study of Honda's Siel India affirms that the advantages of adapting the Japanese management system in India included: 1) the Japanese management system techniques are not capital intensive and therefore their implementation was not difficult; 2) Japanese management techniques are to a large extent based upon training and not formal education; and 3) the Japanese management system is being recommended for high quality and high productivity that could be easily transferred to benefit India by making its products competitive within domestic and international markets (Choudhury, November 2005).

After a through analysis of the compatibility of the Japanese management system in Nigeria, Ghana, Zimbabwe, and Kenya, Tasie (2009) comes to the conclusion that "If African countries are to improve their management styles efficiently and effectively, they must apply, but with caution, the Japanese styles of management." Otherwise, Tasie warns that "... these tools in the absence of the requisite group cohesion, organizational loyalty and flexibility in attitude, may at best serve only a window dressing purpose." (2009). In addition, Anh et al (2011), illustrates that *kaizen* practices can be transferable to non-Japanese cultural environments such as South Korea, Italy, United States, Austria, Germany, Finland, and Sweden. However, he warns his readers that the performance of *kaizen* implementation is contextually dependent.

On the other hand some scholars still assert that *kaizen* practices are embedded in the Japanese culture and are difficult to transfer abroad. Actually, they argue that *kaizen* has been dysfunctional in a number of foreign companies because it is insensitive to domestic cultures, urges foreign-owned companies to emulate the Japanese way of management, and is based on the assumption that what works in Japan has to be uniformly implemented in other countries (Shaari, 2010). Drawing on insights from the cybernetics of Beer (1966), it is possible to argue that *kaizen* categorizes the management of complexity in the management of target-oriented operations.

Many Japanese management systems are not easily adopted by an overseas counterpart due to environmental factors such as differences in national culture and work ethics. Transferred management systems are more likely to be hybridized with locally practiced systems (Yokozama, K. 2010). As mentioned above, to use Lillrank's (1995) conclusion, the direct transfers of Japanese management practices often fail not because of geographical distance but rather due to the mental distance, i.e., culture, history, and strategic paradigms. Moreover, Hayashi (1994) argues that a *kaizen* management system works effectively in

Japan because the Japanese organizations tend to have organic structures with decentralized decision-making, a low degree of specialization and formalization, and above all the culture of horizontal communication. Lincoln and McBride argue that the Japanese management system which is based on teamwork, participatory decision-making and quality circles is a result of the collective culture that views self-development to be occurring through harmony and reciprocity in interpersonal relations. Thus, Japanese companies by and large use consensus decision-making with everyone in the company being consulted on each decision (cited by Chow, C. et al., 1991).

More specifically, the transfer of *kaizen* to other countries does not appear to be successful because of a lack of synergy between the requirements of *kaizen* and the work ethics of local industrial workers. Out of respect, or fear, local workers may not feel comfortable making suggestions to their managers (See for example, Fukuda, 1988). For instance, Yokozawa, Steenhuis and Bruijin succulently argue that though Japanese companies are attempting to transfer *kaizen*, they are finding it difficult to create a pleasant and reassuring organizational climate because they fail to pay enough attention to the host country's national culture (2010). A case in point, Yokozawa, Steenhuis and Bruijin (2010) established that the *kaizen* management system in Indonesia has not been operating as expected because the Indonesian workers feel that they are less responsible for their jobs. In a similar vein, some Japanese companies have found it very difficult to transfer *kaizen* to Germany because German enterprises have rigid job descriptions and the bureaucratic organizational structure of their firms prevents workers from sharing responsibility, having open communication, or developing teamwork, aspects that are paramount to fulfilling the functions of *kaizen* (Yokozawa, Steenhuis and Bruijin, 2010). Along with a nation's cultural characteristics, Recht, R and Wilderom , C (1998) and Anh et al (2011) assert that the adoption of *kaizen* is to a large extent dependent on some specific organizational features such as centralization of authority and cooperation that cuts across functional lines.

Furthermore, Ishiwata, A. (2009) argues that implementation of *kaizen* in Africa and in particular in Ethiopia may be facing challenges because in African countries with a "socialistic nature like Ethiopia, power is mainly concentrated in the hands of a top manager, whereas the basic concepts of *kaizen* are to empower the workers." Because the *kaizen* method focuses on visualization of production and quality performance, workers without sufficient educational backgrounds may not be able to understand the tables and figures. Thus, separate, in-depth training for workers needs to be provided in order for them to develop a full understanding of the tools used in the *kaizen* work environment. Furthermore, Ishiwata argues that the sources of the loss in productivity in Africa are mainly found outside the company. There are delays in the delivery of materials and sudden interruptions of orders from retailers and traders. Given this, Ishiwata suggests that there needs to be improvement in business networking, both backward and forward, if business productivity is to improve for most African manufacturers.

Conceptual Framework

From the foregoing discussion, the conceptual framework that could be developed to study the success of *kaizen* overseas transferability and implementation of the *kaizen* practices in Ethiopia depend on the degree of compatibility between the Japanese company's *kaizen* culture and the host country's national culture. As articulated by Anh, et al., (2011) though not a universal model for successful *kaizen* transferability to other countries, *kaizen* practices should be adapted to the local culture in order to have the highest probability of success. Given that *kaizen* is a vital approach to problem solving, its application requires restructuring the organizational culture and then use formal root cause analysis to identify and correct the problem at the source. Thus, *kaizen* practices could be implemented by the manufacturing companies of host countries provided that the host companies have a low level of centralization of authority, and practice cross-functional team cooperation of eight to 12 people with a skilled facilitator to identify, measure, and correct the problem associated with the process (See for example, Anh, et al, 2011). In short, manufacturing companies in the *kaizen* host countries may be in a position to generate significant value-added products that could effectively compete in the global market provided there is a synergy between the work ethics of the Japanese *kaizen* system and a host company's organizational culture. In addition, the *kaizen* host companies need to be fully committed to boosting the morale of their workers to develop members' capabilities, to achieve self-actualization, and to work cooperatively. These commitments are vital to the process for improving the quality of the company's output. As discussed by Zimmerman (1991) and Imai (1997), as a process *kaizen* utilizes various tools and methods to make the problem visible, and uses formal root tool cause analysis and other means to identify and correct the problem.

Given this conceptual framework, the introduction of *kaizen* as a management tool and success in the transfer of technology to improve and enhance productivity and managerial capability in Ethiopia needs to be seen in the establishment of several building blocks in addition to conceptual issues related to:

1. the fit between *kaizen* culture and the organizational culture of Ethiopia's manufacturing practices;

2. changes in the mindset of Ethiopian manufacturing workers so they will adhere to the *kaizen* work ethics;
3. workers' training and discipline so that workers follow standard operating procedures;
4. the existence of a hungry mentality so Ethiopian factory workers will do work which is above and beyond their responsibility; and
5. the empowerment and involvement of workers in decision-making to cooperatively identify problems, generate solutions, implement them and then follow up to evaluate quality and productivity.

Conclusion

On May 2008, at the Fourth Tokyo International Conference for African Development (TICAD IV) also known as the Yokohama Action Plan, Japan promised to cooperate in the reinvigoration of Africa's economic growth. Given that Ethiopia's manufacturing sector was only about 5% of the country's GDP, it showed no hesitation and jumped to take advantage of the Japanese offer help Ethiopia across its industries. Japan's offer proposed techniques that could accelerate and improve the quality and productivity of Ethiopia's manufacturing enterprises. After Japan showed its willingness to help with Ethiopia's industrial development, it gave a seminar in collaboration with the Ethiopian Ministry of Trade for about 300 attendees in Addis Ababa on November 4, 2009. As a result, the Governments of Ethiopia and Japan agreed to conduct a Development Study on quality and productivity improvement (KAIZEN) in Ethiopia. Accordingly, the Japan International Cooperation Agency (JICA) and Ministry of Trade and Industry (MoTT) in Ethiopia were made responsible for setting up *KAIZEN* Institute in Ethiopia, the implementation of *Kaizen* pilot Project, and then the selection and training of pilot project companies.

The *Kaizen* project in Ethiopia consisted of three phases. The first phase which started in August, 2009, reviewed the quality and productivity of 63 companies. After preliminary diagnosis of these factories, 30 companies were selected based the following criteria: 1) proximity to Addis Ababa, within 100km distance, 2) contributions to exports and /or imports, 3) scale of capital, and 4) number of employees. Then, the employees of the pilot companies were sent to Japan to undertake work-site observation and learn from the experience of the Japanese kaizen practitioner. In October 2009-2010, by the end of the first phase of the project, from the thirty pilot companies, only 6, 4, and 8 companies were finally chosen by Ethiopia's Kaizen Institute for having high possibility, good possibility, and some possibility respectively to become kaizen model companies (Ethiopian Ministry of Trade, 2011). Therefore, in order to understand the mechanisms needed for the transference of the Japanese *kaizen* management system from Japan to Ethiopia, it is worthwhile to review the literature and identify the important variable needed for the transferability of the Japanese *kaizen* management techniques to other countries.

Over the years *kaizen* has become a global activity. Japan, either through its multinational enterprises or through the support of the Japanese International Cooperation agency (JICA), has attempted to transfer its factory-level model for improving quality and productivity, known as *kaizen,* to a number of countries. Particularly, since *kaizen* can realize productivity improvement with little additional investment, it has been adopted by a number of developing countries with different cultures and business environments. Over the years, *kaizen* becomes internalized and institutionalized in some host countries because it is generally regarded as a philosophy of life. For example, *kaizen* has been adopted by highly disciplined workers and by workers with an unwavering hungry mentality conducive to innovation that makes them eager to learn advanced technologies and management systems in order to survive in international competition.

In some countries, however, the implementation of *kaizen* has been challenging because of a lack of synergy between the requirements of *kaizen* and the work ethics of local industrial workers. *Kaizen* practices are embedded in the Japanese culture and are very difficult to transfer abroad. The dysfunction of the *kaizen* management techniques occurs when Japan is insensitive to domestic cultures of foreign manufacturing companies. Japan has assumed that what works in Japan has to be uniformly implemented in other countries, and Japan insists that foreign-owned companies must emulate its management system (Shaari). 2010).

Given that *kaizen* is a vital approach to problem solving, the transferability and practical implementation by foreign companies involves bottom-up decision-making and an employee-driven management style that adheres to cross-cultural cooperation. In short, manufacturing companies in the host countries could generate value-added products and effectively compete at the global market provided they maintain their synergy with the work ethics of *kaizen.* Their organizational cultures must be fully committed to boosting the morale of their workers and developing their ability to achieve self-actualization. As a result of such coordinated efforts by all employees, they will all be rewarded by the improvement of the quality of their products.

Chapter 9

CHINA'S SOUTH-SOUTH COOPERATIVE INVESTMENTS AND CO-DEVELOPMENT MODALITIES IN AFRICA

Africa has become more important, due to its growing role in supplying oil, gas, and non-fuel minerals to the world. In response, the United States has launched the Millennium Challenge Account (MCA) and the President's Emergency Plan for AIDS Relief (PEPFAR). In addition, the United States has designed a new military command Africom, to counter attacks from the supposed terrorist cells in the African continent (Lake and Whitman, 2006).

In recent years, a number of African countries have shifted their focus to cooperative investments with private corporations or state-owned enterprises as sources of future dynamism. These investments are originating primarily in the industrializing or newly industrialized countries of Asia, rather than Western European and US multinational companies. Because of an exponential and sustained growth in its economy, the Peoples' Republic of China (hereafter referred to as China), has positioned itself at the forefront of being a very vital and influential player in Africa's cooperative pro-business investments. As discussed by Alden and Davis:

> *The marked presence of Chinese multinational corporations on the global stage is changing the landscape of international business and politics. Western firms, once with virtually undisputed command over the financial resources and requisite political ties to dominate global business, are now being challenged by a host of emerging country corporations with China being at the forefront (2006).*

China is attempting to accomplish this objective by capturing key resources and market share across Africa using the South-South Cooperation Investment business strategies (i.e., joint activities between the newly industrialized southern countries and the lesser-developed nations of the Southern Hemisphere). African governments have appreciated and responded enthusiastically to this new source of bottom-up, multiple, bilateral investment, trade, and aid because China has a professed willingness to ignore political conditions placed on Western assistance (Alden, 2005).

Contrary to Western debt and assistance marked by various forms of economic and political overtones, China is in the process of bestowing a mix of loans with generous terms, debt forgiveness, infrastructure development, and other assistance to African nations so that they could be relieved from Western cultural, political, and economic hegemony (Habib, 2008). For example, Large argues "...a new wind from the East is blowing across Africa, and is attracting unprecedented attention. This is driven in part by the wider resurgence of China in world affairs, but much is also the result of the recent visibility and interest in the growing presence, roles, and impacts of Chinese actors throughout the continent" (2008).

The Western investments have overtones of various forms of conditionality, such as the formation of free trade, building private companies, or loosening of government regulations. On the other hand, the Chinese investments in Africa's infrastructure rejuvenation and the various types of China's multifaceted influence as market, donor, financier, contractor and builder of investment projects are claimed to be based on flexible soft loans and are tailored to lift the overall economic performance of the borrowing and assistance-getting African countries. At the opening of the summit held in Beijing in October 2000, for example, the Forum on China-Africa Cooperation (FOCAC), President Hu Jintao of China promised to the 48 heads of African states that China would offer $3 billion in preferential loans and $2 billion in export credits over the next three years.

In addition, at the landmark FOCAC Beijing meeting in November of 2006, China adopted a declaration proclaiming "a new type of strategic partnership" and promised to double its foreign aid to African counties (BBC, 2006; Corkin & Burke, 2008; Jian-Ye, 2007). In May of 2007, China captured international attention when it hosted the annual African Development Bank (AfDB) conference in Shanghai. At the annual meeting, "China agreed to make an additional $20 billion pledge for infrastructure development in Africa over the next three years" (Gill, et al., 2007).

China's deepening involvement across Africa can be viewed from two perspectives. The protagonists of political warfare theory argue that China's policy in Africa is a nonviolent instrument of grand strategy. It involves coordinated activities that could precipitate in tangible effects on intended targets such as economic aid and development assistance, as well as training, equipping, and arming military and security forces to achieve political and economic clout. Given this thesis, the proponents of the political warfare theory argue that China's investment in Africa is not only meant to fulfill China's immediate convenience, it is meant as a grand strategy designed to give it clout and leverage to access and develop further business opportunities in Africa (Chau, 2007). Based on this argument, the proponents of political warfare theory predict that China's investment in Africa is nothing creative but rather is an offer of old wine in a new green bottle, tailored to establish China's "new imperial power" in Africa. Chinese assistance to Africa is mainly in the form of colonialist projects that will perpetuate Africa's underdevelopment through exploitation, extraction, and destruction of Africa's resources and industrial capacity (Chau, 2007).

The South-South development cooperation school of thought, on the other hand, views China's increased aid, trade, and investment in Africa as a means to foster Africa's self-sufficiency and sustainable development in the 21st century (Naidu, 2008). The protagonists of the South-South Cooperative (SSC) model of development forcefully argue that China should be left alone to forge its unique partnership with Africa and the West must simply learn to compete. According to Okonjo-Iweala, the former Nigerian Finance Minister, China, "... the new economic giant...knows what it means to be poor and has evolved a successful wealth creation formula that it is willing to share with African countries" (October 24, 2006). China's growing investment commitment in Africa is more likely to boost the huge infrastructure deficit of the continent (Ezekwesili, July 11, 2008). In short, the proponents of the SSC model argue that China is acting as a model for Africa's approaches to international and domestic problems.

The central motive of the pursuing study is to investigate if the opportunities and challenges of Chinese investments in Africa are based on a win-win strategy. Thus, the first part of the chapter reviews existing studies in order to explore the conceptual framework needed to map out the determinants of South-South Cooperation's (SSC) ventures and examines the extent to which China conducts to compliment or undermine the SSC model. The second portion reviews and contextualizes China's investment in Africa. The third section scrutinizes the appropriateness of Chinese capital and technological flows to Africa. Finally, after summarizing the main findings of the study, the chapter concludes by drawing some relevant policy implications and suggests relevant future research directions.

China's South-South Cooperative Investments

Many developing countries emerged from colonial rule in the 1950s. Between 18 and 25 April, 1955, the Prime Ministers of Burma (Myanmar), Ceylon (Sri Lanka), Indonesia, India, and Pakistan organized the South-South meeting in Bandung, Indonesia to discuss the themes and problems of economic cooperation, human rights, self-determination, dependent people, and the promotion of peace (Lumumba-Kasongo, 2007). The African region was represented by six delegates from the then independent governments of Egypt, Ethiopia, Liberia, Libya, and Sudan, and the semi-independent country of the Gold Coast (Ghana).

In the South-South Bandung Conference of Afro-Asian Developing Countries in 1955, China identified itself with African and Asian countries and set out to advance a new international system of economic relations in a more equitable direction. More specifically, China presented its "Five Principles of Mutual Coexistence." Included in the five principles were 1) respect for territorial integration; 2) rejection of aggression; 3) non-interference in the internal affairs of other countries; 4) equality and mutual benefit; and 5) peaceful coexistence (See Asche, 2008 and Harris and Worden, 1986).

Based on the principles of self-determination prompted by the United Nations and the collective action by the Bandung Conference, the South contributed to the formation of the Non-Aligned Movement within the United Nations in 1961 (Ohiorhenuan and Rath, 2000). Starting in 1964, this paved way for the rise of the Non-Aligned Movement of the Third World nations—also known as the Group of 77 (G-77)—an international organization of over 100 independent nations which were either formally colonized by the Western powers or those with economic and political characteristics of the Global South (Lumumba-Kasongo, 2007).

Following the substantial increase in the price of oil by the Oil Producing and Exporting Counties (OPEC) in 1973, China, along with most of the developing countries, strongly advocated for the formation of fair trade between the developed and the developing. In 1974, the United Nations Conference on Trade and Development (UNCTAD) established the New International Economic Order (NIEO) to assist the South in the area of trade policy and promotion. Like other Third World countries, China clearly saw that the existing international economic order was fundamentally flawed. Thus it supported the United Nations resolution which called for: 1) an integrated approach to price support for commodity exports, 2) the attainment of official development assistance to reach the target of 0.7 percent of the GDP of the developing countries, 3) the lowering of tariffs on the export of manufactured goods from developing countries, 4) full permanent sovereignty over the natural resources and economic activities of western-oriented multinational firms, and 5) the establishment of a mechanism for the transfer of technology to developing countries separate from foreign direct capital investments (Looney, 1999).

Given the perspective of the developing countries—that the multilateral organizations, led by the developed nations, particularly the United States, have financially controlled and have devised rules at the inception of the developing nations to make them dependent on Western hegemony (Worden, 1986)—China stood by and supported the core idea of the G-77. Also, China strongly argued that SSC was the way out of the zero-sum game purposely created by advanced West to impede the ambitions of the developing countries.

Initially, SSC highlighted the anti-colonial movement and emphasized the solidarity of Third World Countries. By de-linking themselves from the advanced countries of the North, the Southern nations aspired to pursue their collective development through cooperative exchange of knowledge, skills, resources, and technical know-how—only among themselves.

In short, by initiating the SSC model, developing countries became fully convinced that they could address and solve their economic problems by sharing and learning from the experiences of other developing countries. Thus, the SSC platform was by and large tailored to the exchange and creation of cooperation and development relevant to the developing countries.

> *The pivotal role that SSC could play in the arena of development comes from the fact that the developing countries account for a major proportion of the people in the world and some of them are large economies, which have a major share of the world GNP. As the South unites into a single mass, they can voice their concerns as a large economic, moral, political and social force (Doha, 2005).*

Many developing countries were battered by debt and negative economic growth rates in the 1980s. As a result of external shock, in the 1990s the SSC movement undertook a pragmatic approach to liberalize their macroeconomic policies (i.e., follow the rigid implementation of the structural adjustment programs) and decided to integrate themselves into the global market. In short, the Southern countries have evolved—not divided—to participate more effectively in the newly emerging economic order, to respond to the new global challenges, and to achieve the targets set forth by the founders of G-77. To highlight: "The differentiation and fragmentation of economic interests among developing countries will likely make it more difficult for the South to maintain common positions across the board in future North-South dialogue" (Ohiorhenuan and Rath, 2000).

At the First South Summit in Havana in 2000, the Southern countries came out with a strategy to learn from each other in different arenas such as foreign investment and trade promotion policies. The joint development and dissemination of solutions was called the Havana Plan of Action. In 2003, the United Nations General Assembly adopted Resolution 58/220, declaring December 19th the annual United Nations Day for South-South Cooperation. In June 2005, at the Second South Summit in Doha (Qatar), a Plan of Action was adopted by the United Nations. Finally, an internationally agreed set of goals—known as the Millennium Development Goals (MDGs)—was officially declared in 2005 (UNESCO, June 2006).

More recently, as a natural growth of the South-South Cooperation, Africa is giving considerable attention to drawing knowledge, experience, and policies from China to build its capacity for stimulating environmentally sustainable development. As narrated by Rocha (2008), the Sino-African partnership is envisioned "...to stimulate backward and forward linkages with the local economy; generate additional employment opportunities; bolster revenues for the state; enhance economic growth; and boost the continent's development prospects. In foreign direct investment flows alone, the South-South flows have grown far faster than North-South flows...One recent estimate suggests that South-South flows rose from $4.6 billion in 1994 to an average of $54.4 billion between 1997 and 2000, equivalent to 36 percent of total FDI inflows to developing economies in the latter period (Akkurt and Ratha, 2004). Chinese investment increased from $20 million from 1990 to 1997 to $120 million from 1998 to 2002. "In value terms, extractive and resource-related projects comprise a much higher share at 28 percent, but nonetheless 64 percent of the value of Chinese investments in Africa is in the manufacturing sector" (Akkurt and Ratha, 2004). The question that needs to be addressed is, have the Chinese Cooperation ventures contributed to driving new forces, generating positive spin-off, and serving as effective leapfrogging vehicles for Africa's development in the 21st century?

China's Cooperative Investment in Africa

Despite the arrogance of Western colonialists, who state that Europe should not hand over its African commitments to the recently-emerging China, it needs to be underlined at the outset that the establishment of modern Sino-African relations goes back "six hundred years ago. Zheng He, the chief navigator of China's Ming Dynasty and commander of the largest fleet in the world, discovered almost a century before the much heralded visits to Africa by Vasco Da Gama (Sebastian, 2008). However, the resurgence in Chinese-African relations started with Chairman Mao's observation that "We don't have a clear understanding of African history, geography, and the present situation" (Anshan, 2005). In 1963-64 Prime Minister of the Peoples' Republic of China Zhou Enlai made a ten-country visit to Africa. The general aim of Premier Zhou

Enlai's visit to Africa were to: 1) underscore the implementation of the One-China policy and foreclose Taiwan's diplomatic relations with Africa, 2) respect the principles of sovereignty and non-intervention, 3) promote development on the basis of equality and mutual benefit, 4) seek prestige by presenting itself as mentor or a de facto leader or a moral leader of the developing world in the United Nations, 5) de-link the progressive African nations from the hegemonic relations they had with the then-revisionist Soviet Union, and 6) sow anti-Western imperialist sentiments in Africa (Muekalia, 2004; Harris, 1985).

Prior to the 1970s, Sino-African relations were by and large ideologically driven. It provided financial support, equipment and training to a variety of liberation movements, particularly in Algeria, Angola, Congo, Mozambique, Namibia, South Africa, Rhodesia, etc. China's "...involvement in the Non-Aligned Movement and other Third World conference-type activities...were designed to demonstrate its own anti-imperialist approach to aid and to identify it with those nations that continued to suffer the effects of colonialism (Hamrin, C.L., 1986). As stated by Gu and Humphrey:

> *By blaming Africa's underdevelopment on colonialism, Beijing believes it has established the moral ground. From training "fighter for freedom" in the revolutionary 1960s and early 1970s to providing scholarships to children of African elites, China has been exporting its values for years. By successfully linking neo-colonialism with the neo-liberalism of Western countries, China has been able to win the hearts and minds of African elites (2006).*

To exemplify its commitment to a non-imperialist stand, starting in 1967, China began building the TanZam Railway between Tanzania and Zambia. Following the death of Mao Zedong, however, the Chinese government gave less attention to Africa. Instead, China turned inward throughout the 1980 and 1990 to experiment with its new economic reform programs. "When Chinese economic reform began in 1978, the political leadership initially concentrated on a swift economic catching-up process, and attracted only relatively little importance to Africa in comparison with Western industrialized countries and Japan. For instance, between 1980 and 1987 the contribution pledged each year amounted to about $200-300 million, falling to a low point in 1988 of only $60.4 million. This comparatively low status was reflected in the rather sporadic visits by high-ranking politicians to Africa, a stagnating volumes of trade, and stagnating or even declining development assistance inputs" (Asche, 2008).

Because of the global domination by the World Bank and International Monetary Fund's structural adjustment programs (which advocated extensive economic liberation and privatization), the Sino-African relations were partially eclipsed during the Cold War. Following the Tiananmen incident of 1989 (under the economic transformation initiated by President Deng Xiaoping), China renewed its SSC program and attempted to reconnect with Africa mostly to satisfy its economic need for resources—oil, minerals, timber, etc.—and to market its manufactured goods in the Africa.

China resumed its economic relations with Africa through an institutional framework known as the Forum on China-Africa Cooperation (FOCAC). As stated by Holslag:

> *The China-Africa Cooperation Forum (FOCAC) is another means for bolstering commercial and political relations. Established in 2000, the FOCAC forms an interface for officials and business leaders through ministerial conferences, senior officials' meetings, and the China-Africa Joint Business Council. Its current goals are stressed in the Addis Ababa Action and entails issues related to peace and security, multilateral cooperation, economic development, and social development. A first priority in this regard is the development of Africa's agriculture in order to strengthen the food security of Africa and to increase its exports to China and other markets. China will continue to support and encourage strong and viable Chinese enterprises, through financial and policy incentives schemes (2006).*

In contrast to the West's view of Africa that chaos, conflict, corruption, and poor governance characterize its underdevelopment, China propagates that the African continent is rich in culture, religion, social dynamism, and energy. Realizing that the African continent has a great opportunity for business, the Chinese government encourages the following industries and projects to be invested in Africa: a) processing industrial products in the fields of electronics, machinery building, textiles, and garments, b) investing in agricultural products in order to add value to Africa's exports and improve Africa's terms of trade, c) extracting natural resources, such as petroleum and high-value minerals, and d) investing in infrastructure, power supply, and real estate development (United Nations, UNDP, 2007).

Realizing that Africa is marginalized in the worldwide distribution of foreign direct investment (FDI), China pledged government-backed foreign direct investment to African countries. In 2007, over 700 registered Chinese state-owned and private companies (provided with government financial backing) have entered into a number of business ventures in collaboration with African national governments, state-owned corporations, and private firms. For instance, the Chinese government has designated about 180 companies to benefit from preferential finance, tax concessions, and political backing to "go global" and become true multinationals (Alden and Davies, 2006).

Despite the government's support in leveraging Chinese businesses to go global, at this stage, Chinese investment in Africa is very low in comparison with other areas. For example, "Africa is attracting less investment, ranking in a mere US$317 million corresponding to 5.8% of total Chinese FDI outflows in 2005, in comparison to Latin America, which attracted US $1.7 billion accounting for 32%. Asia pulled off US$3 billion, representing 54.6% of total Chinese FDI outflows" (Rocha, 2008). Though the motives of foreign direct investments might be 1) securing new markets, 2) raising efficiency, 3) securing raw materials, 4) obtaining cheap labor, and 5) securing defensive or offensive strategic advantages, the Chinese investments in Africa seemed be exclusively focused on securing raw materials and developing the markets for Chinese goods and services.

The basic forms of the Chinese Development Cooperation, which is almost exclusively project-based, includes 1) giving grant aid (non-repayable loans to social projects such as schools, hospitals, housing, etc), 2) interest-free loans to finance infrastructure projects, and 3) preferential credits or concessionary credits (reserve-backed lending) with interests rates below the market level. Through the Export and Import (EXIM) Bank of China (the official credit agency of China established in 1994 to extend export seller's and buyer's credits, credits for investment, and construction projects, and guarantees to promote Chinese investment in Africa), it lends to China's state-owned enterprises (SOEs) to promote their "Going Global" strategy. Though there is no distinction between development cooperation and commercial cooperation, the EXIM bank mainly assists the financing of infrastructures regarded very vital for extracting and transporting energy and mineral resources.

It needs to be highlighted that the Chinese government chooses Chinese construction companies to undertake large-scale projects and infrastructure development to encourage the expansion of markets and the entry of smaller firms in Africa. For instance, as of September 2006, China's committed 79 percent of its contracted investment in infrastructure development (Ellis, 2007). Between 2000 and 2005, China-Africa trade was $39 billion and is projected to reach $100 billion by 2010 (Alden, 2005). Since 2000, Africa's exports to China have grown at a rate of 56 percent. Oil and mineral exports account for 85 percent of African exports to China. "The share of Africa's exports to China rose from 1.3% in 1995 to 9.3% in 2004, accompanied by a significant decline in African exports to OECD countries in the same period" (Broker, 2007).

In its socially responsible development programs, China is donating development assistance and soft loans to various African states to finance their infrastructure projects, including roads, railways, access to fishing waters, hydropower stations, agricultural land, schools, and medical personnel. In 2006 alone, "There were more than 1000 Chinese doctors and nurses working in 36

African countries. At the Beijing Summit, Hu Jintao also announced support for 30 new hospitals in Africa, 30 malaria prevention and treatment centres and an additional US $38 million for the provision of artemisinin (a derivative of the Artemissia shrub) over the next years. ...By 2009, government scholarships for African students to study in China will be doubled from their present 2000; and 15,000 African professionals will be trained in technical, scientific and administrative fields in 2007-09" (le Pere, 2008). In addition, "with 26 African countries now being accorded 'Approved Destination Status' by China, it is projected that there will be 1 million Chinese tourists traveling to Africa by 2020, compared to the 110,000 in 2005" (le Pere, 2008).

In short, in contrast to Western hegemonies, China's bilateral state-centric engagement in Africa is based on the principles of sovereignty and non-interference in internal affairs. China's investment in Africa is driven to:

1. acquire the natural resources, energy supplies, and export markets to sustain its growing economy. Also, as stated by Alves, "Africa's long-standing preferential access to western markets offers 'back door' entry for some Chinese producers" (2008);
2. ascertain its belief that its development model is instructive for Africa; and
3. strengthen diplomatic alliances essential to support its global ambitions.

In other words, China's strategic incursions into Africa include 1) the use of public diplomacy, including high-powered official visits and a triennial Forum on China-Africa Co-operation (FOCAC); 2) China's pledge of large amounts of aid and investments in Africa's infrastructure and other sectors with no political strings attached, except withdrawal of diplomatic relations with Taiwan, and 3) the use of aid donations to encourage Chinese companies to acquire overseas assets, such as oil and industrial raw materials so that Africa could become a strategic training ground for Chinese companies (JETRO, 2007).

In addition to being diplomatic, the Chinese investment, trade, and infrastructural assistance help the African continent diversify its exports. But, it needs to be underlined that through government-endorsed contracts, the Chinese EXIM Bank requires that in all overseas financing, the Chinese contract must ensure that they include export spin-offs in the long run from China. For instance, in the short run, while local and other foreign construction companies operate on profit margins of 15-25%, Chinese companies usually operate on margins of under 10%, making them extremely competitive. Large owned enterprises (SOEs) generally slice their profit margin to undercut other competitors.

> *[D]espite the enormous challenges China faces concerning its own development, Beijing's focus on infrastructural development in Africa, with the construction of roads, bridges, hydroelectric and irrigation schemes, schools, hospitals, health centres and an array of government buildings, has driven private sector competition and made a clear and definite contribution to improving the lives of people across Africa (Corkin & Burke, 2008).*

Africa needs to ascertain that the Chinese investments are transformative and are likely to extricate the African continent from the doldrums of underdevelopment. However, instead of mirroring Africa as a mere beneficiary of Chinese benevolence or as a renter continent—that is, the African state governments are recipients of the external rent and do not require a strong domestic sector—the Chinese cooperative assistance offers need to inspire alternative routes to an environmentally-sensitive development based on a win-win strategic partnership.

For example, some other African countries state that the presence of the Chinese in their countries is not only instructive but also contributes to positive results. For example, Mr. G. D. Boateng, Executive Secretary at Ghana's Secretariat of the Chinese funded Bui Dam Project argues that "With Chinese assistance, old development plans that were jettisoned at the insistence of development partners are now being revived and are being executed at much lower costs. Before the Chinese came, the BUI Dam project had been on the shelf since the 1960s. We had expressions of interest from a number of Western companies in the 1960s and in 2001, but they all fell through because those companies didn't see the project as a worthwhile project. Now with Chinese assistance the project has gone off the shelf to the ground and this time it is an integrated project that includes the building of a new city around Bui" (JETRO, 2007). Also, in Lesotho, very important growth in the textile and clothing industry has been recorded as a result of investment from Asian firms. What is achieved in Lesotho "...is the process of growth leading infrastructure as Chinese and Taiwanese investors demand improved infrastructure in transport, energy and water, all necessary for profitable operations in the sector" (Gelb, 2005).

On the whole, unlike the Western competitors, China makes no value demands that its aid be intertwined with investments and provides generous support for the expansion of Chinese companies into the African markets in order to diversify its source of supply for its industrial inputs. Based on this, a number of African governments seem to be satisfied with the Chinese contributions to the expansion of their infrastructure, tapping unexploited resources, integrating Africa's economies into global value chains, and visualizing China as a model for Africa's development. Despite the fact that domestic companies feel that they are being crowded out and there are shortfalls in the transfer of know-how and employment to local workers (Asche, 2008), a number of policy makers in Africa go one step further to justify that China has brought economic sanity to impoverished and conflict-ridden neighborhoods in Africa. To make China be influential and a credible source for Africa, a number of African countries have endorsed themselves to be a strategic training ground for Chinese state-owned enterprises, as well as private enterprises, in order to quench their thirst for oil and industrial raw materials (JETRO, 2007). Being the trailblazer from Western dictates, the Chinese Export-Import Bank has played a major role in low-cost financing development, cooperative projects, and coordinating the effort of Chinese state-owned corporations and private enterprises. Nevertheless, it is worth noting that the growth of South-South development cooperation in Africa is not likely to fundamentally change the terms of the relationship between Africa and the Western industrialized countries (North), but it can definitely be ascertained that the Africa continent has leveraging power to bargain with prospective Western investors (Gelb, December 2005).

The Sino-investment projects are in the process of generating development cooperation in resources (i.e., oil, mining, timber, agricultural commodities), trade and investment, and contracts for construction and engineering projects (roads, bridges, schools, shopping centers, housing and office buildings, water conservancy, and power plants) for Africa's present and future generations. Though very vital, African states thus far "have not developed strategies of their own that underpin their cooperation with China" (Asche, 2008). Therefore, if Africa is to extricate maximum benefits from its enhanced cooperation with China it needs to design its own game plan and allocate a specific role for China based on a common agenda at the continental level.

For example, in 2006, Angola signed with China for the construction of an oil refinery to enable Angola to meet increasing domestic demand and increase supply to regional markets with the Southern African Development Community. However, the negotiations broke down because instead of abiding by the intra-Africa trade, China insisted that the bulk of the refined oil be exported to China.

Since China has not come out with environmentally sensitive programs, 30% of the forest logging concessions given to China in Central Africa is expected to precipitate an increase of carbon emissions. If the various mining concessions held by China in Africa do not comply with environmental laws, it is possible that they might be a health hazard and could impair human security. For instance in Gabon, the Chinese oil company was accused of "a whole range of unacceptable practices including pollution, exploding dynamite, and carving roads through parks. In addition, environmental groups, human rights groups, and businesses are irked by some unsavory aspects of [the] Chinese profile, such as the deployment of Chinese labor, which limits local employment opportunities, destroys local manufacturing capabilities, [and] sustains poor labor and environmental standards" (JETRO, 2007). As articulated by Rocha:

> *Since Cameroon, Congo, [the] Democratic Republic of Congo, Equatorial Guinea,Gabon, and Liberia are all major suppliers of timber to China, the conduct of industry in theCongo Rainforest has serious ecological and other implications for the entire continent. There are already indications that the effects of climate change will be most severe in Africa. Thus, continued mismanagement, in all its dimensions, of Africa's natural resources, renewable and non-renewable, will have catastrophic consequences for the continent (2008).*

Due to limited cross-cultural communication, there seems to be lack of collaboration between the Chinese and African employees. Examining the composition of personnel in most of the over 800 state-owned Chinese firms, Africa seems to be dependent on Chinese experts. The African workers are busy accomplishing semi-skilled and manual types of work in textiles and clothing and the logging of tropical timber. The highly skilled and senior managerial personnel are brought from China and are mostly engaged in extractive industry (oil, gas, and mining), hydroelectric, and civil engineering. In addition, with Chinese infrastructure projects, local construction firms are crying foul with respect to Chinese bidding practices and with the overwhelming Chinese involvement in the composition of the semi-skilled labor force. This might be possible because the Chinese are not adequately trained in cross-cultural communication skills to effectively deal with their African counterparts. Even if the Africans are not highly trained in engineeringand construction, as part and parcel of the Chinese co-development strategy, the main purpose of Chinese investment in Africa should have been to train and upgrade the skills of local personnel so that Africa could be in a better position to replace the highly skilled Chinese employees and investors in the near future. African governments should be in a position to monitor that the Chinese companies are contributing to improve the skills of the local workforce even if they may initially employ expatriate skilled technical and management personnel. Thus, the Chinese need to establish local educational infrastructure and provide training opportunities to adequately prepare prospective African employees (See the United Nations, UNDP, 2007).

Based a review of the literature, the socio-economic impacts of some of the Chinese cooperative investments in Africa are summarized using the following dimensions: a) Human Capital (local employment) b) human management skills (control of decision making process) , c) technological transfer, d) local content requirements, e) efficiency, and f) the terms of trade (See Table 1).

1. **Human Capital**: The Chinese investors seem to be in control of decision-making and are involved as heads of human development, accounting, finance, marketing, production, and operations. Research and development (R&D) for all Sino-African investments are also conducted in the Chinese headquarters, controlled by state-owned enterprises and government-approved private agencies.
2. **Technology Transfer**: Typically, state-owned companies arrive in Africa with their own work force, mainly project managers, engineers, technicians (Jian-Ye, 2007). Unless corrected, the Sino-African investment is likely to fatten the pockets of state elites and marginalize the African masses. In line with the objectives of the SSC, the degree of control must be reversed if there are going to be technological transfers from China to Africa. Also, China has done little to integrate Africa into the global value chains though it is considered to be an essential part of the technology transfer package.
3. **Local Continent Requirements and Environmental Externalities**: More than 50 percent of the intermediate products for Chinese investments in Africa originate in China. Thus, though it is claimed that the Chinese-capital investments in Africa are new (Greenfield) rather than takeover investments, but it needs to be underlined that the Chinese investments in Africa are constrained by not being environmentally friendly. Similar to the Euro-African investments, the Sino-African investments have failed to address their negative environmental externalities.
4. **Efficiency:** African firms generally lose about 8 percent of sales due to power outages, and transportation delays account for about 3 percent lost sales (World Economic Forum, 2007). The Chinese construction companies are currently able to wind up to a third of all public tender processes in Africa to electrify a number of places and speed up the transportation process. The African governments see this as a means of obtaining construction services more cheaply and more quickly than obtaining them from Western construction firms. Nonetheless, it is instructive to notice that about 30 to 40 percent of the orders that come from China are being executed by Chinese firms with little collaboration with local African personnel and subcontractors (see for example, Asche, 2008).
5. **Foreign Exchange:** As discussed above, most of the foreign exchange generally used for the Chinese investments in Africa originates from the China's EXIM and development banks. Employing Article 4 of the special regulation called the "Guidance for Granting Loans to Support the Overseas Processing of the Investor's Raw Materials and Assem-

bling Operations" the Export-Import Bank of China has been granting long-term and short-term loans to companies investing abroad to purchase Chinese equipment and technology necessary to build factories abroad (Zhaoxi, 2009).

6. **Terms of Trade:** In 2006, Africa's exports to China were composed of oiland gas (about 62 percent), minerals and metals (about 13 percent), and manufactured goods (8 percent). The main imports of Africa from China included about 45 percent manufactured products, 31 percent machinery and transport equipment, and about 24 percent primary products. "Rough estimates suggest that Africa's terms of trade (the ratio of Africa's export price index to its import price index) in relation to China improved by 80 to 90 percent between 2001 and 2006 (Jiang-Ye, 2007). More specifically, the terms of trade of the 48 countries of Sub-Saharan Africa can be divided roughly equally into winners (for example, oil exporting countries), winner-losers, and losers (oil-importing textile producers such as Madagascar and Mauritius, coffee producing and other agricultural exporting countries) (Kennan and Stevens, 2005).

While Chinese exports to Africa are poor in quality, they are generally cheaper to African consumers. The export driven strategy of China has heavily contributed to huge job losses in a number of manufacturing industries throughout the African continent. For instance, instead of supporting domestic enterprises through backward and forward linkages within the domestic economy, the footwear industry in Ethiopia has been facing pressures from cheap Chinese imports (Gebre-Egziabher, 2007). In addition, although cotton growers in West Africa have benefited from increased exports of raw cotton to China,"nevertheless most observers today share the concern that by purchasing raw materials from the continent and selling value-added products back, China's increased involvement will create unfavorable trade balance for many African countries" (Broker, 2007). The importation of Chinese manufactured textiles to Lesotho, Kenya, and South Africa with well-established clothing industries has flared up social unrest and disruption by trade unions (Alden and Davies, 2006). As stated above, Chinese economic involvement on the African continent has contributed to a surge of low- cost consumer goods. But, the importation of higher value-added products such as refrigerators, air conditioners, and other machinery products have not stimulated but displaced local products and laborers.

TABLE 9. 1: IMPACT OF CHINESE COOPERATIVE INVESTMENTS IN AFRICA

INDICATOR	AGGREGATE ANALYSIS OF THE EFFECTS OF CHINESE INVESTMENTS IN AFRICA
a) Human Capital	
Local employment	In general, the Chinese are employed in highly skilled jobs where as African are mainly engaged in lower skill jobs
Chief Executive officer/ organizational structure	Mixed
Accounting & finance	Mixed
Marketing	Local people are used to market local products. Thus far, most of the products are sold in the domestic markets and Chinese investors are not helping African countries to sell their products internationally.
Production and Operations	Mostly Chinese
R&D and Product Design	Mainly Chinese
b) Technological Transfer	
Engineering Specification	Mostly accomplished by Chinese
Human Capital and Development	Very minor training given to local employees
Productivity	The Sino-African firms are very productive
Technological Infrastructure for Backward and Forward Linkages	Mixed impact
c) Environmental Effect and local content requirement	Generally negative impact on the continent and less than 50 percent of supplies are obtained from domestic sources.
d) Efficiency	Per unit cost of goods and services produced by the Sino-African investment is cost effective
e) Foreign Exchange	Mostly supplied by China's EXIM and China Development Bank
f) Term of trade	
Boosting Exports	Limited domestic manufactured products for the international market, China heavily exports Africa's primary products
Boosting Imports	The Chinese have heavily flooded African markets with cheap and poor quality products from China

Chinese investments that seek efficiency and use local content inputs for export-oriented manufacturing have been very limited in Africa (United Nations, UNDP, 2007). " In recent years, individual small entrepreneurs, often traders, have been traveling or migrating to Africa to seek business opportunities. Once established (teaming up with local business) in African towns, these entrepreneurs set up wholesale or retail outlets and import from China consumer goods like electronic appliances, textiles, and clothing, competing with local traders" (ECOWAS-SWAC/OECD, 2006).

Summary and Policy Implications

The internationalization of Chinese investment in Africa has been accelerated in recent years in manufacturing (textiles), resource extraction, construction, and other services. China's incentives to promote FDI outflows to Africa take four forms: a) special and general tax incentives (All Chinese enterprises overseas are exempt from corporate income tax for five successive years after beginning operations); b) loans and credit (Chinese enterprises with investments abroad are accorded medium- and long-term commercial loans or soft loans from government-owned Chinese banks); c) foreign exchange (China's foreign exchange administration stipulates that Chinese enterprises are eligible for foreign exchange for foreign investment projects); and d) a favorable import and export of raw materials and services (United Nations, UNDP, 2007).

Based on the current Chinese investments and co-development projects existing in Africa, the supporters of Chinese investment in Africa argue "Africa registered 5.8 percent economic growth in 2007, its highest level ever, in part because of Chinese investment. Experts say the roads, bridges, and dams built by Chinese firms are low cost, good quality, and completed in a fraction of the time such projects usually take in Africa" (Hanson, 2006). In short, proponents of Chinese investment in Africa claim that China has not only provided assistance but has also invested in Africa in areas that the Western aid agencies and private investors have long neglected. For instance, though agriculture is regarded as vital for Africa's development, both the United States Agency for Development (USAID) and the World Bank reduced assistance to Africa's agricultural sector by as much as 90 percent in the 1990s. The Chinese state-owned enterprises, on the other hand, provided human and capital assistance to Africa without any conditionality (Lake and Whitman, 2006). As argued by Sebastian:

> *The concurrent economic development of China and African countries is truly complementary—rapid Chinese growth requires constant fueling from natural resources, in which Africa is abundant. While Africa is lacking in infrastructure, China possesses an expertise in the*

> *construction and manufacturing sector that is willing to share. This symbiotic relationship has resulted in an unprecedented scale and pace of trade and investment flows between China and Africa (2008).*

On the other hand critics argue China has shipped entire workforces across to Africa for many of its projects. Also, China has flooded the African markets with cheap consumer goods and devastated the local textile and consumer product industries. In addition, some of the Afro-pessimistic intellectuals argue that as yet a) there is little evidence whether China's renewed, and most probably lasting involvement in Africa will serve the continent better than the decades of aid from Western governments, which have scarcely delivered on their promises; b) while Chinese FDI is contributing to economic growth (especially in resource-endowed states), apart from an infrastructure construction boom, "there is little evidence of a positive impact on broader human development" (Broker, 2007); and c) "China has an African Policy. Africa doesn't have a China policy" (the daily newspaper *Nation,* Nairobi, Kenya, 2006). Instead of being dictated, it is up to Africa states to determine how they can use their relations with China. "African political leaders should sit in the driver's seat with their national policy guidelines and their priorities (Lumumba-Kasongo, 2007)."

In short, Lumumba-Kasongo argues that under the pretext of the SSC model China has introduced the "Beijing Consensus," which is to a large extent based on China's self-representation as Africa's help-mate rather than the "Washington Consensus," "which is the dogma of White House, Pentagon, the [World] Bank, International Monetary Fund, and multinationals representing the interests of big private business" (2007).

Instead of the two diametrically opposed perspectives of the Chinese engagement in Africa presented above, Holslag's (2006) point of view is eclectic. According to Holslag, China's vision on its economic relations is to beckon Africa with sweet carrots largely tailored to derive goodwill and permit it to do business suavely (2006, p.15). Being engaged in constructive exchange, Africa simply needs to redefine the rules of the game to make it more amenable and less threatening to its own interests (Rocha, 2008). For example, in South Africa, Chinese investments are "the product of lengthy and detailed negotiations that–apparently unlike some deals struck in other African settings–are framed in terms which conform to international legal norms and responsibilities" (Alden and Davis, 2006). African governments should be in a position to monitor that the Chinese companies are contributing to improve the skills of the local workforce even if they may initially employ expatriate skilled technical and management personnel. Finally, African leaders need to encourage the Chinese investors to adopt production techniques that are ecologically sensitive and are in line with the Chinese environmental guidelines (See, Bosshard, 2008). In chapter 10 Chinese investment in Ethiopia will be discussed.

Chapter 10

CHINA'S INVESTMENT IN ETHIOPIA: DEVELOPMENTAL OPPORTUNITY OR DEEPING CHINA'S NEW MERCANTILISM?

After China became a member of the World Trade Organization (WTO) in 2001 it faced severe competition in its home markets. To face the globalization challenge, Chinese companies actively participated in international competition, developed their global vision, established overseas distribution networks, trained international management talent, and embarked on promoting their brand internationally. Also, the gradual internationalization process demanded changes in China's investment modes and geographical targets (Zhaoxi, 2009). Because of tough competition and an exponential and sustained growth in its economy, the Peoples' Republic of China (hereafter referred to as China), has positioned itself at the forefront of being a very vital and influential player in Africa's cooperative pro-business investments

As discussed in Chapter 9, China's deepening involvement across Africa can be viewed from two perspectives. The political warfare perspective argues that Chinese investments in Africa in the twenty-first century are not only based on the need for natural resources, such as oil, timber, minerals, but are also focused on financial resources and political influence designed to pursue Chinese neo-imperialist objectives vigorously. Based on this, the adherents of the political warfare theory argue that if the U.S. fails to design a profound strategic approach to emancipate Africa from China's silver-coated ulterior motives, China may eventually contribute to "doomsday" and the New African Scramble (Lake and Whitman, 2006).

Applying the opinion of the political warfare theorist to the Sino-Ethiopian situation, Leggett argues, "A poor landlocked nation...Ethiopia lacks the vast natural resources that have drawn China's interest in other countries. But it has something else Beijing craves: geopolitical clout in the region. Ethiopia is the source of the Blue Nile, the river that slakes Egypt's thirst. It is the meeting ground between largely Muslim North Africa and the Christian south. And it is the seat of the African Union, the political body that represents the continent" (Leggett, 2005).

Chau also argues that by providing free financial contributions and other infrastructural investments at opportune times, China is using political warfare to demonstrate Chinese support for the Ethiopian people, possibly gaining an immediate favorable impression and benefits in the future. Since late 1999, China's political warfare led to fruitful opportunities at the grand strategic level in Ethiopia. Finally, Chau concludes that political warfare operations have helped China achieve the central objective of its grand strategy in Ethiopia (2007).

On the other hand, the South-South development cooperation school of thought, views China's increased aid, trade, and investment in Africa as a means to foster Africa's self-sufficiency and sustainable development in the 21st century (Naidu, 2008). The protagonists of the South-South Cooperative (SSC) model of development forcefully argue that China should be left alone to forge its unique partnership with Africa and the West must simply learn to compete.

The thrust of Africa's interest in following China's model of development emerges because prior to 1949, "...China was devastated by war, and levels of 'development' in certain African states were above that of China and other East Asian countries, today China offers an impressive, if highly mixed demonstration of a developing yet already significantly advanced economy (Large, 2008)." Following the FOCAC Summit and the third Ministerial Conference of 2006 held in Beijing, it is no wonder that China has not only emerged as a model for development but has spearheaded pro-business cooperation investments across Africa.

For example, according to Ethiopia's Foreign Minister, Mr. Mesfin, the Ethio-Chinese joint-partnership projects are not only related to agricultural projects and capacity building but are vital for generating the harmonization of common strategies for the two countries (2008). In addition, Ethiopia's former Prime Minister, the late Meles Zenawi ascertained that with the establishment of a new strategic partnership with China, the Ethiopian workers are reasonably paid and their work places are environmentally friendly. Also, the former Prime Minister highlighted that Ethiopia's exports have added value and have resulted in dividends for the joint-venture partners. "Ethiopia's exports to China have jumped following China's declaration of duty-free market access to African goods. Ethiopia admires China's technological level and expects China to expand technical assistance to Ethiopia" (2006).

Based on theoretical synthesis, the political warfare theorists argue that the so-called "cooperative" investments undertaken by China in Africa are devastating and exploitative. In contrast, the position of the South-South Cooperative school of thought (on China's cooperative assistance programs to Africa and particularly to Ethiopia) seems to be drenched with lofty phrases and promises. Therefore, before romanticizing on illusions, the practical synthesis of the theories of the two schools of thought needs to be systematically and empirically tested. For example, China's respect for the sovereignty of the aid-getting African nations and not interfering in their internal affairs seems to be a very commendable. But we need to take into consideration Alves' point that China is "coddling human rights violators, undermining international efforts to improve governance standards, and contributing to potentially unsustainable debt levels (2008)." In addition, it worth testing the validity of Habib's argument that by turning a deaf ear to human rights violations and being blind to the existence of human rights violations in its aid engagement scheme, China is contributing to adverse consequences for some of Africa's citizens (2008). From China's politico-diplomatic "African strategy," it is quite obvious that China has shown its strategic interest in Africa and has particularly mapped out its interest in Ethiopia. China's interest in Ethiopia has provided Ethiopia a "window of opportunity" to navigate other possible Western investors. But, do the Chinese infrastructural imperatives mirror Ethiopia's developmental goals?

The two perspectives of the Chinese engagement in Africa are very instructive. But in order to have a clear picture, the two points of view need to be rigorously analyzed from a specific African country's point of view. Therefore, the empirical part of this study will be to advance the understanding and rationalization of the various Chinese investments in Ethiopia. Ethiopia is chosen because in the last five years, Ethiopia has achieved a high and sustained rate of growth. Given that Ethiopia has been the major beneficiary of Chinese investment and cooperative development projects, the question which needs to be pondered is: can some of Ethiopia's spectacular growth rate be attributed to Chinese investments? More specifically, have the Chinese cooperative investment footprints enabled the Ethiopian economy to master high-valued technology and generate productive employment or have the various co-development Chinese investments deepened Ethiopia's dependence on the Beijing Consensus model? The first part of the paper reviews and contextualizes China's investment in Ethiopia. The second section of the paper scrutinizes the appropriateness of Chinese capital and technological flows to Ethiopia. Finally, after summarizing the main findings of the study, the paper concludes by drawing some relevant policy implications and suggests relevant future research directions.

Chinese Investment in Ethiopia

Ethiopia's bilateral trade relations with China date back to before the founding of the Peoples' Republic of China. But Ethio-Chinese relations formally began in 1964, when the Prime Minister of China, Zhou EnLai, visited Ethiopia. Though marginal, economic and technological cooperation between Ethiopia and China started in 1970 after the two countries issued a joint communiqué on the establishment of full diplomatic relations. From 1977 to 1985, China suspended its diplomatic relations with Ethiopia because it felt that Ethiopia was pursuing a pro-Soviet revisionist model. However, as Ethiopia slowly disentangled itself from its hegemonic dependency on the Soviet Union in 1985, China normalized its diplomatic relations with Ethiopia. As stated by Xiaojie, since 1985, Ethio-Chinese relations have manifested a high-level of exchanges in cooperative politics, economy, culture, and education as well as in the international arena (2008).

For instance, in 1986, a limited a number of Chinese companies started bidding on projects for the Ethiopian Government. As narrated by Chau (2007), bilateral relations between the two countries were limited until the mid-1990s, but reciprocal high-level visits by Ethiopia's Prime Minister Meles Zenawi and China's President Jiang Zemin occurred in 1995 and 1996. This led to a series of agreements between the two countries, including the China's provision of free assistance to Ethiopia for a period of five years (i.e., from June 1, 1996 to May 31, 2001). As a goodwill gesture, in October of 2000, China donated office equipment to the Ministry of Information on the eve of the 30th anniversary of the establishment of diplomatic relations between the two countries. In accordance with the exchange of letters signed by the governments of China and Ethiopia, in October of 1997, Chinese construction workers completed houses that could accommodate 85 families and delivered them in August 2000 to the Addis Ababa mayoral office.

To be engaged in contracted projects, such as building of houses, bridges and roads, Chinese construction and sewage workers were sent to Ethiopia to work in these small and medium projects. By sending labor abroad, China provided job opportunities for its labor force, enhanced the quality of labor, and improved the development of relevant domestic industries such as domestic airlines and telecommunications. Put simply, in the earlier period, Chinese officials embarked on sending labor and getting involved in contract projects as the most competitive export pattern for China's domestic service sector.

China's earlier outward FDI entry strategy has already had extremely positive effects on the Chinese economy. It helped it to expand production capacities and enter new markets by creating new opportunities to increase Chinese companies' competitiveness and facilitate the emergence of top-quality enterprises through various forms of cooperation (Zhaox, 2009). After Ethiopia made unique contributions to the 2nd Ministerial Conference of FOCAC in 2003, Chinese President Hu Jintao announced the following measures to further cooperation with Ethiopia. China:

- gave zero-tariff treatment for Ethiopian exports. As a result, Ethiopia's export to China soared by 607 percent from 2004 to 2005 (i.e., from US$14 million in 2004 to US$ 85 in 2005).
- increased the preferential treatment of Ethiopia's exports from 192 export items to 442 items.
- extended debt cancellation to Ethiopia.
- wrote off Ethiopia's interest-free government debt which was supposed to mature by the end of 2005.
- pledged to set up the fund in order to encourage Chinese companies in Ethiopia. As a result, the fund was used to build the Ethiopia China Glass Company (CGC) in Addis Ababa.
- decided to build three rural schools and a malaria treatment center in Ethiopia.
- sent Chinese young volunteers to Ethiopia to assist in Ethiopia's development efforts, and
- granted Ethiopia the Approved Destination Status for Chinese tourists in 2004 and in the sector of human resources cooperation, China helped to train about 348 Ethiopian professional between 2007 and 2008 (Xiaojie, August 2008).

As a result of China's diversified global entry mode and portfolio of activities which it has learned over the years, China also offered a three-point proposal to boost its relations with Ethiopia. The projects include "...agricultural technology, demonstration center, and an all-packed economic and trade project including the construction of hydropower stations and the establishment of an oriental zone to attract investment from Chinese companies (Chinese News Agency, Xinhua, 2008).

On March, 19th 2008, the Jiangsu Yong Yuan Investment Group of China promised to construct the first private Eastern Industry Zone in Dukem, Oromia Regional State, in order to build the industries and to invite local private and international companies. It is estimated that about 30 Chinese companies have shown interest to invest in the industrial zone. As stated by Tamene, the Ethiopian Eastern Industrial Zone is envisaged to incorporate multi sector industries ranging from investment in textile, garment, shoe, cotton, jeans processing, leather, construction machineries, electrical materials, and steel manufacturing sectors (2008).

After the completion of the industrial zone, the following economic and social outcomes are expected. Economically, approximately 80 projects will be established in the zone. The annual total sales revenue of the environmentally-friendly building materials, power transmission lines and transformers, and telecommunication equipment is expected to generate about RMB 16 billion every year. Exported products from the zone will generate RMB5 billion. In addition, after the tax exemption period, the Ethiopian Government will collect about RMB 5 billion tax revenues. Socially, the Industrial Zone, equipped with advanced technology and professional management skills, is expected to create about 10,000 to 20,000 local jobs, out of these 3,000 will be trained skilled domestic workers. As part of its social responsibility, the Eastern Industry Zone will contribute to fund local education, hospital, and other public services and to strengthen the country's Sustainable Development and Poverty Reduction Program (Committee, Ethiopian Eastern Industrial Zone, 2009).

The literature and empirical studies indicate Chinese global entry modes vary from contractually based agreements, exporting, joint ventures, and wholly owned strategies. For example, Rongping argues that Chinese aspirant multinationals prefer to use joint ventures to enter developing countries (2000). Zhaoxi, on the other hand, empirically shows that China's overseas investment is about 60 percent trade-oriented investment, while manufacturing and resource-oriented investments together account for about 30 percent (2009).

Chinese investors seem to have carefully engineered their entry strategy into Ethiopia. With considerable oscillation and no discernible trend before 1991, China devised trade and biddings on government sponsored contractual projects, mainly infrastructural landscape, to gain access and expand into Ethiopia's downstream resources. With a wave of privatization and structural reforms that gained momentum in Ethiopia spurred a flurry of various types of foreign direct investments that originated from the Southern Countries (i.e., China, India, South Africa, etc). For example, from 1992 to 2005, Chinese investments in Ethiopia got organized under the wholly owned type of organizational structure (i.e., 86 percent wholly owned compared to 12 percent in joint ventures) in order for Chinese companies to acquire upstream assets (See Table 1). In recent years, the presence and conduct of China's foreign direct investment in Ethiopia is fast becoming one of the prominent features of the Ethiopian economic landscape either by infrastructure exchange for access to natural resources or by denoting Chinese development assistance or providing favorable lending and capital contribution.

However, though Ethiopia intends to use Chinese cooperative investment as means of enhancing its regional development, the inflow of Chinese investment has not been equally shared. Geographically, most of the Chinese Cooperative investments are located within the Addis Ababa and Oromia

Table 10.1: List of Chinese Investment Projects in Ethiopia, 1992-2008

1. Region	Wholly-owned	Joint-ventures	South Africa-Chinese	Canadian-Chinese	Djibouti-Chinese	Dutch-Chinese	American-Chinese	Chinese-Yemeni	Chinese-Pakistani
Tigray	1								
Afar	2								
Amhara	7		1						
Oromia	63	31	1						
Somalie		1							
Benishangul-Gumuz	2	1							
SNNPR	7	1							
Gambela									
Harari	1								
Addis Ababa	555	55		5	1	1			1
Dire Dawa	3	1							
Multi-regional	71	13	1				1	1	
Total %	712 86.1%	103 12.3%	3 0.4%	5 0.6%	1 0.1%	1 0.1%	1 0.1%	1 0.1%	1 0.1%
2. Capital (000 birr)	7,875,400	4,489,954	107,554	51,862	6,000	1,000	5,124	3,310	1,500
3. Invest. Status:									
Pre-impl.	552	89	2	2	1	1	1	1	0
Operation	163	14	0	1	0	0	0	0	1
4. Employee:									
Permanent	34,962	13,233	3,700	420	100	100	94	65	50
Temp	50,017	13,380	2,937	352	200	10	0	50	10

Computed from the data obtained from the Ministry of Trade and Industry: "List of Investment Approved from China from July 1992-December 28, 2008."

Regional State. While 78 percent of the wholly owned Chinese companies are located in the Addis Ababa Regional Zone and about 9 percent are situated in the Oromia Regional State, without any significant catching up by the other regional zones. In addition, of the 103 joint-venture companies, 53 percent are situated within the Addis Ababa region while 30 percent are launched within the Oromia Regional State. In addition, the small- and medium-size state-owned Chinese Enterprises operating in Ethiopia are fully operating while the remaining 78% (647/828) are partially or yet to be fully implemented. To fully implement the various investments, the Chinese investors employed 44% (i.e., 52,714/119,670) full-time workers and 56 percent (66,956/119,670) temporary workers.

Analytical Framework

As mentioned above, China has positioned itself at the forefront of being a very vital and influential player in Southern Cooperative pro-business investments in order to speed up the development ambitions of the host countries and to acquire cardinal natural resources essential for its development. Chinese multinational enterprises are more effectively investigated in other developing countries than the industrialized countries' multinational enterprises because: 1) state-owned and state-associated Chinese firms could have capital made available to them at below-market rates due to imperfect capital markets (Warner et al., 2004); 2) inefficient banking systems may make soft loans to potential outward investors (Antkiewiez and Whally, 2006); and 3) family-owned firms may have access to cheap capital from family members.

Based on this investment policy, China is increasing its presence in all key dimensions of international business: foreign trade, contracting overseas projects, labor service cooperation, foreign direct investment, agricultural cooperation, investment in international high-tech ventures, and development of overseas resources (Zhaoxi, 2009). The Chinese investment encompasses packages of capital, managerial, and organizational know-how. Thus, based on the South-South win-win cooperative model the Chinese are expected to 1) transfer advanced technology, 2) diversify the export profile, 3) stimulate spillovers to domestically owned firms, 4) generate human capital formation, 5) generate additional global marketing opportunities, 6) stimulate backward and forward linkages with the local economy, 7) bolster revenues and foreign exchange, and 8) create a more competitive business environment in the developing countries.

As mentioned above, Ethiopia, like a number of African countries, has provided conducive investment climate and rendered incentives to attract various forms of Chinese cooperative investments. According the Ethiopia Investment Administration, China-funded enterprises had invested US$960 million in Ethiopia by July 2008. The Chinese investments are diversified into many sectors, such as construction, telecom, textile, healthcare, and agriculture. It is supposed to bring to Ethiopia much-needed capital, know-how, and management experience. It is also expected to play a notable part in increasing local employment (See for example, Waltainfo.com, 2009). According to win-win theory, the SSC ventures are supposed to induce "...liberal economic cooperation through trade flows (export and import relations, foreign domestic flows, technology transfer and integration in global value chains, and aid flows, should bring proportional benefits, which otherwise the partners would not have access to before entering into these relations" (Lumumba-Kasongo, 2007).

As part of SSC, is the economic cooperation between Ethiopia and China complementary and does it result in a win-win situation? In short, the central question of the study addresses: do the Chinese Cooperation ventures in Ethiopia fare in terms of transfer of technology, diversifying exports, and the creation of linkages with domestic economy? To answer the above question, an analytical framework that incorporates the impact, the process of ownership and operational effects of the foreign investment on the local economy is very vital. The Sino-Ethiopian investments are analyzed using the following conceptual framework (See Desta, 1993).

A. Ownership of the Chinese investments in Ethiopia:
   Ownership (wholly owned, joint venture, production sharing, turnkey)
B. Operational setup of the Chinese investments in Ethiopia:
   1. structural (organizational setups)
   2. management skills (more training, knowledge transfer, and creating new and sustainable jobs)
   3. higher local investment (increasing domestic investments as local companies gain access to distribution channels and suppliers of local supplies
   4. labor (availability of skills, management-labor relations)
   5. degree of integration with headquarters (ethnocentric, polycentric, geocentric)
   6. project (location, nature, and relevance)
   7. Chinese affiliates versus other local companies and community
   8. business leaders attitude
   9. degree of competition and competitiveness (improving overall economic growth by increasing competition, raising quality levels and delivery reliability)
   10. present/prospective growth of domestic demand for the Sino-Chinese products
C. Prospective contributions of the Chinese investments in Ethiopia:

1. Technology transfer (improvement in access to relevant technology)
   a) infrastructural development
   b) net value added
   c) training of local employee and other production (demonstrative) effects
   d) wages paid to local labor
   e) interests paid to local capital
2. Trade effects
   a) export promotion effects (using their access to overseas marketing and distribution networks)
   b) diversification of exports
   c) import substitution effects
3. Revenue benefits (widening local tax bases and contributing to government revenues)
4. spill-over effects (positive and negative)

Methodology of the Study

When the researcher visited Ethiopia during the summer of 2008, he had the opportunity to informally observe a number of Sino-Ethiopian projects. Additional information on the Ethiopian perspective about the activities on contractually based projects, Chinese wholly owned investments, and some of the Sino-Ethiopian joint ventures were obtained from government officials, local residents, and employees. In addition to reviewing existing literature, the annual reports published by the Ethiopian Ministry of Industry were carefully analyzed in order to establish a better understanding of the operations of the selected case studies. As shown above, the aggregate profiles of the firms established by the Sino-Ethiopian cooperative investments presented in Table 10.1, about eighty-six percent are wholly-owned and 12 percent are Sino-Ethiopian joint-venture enterprises.

The Chinese-Ethiopian cooperative and co-development investments case studies for this include: 1) the Ethiopia Hansom International Glass, PLC, a Chinese wholly-owned investment, located suburb of Addis Ababa, 2) the Red Fox International Cement Investment Business, PLC, established in 2008 in Oromia Regional State, and 3) The Sino-Ethiopian Associate Africa, PLC, a pharmaceutical joint venture established in 2001 in the Oromia Regional State. And as a background, a brief description of the contractually-based projects undertaken by the Chinese companies, the Addis Ababa Ring Road Project and the Takeze Hydro Water Contractual Project is in order.

Contractually-Based Projects

The Addis Ababa Ring Road Project, under construction by the China Road and Bridge Construction (CRBC) commenced in March 1998 and was completed in June 2004, while the Gotera interchange was open to traffic May 1, 2009. As shown in Table 2, under the Chinese claim that they lack skilled and semi-skilled Ethiopian labor force, the Chinese investors have hired about 39 percent skilled Chinese workers (i.e., site engineers, technicians, management staff and top managers) compared to 61percent (i.e., 432/705) of the Ethiopian work force in this category. Nonetheless, 100 percent of the unskilled workforce is composed of Ethiopians (See Mo, 2007). Though undertaken by Chinese companies, the Addis Ababa Ring Road projects are financed by multilateral grants, soft loans, and technical assistance denoted to Ethiopia and but tendered and financed by the Ethiopian Government (GebreEgziabher, 2006).

The Takeze Hydro Water Project, a key for poverty reduction, the Takeze hydro power station was initiated by the Ethiopian Government and financed by the World Bank and other international financial organizations in 2005 for the electrification programs of the Tigraye Regional State. The hydro power station is located near the boarder with Sudan and Eritrea and is rising in the headwater of the Blue Nile River. The hydro power station is envisioned to interconnect neighboring countries and share available plant capacity. As shown in Table 10.2, about 600 Chinese engineers were involved in carving out a vast underground tunnel. The Chinese engineers have a plan to pour an approximately 188m high cement dam stretching 1.6 kilometers long and containing deep caves that will hold massive power turbines. "At 188m high, the Tekeze Arch Dam ranks as the highest dam in Africa, eclipsing the previous record height for an African dam of 185m held by the Katse Arch Dam in Lesotho" (Waterpower Magazine, 2009). Of the total work force, 100 percent are unskilled Ethiopians. But the Chinese skilled labor force controls 53 percent (i.e., 470/880) of the internal operations of the project.

TABLE 10.2: PROFILE OF THE ADDIS ABABA RING ROAD AND THE TAKAZE HYDRO WATER CONTRACTUAL PROJECT PER YEAR

COMPANY	ADDIS ABABA RING ROAD*		TAKEZE HYDRO PROJECT**	
YR. STARTED	1998		2005	
NO. EMPLOYED	ETHIOPIAN	CHINESE	ETHIOPIAN	CHINESE
Unskilled	780	---	1000	--
Skilled	400	180	200	250
Site Engineer Technician	30	90	100	150
Mgmt Staff	1	2	100	50
Top Managers	1	1	10	20
Remark	Completed in 2003		Continues	

Source: * Peng Mo, "Addis Ababa Ring Road Project: A Case Study of a Chinese Construction Project in Ethiopia," Shanghai, 16, May 2007. ** Computed by the author based on the information obtained from an oral interview of reliable sources.

Wholly-Owned and Joint-Venture Chinese Enterprises in Ethiopia

Ethiopia has issued and subsequently revised investment proclamations and codes since 1992/93, to attract foreign direct investment (FDI). The reforms undertaken by the Ethiopian government include the privatization and creating favorable conditions for the inflow of foreign private investment and the diversification of the ownership of the industries. For Example, Ethiopia has instituted public enterprises, wholly (sole) owned foreign enterprises, shareholding corporation, partnership enterprise and individual enterprises. As discussed by Gebeyehu, December, 2004) the main incentives offered to foreign investors by the Ethiopian Government include:

- Foreign investors are fully exempted from customs duties and import tariffs on capital equipment and export taxes. Income tax holidays are given for investors that favor exporting their products.
- Research & Development expenditures and remittance of capital are tax exempted.
- Foreign investors could carry forward initial operating losses and can use any depreciation method to apply in their financial statement.
- Investment guarantees for FDI include full repatriation of capital and profits. Foreign investors could remit profits and dividends accruing

from investment, principal and interest payments on external loans, payments related to technology transfer agreement, proceeds from the sale or liquidation of an enterprise and proceeds from the transfer of shares or of partial ownership of enterprise to a domestic investor.

As outlined before, the Chinese wholly owned enterprises in Ethiopia are one hundred percent owned by the Chinese private limited companies (PLC). Unlike state-owned enterprises, PLCs are privately owned, non-governmental entities and are not allowed to trade their shares in the stock market and offer shares in the company to the general public. Based on the protection offered under the standard Ethiopian foreign company rules and regulations, one hundred percent of profits of the Chinese solely owned enterprises can be exported. In addition, some technology and components can be imported duty free. Finally, substantial tax holidays are accorded to certain favored industries. Included in the Case Study are three wholly owned Chinese companies: Ethiopian Hansom International Glass, PLC; Red Fox International Investment Business, PLC; and Sino-Africa Overseas Leather Product, PLC. Additionally, the Sino-Ethiopia Associate Africa joint venture company is examined as well.

1. **The Ethiopia China Glass Company (ECGC)**

   Funded by China-Africa Development Fund (CAD-Fund) at a cost of 35 million US dollars, the first ever glass manufacturing industry (ECGC) is located suburb of Addis Ababa. The ECGC glass factory, jointly established by CGO Co. Group Ltd, and China Africa Development Fund has a capacity of producing 42,000 metric tons of quality sheet glass per annum. About 30 percent of the glass sheets produced by the factory will be for local use and the remaining 70 percent for export to East African countries. Most raw materials such as silk, sand, and dolomite will be obtained locally but soda ash will be imported.

2. **Red Fox International Investment**

   The company was launched as a turnkey project in April of 2008 in the Oromia Regional State to produce 150,000 tons of cement per year. As envisioned, the company is producing at full capacity, that is, about 350 to 400 tons of cement per day.

3. **Sino-Africa Overseas Leather Products, PLC**

   Sino-Africa Overseas Leather Products was launched on June 2, 2008 in the Oromia Regional Zone in order to process domestic raw leather products into highly valued leather products using Chinese high-

Table 10.3: Strategic Variables Showing the Operational Relationship of the Wholly-owned Chinese Investments & Sino-Ethiopian Joint Ventures

Company	Ethiopia Hansom International Glass, PLC		Red Fox International Investment Business, PLC		Sino–Africa Overseas Leather Product, PLC		Sino-Ethiopia Associate Africa, PLC	
Year started	March 12, 2008		March 14, 2008		June 2, 2008		2001	
Region of Investment	Suburb of Addis Ababa		Oromia		Oromia		Oromia	
Investment type	Wholly-owned Chinese Investment, manufacturing glass sheet products		Wholly-Owned Chinese Investment		Wholly-owned Chinese investment, manufacturing of finished leather products		Joint-venture	
Ethiopia's Motivation for investment	It enhances the development of Ethiopia's sub-sector of the construction industry. Besides boosting foreign currency earnings, the factory is expected to create lots of job opportunities,		Enhancing the development of the construction industry sub-sector. Currently the project is producing 350-400 tones of cement per day		Export high quality leather products to earn foreign exchange		Developing the pharmaceutical industry sub-sector	
Chinese Motivation for Investment	About 30 percent of the glass sheet produced by the factory will be for local use and the remaining 70 percent are to be exported to East African countries.		About 100 percent cement produced by the company is intended for local consumption.		Convert Ethiopian leather resources using Chinese capital, leather technology, and highly skilled manpower.		Favorable investment opportunity in the country	
Total number of Employees	Chinese	Ethiopia	Chinese	Ethiopian	Chinese	Ethiopian	Chinese	Ethiopian
	30	308	18	70	10	1300	3	118
CEO	1		1		1		1	
Human Resources personnel	1	23	1		1	13	1	2

Production mgmt	25	270	16	67	3	18	1	112
Marketing mgmt	2	12	1		3	10	1	3
Research and product Design mgmt	1	3	1					
Production capacity	42,000 tons of glass per annum		150,000 tons of cement per annum				1.2 billion capsules per annum	
Total Sales:	$______________		ETB42,870,027				ETB8,203,500	
Export					$98,000,000 (USD)			
Domestic			Marketing domestically					

skilled labor, capital, and technology. The export of processed leather products is in its infancy in Ethiopia. Thus, to process high quality shoe and leather products for export, it was established as wholly-owned company. For instance, in 2009, the company earned close to US$98 million from its export ventures.

Foreign Direct Investment

The Sino-Ethiopia Associate Africa, PLC is pharmaceutical industry sub-sector located in the Oromia Regional State. Currently the factory is producing 900,000,000 capsules per annum. Of these, 70 percent are to be sold domestically and 30 percent are to be exported and sold in the international market.

Data Analysis

The four Sino-Ethiopian Cooperative Investments Case Studies given above are analyzed in terms of their effects on Ownership and Human Capital, Production Management and Operations, Export Effects, Technological Transfers, Efficiency, Foreign Exchange Effects, Local Content Requirements and Spillover Effects, and Environmental Effects (See Table 10.3).

Ownership and Human Capital

When Chinese enter a joint-venture or create a wholly-owned subsidiary, they send experienced managers or top specialists abroad. As discussed by Donghong, Chinese companies " They usually send their best people, recruit local managers and train them all in view of their international assignment" (2009). Rightly so, it is shown in Table 3 that while the Chief Executive Officers (CEOs) or heads three Chinese wholly-owned Chinese companies are Chinese whereas the CEO of the Sino-Ethiopia Associate joint-venture company is an Ethiopian.

Production Management and Operations

Given that Chinese investors in Ethiopia are unfamiliar with cultural makeup of the local situation and the Ethiopian labor laws that pertain to wages, holidays, housing and other benefits, in the solely owned Chinese firms and the joint venture firm, Ethiopian employees are in charge of human resources management. In view of this, it can be assumed that there is a smooth cross-cultural communication within these enterprises and between the enterprise and its external suppliers and customers.

Export Effects

The process of inviting foreign investors to developing countries is not an objective per se, it is rather a means to increase value added exports. Thus, due to the widely held expectation that foreign companies can bring in competitive assets and that they can enhance the export sector of the respective host countries; foreign companies are given numerous incentives to invest in a number of developing countries. In addition, it is assumed that foreign affiliates could indirectly create positive externalities that could entice the export prospects of local firms. In addition, imports to a home country from a host country also capture the intensity of trade relations. The empirical evidence on the role of FDI in export performance is mixed. For instance, FDI seems to have played a pivotal role in the structural transformation of Mauritius by bringing in technology, capital, entrepreneurship, and has helped the Mauritanian economy diversify its export base, and move drastically away from total dependency on sugar (Desta, 1998).

Based on the Sino-Ethiopia Associate Africa pharmaceutical joint venture company, it is possible to argue that both partners handle aspects of the international marketing sector. Since the Chinese marketing officers are well versed in some aspects of the international marketing, they might have trained local employees in export management and foreign marketing strategies. Also, it is possible that local firms could have acquired international marketing techniques by hiring some of the Ethiopian workers who might have left the Sino-Ethiopian joint venture to start their own businesses. The three wholly owned enterprises mostly produce for the domestic market, it is very likely that they might have facilitated some type of interaction with local suppliers and domestic customers. But it is possible to assume that since the wholly-owned enterprises mostly produce for the Ethiopian domestic market they might have done little to integrate Ethiopian products to the global value chain. Thus based on the three case studies, it is possible to ascertain that the Chinese wholly-owned companies (i.e., Ethiopia Hansom, Glass and the Red Fox, Cement Factory) don't seem to act as a platform for exports and their goal is to seek for themselves efficiency in their production process by taking care of Ethiopia's factors of endowment. Since the Sino-Africa produces leather products that are designed to compete in the international market, it does not seem to crowed out the low quality local products. The Sino-Ethiopia, a pharmaceutical joint-venture enterprise is of higher quality base and is more efficient; therefore it is complementary and generates foreign exchanges indispensable for the country.

Technology Transfer

As discussed before, to obtain investment authorization, foreign investors in Ethiopia are given incentives to meet technology transfer requirements. Typically, Chinese arrive in Africa with their work force to manage and control the investments. As shown in Table 3, ninety seven (i.e., 1678/1726) percent of the project managers, engineers, and technicians working in the wholly owned Chinese enterprises are Ethiopians. Research and product design on the other hand seems to be forged in the headquarters rather than basing it on equity ratio to include the Ethiopian partner.

Efficiency Effects

African firms generally lose about eight percent of sales due to power outages, and transportation delays account for about three percent lost sales (World Economic Forum, 2007). In line with Gebeyehu's argument that FDI enterprises are often more efficient and provide positive externalities for local firms in terms of sharing experiences of doing things in new and cost effective ways (2004), the Ethiopian Government envisages to obtain construction and transportation services cheaply from China's investors. Nonetheless, since more than 50 percent of input materials executed by the Sino-Ethiopian firms come from China, it is very difficult to ascertain the contribution of efficiency to the new products made by the Sino-Ethiopian investments.

Foreign Exchange effects

As discussed above, most of the foreign exchange generally used for the Chinese investments in Ethiopia originates from China's EXIM and China's development banks. For instance, the Export-Import Bank of China has been granting long-term and short-term loans to companies investing abroad to purchase Chinese equipment and technology necessary to build factors abroad (Zhaoxi, 2009). Thus, the projects in Ethiopia have enabled it to conserve the foreign exchange which it could have spent on establishing these projects and has helped it to earn the necessary foreign currency by selling some of the Sino-Ethiopian investment products abroad.

Local Content (value added) and spillover effects

While the dependency school theory views foreign investment from developed countries at the core of the world economic system as harmful to the long-term economic growth of developing countries out in the periphery, other studies seem to demonstrate that foreign direct investors can potentially benefit domestic firms through spillover effects. Spillover effects are therefore regarded as very important conduit through which foreign direct investment promotes economic growth in the host country. "The competitive pressure may spur local firms to operate more efficiently and introduce new technologies earlier than would otherwise have been the case. Because foreign firms are not able to extract the full value of these gains, this effect is commonly referred to as the spillover effect" (Fan, 2002).

More specifically, Elmawazini (2005) conjectured that foreign direct investment entails a cross-border transfer. The linkages between foreign affiliates and local firm include

- training workers who may subsequently move to local firms,
- demonstrating new technologies (learning from watching benefits), and
- providing technological assistance to their local suppliers.

Rhee and Belot (1990) also argue that through the formation of linkages, local firms could be engaged as suppliers and sub-contractors to foreign investors and these linkages provide channels through which knowledge about technologies and foreign market conditions may be transmitted (1990).

Though the spillover effect of FDI on the productivity growth of local firms does not occur automatically (See JBIC, 2002), based on the incentives given by the Ethiopian Government to Chinese investors, the four case studies utilize local content. Adhering to backward linkages, the Chinese investors purchase their factors of production from local suppliers. In addition, since they mostly sell their outputs in the domestic market, they have contributed to forward linkages. The four case studies act in creating complementary activities rather than "crowding out" domestic firms. In short, the Sino-Ethiopia foreign investments have forced the local firms to restructure their institutional structures to be more competitive and adequately fulfill the domestic demand, thereby, maintaining their market shares. Thus, the Chinese investments have contributed to positive productivity spillovers.

Environmental Effects

Since the "Earth Summit" (United Nations Conference on Environment and Development or UNCED) of 1992 in Rio de Janeiro, Brazil, the environmental and social dimensions of foreign investment have become a matter of intense controversy between certain home and host countries. In some countries, "The high local visibility of larger multinational investors can make them particularly attractive targets for local enforcement officials. ...This reflects the growing desire for corporate managers to locate these activities in communities where their productivity levels and competitiveness benefit from high standards of environmental protection." (JBIC, 2002).

To attract Chinese investors, the Ethiopian government seems to covertly relax the enforcement of environmental standards. For example, the Chinese contractual-based projects, wholly owned, and the joint venture cases analyzed in this paper are by and large operating in ecologically sensitive regions. They are facing serious environmental problems because the Ethiopian Government has prioritized short-run economic growth over the achievement of environmentally sustainable economic growth in the long run. Ethiopian environmental protection officers at each level of the political system do not seem to fine the Chinese investors for their transgressions or for negatively imprinting their environmental footprints on the country or they fail to encourage the Chinese investors to adopt production techniques that are less harmful to the Ethiopian environment. Like other international financial institutions, the Chinese investors and financiers (such as the Export-Import Bank of China) fail to undertake their environmental guidelines when lending the concessional loans as part of the country's official development assistance program (See for example, Bosshard, 2008).

Undoubtedly, Chinese investments in Ethiopia are an indispensable part of the economic system (they have contributed to infrastructural development, provided capital, new technologies, modern management know-how, and enhanced demonstration effects). Nonetheless, little or no attention is paid by the Ethiopian Government to check the environmental implications of most of the Sino-Ethiopian investments. For example, the Addis Ababa Ring Road has reduced the traffic pressure in the densely populated central zones and curtailed heavy traffic passing through the center. But, the ring Road has inevitably contributed to environmental challenges, such as air and noise pollution. For example, since most of the country's vehicles run on diesel and leaded gasoline, they constantly emit suspended particulate matter (spm), carbon monoxide, lead and hydrocarbons into the surrounding neighborhoods, which could cause bronchial asthma and a loss of vision and mental alertness (See for example, Lund, 2008).

The Tekeze hydropower project is a non-polluting renewable energy thought to be the cheapest form of power and the lowest-cost renewable resource. Though the advantages of the Tekeze hydropower project outweigh its limitations, it needs to be underlined that its social and environmental impacts are tremendous. Socially, it has forced displacement of residents from the area to other semi-arid locations. Environmentally, it has caused ecological deterioration from erosion and landslides on steep hills around the dam. Finally, the

Tekeze and Atbara Rivers depend on the arrival of the East African Monsoon during the months of July, August, and September, though its ability to recharge groundwater is likely to be limited. Moreover, its impact on sedimentation, silt loss, and endangered species is likely to be very substantial.

Concerning the case studies, of the three Chinese wholly owned firms, the Ethiopia Hansom Glass factory is the least environmentally sensitive because the glass sheets that it produces are subject to air pollution and resource degradation. The Red Fox cement factory contributes to water pollution and degrades the environment. The Sino-Ethiopia Associate Africa pharmaceutical company uses hazardous chemical products while producing drugs. The Sino-Africa Overseas Leather Product Company uses various types of chemicals to process the local raw hides into leather products.

Summary, Policy Implications, and Future Research Directions

As the Chinese economy booms, Chinese multinational corporations are embarking on an acquisition drive to capture the oil, natural resources, and unexploited markets of Africa to sustain its rapid economic growth. Based on the current Chinese investments and co-development projects existing in Africa, supporters of Chinese investment in Africa argue that the recent increase in Africa's gross domestic product is because of Chinese investment. Unlike the Western investments in Africa, the Chinese state-owned enterprises provide human and capital assistance to Africa without any conditionality.

Critics on the other hand argue that China has shipped entire workforces across to Africa for many of its projects. In addition, China has flooded the African markets with cheap consumer goods and devastated the local textile and other consumer product industries.

The two perspectives of the Chinese engagement in Africa are very instructive. But in order to have a clear picture, the two points of view were analyzed from Ethiopia's perspective. The presence and conduct of China's foreign direct investment in Ethiopia since 2000 is fast becoming one of the fronts in reshaping Ethiopia's economic architecture. With considerable oscillation and no discernible trend before 1991, China devised trade and biddings on government sponsored contractual projects, mainly infrastructural landscape, to gain access and expand into Ethiopia's downstream resources. With a wave of privatization and structural reforms that gained momentum in Ethiopia spurred a flurry of various types of foreign direct investments that originated from the Southern Countries (i.e., China, India, South Africa, etc.). For example, from 1992 to 2005, Chinese investments in Ethiopia got organized under the wholly owned type of organizational structure (i.e., 86 percent wholly-owned compared to 12 percent in joint-ventures) in order for Chinese companies to acquire upstream assets. In recent years, the presence and conduct of China's foreign direct investment in Ethiopia is fast becoming one of the prominent features of the Ethiopian economic landscape either by infrastructure in exchange for access to natural resources or by denoting Chinese development assistance or providing favorable lending and capital contribution.

However, though Ethiopia intends to use Chinese cooperative investment as means of enhancing its regional development, the inflow of Chinese investment has not been equally shared. Geographically, most of the Chinese Cooperative investments are located within the Addis Ababa and Oromia Regional State. While 78 of the wholly owned Chinese companies are located in the Addis Ababa Regional Zone and about 9 percent are situated in the Oromia Regional State, without any significant catching up by the other regional zones. In addition, of the 103 joint-venture companies, 53 percent are situated within the Addis Ababa region while 30 percent reside within the Oromia Regional State. In addition, 22 percent of the small- and medium-size state-owned Chinese Enterprises operating in Ethiopia are fully operational while the remaining 78 percent (647/828) are partially or yet to be fully implemented. To fully implement the various investments, the Chinese investors have employed 44 percent (52,714/119,670) as full-time workers and 56 percent (66,956/119,670) as temporary workers.

Ethiopia's main objectives for allowing Chinese investment to operate in country are to have access to high technology, to increase employment, to acquire know-how, to increase foreign exchange through export, and to benefit from both backward and forward linkages. Thus, the four Sino-Ethiopian Cooperative Investment case studies given above are analyzed in terms of their effects on 1) Ownership and Human Capital 2) Production Management and Operations, 3) Export effects 4)Technological Transfers 5) Efficiency 6) Foreign Exchange effects7) Local Content requirements and spillover effects, and 8) Environmental effects of the Sino-Ethiopian investments. However, since the analysis is based on four case studies, it needs to be underlined that the results of these case studies are anecdotally based and are not sufficient to generalize about characteristics of the entire Sino-Ethiopia Cooperative investments. Also, it needs to underlined that host countries will not be able to capture the full benefits associated with foreign direct investment until they reach a certain threshold level in terms of educational attainment, provision of infrastructure services, local technological capabilities, and development of local financial markets, thus the analytical outcome of this study needs to be considered tentative.

In terms of ownership and human capital, most of the Chinese investments are wholly owned. When Chinese enter a joint-venture or create a wholly owned subsidiary, they send experienced managers or top specialists from abroad. Based on the four case studies, while the CEOs of the three wholly owned Chinese companies are Chinese, the CEO of the Sino-Ethiopia Associate Africa joint-venture company is an Ethiopian. Given the Chinese investors in Ethiopia are unfamiliar with cultural makeup of the local situation and the Ethiopian labor laws that pertain to wages, holidays, housing and other benefits, in the solely owned Chinese firms and the joint venture firm, Ethiopian employees seemed to be in charge of the human resources management. In view of this, it can be assumed that there exists a smooth cross-cultural communication within the enterprises and between the enterprise and its external suppliers and customers.

The process of inviting foreign investors to developing countries is a means to increase the valued-added exports of the host country. Based on the Sino-Ethiopia Associate Africa pharmaceutical joint venture company, it is possible to argue that both partners handle the international marketing sector. Since the Chinese marketing officers are well versed in some aspects of the international marketing, they might have trained local employees in export management and foreign marketing strategies. Also, it is possible that local firms could have acquired international marketing techniques by hiring some of the Ethiopian workers who might have left the Sino-Ethiopian joint venture to start their own businesses. Nevertheless, since the three wholly owned enterprises mostly produce for the domestic market, it is very likely that they might have facilitated some type of interaction with local suppliers and domestic customers. It is likely that the wholly owned enterprises mostly produce for the Ethiopian domestic market and have done little to integrate Ethiopian products to the global value chain. Thus based on the three cases, it is possible to ascertain that the Chinese wholly owned companies don't seem to act as a platform for exports and their goal is to seek for themselves efficiency in their production process by taking care of Ethiopia's factors of endowment. The wholly owned Sino-Africa produces leather products that are designed to compete in the international market—it does not seem to crowd out the low quality local products. The Sino-Ethiopia pharmaceutical joint venture enterprise is of higher quality base and is more efficient; therefore, it is complementary and may generate foreign exchanges indispensable for the country. Nonetheless, since the Ethiopian employees do not receive the necessary training in international marketing know-how, the leather products seem to be totally dependent on the Chinese joint venture partners in order to promote and distribute their products in overseas markets. In addition, as argued by GebreEgzibher, "The major types of products exported to China are agricultural products which are unprocessed or semi-processed. These include skins, leather and leather products, oil seeds, pulses, coffee, and tantalum. The bulk of leather, skin, and hides are semi-processed. Ethiopia has huge potential in other products which are allowed to be exported to China.

These include coffee, natural gum, bee wax, edible oil, horticultural and textile products, precious stones, and other organic products." (2006)

Typically, the Chinese PLCs arrive in Africa with their work force. The project managers, engineers, and technicians working in Ethiopian government project contracts and wholly owned enterprises are mostly Ethiopians. On the other hand research and product design is forged in the headquarters rather than basing it on an equity ratio to include the Ethiopian partner. In terms of efficiency, since more than 50 percent of input materials executed by the Sino-Ethiopian firms come from China, it is very difficult to ascertain the contribution of efficiency to the new products made by the Sino-Ethiopian investments.

Most of the foreign exchange generally used for the Chinese investments in Ethiopia originates from the China's EXIM and China's development banks. For instance, Export-Import Bank of China has been granting long-term and short-term loans to companies investing abroad to purchase Chinese equipment and technology necessary to build factories abroad (Zhaoxi, 2009). Thus, the projects in Ethiopia have enabled it to conserve the foreign exchange, which it could have spent on establishing these projects, and helped it to acquire the necessary foreign exchange by selling some of the Sino-Ethiopian investment products in the overseas market.

While the dependency school theory views foreign investment from developed countries at the core of the world economic system as harmful to the long-term economic growth of developing countries out in the periphery, other studies seem to demonstrate that foreign direct investors can potentially benefit domestic firms through spillover effects. Spillover effects are therefore regarded as a very important conduit through which foreign direct investment promotes economic growth in the host country. Though the spillover effect of FDI on the productivity growth of local firms does not occur automatically (See, JBIC, 2002), based on the incentives given by the Ethiopian Government to Chinese investors, the four case studies utilize local content. Adhering to backward linkages, the Chinese investors purchase their factors of production from local suppliers. In addition, since they mostly sell their outputs in the domestic market, they have contributed to forward linkages. The four case studies act in creating complementary activities rather than "crowding out" domestic firms. In short, the Sino-Ethiopian foreign investments have forced local firms to restructure themselves to be more competitive and adequately fulfill the domestic demand, thereby maintaining their market shares. Thus, the Chinese investments have contributed to positive productivity spillovers to the Ethiopian economy.

Since the 1992 Earth Summit in Rio de Janeiro, the environmental and social dimensions of foreign investment have become a matter of intense controversy between certain home and host countries. For example in Ethiopia, to attract the Chinese investors, the Ethiopian government seems to covertly relax the enforcement of the environmental standards. The Chinese contractual-based projects, wholly owned, and the joint venture cases analyzed in this paper are by and large operating in ecologically sensitive regions. They are facing serious environmental problems because the Ethiopian Government seems to have prioritized its short-term economic growth over the achievement of environmentally sustainable economic growth in the long run. Ethiopian environmental protection officers at each level of the political system do not seem to fine Chinese investors for their transgressions or for negatively imprinting their environmental footprints on the country, or they fail to encourage the Chinese investors to adopt production techniques that are less harmful to the Ethiopian environment. Unlike other international financial institutions, the Chinese investors and financiers (such as the Export-Import Bank of China) fail to undertake their environmental guidelines when lending the concessional loans as part of the country's official development assistance program (See, Bosshard, 2008). Undoubtedly, Chinese investments in Ethiopia are an indispensable part of the economic system (they have contributed to infrastructural development, provide capital, new technologies, modern management know- how, and enhanced demonstration effects). Nonetheless, little or no attention is paid by the Ethiopian Government to check the environmental implications of most of the undertaken Sino-Ethiopian investment case studies.

It needs to be underlined here that host countries will not be able to capture the full benefits associated with foreign direct investment until they reach a certain threshold level in terms of educational attainment, provision of infrastructure services, local technological capabilities and development of local financial markets. As an essential element of avoiding economic and social disparities among the different regions, the Ethiopian government needs to enhance the attractiveness of Ethiopia's hinterland and other relatively neglected regions by 1) undertaking fundamental infrastructural development (i.e., electricity, water, good transport, and telecommunications), 2) improving and encouraging labor mobility to the undeveloped regions by creating schools, hospitals, parks, etc., 3) create local development agencies to promote FDI in each region. In short, further work is necessary to untangle the effects of social responsibility, to enforce environmental safeguards, to train local labor, and to transfer the technology of the Chinese cooperative investments into the Ethiopian economy.

Though anecdotally focused, the modest contributions upon which we hope other researchers will build is that more case studies need to be collected to analyze if Chinese investments in Ethiopia are politically motivated or are meant to fulfill the ideals of the SSC investments. Nonetheless, based on Lummumba-Kasongo's argument that according to the win-win approach theory, the SSC ventures are supposed to induce "...liberal economic cooperation through trade flows (export and import relations), foreign domestic flows, technology transfer and integration in global value chains, and aid flows, should bring proportional benefits, which otherwise the partners would not have access to before entering into these relations" (2007); it is possible to ascertain that in the short term Ethiopia has substantially benefited from the Chinese cooperative investments. Thus, the argument of the proponents of political warfare theory—that China's investment in Ethiopia would perpetuate underdevelopment through exploitation, extraction, and destruction of Ethiopia's resources and industrial capacity—needs to be challenged at this juncture. As outlined by China's politico-diplomatic "African Strategy," it is quite obvious that China has shown its strategic interest in Africa and has particularly mapped out its interest in Ethiopia. Except for their significant negative environmental effects it is perpetuating on the Ethiopian soil at this juncture, it possible to assert that China's investment in Ethiopia is closely aligning with the SSCs stated goals. In assessing the environmental impact, it should be noted that some of the negative externalities could have been easily corrected if the Ethiopian authorities had proactively asked the Chinese enterprises to adhere to the Chinese domestic environmental policy (See, Bosshard, 2008).

Thus, the tentative conclusion we can arrive at from the four case studies is that by using its new standards of economic diplomacy China is slowly gaining ground in Ethiopia. Nevertheless, it looks farfetched to make assertions like the proponents of "New Mercantilism" school of thought—that "China's rise confirms the current position of African countries: that of a commodity supplier and a modest consumer's market" (Holslag, 2006).

Chapter 11

ECONOMIC GROWTH FOR INFLATION: THE ETHIOPIAN DILEMMA

By and large, Ethiopia has recorded seventeen years of economic stagnation under the leadership of the Derg, a military government. For example, in 1990/91, the growth rate of the Ethiopian Gross Domestic Product (GDP) was -3.2 percent, cyclical unemployment was about 12 percent, the rate of inflation was about 21 percent, and the country's budget was at a deficit of 29 percent of GDP. For the last five years, contemporary Ethiopia has gathered momentum by recording a steady economic growth. Along with this growth, however, the country has seen an accelerated, double-digit increase in the price of goods and services. Thus, inflation has remained a scourge of the Ethiopian economy (See for example, Tadesse, 2008; Demissie, 2008; Goodo, 2008; Kassahun, 2002).

Stated in simple words, over the years, Ethiopia has been facing with an overheating economy. With the global soaring price of oil, wheat, corn, and minerals, this condition cannot be regarded as unique to the Ethiopian situation. What makes this a special case is that Ethiopia is a low-income country. The increase in National Consumer Price Index (the main gauge of inflation) has become very detrimental to the low-income groups and retirees who live off a fixed income. The risk of inflationary pressure is reducing the purchasing power of the Ethiopian birr. The inflation rate in Ethiopia was "almost 40 percent year-on-year,... driven largely by rapidly rising domestic food prices" (IMF,2008). Therefore, an item which used to cost one birr a year was costing one birr and 40 cents in 2008 to 2011. That is, the value of one birr was approximately 71 cents (i.e., 1/1.40).

Given that a large portion of county's population lives in absolute poverty (i.e., less than one dollar per day), it is time that the regime in power identifies the salient factors that might be contributing to inflation in Ethiopia. Also, it is absolutely vital that economic policymakers design strategies that could curtail the on-going erosion of purchasing power—to curb inflation before it deepens the economic crisis and contributes to political instability (Desta, 1993).

The focus of this chapter is to examine both the main causes and the consequences of existing inflationary pressure in Ethiopia. The first section provides the literature review, which briefly discusses the theoretical formulations of inflation as well as empirical findings in the context of the causes of inflation in developing countries. The second part provides empirical analysis of the determinants of inflation in Ethiopia using an econometric technique. The final section contains the conclusion of the study and provides some suggestions on how policymakers may control the current inflationary pressure in Ethiopia and prevent the resurgence of inflation at a minimum cost in terms of output loss.

Determinants of inflation

There are various theories proposed by various economists to explain the determinants of inflation. In this study, the various theories of inflation are grouped into a) inflation as an economic growth phenomenon, b) demand-pull and cost-push theories of inflation c) the monetarist explanation of the causes of inflation, and d) fiscal budget deficit as a source of inflationary pressure.

Inflation as an Economic Growth Phenomenon

From theoretical and empirical perspective, determining the direction of causality between economic growth and inflation in the developing countries is very controversial (e.g., Hossain & Chowdhurry, 1996). In 1950s, the Structuralist Economist view of inflation, as pioneered in Latin America, persuasively argued that moderate inflation and economic growth are positively related. This was in contradiction to the policy advice of the international lending institutions (Meier, 1995; Mallik & Chowdhurry, 2001). Stated in simple terms, inflation stimulates the economy since nominal wages may lag behind prices, allowing for slower adjustment to wage expectation.

Similarly, the Keynesian economic perspective assumed that moderate inflation might accelerate economic growth by raising the rate of profit, thus increasing private investment (Jung & Marshall, 1986). According to Meier, inflation accelerates economic growth in two ways: "by redistributing income from workers and peasants, who are assumed to have a low marginal propensity to save, to capitalist entrepreneurs, who have assumed to have a high marginal propensity to save and invest; and by raising the nominal rate of return on investment relative to the rate on interest, thus promoting investment" (1995). Capitalizing on the Keynesian theoretical framework, the ruling party in Ethiopia seems to attribute the surge in inflation to macroeconomic growth. As stated by Goodo, "The Ethiopian government admits that inflationary pressure has become very severe. However, it also claims that the economy has been growing at 10% for five consecutive years and it is healthy at present." (2008; Hassan, 2008).

Using the full-employment model, it is possible to assume that if a nation achieves full employment, economic growth is likely to precipitate an inflationary situation. Since the 10 percent increase in nominal GDP cannot keep pace with a 40 percent inflation rate, the acceleration of economic growth seems to be overstated. In fact, it is possible to assert that double digit inflation in Ethiopia is nothing but a clear sign of an unhealthy economy (See for example, Goodo, 2008). As persuasively argued by Barro, the inflationary situation in a country could have a negative-structural-break effect on economic growth, if the sustained increase in prices is more than 15 percent (1996).

The inflationary economic growth process generates distortions in the allocation of resources under the free market system. It may not bear fruit if the Ethiopian citizens do not "have confidence in the stability of the value of money, and . . . if inflationary financing is not accompanied by governmental policies of holding down the wage and interest costs of business enterprises" (Meier, 1995, pp. 180). It needs to be appreciated that following a rise in the Consumer Price Index, the Ethiopian government not only scrapped taxes on flour and grains but also started selling edible food items at subsidized prices in order to repress inflation. The government claims "greedy" businesses and speculators are the cause of the inflation. They subsidize food to placate the vulnerable urban poor and the salaried government employees. The efforts of the Ethiopian government to curtail inflation are in the right direction. However, the governmental subsidization programs may be effective only for a short period of time. They are likely to result in shortages; inefficient production and distribution; and black markets. To suggest possible solutions for curtailing inflation in the long run, the articulation and disarticulation between aggregate demand and aggregate supply will be investigated. Additionally, the monetary policy Ethiopia will be assessed in relation to the chronic inflation that has manifested in the country.

The demand-pull and cost-push factors for inflation

Keynesian economists often classify inflation according to the source of the inflationary pressures. The most straightforward method defines inflation in terms of sustained pressure from the demand side of the market or the supply side of the market. By and large, a rampant inflationary situation in any country occurs because of an imbalance between demand-pull and cost-push factors. The demand-pull inflation scenario occurs when a sustained increase in prices is preceded by a permanent acceleration of the nominal gross domestic prices growth (e.g., Gordon, 2009). Stated differently, inflation occurs when increases in total spending are not offset by increases in the supply of goods and services. When many consumers are trying to buy the same good, the price of that good inevitably increases, as there is a limited supply. Also, demand-pull inflation could be a result of an increase in consumer and business confidence, an increase in the money supply, and/or government budget deficits.

On the other hand, cost-push inflation is an increase in production costs that force firms to raise prices to avoid losses. In broad aggregate terms, these could be as a result of increase in wages, energy shocks, weather shocks, increase in the prices of agricultural inputs, or import price hikes, which might cause exchange rate depreciation or a decline in land holding sizes. While the demand-pull explanation suggests restrictive monetary and fiscal policies, the cost-push theory endorses price formation and wage determination as stabilizing mechanisms.

Inflation as a monetary phenomenon

According to Monetarist economists, in every case where the inflation rate of a country is high for any sustained period of time, its rate of money supply growth is also high (e.g., Friedman, 1959). In accordance with this, the National Bank of Ethiopia has recently responded by tightening the monetary policy in order to tackle the chronic level of inflation. However, to examine if a relaxed monetary policy has been the source of inflation in Ethiopia, the role played by financial and non-financial intermediaries in the supply of money stock needs to be factored out.

In Ethiopia, financial intermediaries may accelerate inflation if the National Bank of Ethiopia relaxes its financial and monetary policies that regulate the Ethiopian financial intermediaries to maintain the statutory liquidity requirement of demand and time deposits. In addition, an increase in money supply could accelerate inflation if the central bank substantially reduces the discount rate or buys existing government bonds from investors. The discount rate is the interest rate charged by the National Bank of Ethiopia when member banks borrow from it.

As shown in Table 11.1, Ethiopia seems to have been driven into an inflationary trap because there was an increase in the country's broad money supply (i.e., currency in circulation, demand deposits, savings deposits, and time deposits) from 19.4 percent in 2002 to 23.3 percent in 2006. That is, Ethiopian banks adopted a relaxed monetary policy to help promote the financial markets.

Ethiopian banks overused their reserve facilities to boost their credit portfolio (Teshome, 2008). The excess reserve in Ethiopia occurred due to more savings. As persuasively argued by Demissie, "the demand for bank credit rose sharply to finance large-scale investment projects by the public enterprises and the rapidly expanding private sector. Substantial negative real interest rates and commercial banks' excess reserves facilitated the rapid expansion of credit" (2008).

From 2002 to 2006, Ethiopia's real GDP increased by 6.8 percent (See Table 1). Instead of adjusting the money stock with the increase in GDP, the country's money supply accelerated by about 18 percent, contributing to an average 12 percent increase in the rate of inflation. The link between money supply and other determinants of growth is not an automatic process. However, if we abide by the principles of the transmission mechanism, we might argue that the increase in money supply in Ethiopia might have contributed to an increase in investment. However, the problem of inflation in the Ethiopian environment cannot be tackled without addressing the large budget deficit.

TABLE 11.1: ETHIOPIA'S GDP, INFLATION, BROAD MONEY, PUBLIC FINANCE, INVESTMENT, SAVINGS, AND CURRENT ACCOUNT BALANCE, 2001-2007

YEAR	REAL GDP GROWTH RATE (%)	INFLATION RATE (%)	BROAD MONEY INCREASE (%)	GOV'T BUDGET/ GDP (%)	GROSS CAPITAL FORMATION, % GDP	DOMESTIC SAVING, % GDP	CURRENT ACCOUNT BALANCE (%)/ GDP
2001/02	1.6[d]	7.2[b]	19.4[b]				
2002/03	-4.5[b]	15.1[b]	12.3[b]				
2003/04	11.5[b]	8.6[b]	20.0[b]	-7.4[d]	12.4[d]	5.4[d]	
2004/05	10[c]	9.2[c]	16.4[b]	-5.8[d]	11.4[d]	2.6[d]	-9.1[a]
2005/06	9.7[c]	9.0[c]	23.3[b]	-7.4[d]	11.4[d]	5.2[d]	-10.2[a]
2006/07	9.0[a]	18.0[a]	29.7	-5.8[d]	12.0[d]	8.1[d]	-14.4[a]

Notes: [a] Economic Intelligence Unit (1997, 1998, 1999, 2006). Ethiopia: Country outlook. *EIU Views Wire.* [b] International Monetary Fund (2008, April). *International Financial Statistics.* [c] The World Bank Group (2007, April). Ethiopia. *World Development Indicator Database.* [d1] International Monetary Fund (2007, June 15). [d2] AfDB/OECD (2007). African economic outlook: Ethiopia.

Fiscal Deficit and Inflation

Tax levy in underdeveloped countries is generally very low. In addition, a government cannot or does not find it politically feasible to raise taxes when it needs to increase government spending. During wartime, the need to rapidly increase military spending results in government expenditures rising faster than tax revenues. The desire of the government to reduce taxes in the face of a continued high level of spending can lead to large budget deficits. Large budget deficits can be the source of inflationary monetary policy. As argued by Meier, "When financing of government expenditures by money creation exceeds the non-inflationary limit, total spending in the country becomes greater than production valued at stable prices (1995, pp. 176; see also Johnson, 1966).

To promote more investment; to maintain law and order within its highly volatile domestic environment; and to ascertain peace and tranquility with its neighbors, the Ethiopian government has been running a budget deficit of between five and six percent of GDP per year (See Table 11.1). Government deficit could be financed by selling government savings bonds (monetization of the debt) if there is a highly developed capital market. However, capital markets barely exist in Ethiopia. Thus, the Ethiopian government has either depended on external sources of finance or has financed its budget deficit by printing high-powered money (currency and deposits at the National Bank), which serves as a reserve for commercial banks and allows commercial banks to expand their loans (Johnson, 1966; Meier, 1995, pp. 177; Hassan, 2008). Since donor funds have not greatly increased in 2007/08, it is reasonable to assume that the government's commitment to finance large-scale capital projects and infrastructure improvements has contributed to the sustained inflationary period (AfDB/OECD, 2007).

Methodology and Data Analysis

To determine the factors that have contributed to inflation in Ethiopia, time series data (1991-2 to 2006-7) are used. The main source of data is from the World Bank, International Monetary Fund, and the Ethiopian Statistical Office. The regression coefficients are estimated using ordinary least squares. Based on the theoretical and empirical discussion presented above, the inflation function for Ethiopia has been specified using the following econometric model:

$$\text{INF Rate}_t = \beta\, GDP_{t-1} + \beta\, IM_{t-1} + \beta\, BD_{t-1} + \beta\, LR_{t-1} + \beta\, MS_{t-1} + \beta\, EX_{t-1} + \mu_t \ldots$$

Where

INF RATE = Ethiopia's Consumer Price Index (1992/93-2007/8)

GDP = Real GDP growth rate (%), 1992/93 - 2006/7

IM = Import /GDP (%), 1992/93 to 2006/7

BD = Government budget/GDP (%), (1992/93 to 2006/7

LR = Lending interest rate (%), 1992/93 to 2006/7
EX = Nominal Exchange rate, 1992/93 to 2006/7
β = Standardized coefficient data
μ= represents all relevant variables omitted from the model as well as random errors

As shown above, the predictor variables which are lagged by one year include real GDP, nominal exchange rate, money supply, lending interest rate, government budget/GDP (%), foreign exchange rate. Ethiopia's consumer price index (CPI) is the dependent variable. Instead of GDP deflator, CPI is used to gauge the inflation rate in Ethiopia because it reflects the real prices faced by the Ethiopian consumers.

To standardize and adequately represent the constructs under study, the dependent and independent variables depicted in the above regression equations are estimated based on percentage increase rate. The relative influence of the predictors on the dependent variable (the level of inflation in Ethiopia using annual data for the period 1991-2 to 2007-8) is ascertained by using beta coefficients. Holding other variables constant, beta coefficients measure change in the dependent variable (in standard deviation units) for a unit of change in each explanatory variables. In short, since beta coefficients are independent of the units of measurement of each explanatory variables they are used to compare compared the effects of the independent variables on the dependent variable directly.

As shown in Table 11. 2, the model explains 69 percent of the determinants of inflation rate in Ethiopia. In the Ethiopian economic environment, as real GDP increases by 1 percent, inflation measured by the consumer price index increased by 0.04 percent. Though not statistically significant, it shows that real GDP propagates inflation in Ethiopia. Also, as import to Ethiopia increased by 1 percent, inflationary pressure was engendered by 1.5 percent. In addition, as exchange rate depreciated by 1 percent, inflationary situation in Ethiopia hiked by 1.5 percent. In recent years, since Ethiopia is attempting to be an open economy, its inflationary instability is heavily dependent on external trade. The depreciation of the *birr* over the period under review implies that the price of imported commodities has increased when expressed in local currency. Therefore, inflation in Ethiopia is subjected to inflationary impulses transmitted by the average prices of imported goods and services that are purchased from abroad.

Table 11.2: Regression results (coefficients)

Model	Un-standardized Coefficients B	Std. Error	Standardized Coefficients Beta (B)	T	Sig.
(Constant)	14.349	9.851		1.457	.183
Real GDP	.050	.238	.038	.209	.840
Import	1.155	.293	1.479	3.938	.004*
GD (budget deficit)	.745	.589	.230	1.264	.242
Broad Money	.339	.225	.257	1.503	.171
Exchange rate	5.839	1.535	1.514	3.802	.01*
Lending Interest rate	-.969	.354	-.475	-2.74	.03*

* significant at .05 level

Inf Rate = .038GDP + 1.479IM + .230GD + .257MS + 1.514EX -.475LR
t-value (.209) (3.938) ((1.264) (1.503) (3.802) (-2.74)
Adjusted R Square = 0.69 F =6.227 Sig. at 0.01 level, N=15

The results also show that as banks increases their lending rates to their domestic customers by 1 percent, inflation pressure in Ethiopia declined by 0.5 percent. In line with the monetarist point of view, as money supply increases, inflation pressure in Ethiopia has been increasing. Also, since deficit financing of the government is positively related to inflation, it could be argued that monetary policy in Ethiopia is to a large extent based on the discretion of the government instead of being independently determined by the country's National Bank.

Summary and policy implications

For the last five years, Ethiopia has recorded sustaining economic growth. Moderate inflation is an inevitable consequence of sustained economic growth. It can enhance economic growth by mobilizing the resources of a country. However, inflation in Ethiopia is beyond the break-even point. Instead of stimulating economic growth, inflationary pressure in Ethiopia seems to be on the verge of distorting the allocation of resources and is likely to be a deterrent to undertaking productive investments.

Based on the multiple regression analysis results, it is quite clear that the main determinants of inflation in Ethiopia are real GDP, percentage increase of the exchange rate (exchange rate of the Ethiopian birr against the US Dollar), and the domestic lending interest rate used as a proxy for broad money supply. Though it is very difficult to document, the inflow remittance through the informal channels from abroad might have contributed to the soaring of prices in the Ethiopian market of goods and services. Thus, the lesson to be ascertained from this analysis is that to successfully jump out of the inflationary trap, the Ethiopian monetary authorities need to tighten the stock of money in the country. In other words, a tight monetary policy could serve as an anchor for inflationary pressure in Ethiopia.

Therefore, as a partial solution to the inflationary pressure in Ethiopia, it could be suggested that let the National Bank of Ethiopia be allowed to function as an institutionally independent body. That is, the National Bank of Ethiopia could be made to be immune from political pressures to tighten its monetary policy, such as auditing of financial institutions to maintain reserve requirements or forcing banks to indulge in prudent lending procedures. However, it needs to be underlined that granting legal independence to a central bank is not sufficient to keep monetary policy effective on a sustained basis unless the central bank also dominates the fiscal policy of the government. In other words, the framework of fiscal policy should result in a monetarily dominant regime. Granting legal independence to the central bank, the fiscal policy regime must be such that it does not allow changes in the price level to become the mechanism through which the condition for government solvency is satisfied (Canzoneri et al., 1998).

With a substantial increase in prices, Ethiopian banks are on the verge of lending to the least solvent borrowers to keep from bankrupting themselves. In addition, as the value of the domestic currency depreciates, domestic savers may decide to invest abroad. Rampant inflation proliferates inefficiencies and disrupts investment. It takes time and proper policy to adequately damp inflationary fires. The supporting price controls implemented by the Ethiopian Government as knee-jerk responses to inflation might be effective for a short period of time. In fact, political and economic agitators may be calmed by government subsides, supplements, and price floors, as well as an increase in interest rates and reserve requirements. Banning speculators in futures trading of edible products and preventing rising prices with government subsides might not halt the rampant inflation. Inflation creates more inflation unless long-term stabilization programs are pursued. Since current inflation causes inflationary expectations. The current inflation rate in Ethiopia can therefore be partly explained by its past history of inflation and the various relative price and institutional adjustments such as indexation of wages, government subsidies, financial contracts, monetary and exchange rate policies which the government might have taken over the years to deter inflation. In other words, based on rational expectation theory we can assume that the Ethiopian people may use all available information including that about current policies to forecast the future.

Therefore a stabilization program to mitigate the inflationary situation in Ethiopia may include a drastic cut in the money supply, reducing government expenditures and a further devaluation of the currency. As shown above, the minor currency depreciation in Ethiopia has lead to a high cost of imported materials for production, which are ultimately passes onto higher prices for goods and services. As indicated before, these policies can have their own inertia and usually induce an unexpected inflation. But they have to be undertaken in order suppress the evolving inflationary pressures encountered by the country.

However, since a large portion of inflation in Ethiopia is due to a price surge in edible and finished products, one of the long run strategies for suppressing inflation and increasing employment in Ethiopia is to balance the aggregate demand with long-run aggregate supply. Aggregate demand is a combination of the price level and real output at which the money and commodity markets are both in equilibrium (Gordon, 2009).

Though not included in the model due to lack of data, with limited land holding, massive land degradation, soil nutrient depletion, and inefficient production techniques, based on the law of diminishing returns, it is possible to argue that, despite economic growth, rapid population growth in Ethiopia might have contributed to low agricultural productivity. For example, the food estimate for the 2004/05 periods in Ethiopia indicates that while the population increased at about 2.5 percent, the food production grew at 3.7 percent (ESSGA, 2006). When compared with the eruption of population in Ethiopia, the food growth is at the margin to provide adequate nutrition (Worku, 2000). In addition, while cereal production in Ethiopia increased by 17.7 percent from 2005 to 2007, the prices of cereals jumped by 15 percent. This is both due to increases in the price of fuel oil and fertilizers, as well as inefficient market structures (Teshome, 2008).

Due to the diversification of the commodity export base that Ethiopia is pursuing under the Agricultural Development Led Industrialization (ADLI) paradigm, farm exports have grown on average by 25 percent (Tadesse, 2008). Nonetheless, it needs to be underlined here that due to an extensive use of chemical fertilizers, the limited rural Ethiopian land is currently facing a number of environmental challenges. The challenges range from land degradation to environmental pollution. Due to the misguided application of chemicals in agriculture, it is estimated that Ethiopia has accumulated one of the largest stockpiles of obsolete pesticides on the African continent (Edwards, 2004). Therefore, we can argue that the sharp increase in the price of agricultural outputs could be attributed to the limited production technologies currently available in rural Ethiopia.

What is more, Ethiopia is indulged on growing horticulture commodities in order to diversify its exports and earn foreign exchange. Given this, Ethiopian farmers are reducing the production of more essential edibles. Instead, they harbor the production of horticultural commodities in order to amass strong foreign currency. More particularly, most of the agricultural land in the proximity of highways is tailored to the production of horticultural crops (i.e., floriculture fruits and vegetables) for export. The reduction of its limited land holdings to the production of horticulture products instead of edible food items has accentuated the price of the staple products. Taking the best land in order to secure the best financial returns by growing floriculture is morally wrong. Since the market for horticultural products is strongly dependent upon knowledge, human capital, and technical inputs, "small producers are frequently eliminated from markets for failure to understand market dynamics or because of their inability to meet new production, sanitary, and quality standards" (USAID, 2005). Given this fact, it can be argued that in the long run, the dependency of Ethiopian farmers on the production of horticultural commodities is not only less lucrative but also environmentally costly. For instance, the pattern was the same in other similar countries that imported agro-chemicals (viz., herbicides, pesticides, and fertilizers) for horticultural products. They would not only exhaust the productivity growth of their agricultural land, but also create toxic and hazardous waste that could pollute the surrounding environment and damage human health (e.g., Desta, 1998; Edwards, 2004).

If Ethiopia is to achieve long-term sustainable growth, its developmental process has to be rooted in the Ethiopian system of thought and its people-centered approach, rather than depending on the Western capitalist model of industrialization by invitation to gain various forms of external assistance. Since agriculture is the backbone of the Ethiopian economy, its sustainable development model must be one of self-sufficiency—to feed its own people instead of producing environmentally-insensitive horticultural products to amass foreign currency. Contrary to expectations, Ethiopian horticultural commodities are sold at very low prices. Additionally, they lack markets to absorb production, often involve a large number of middlemen, and lack marketing institutions to safeguard farmers (Gebremedhin, 2007).

Given the resources and techniques of production, the Ethiopian agricultural sector seems to have exhausted its productivity growth. To improve productivity under these conditions would require substantial investment in research and development. For example, since deforestation, desertification, increase in population, shortage of water, and air-related disease are to a large extent the symptoms of poverty, the poor need to be organized to formulate and implement their own development strategies and ensure that their basic needs are fulfilled.

Based on land security and adhering to environmentally-sensitive, cooperatively-managed systems, it is reasonable to assume that Ethiopia would not only achieve growth and equity (with full employment and modest inflation) but could also empower the Ethiopian people to fully participate in the design and management of long-lasting development paradigms (Kofi & Desta, 2008).

FIGURE 11.3: ETHIOPIA'S GDP, INFLATION, BROAD MONEY, GOVERNMENT BUDGET DEFICIT, POPULATION GROWTH RATE, EXCHANGE RATE, IMPORTS/GDP (%)

YEAR	REAL GDP GROWTH RATE (%)	INFLATION RATE (%)	NOMINAL EXCHANGE RATE $ = BIRR	BROAD MONEY INCREASE (%)	GOV. BUDGET DEFICIT/GDP (%)	POP. GROWTH RATE	EXC. RATE	IMPORT/ GDP (%)
1991/92	-3.7b	20.8b	2.07b	17.0b	-9.6b	2.8b	2.07b	10.7b
1992/93	12.0	10.1	5.00	19.0	-7.6	2.8	5.1	16.9
1993/94	1.7	1.1	5.77	18.4	-11.1	2.8	6.22	21.5
1994/95	5.4	13.4	6.25	26.5	-4.00	2.8	6.32	23.5
1995/96	10.6	-2.6	6.32	18.4	-8.3	2.7	6.35	23
1996/97	5.2	-1.4	6.50	15.9	-5.2	2.8	6.78	25.5
1997/98	-1.4	3.9	6.88	27.6	-4.5	2.6	7.09	25.3
1998/99	6.0	4.8	7.51	14.3	-8.7	2.9	8.12	28.9
1999/00	5.4	6.2	8.14	14.3	-11.7	3.1	8.23	30.0
2000/01	7.7	-5.2	8.33	10.5	-5.5	2.7	8.47	29.9
2001/02	1.2d	-7.2b	8.543	19.4b	-9.3	2.7	8.57	34.1
2002/03	-3.8b	15.1b	8.581	12.3[b]	-8.7	2.7	8.61	44.5
2003/04	11.5b	8.6b	8.62	10.9[b]	-7.4[d]	2.6	8.63	40.2
2004/05	10.0c	9.2c	8.65	19.6[b]	-5.8[d]	2.5	8.67	29.0
2005/06	9.7	12.3c	8.68	17.4[b]	-7.4[d]	2.6	8.69	40.0
2006/07	9.0	17.0a	9.20	29.7	-5.8[d]	2.5	9.20	42.0
2007/08	20.10							

Notes: [a] Economic Intelligence Unit (1997, 1998, 1999, 2006). Ethiopia: Country outlook. EIU Views Wire., [b] International Monetary Fund (2008, April). International Financial Statistics. [c] The World Bank Group (2007, April). Ethiopia. World Development Indicator Database. [d1] International Monetary Fund (2007, June 15). [d2] AfDB/OECD (2007). African economic outlook: Ethiopia.

Chapter 12

THE VIABILITY OF MALAYSIAN DEVELOPMENT STATE FOR AFRICA IN AN ERA OF ECONOMIC GLOBALIZATION

Despite the pursuit of advancement since political independence in the late 1950s, it is very sad to see that a number of African countries are falling behind in human development. For example, the number of extremely poor in Sub Saharan Africa (SSA) has increased from two hundred million to about three hundred and eighty million between 1981 and 2005 (World Bank, 2009). To revitalize Africa's development process and galvanize its people in the 21st century, the Economic Commission for Africa (ECA) has challenged the African states to refute the canons of Neo-liberal policies of the Washington Consensus, which has submerged them into a deep chasm of economic crisis. Instead, it has encouraged the African countries to use the Malaysia developmental state, in collaboration with democratic political values and a system of good governance, promoting the rule of law, with transparency and a free flow of information.

However, in view of the 1997 financial crisis in East Asia and the current economic slowdown in the Japanese economy that has occurred because of globalization, the developmental state model's contribution to high economic growth is now called into question as an absolute, and challenged as irrelevant for application elsewhere. Similarly, a neo-mercantilist model which served the East Asian region for the past four decades as financier, planner and the producer of goods and services, and preserved social solidarity and ethnic cohesion, has now exhausted its effectiveness because the current global economy is fundamentally market-driven and not state engineered (Pang, 2000). In addition, as stated by Pang, the Asian Developmental state model has become incompatible with current globalization because it has encouraged clienteles, cronyism, cartels, official and unofficial favoritism for business firms, and gives state patronage to certain ethnic groups (2000). The purpose of the research described herein is to map out the reasons why a number of scholars and policy makers still strongly argue that the Developmental state model which contributed to the East Asian miracle of high economic growth could still be relevant in an age of globalization for Africa provided the paradigm is adjusted to integrate democratic values and administered by good governance (Meles, 2006; Economic Commission for Africa, 2011; Teshome, A., 2012).

This Chapter proceeds as follows. The first part of the Chapter maps out briefly the various economic development blue prints that have been attempted in Africa since its political independence in the late 1950s. The second part explores the trajectory of the Malaysian Developmental state model. Using the Malaysian developmental state framework, the third part of the Chapter outlines the framework of the Malaysian Developmental State model that has been suggested for Africa's development in the 21st century.

Major Economic Development Blueprints Attempted in Africa

After most African countries achieved their political independence from colonial rule in the late 1950s, the first generation of post-colonial African leaders overwhelmingly used a state-centric developmental model to promote nation-building and foster the unification of their multi-ethnic and multi-religious societies (Laakso, L. and Olukoshi, A. O., 1996). More specifically, to achieve what was described as Africa's development decade, most of the independent African states followed Arthur Lewis' Dual-Sector structural economic model, which was heavily endorsed by the United Nations and other funding agencies as the general theory of development that could mechanically transform the Anglo-Saxon development models for Third World nations.

Briefly stated, the presumption of Lewis' model was that a poor country's economy contained two sectors – a small "capitalist" and a very large "traditional" (agricultural) sector – from which the marginal production of labor was at its minimum. Based on this assumption, Lewis argued that in order to be transformed structurally, developing countries must be converted from an agricultural to an industrial economy in order to use the surplus labor available in the rural sector to enhance capitalistic development in the urban sector. Because of the lack of indigenous private entrepreneurs in Africa in the early 1960s, state intervention in the economy was considered a legitimate strategy to ensure the economic growth that was vital to the delivery of services to African communities (Maphunye, April, 2009; Kofi and Desta, 2008). However, Lewis' model, which is also known as the industrialization of Africa by invitation, failed to materialize in Africa because the model neglected to recognize the importance of agriculture as it simply emphasized an infusion of capital rather than the means to achieve it. Also, irrespective of their industrialization pretensions, the African states that emerged from colonialism were mainly predatory states, highly driven to maximize rent for the ruling classes rather than fulfilling the needs of the down-trodden masses (Meles, 2006).

In the 1970s, the African states attempted to transform their economic system based on the "import substitution model." That is, the African nations initiated a strategy for their domestic industrial growth by reducing the imports of manufactured products and saving foreign exchange. Furthermore, instead of using Gross Domestic Product as a means of measuring the stages of economic growth and to assess people-oriented development, they used the physical Quality of Life Index, composed of the literacy rate, life expectancy, and infant mortality.

However, as a result of oil shocks, political turmoil, and drought, many African economies were weakened in the 1980s. For example, the GDP in sub-Saharan Africa fell from 4.2 percent per annum in the period 1965-1980 to only 2.1 percent in the years 1980-1990, while population in Africa increased by 3 percent and agricultural production hovered around 2 percent per annum (Berry, S., 1995).

Therefore after three decades, it was found that the top-bottom ideological commitment of massive state intervention in the political, economic and social aspects had not only adversely affected the industrialization of Africa but also had an insignificant effect on the desired developmental objectives of eradicating poverty, ignorance and disease. As a result, the African nations were forced to search for a new political economy. They designed the Lagos Plan of Action which emphasized self-reliance and self-sustaining growth based on integrated and dynamic national, sub-regional and regional markets (Adedeji, A., 1985, P.15).

Due to the global economic recession which ensued in the 1980s and 1990s and in order to borrow financial capital from international financial institutions, the African states had no choice but give up the Lagos Plan of Action and embrace the Structural Adjustment Programs (SAP) designed by the International Monitory Fund (IMF) and the World Bank. Briefly stated, the Structural Adjustment Programs, premised on the Neo-liberal model, is also known as the Washington Consensus. It was premised on the assumption that the existence of a) free market systems, b) the privatization of state-owned enterprise, c) promotion of free trade, d) export promotion, and e) the creation of a conducive environment for direct foreign investment, would restore internal and external macroeconomic stability and accelerate economic growth in the long run.

Since the SAP did not take into consideration the African culture and organizational set-up (Deng, L.A., 1998), African states were overwhelmed with the adoption of the SAP. That is, the state's autonomy was eroded and its capacity to foster a developmental agenda was inhibited. In their decision-making process, the African technocrats were partially dominated by and became more accountable to the bureaucrats in international development agencies instead of to their people (Edigheji, 2005). Due to the misuse of abundant resources, rampant unemployment, and the deep recession that followed the implementation of the SAP, Africa's GDP growth rate was drastically reduced to less than 0.5 percent per annum, while Africa's debt as a percentage of GNP increased from 28.6 percent in 1980 to 107.9 percent in 1991. Its ratio of debt to its total exports increased from 96.6 percent in 1980 to 329.4 percent in 1991 (Berry, S., 1995; Kofi and Desta, 2008; and the World Bank, 1980-93). Not only was the political space contrived but entrepreneurial creativity and ingenuity were stifled, and a number of African states became unstable, ruled by military dictators and despots.

To address the low level of economic growth, lack of infrastructure, and political instability that characterized the African continent, the Economic Commission for Africa (2011), hereafter referred to as the African Commission, persuasively challenged the African states to refute the canons of Neo-liberal policies of the Washington Consensus and encouraged them to use the Malaysia developmental state in order to revitalize their economies and reframe their political system to address the basic tenets of democracy and good governance.

The Malaysian Developmental State for Africa

Economically, Malaysia was chosen as the role model for Africa to jump from agriculture -intensive economy to an industrialized and knowledge-based economy in the 21st Century, because like most African states, about five decades ago, Malaysia was heavily dependent on agriculture. However, upon its disillusionment with the Western model of development, Malaysia under the leadership of Prime Minister Mahathir Mohammed (1981-2003) started looking at the developmental interventionist state as the means to industrialize the Malaysian state. That is, Malaysia focused on the institutional and sociopolitical bases of Japan and South Korean states. Malaysia pursued the Japanese developmental state because it was based on: 1) a meritocratic bureaucracy of autonomous government elites (i.e., not elected but less subject to the influence of the corporate class or working class through the political process), 2) economic nationalism (a desire to catch up with the United States of America), 3) an industrial policy of governmental guidance and supervision that functioned with an unusual degree of public-private cooperation, 4) the protection of collective group interests to beget a culture of job over profit, with unhindered access to the U.S. markets (See Pang, 2000; Johnson,1982; Fingleton, 1996). In addition, the South Korean developmental state model was also considered because it emphasized the state bureaucracy's active role in economic growth and industrial transformation (Hyun-Chin, L and Jin-Ho, J., (2006).

To facilitate its industrialization process, the Malaysian Government invited Japanese and South Korean experts to provide technical assistance to the governmental and private sectors and to train the Malaysian labor force. A number of Malaysian students were also sent to Japan and South Korea to be trained in a number of vocational and tertiary institutions so that after their training they could reenergize Malaysia to pursue an effective developmental state (Zalanga, (2012). Domestically, the Malaysian Government embarked on socializing its work force to be well versed in Japanese and South Korea work ethics, values, and managerial styles. Therefore, based on Prime Minister Mahathir Mohammed's instruction, Malaysia adopted a "Look East" policy to emulate Japan and South Korea's developmental state efforts.

Africa's past challenges with despotic rulers, a one-party state and other forms of authoritarian domination denied the continent's citizens the opportunities and the basic rights to play meaningful roles in their countries' governing processes (Maphunye, April, 2009, p.44). However, unlike the pseudo democratic government that exists in Malaysia and other East Asian countries, the African Commission pointed out that an ideal democratic state and good governance is crucial for sustained growth in Africa. In addition, to reconcile its state interventionist economic model with democracy and to achieve Africa's sustainable development at the end of such integration, it was suggested that there should be a harmonious relationship between a capable bureaucracy and state-business in Africa.

Finally, to achieve an economic renaissance like Malaysia's, the African Commission has encouraged the African developmental states to attract foreign investors to provide capital, management, and marketing expertise so that the states may effect the structural transformation they so need and desire. To stimulate investor-friendly environments conducive to foreign investors, African countries were also encouraged to have fully equipped infrastructures, trained human capital, and politically stable environments that have well established rules of law, independent judiciary system, and effective regulatory bodies (2011).

In recent years, because of the financial crisis in Asia and economic slowdown of the Japanese economy, it is widely proclaimed that the state guidance of all economic activities in East Asia that contributed to the East Asian miracle of high economic growth is being challenged. Also, in an age of economic globalization, the East Asian developmental model is considered now to be outdated.

As argued by Pang, the neo-mercantilist model, which served the region for the past four decades, has exhausted its effectiveness. It must be acknowledged that the global economy is fundamentally market-driven, not state-promoted. The state needs to reduce voluntarily its role as financier, planner, and producer of goods and services. The state should not row, but steer social solidarity and ethnic cohesion should be preserved and built on economic dynamism and income equity (Pang (2000), and needs to adhere to democratic values and good governance.

The comparison of the developmental strategies of Malaysia and African states is based on the following characteristics of the developmental state model as suggested by Johnson (1982), Wade (1990), Fingleton (1996) and Dadzie (2012). According to their assessment, a developmental state is:

- autonomous and heavily involved in a macroeconomic planning process, needed to promote structural transformation and which plays a strategic role in economic development;
- staffed by highly qualified, professional government elites (i.e., insulated from the political process and not influenced by politicians, workers or the corporate class through the political process) who are given sufficient latitude to develop initiatives and operate effectively;
- selfless in designing strategic visions, planning innovative processes, formulating appropriate policies and implementing plans to transform their societies;
- a catalyst for efficiently executing the developmental (industrialization) goals of the nation;
- democratic, allowing the citizens to play meaningful roles in the country's governance process;
- encouraging to public-private strategic coalitions or cooperatives that are shaped by societal forces;
- supportive of entrepreneurs who undertake risky ventures;
- equipped with infrastructures, trained human and social capital and politically stable environments to entice foreign investors with capital, management, and marketing expertise to invest in the country.

Chapter 13

THE CONTINUING SAGA OF GLOBALISM: COMPARING ETHIOPIA'S DEVELOPMENTAL STATE STRATEGIES TO MALAYSIA

As discussed in detail in the first part of Chapter 13, it was proposed by the Economic Commission for Africa (2011) that African States would catch up and accomplish a vibrant economic system if they could emulate the Malaysia developmental state model along with addressing democratic values that would allow the citizens to play meaningful roles in the country's governance process. With this understanding in mind, the purpose of this Chapter is to assess if 1) Ethiopia has established the groundwork necessary for the implementation of a developmental state that is similar to the Malaysian developmental state model? and 2) Unlike the East Asian authoritarian developmental state which have postponed democracy until economic development is achieved, is the Ethiopian developmental state model moving towards establishing a participatory democratic developmental state?

The comparison of the developmental strategies of Malaysia and Ethiopia is based on the following characteristics of developmental state model as suggested by, Johnson (1982), Wade (1990), Fingleton (1996) and Dadzie (2012). A developmental state

- is autonomous and is heavily involved in macroeconomic planning process needed

- to harness structural transformation and plays a strategic role in economic development;
- is staffed by highly qualified professional governmental elites (i.e., insulted from the political process and not influenced by politician, the workers and corporate class through the political process) which are given sufficient scope to take initiatives and operate effectively;
- is selfless in designing strategic visions, planning process, formulating appropriate policies and implementing plans to transform their societies;
- is a catalyst for efficiently executing the developmental (industrialization) goals of the nation;
- is democratic and allows the citizens to play meaningful roles in the country's governance process;
- encourages public-private strategic coalitions or cooperation that are shaped by societal forces;
- supported entrepreneurs to take risky ventures, but the state would resort to taking risk;
- is equipped with infrastructures, trained human and social capital and politically stable environments to entice foreign investors with capital, management, and marketing expertise to invest in the country.

More specifically, to assess the Ethiopian developmental states based on the attributes forwarded by the Economic Commission for Africa the following vital questions are used:

1. Is Ethiopia's commitment to the democratic development state goal supported and has a strong vision that is tailored to trigger a process of profound societal transformation?
2. Is the developmental state planning process in Ethiopia designed by competent, efficient and autonomous professional bureaucrats that work collaboratively with the private sector in policy making efforts?
3. Is the developmental state plan in Ethiopia managed by competent and professional bureaucrats that are solely recruited on meritocracy to work autonomously—free from forming close relations with the politico-legislative elites?
4. Are the Ethiopian bureaucratic elites devoid of corruption and rent-seeking mechanism in order to effectively manage and perform their duties?
5. To attract foreign investors with capital, management, and marketing expertise, is the Ethiopian environment equipped with investor-friendly permissive environments equipped that include 1) the neces-

sary infrastructures, 2) trained human capital, and 3) a politically stable environment that includes well established rules of law and other social accountability stand?

6. Is the Ethiopian developmental state operating in a democratization process that calls for accountability, transparency and the participation of the public in policy-making?

THE VISION OF A DEVELOPMENTAL STATE

The history of development in Malaysia points out that an important recipe for development rests on state action. That is, the state action in industrial upgrading, employment generation, reduction of inequality, and the protection of civil liberties is regarded as the necessary condition to escape underdevelopment. Embedded with the private sector ingenuity, the autonomous public sector in Malaysia has been used as a catalyst for development to meet the overarching the 2020 Malaysia developmental Vision. That is, the 2020 Malaysian Vision was planned by the Malaysian government to make the country be a fully developed nation and facilitate growth with improved equity and poverty reduction in the Malaysian nations. As a result, the preponderance of economic coordination and due to judicious state intervention within the Malaysian developmental state, schools, roads, health centers and public housing has made a steady transition from poverty to achieving its developmental state agenda (Khoo, S. 2007).

As in Malaysia, since 2004, Ethiopia has identified agricultural development-led industrial development as a priority policy. Recently, the policy makers in Ethiopia have embarked on the five-year Growth and Transformation Plan (GTP) for the period 2010/11 to 2014/15 to achieve not only the United Nations Millennium Development Goals but also to make Ethiopia as one of the middle income countries by 2020-2030 (Kunama, G. May 12, 2011).

To rekindle the Ethiopia economy which was on the brink of a colossal failure during the military (Derge) regime, the current Ethiopia's Democratic Developmental State Model has been guided by very strong government intervention in the market, giving power and authority to the government bureaucracy to plan, supervise, and implement the developmental processes of the country. The developmental state governs the process of investment in key economic sectors. The matrix presented in Table 13.1 gives a template that could be used to compare the conditions of the developmental states operating both in Malaysia and Ethiopia. For the last seven years, (i.e., 2005-2011), while Malaysia's GDP grew at 5.23 percent, Ethiopia without speeding the direction of industrialization and mainly being plan-oriented rather than full market-oriented, it has achieved an average of 9.9 percent growth rate in its GDP.

As targeted by the Malaysian Developmental target, the incidence of poverty in Malaysia declined from 49% in 1970 to about 5% in 2000 (Khoo, 2007). With recorded economic growth, the poverty reduction measured by poverty head count in Ethiopia has declined from 41.9 in 2005 to 29.6 percent in 2011. Similarly, Ethiopia has achieved a remarkable trend in establishing health services of 0.619 health index (compared to Malaysia's health Index of 0.855). For example, while sub-Saharan African achieved only 39 percent of the reduction in child and maternal deaths, Ethiopia recorded about 40 percent reduction in child mortality among children under five years of age (Shah, 2013).

Similarly, due to poverty reduction and access of health benefits and the expansion of the Ethiopian economy, the Human Development Index (HDI), measured using life expectancy (living long), level of schooling (adult literacy rate) and real GDP per capita (standard of living) of Malaysia' HDI improved by 3.1% (i.e., from 0.738 in 2005 to 0.761 in 2011), whereas, even though Ethiopia's HDI improved by 16% (i.e., from 0.313 in 2005 to 0.363 in 2011), its HDI score is about 22% less than the average score of the sub-Saharan countries.

It needs to be underlined that the Ethiopian developmental state seems to have played an important role in underpinning in terms of quantitative economic growth. However, the low income people don't seem to benefit from the staggering economic growth of the country. The poverty ratio of people living below $1.25 a day in Ethiopia is rather very close to about 30 percent. Based on the extreme social inequalities and abject poverty that exists in the country, it is possible to indicate that the majority of Ethiopians have not been able to share the benefits of economic growth which the country has achieved for the last seven years. What is surprising due to fuel prices, loose monetary policy mainly used for public infrastructure investment, and high prices of edible food products, it is possible that Ethiopia may not achieve what it has set for the 2015 Millennium Development Goal.

The Ethiopian government is supposed to spend 4.5 percent of GDP to attain the Millennium Development Goal of 100 percent primary school completion by 2015 (World Bank, 2005, p. 172), but as shown in Table 1, Ethiopia's GDP expenditure on education is 5.5%, compared to Malaysia's (4.6%). Nonetheless, the education index of Ethiopia is only 0.237 compared to 0.73 for Malaysia. That is, while 73 percent of the school age children in Malaysia complete primary and secondary schools only 24 percent of Ethiopian children complete their primary and secondary schooling. In addition, in terms of quality and equity, Ethiopia has the highest student-teacher ratio in the world. It was reported by the World Bank that since 1993-94, the pupil-teacher ration is 65: 1 and the number of pupils per section is 75 to 82 in government primary schools compared with about 30 in privately operated schools in non-governmental organizations (2005, p. xxiv). Thus, when compared with Malaysia, Ethiopia gives less emphasis on investment in human capital as an important ingredient for economic transformation and the assertions of the developmental state model.

Therefore, if the intended Ethiopia plans and visions have been fully implemented, there is no doubt that they could have achieved their intended goals. However, many of the fruitful projects were unduly delayed because the governmental functionaries lacked the professionalism and commitment needed to mobilize the limited resources of the nation (See Desta, July 7, 2011). Put differently, if the Ethiopian functionaries had been willing to operate efficiently to address the economic challenges of the country and if government intervention had been implemented carefully, there is little doubt that these plans would have generated the greatest welfare for the largest numbers of Ethiopians.

One of the missing preconditions that caused the failure to adopt sound developmental policies in Ethiopia might be due to the prevalence of rent-seeking behavior. As pointed out by Fischer (2011; Kaufmann, 1998, p. 524) since rent-seeking is a means of resistance to reform, it may be seen as a kind of 'legitimized theft' purposely designed by government officials to appropriate rent in order to maximize their utility for embezzling funds and demanding bribes from their clients. In addition, rent-seekers may also be powerful interest groups or lobbyists who exert considerable influence and who bribe government bureaucrats to hinder other competitors so that their inefficient companies win governmental tenders. Thus, as a result of rent-seeking, the policy outcomes of the various projects have not been implemented adequately in Ethiopia. Because of the possibility that the existence of various rent-seeking groups took strategic advantage of resisting reforms and implemented rent-seeking delays and setbacks because the donor's austerity measures might have not been whole- heartedly endorsed by the ruling party. That is, the government's decisions to introduce reforms might have lacked coalition support by policy advisers and technocrats. As stated by Pang (2000), Technocrats generally make decisions with national interest at heart, but with an eye to global realities. "what matters to them is what their colleagues overseas think of their actions. They are interchangeable technocrats, moveable parts of the their governments, often influenced by the views of those sitting in Washington, London , Bonn , Paris...". Finally, Ethiopian government vision is to enhance large and ambitious development projects such as to accomplish the five year Growth and Transformation Plan in the short run, end poverty and become a middle income country in the long run. Instead of searching for the optimal combinations of local resources, Ethiopia's developmental state calls for foreign capital to finance its yearly budgets deficits, thus it might be very difficult to accomplish its ambitious plans (See for example, Ohashi, Nazret.com, 6/9/2011).

TABLE 13.1: THE ECONOMIC AND SOCIAL PERFORMANCE OF ETHIOPIAN DEVELOPMENTAL STATE (2005-2011)

INDICATORS	MALAYSIA			ETHIOPIA		
	2000	2005	2011	2000	2005	2011
Economic status						
Human Dev. Index (value)	0.705	0.738	0.761	0.274	0.313	0.363
Life Expectancy(years)			74.2		52	59.3
Health index			0.855			0.619
Expenditure on health (% GDP)			1.9			2.2
GDP/ capita ($)	4029.9	5381.8	12,724	123.8	164.6	848
Annual GDP Growth (%)	8.9	5.3	5.16	6.1	11.8	8.0
Poverty ratio, living below $1.25/day (%)				41.9	39.0	29.6
Consumer price index		9.0	22.0		38	40..0
Real GDP/capita ($)		4937.43	10,429.51		119.28	605.71
Education						
School life expectancy			11.5			4.3
Education index			0.73			0.237
Primary school enrollment			0.70	61.6	74.2	90.7
Secondary school enrollment				17.1	23.1	20.3
Educ. Exp/GDP			4.6			5.5

Source: CSA abstract, 2003-2011;LISANE MASIE, March, 2012; World Bank (2011), World Bank Indicators 2011, Washington, D.C.

MERITOCRATIC BUREAUCRACY

For the elites and the state institutions to play leading economic steering roles, the developmental states needs to be relatively autonomous. As stated by Nordlinger (1987:361), autonomy is defined simply to mean that the state achieves independence from the demanding clamor of special interest groups. Evans (1994) argues that a developmental state is more effective and efficient than a predatory (parasitic) state because it is managed and run autonomous professional elites.

Starting in the 1990s, though accountable to the public, the civil service in Malaysia has become embedded and has been able to co-ordinate the economy with the private sector. Thus, as stated by Zalanga (2012), using the "Client's Charter" reform, Malaysia has empowered the public by letting them know the minimum to expect from public servants.

In line with highly selective meritocratic recruitment and long-term career rewards, the civil servants in Malaysia are recruited through vigorous national examination system. Once, employed, the employee undergo through extensive training in their respective ministers. The skills and knowledge they acquire allow the bureaucrats to carry out their administrative duties with no major interruptions from politicians. In addition, the remarkable economic growth in Malaysia reveals the positive impact that a professional and comparatively meritocratic bureaucracy can contribute to economic growth if the economic decision making is insulated from political whims.

In the Ethiopia polity on the other hand, the private economic interest is carefully monitored and the possibility of an emerging leadership is limited. The functional requirements of economic growth and diversification by and large are left up to the prerogative of the developmental state. The bureaucracy is managed by civil servants functionaries that are primarily recruited on meritocracy and have clearly spelled out functional obligations to serve competently. While in service, the state functionaries are required to attend various in-service seminars inside the country or sent abroad to upgrade their professional standards. But the institutions whereby the various functionaries operate are not autonomous. "From equal representation point of view, the higher positions in the various governmental departments are assigned according to ethnic-based quota system. ...the perception held by the public is that the bureaucrats are made to operate in line with their ethnic affiliation rather than in pursuit of the goals of the organization" (Desta, 2012, p. 20). In addition, the state-driven developmental model is conditioned to a set of paradigmatic practices such as cronyism and unofficial favoritism to select and allocate a number of business firms to certain ethnic groups.

Insulation of Bureaucracy from Political and Societal Forces

The Malaysian developmental state goal is to achieve rapid economic development. Thus, it gives power and authority to the bureaucracy to plan, supervise and implement efficient policies. Like the Malaysian bureaucrats, Ethiopian elites are highly skilled and well-motivated individuals who are the most talented graduates of the best universities in the country and abroad. Nonetheless, because they are recruited to fulfill ethnic affiliation, they are strongly influenced by the ruling elites. They seem to be politically accountable to their regional state. Thus, Ethiopia like Malaysia can be seen as developmental state that have practiced judicious state intervention at some points, but state interventions at other points seems to be based through ethnic political bargaining. Given this, the bureaucratic leaders and high-ranking civil servants in Ethiopia are involved in widespread corruption and scan. Instead of having selfless devotion to Ethiopian economy, the civil servants are political cadres recruited for the existence of the ruling party in power. .

To summarize, though non-partisan professional public service is a prerequisite to a developmental state, the designed plans in Ethiopia did neither take feedback from the private sector nor established an interface relationship between the ruling party cadres (who are appointed to public service positions even when they do not qualify for such positions mainly focus on mostly on policy-related and political matters in their departments or ministry) and those appointed as civil servants or also known as the "politics-administration interface" (See for example, Maphunye, April 2009). The developmental plans are too ambitious and are not initially established on a well established infrastructural base that could have engineered Ethiopia's take off strategy. For example, unlike what is heavily practiced in Japan and to some extent in Malaysia, the bureaucracy is far removed from the corporate sector. Former government officials of Ethiopia are hardly encouraged to take positions in top posts in private corporations after retirement so that they could be engaged in transform the institutions.

Market-orientations and Foreign Direct Investment

To get feedback from the private sector and allowing the market to operate freely, the Malaysia developmental state is heavily involved in designing the developmental plans, developing the various implementation strategies and formatting summative evaluative techniques. To serve its national developmental goals the Malaysian developmental state has a stable state, heavily invested in infrastructure such as highways, electricity, telecommunication, information technology, provided health, quality housing, schools to its citizens and introduced long-term state determined incentives, necessary for development. This approach enabled Malaysia's phenomenal success in attracting foreign direct investors to invest in the country. To make its products globally competitive, Malaysian economy is open and has upgraded the quality of its administrative and production system to the level of receiving international recognition in form of the ISO 9000 certification. Thus, the Malaysian government is doing everything possible to make the Malaysian economy be competitive and also achieve sustainability. As stated by Khoo (2007), the Malaysia's rapid growth trajectory is based on the globally market.

Though embarking from agricultural to industrial stage is very strenuous, to speed up Ethiopia's industrialization process and climb higher on the developmental ladder, Ethiopia is spending about 20 percent of its GDP to reengineer its infrastructural services, such as roads, schools, railways, air transport, dams, and telecommunication services. The economy is not entirely tailored to the market but is controlled by the government. To entice foreign investors, the Ethiopian government is giving special deals as investment incentives to create conducive environment for foreign investors. For example, contrary to the argument that the country could face devastated soil, dry aquifer, ruined ecology from chemical infestation (Mersha, 2009), Ethiopia is leasing virgin farmlands and bestowing tax holidays and tax relief on imported capital to foreign investors. But foreign investors in Ethiopia are crowding out domestic investors. Being less regulated to follow domestically-mandated standards and reinvest some of their profits in Ethiopia, foreign corporations in Ethiopia are creating problems such as land grabs more than they can create jobs, bring capital, technology, and help Ethiopia have access to world markets.

Democratic Governance

According to the Malaysian government, democratic values are Western constructs, purposely designed to impose Western values on non-Western countries, therefore they can not be transferred to the Malaysian environment (Mohammed, T. 1994). Based on this stand, it is generally argued that development in Malaysia requires better state action and not Western induced democratic values. Currently, the Malaysia state is governed by a powerful bureaucracy, incomplete democratic institutions, and limited political freedom.

Unlike the Malaysian Developmental state, though Ethiopia at times has been appalling human rights, the EPRDF Party without undertaking institutional reforms seems in the process of implementing simultaneously the twin-tracked approach democratization and developmental state. The EPRDF ruling party in Ethiopia constantly argues that it is applying far good governance and equitable administrative, fair judicial and electoral practices to make Ethiopia appear a democratic developmental state. The various opposition groups on the other hand feel that there is a strong state-centered and the ruling party in Ethiopia is using democratic governance for a window dressing purposes. Instead of holding elections on broad suffrage basis, the opposition parties argue that the outcomes of elections in Ethiopia have been fraudulent and undemocratic. The elections held in Ethiopia are based on broad suffrage, those elected are mainly political cadres and the outcomes of the elections have been predetermined. During the 2010 election, for example the US Assistant Secretary of State for African Affairs, Johnnie Carson, the Chief European Union (EU) observer, Thijis Berman argue that while the elections were peaceful and well organized, they were not on uneven playing fields (BBC news, May 25, 2010). Moreover, the judiciary system in current Ethiopia is executively controlled and is an appendage of the ruling party. Thus, since the participation of all concerned citizens, access to information held by public authorities, and the opportunity to participate in decision-making process is a prerequisite for democracy, the Ethiopian governance system needs to be restructured its institutions and empower the masses to be ensured through representation if the developmental state model is expected to bear fruits.

Summary and Looking Forward

Based on the analysis given in Table 13.2, it can be concluded that unlike the conceptual framework forwarded by the Economic Commission for Africa, Ethiopia's democratic developmental state is unique and is different from the Malaysian developmental state model. Economically, Ethiopia more than Malaysia has recorded a staggering economic growth. From 2005-2011, as targeted by the Developmental state, Malaysia's GDP grew at 5.23 percent. The incidence of poverty in Malaysia has declined from 49% in 1970 to less than about 5% in 2000. Without speeding the direction of industrialization and mainly being plan-oriented rather than being a full market-oriented system, from 2005 to 2011, Ethiopia achieved an average of 9.9 percent growth rate in its GDP. With the miraculous economic growth, the poverty reduction in Ethiopia as measured by poverty head count has declined from 41.9 in 2005 to 29.6 percent in 2011. However, unlike the Malaysian developmental plan which is based on free market economic system, Ethiopia seems to be portrayed as a predatory state and has embarked on state-led market system.

The developmental State Model assumes that the organizational set-up of the state needs to be manned by highly disciplined professional government functionaries and technocrats, recruited based on meritocracy to fulfill clearly spelled out functional obligations. Also, it is assumed that non-partisan professional public service is a prerequisite to a developmental state. However, the developmental plans in Ethiopia are too ambitious and are not initially established on a well established financial and infrastructural base that could have engineered Ethiopia's take off strategy. In fact it could be argued that the designed plans in Ethiopia are solely established by politicians without taking feedback from the private sector. As it stands now, Ethiopia's developmental state is not operating in a market-friendly environment. A number of the government-initiated developmental plans are either obstructed or unduly delayed for implementation because the professionalism of some of the government functionaries lacks commitment to mobilizing the limited resources of the nation for development purposes. They appear to be interested in maximizing their utilities by imposing hidden rent-seeking agendas.

Table 13.2: Developmental State or Democratic Developmental State in Malaysia and Ethiopia: A Comparative Overview

Indicators	Malaysia	Ethiopia
Economic Growth	For the last seven years, (i.e., 2005-2011), Malaysia's GDP grew at 5.23 percent. As targeted by the Malaysian Developmental target, the incidence of poverty in Malaysia declined from 49% in 1970 to about 5% in 2000. Similarly, due to poverty reduction and access of health benefits and the expansion of the Malaysian economy), the HDI of Malaysia improved only by 3.1% from 2005-2011. Seventy percent of the school age children in Malaysia complete primary and secondary schools only 24 percent of Ethiopian children complete their primary and secondary schooling. Thus, Malaysia gives more emphasis on investment in human capital as an important ingredient for economic transformation as asserted by its developmental state model.	From 2005-2011, Ethiopia without speeding the direction of industrialization and mainly being plan-oriented rather than full market-oriented, it has achieved an average of 9.9 percent growth rate in its GDP. With recorded economic growth, the poverty reduction measured by poverty head count in Ethiopia has declined from 41.9 in 2005 to 29.6 percent in 2011. Due to poverty reduction and access to of health benefits and expansion of the economy, the Human Development Index (HDI) of has by 16% but it is about 22% less than the average score of the sub-Saharan countries. The Ethiopian developmental state seems to have played an important role in underpinning in terms of quantitative economic growth. However, the low income people don't seem to benefit from the staggering economic growth of the country. The poverty ratio of people living below $1.25 a day in Ethiopia is rather very close to about 30 percent. Ethiopia's GDP expenditure on education is 5.5%, compared to Malaysia's (4.6%). Nonetheless, the education index of Ethiopia is only 0.237 compared to 0.73 for Malaysia.

INDICATORS	MALAYSIA	ETHIOPIA
Vision of Developmental State	Modeled development along Japan and South Korea. Malaysia has a clear vision of developmental to attained a fully developed nation and works cooperatively (or is embedded with the private sector to bring about growth with improved equity and poverty reduction. The 2020 Malaysian Vision was planned by the Malaysian government to make the country be a fully developed nation and facilitate growth with improved equity and poverty reduction in the Malaysian nations.	Modeled developmental along Malaysia. In addition, the Ethiopia state envisages ensuring democracy and popular participation. Furthermore, it entails not only to attained the Millennium Development Goals by 2015 but also becoming a middle income country by 2020- 2030.
Professional and Meritocratic Bureaucrats	The government bureaucrats are recruited through vigorous national examination system and carry out their duties autonomously without interruptions from politicians.	The civil servants in Ethiopia are by and large recruited on meritocracy but are under the whims of the Ethiopian People Revolutionary Democratic Front (EPRDF).
Insulation of bureaucracy from Political and Societal Forces	The Malaysian developmental state goal is to achieve rapid economic development. Thus, it gives power and authority to the bureaucracy to plan, supervise and implement efficient policies	Ethiopian elites are highly skilled and well-motivated individuals who are the most talented graduates of the universities from the country and abroad. Nonetheless, because they are recruited to fulfill ethnic affiliation, they are strongly influenced by the ruling elites.
The Economic System and Foreign direct investment	The Malaysian economy is largely market driven. The Malaysian economy is planned by professional elites and also gets feedback from the private sector and is accountable to the public. The Malaysian economy being competitive and its growth trajectory is based on the globally market.	The Ethiopian economy is not entirely tailored to meet market demand and supply. Most of the time, t is controlled by the government. To entice foreign investments, the Ethiopian government is in the process of creating investment-friendly environment for foreign investors. But, foreign investors are crowding out domestic firms.

INDICATORS	MALAYSIA	ETHIOPIA
Democratic Governance	Malaysia looks at democratic values as Western constructs and not transferrable to the Malaysian environment. Therefore, It is generally argued that development in Malaysia requires better state action and not Western induced democratic values to achieve sustainable development. In short, the basic argument in Malaysia is development first and then democracy later.	Ethiopia at times has been appalling human rights, however, the EPRDF Party without undertaking institutional reforms seems to be committed to process of implementing simultaneously the twin-tracked approach of democratization and developmental state.

The bureaucratic elites who design and manage the short and long term plans are not politically neutral and do not get the necessary feedback from the public. Therefore, if Ethiopia desires to use the state as a very important vehicle to tackle the deep-rooted developmental problems, it needs to create constant improvement in its public administration sector that could make the employees of various institutions to be politically neutral and professionally competent. As undertaken in Malaysia, a genuine developmental state in Ethiopia could be made to be vigorous, if the Ethiopian Government institutionalizes a free market system. Therefore, if Ethiopia desires the Malaysian developmental state to be served as its role model, it needs to retool its infrastructure, create institutions capable of staging the necessary developmental state and the bureaucratic elites need be autonomous from being influence by the political cadres. Finally, since the foundation of developmental state is based on good governance, Ethiopia like Malaysia needs to form a state run by autonomous professional elites that have the capacity to map out the direction of the country by getting the necessary feedback from the public. The state needs to be embedded with the private sector to sustain future economic growth.

Given the above analysis, the Ethiopian political system is neither a developmental state like Malaysia nor striving towards the ideal of democratic development state. It seems confounded giving the appearance of operating as a centrally-planned economic system. Unlike to adhering to the principles of developmental state, the bureaucracy is not disciplined. Its management system manifests extreme forms of inefficiency and endemic corruption. Given that the existing developmental state model is dysfunctional, it has been an obstacle to the implementation of the well intentioned poverty-minimizing reforms. It is engulfed by rent-seeking attributes and located in an inefficient organizational set up. Thus, if Ethiopia desires to use the state as a very important vehicle to tackle its deep-rooted developmental problems, it needs to improve the competence of its public administration sector and has to encourage its public employees to remain politically neutral, work in collaboration with the private sector, and make sure that appointment of the government elites is transparent and based on due process.

Nonetheless, given that the era of economic globalization has caused the appreciation of currencies and precipitated a huge influx of direct foreign investment and portfolio capital in Malaysia. In addition, the lack of prudent financial market regulations and the emergence of new innovative investment practices Malaysia has resulted in excessive private debt in hard currencies, fluctuation in asset prices and severe exchange rate fluctuation. It is possible to argue that the distinctive Malaysian developmental state model that is suggested by the Economic Commission of Africa is too outdated to be replicated in Africa. In short, given that in the continuing saga of globalism, Malaysian type of developmentalism may not provide something of a template to be emulated by Ethiopia. If the Ethiopian government is willing to relinquish its direct control over many community organizations and abide by democratic values, it could sustain its economic growth and adequately feed its people, it needs to go back to practicing sustainable agricultural because agriculture is the backbone of the Ethiopian economy. Ethiopia's sustainable economic model needs to be largely based on integrated, environmentally sensitive, and cooperative agriculture because the lives of more than 80 million Ethiopians are at stake (see for example, Kofi and Desta, 2008). Stated differently, if democratic sustainable developmental state is suppose to be effective in Ethiopia, a radical and far-reaching set of constitutional revisions need to be established to dismantle the bureaucratic-executive state. Since more than 80 percent of the Ethiopia population live in rural areas, Ethiopia needs to intensify its agricultural base to feed its own people rather than aimlessly flirting with irrelevant Western capitalist models and optimistically dreaming of replicating the East Asian Developmental state model.

Chapter 14

OVERVIEW AND SOME PERSPECTIVES FOR THE FUTURE

A historical account of the nature of the socio-economic and political formation of Ethiopia and its dependent and subordinate relations to the hegemony of the United States from the early 1950s to 1974 reveals that though the country was highly centralized and ruled by semi-feudal authoritarian regime, the Ethiopian economy was inserted into the capitalist economic system (See Eshetu, 1992). Also there was a closer correspondence between the educational system and the socio-economic structure.

Upon the decline of British imperialism at the end of World War II, in line of the United Nations, First Development Decade that advocated the modernizing potential of industrialization as a means of overcoming the traditional dependence on agriculture, Ethiopia was integrated into the sphere of U.S. imperialism through economic, military assistance, the establishment of U.S. military base and foreign investments. In accordance with this development and through the advice of American experts and nationals trained in the United States, the Ethiopian education system was restructured to mirror U.S. interests and fulfills the international division of labor.

In contradistinction to the over-simplified mechanistic view that educational institutions fulfill a conservative role and serve in the continuation of the existing social relations of production, starting 1965, there occurred a breakdown of correspondence between the economic base and the Ethiopian educational system. Ethiopian schools started producing politically conscious and highly militant students. The few foreign-owned industries that were set up had often limited commitment to local development and as they were largely capital intensive, they produced few jobs for the local people. In general, in the

1970s, Ethiopia was faced with sharply declining living standards, recurring financial crises, rampant inflation and a resulting high rate of unemployment. At the economic level, Ethiopia was marked by 1) low domestic capital formation, 2) dependence on foreign aid, and 4) heavy indebtedness. After the liberal prescriptions failed to charter any significant alternative, massive student unrest contributed to the dismantling of the Haile Selassie's regime in 1974.

The Military Government (Derge) which replaced the Haile Selassie regime, first gave up adhering to the required draconian conditions laid out by the multilateral financial institutions to borrow funds and embarked on socialism to restructure the Ethiopian socio-economic order. In the economic arena, the Derge nationalized the major enterprises of the economy. In the field of education, the military regime formally declared equality in the distribution of education and the school system was ordered to follow the enunciated socialist ideology.

After seventeen years, however, it was revealed that the socialist state-led economic systems in Ethiopia were promising a lot but producing nothing tangible. Instead it was hobbled by incompetence and ravaged by corruption in malfunctioning bureaucratic systems. More particularly, the peasants and workers were promised much but were given little. In contradiction to the Derge's lofty ten year plan (1984/85 -1993/94) of building a socialist Ethiopia on an expanded agricultural base and making it self-sufficient in food production, the growth in the agricultural sector, the most dominant sector in the country, was disappointingly low. That is, agricultural productivity declined sharply from 1.2 percent during 1973/83 to a negative growth rate of 1.1 percent during the 1980/88 period. In addition, while land reform abolished the existing feudal serfdom and redistributed land to the farmers, subsequent agricultural collectives were not meant to increase productivity but were meant to subjugate and control the farmers. As pinpointed by Getachew (2010), the military junta that dressed itself in socialist garb used the instruments of the state to control and regiment the masses. "...efforts to consolidate and expand mechanized state farms ...faced a number of technical, financial and managerial difficulties. Famine and the insidious civil war also ravaged the country's economy." For example, with the establishment of the "Villagization Program" in 1985, though 12 million peasants were relocated and collectivized, the famine of 1984/85 also contributed to the mass exodus of Ethiopian refugees to neighboring countries.

In short, the Derge's failure could be attributed to the following misguided policies of: a) nationalization of farm land, b) the villiagization program, c) the Agricultural Marketing Board pricing strategy, d) the inadequate attention given to private sectors in economic construction of the country, and e) the economic hardship faced by the Derge (i.e., the Soviet Union mired in its internal turmoil because of Mikhail Gorbachev's *glasnost* and *perestroika*) because it could no longer get aid from the Socialist countries. Furthermore, the economy was in disarray when the Derge started persecuting and eliminating intellectuals and imposing the Red Terror. As a result of the Red Terror, a number of the intellectuals left the country. By the time the head of the Military Junta, Mengistue, left the country, Ethiopia was characterized by economic crises. For instance, in 1984-84, the economy plummeted to -5.3 percent because of severe drought. In 1986-87, the economy grew by 7.9 percent to decline to about 1 percent in the 1989-90 period (see for example, Eshetu, January 1992).

In 1989, a coalition that included the Ethiopian People's Democratic movement (EPDM), the Oromo People's Democratic Organization, (OPDO), the Southern Ethiopian People's Democratic Front (SEPDF), and the Tigray People's Liberation Front (TPLF) formed an umbrella of Ethio-national front, known as the Ethiopian People's Revolutionary Democratic Front (EPRDF) to dismantle the Military Junta and its functionaries from the Ethiopian power structure. The political landscape was redefined by the EPRDF in July 1991. Thus, 30 ethnic-based opposition parties, "...adopted a provisional national charter, created an 87-member Council of Representatives and formed the transitional Government of Ethiopia (TGE) led by the EPRDF" (Crisis Group, September 2009). Though the Oromo Liberation Front withdrew from the transitional government in 1992 and some members of the Southern Ethiopian Peoples' Democratic Coalition also abandoned the coalition government, the remaining members of the coalition started implementing its new constitution with a bicameral legislature and a judicial system on August 21, 1995 to form the Federal Democratic Republic of Ethiopia.

The cardinal principles of the 1995 constitution were to establish federal governance based on unity and diversity, and to achieve stability in the remaining Ethiopian polity. The Ethiopian polity was predominantly divided into nine ethnic regional states (i.e., Tigray, Afar, Amhara, Oromia, Somali, Benishangual-Gumuz, Gamebella, and Harar); the Southern Nations, Nationalities and Peoples (SNNP-- a voluntary merger of 5 regions); and the cities of Addis Ababa and Dire Dawa (see Habtu, 2003; Serra-Horguelin, A. 1999). To achieve this, in line with Article 39 of the constitution, each Nation, Nationality and Peoples in Ethiopia were assured the unconditional right to self-determination, including the rights to secession.

To assess the implementation of the 1995 constitution, a brief review of the literature indicates that about three outstanding perspectives seem to have been advanced over a period of fifteen years as possible explanations of Ethiopia's current federal status. The first perspective argues that the federal state is moving in the right direction to rendering its people self- and shared rule. Opposing the first view, the second perspective strongly argues that the ethnic federalism designed by the Ethiopian Peoples' Revolutionary Democratic Front

(EPRDF) and in particular Article 39 of the Constitution is a threat to the unity and territorial integrity of Ethiopia. The third perspective, highly endorsed by the writer of this book, holds the opinion that the type of ethnic and regional federalism created in Ethiopia in 1995 was not carefully worked out and is too cumbersome to facilitate adequate communication among the constituents in the New Age.

As mentioned before, the combination of the state-led economic models and Neo-liberal economic models that were super-imposed on the Ethiopian environment before the EPRDF came to power did cause more serious deterioration than benefits. In line with the challenges of the African Economic Commission, instead of undergoing marginal adjustments under the state-led economic model and the open Neo-liberal economic system, Ethiopia is attempting to make dramatic structural changes under a democratically-nested developmental state model (Economic Commission for Africa, 2011).

Given the conceptual framework of the developmental state that is framed by the Commission for Africa (2011) and bearing on the specific operational definitions of a developmental state forwarded by Bolesta (2007), the vital query at this juncture is if Ethiopia is engaged in the process of applying a developmental state, will it attain: 1) socioeconomic development transformed via an industry-led growth strategy, 2) a stable democratic framework and developmental government, 3) the transformation of the state managed by competent bureaucracy that is assigned based on meritocracy, 4) an autonomous institutional environment that is less likely to be influenced by the ruling political elite and political cadres, 5) a capitalist economic environment where private sectors play a crucial role in the development process, and 6) a sustained economic system largely based on export-led growth to combat poverty and generate full employment at a stable price?

As discussed before, over the last seven-years, Ethiopia has recorded steady economic growth and has achieved a remarkable up trend in establishing health services and social development programs. (See for example, Tolina, 2007) Some of the infrastructure services, such as roads, railways, air transport, and telecommunication services are in the process of being reengineered and a few are now in use. Though worthwhile attempts have been made to electrify the rural areas, still a large segment of the rural population and especially women become covered by toxic smokes that result from the burning of wood or cow dung while cooking, and the use of kerosene lamps for lighting their shattered houses. The health facilities available in the country seem to be better than under previous regimes, but it is sad that the health care service centers operating in Ethiopia are still ill-equipped. While 45 percent of births in urban areas of Ethiopia are attended by skilled health personnel only 3 percent of the births in rural areas are attended by skilled heath personnel (IRIN, 2013). Actually, a number of households in rural Ethiopia fetch their water for home use from contaminated streams and rivers. Because of this, priority has been given in the five-year GTP to provide universal potable water services to a large section of the country (Yacob, T. September 30, 2010).

In quantitative terms, it is remarkable to notice that Ethiopia has achieved almost universal primary education. However, when we examine the quality of the rest of the public school system, the second-class public schools seem to be less conducive to learning. The teaching materials and the teachers are inadequate. Given the dual system of education in the country, consisting of well furnished private schools teaching children of the emerging upper class alongside the ill-equipped public schools that are supposed to educate the children of the poor, it is likely that this situation may not only perpetuate class differentiation and but will also likely deter the government's plans for growth and transformation.

In order to achieve Ethiopia's socioeconomic development via the industrialization process, at least on paper, the Ethiopian state has systematically planned for the necessary human capital, the amount of foreign debt and assistance, domestic savings and technology, foreign technical information and technical knowledge available from foreign investors (i.e., via licensing, joint venture or turn-keys). In addition, based on the lessons learned from the 1995 Agricultural Development-Led strategy, the 2002/03 to 2004/05 Sustainable Development and Poverty Reduction Program (SDPRP) and the 2005/06 to 2009/10 Plan for Accelerated and Sustained Development to end Poverty (PASDEP), the Ethiopian government strongly felt that it has a mandate to launch the Growth and Transformation Plan (GTP) for the period 2010/11 to 2014/15 in order to achieve not only the Millennium Development Goals but also to make Ethiopia one of the middle income countries by 2020-2023 (Kunama, G. May 12, 2011).

Although it is a paradox for democracy and developmental states to coexist, by promising good governance and at the same time pursuing the democratization process, the Ethiopian developmental state is planning to reconcile the contradiction by undergoing the industrialization process in order to achieve the goals of the five-year Growth and Transformation Plan. To speed up Ethiopia's industrialization process and to generate foreign exchange, the Ethiopian government has been leasing virgin farmlands to foreign investors (i.e., to Saudi Arabia, India, China, some of the European Union countries, Israel, United States, etc.) by bestowing incentives such as tax holidays, exemption from the payment of custom duties, relief taxes on imported capital, and exemption from payment of sales and excise taxes for export commodities. Nonetheless, it is worth stating again that like other host countries in Africa, Ethiopia is not likely to see capital, know-how, or technology from the foreign investors. (See Desta,

January 10, 2010). Also, those who were evicted from their land will not get productive employment. The evicted local people are likely to face food scarcities and starvation. In short, from capital intensive use by the foreign investors, the country will face devastated soil, dry aquifers, and a destroyed ecology from chemical excesses (Mersha, 2009).

The overall developmental goal of the developmental state could achieve the intended results if the means are systematically strategized (Castellis, 2000, p.284). Since 2004, the EPRDF government has identified industrial development as a priority, but it has been allocating less budget to the industrial sector when compared with other sectors (Tegenu, T. (June 6, 2011). Even now, to accomplish the five-year (2011 -2015) Growth and Transformation Plan, the Ethiopian government is heavily relying on some of its international development partners to allocate aid for funding the five year GTP (Yacob, T. (October 1, 2010).

With the exception of democratic Japan, the developmental states in Asia regard democratic values as Western constructs, purposely designed to impose Western cultural values on non-Western countries (See Mohamed, 1994). However, contrary to the functions of Asian developmental states, the Commission for Africa (2010) strongly challenged the African states including Ethiopia to be managed by competent bureaucracy and operate in a relatively stable democratic environment where: a) power and civic responsibility are exercised by all adult citizens directly or indirectly through their elected representatives, b) decisions are based upon the principles of majority rule, c) there is an understanding that its function is to protect human rights (such as freedom of speech and religion, the rights to equal protection under law and the opportunity to organize, etc.), d) there is broad suffrage and regular free and fair elections open to citizens of voting age, and e) it conforms to the rule of law, which means that the law is supreme and binding on everyone (See for example, Lipset, 1963, Huntington, S, 1991). On the other hand, from the Ethiopian perspective, Habisso (2010) argues that imposing democracy on the poor and ethnically divided, might trigger bloody national struggles. Therefore, can the Ethiopian state simultaneously embark on establishing democracy while pursuing a developmental state to achieve socio-economic growth in the long run? To be regarded as developmental-oriented state, does Ethiopia posses a competent bureaucracy that is able to assign work and hire personnel based on meritocracy, competence, and experience?

When compared with its previous political environments, it is possible to regard current Ethiopia as an emerging democratic state. Viewing it from the surface, the country at times seems to abide by the rules of law. Elections are regularly conducted every five years. Since the government has established various developmental plans as a means of achieving legitimacy, it assumes that it has the support of its own people. Opposition groups on the other hand feel that the outcomes of all elections held thus far in the name of democracy have been used for window dressing. In addition, competing political groups claim that since the elections held in Ethiopia are not based on broad suffrage, those elected are mainly political cadres and the outcomes of the elections have been predetermined. Also, the opposition groups assert the country lacks parliamentary democracy and decisions are not based on the principles of majority rule. During the 2010 election, for example, the incumbent party, the Ethiopian People's Revolutionary Democratic Front (EPRDF) won almost 99 percent of the seats in parliament. Given the discrepancies that existed in 2010, a number of Ethiopian opposition groups have attempted to discredit the results and claim the results of the 2010 election were rigged, and allege that the election process was fraudulent and undemocratic.

The Ethiopian bureaucracy is managed by civil servants that have clearly defined functions. The government functionaries and technocrats are by and large recruited on meritocracy and are expected to serve competently. While they are on the job their skills are improved via various experiential learning seminars. However, the institutions in which the functionaries operate are not autonomous. They are strongly influenced by the ruling elite. From the point of view of equal representation, the higher positions in many governmental departments are assigned according to an ethnic-based quota system. Thus, though the functionaries might be recruited on meritocracy, due to the perception held by the public, willingly or unwillingly the bureaucrats are expected to operate in conformance with their ethnic affiliation rather than in pursuit of the goals of their organization. Because of this, instead of transparency, the desire to fulfill the wishes of the political agenda introduces the temptation for corruption that has become endemic in the functioning of the Ethiopian bureaucracy.

With the benefit of hindsight, it is possible to say that though some of the government-initiated development plans were very rational and if systematically implemented, they could have successfully achieved their intended goals. But, many fruitful projects were unduly delayed because the functionaries lacked the professionalism and commitment needed to mobilize the limited resources of the nation for development. Therefore, if Ethiopia desires to use the state as a very important vehicle to tackle its deep-rooted developmental problems, it needs to improve the competence of its public administration sector and keep public employees politically neutral.

The foregoing analysis suggests that the state has to design the developmental plans, intervene in the implementation of its strategies, evaluate the outcome of the results but leave the market to be free from government interventions. Following the pattern of logic under which the Ethiopian government is functioning, it is very difficult to assume that current Ethiopia is an example of a market-friendly developmental state. Though not explicit, the regime appears to be pursuing a centrally-planned economic system. The Ethiopian regime has openly declared it is in the process of transforming its political system toward democracy in order to bring about a "renaissance for Ethiopia." Given this pronouncement, it could be said that the Ethiopian government is struggling to operate in a democratic way. The Ethiopian government seems to be stumbling in its pursuit of democracy and is not effectively operating to fulfill the requirements for an open market-oriented developmental state. Thus, the Ethiopian political and economic environment seems to be confounded and appears to be operating like a centrally-planned economic system.

What is to be done?

Instead of navigating with an ambiguous plan that may lead nowhere, the Ethiopian government needs to coordinate the objectives of its developmental plans with its institutional characteristics. To bring about environmentally sustainable development projects that could generate structural transformation and growth with full employment, Ethiopia needs to create a favorable business climate so that public and private investments in the country could function successfully. An important lesson to draw from the East Asian developmental experience and more particularly from the Malaysian experience that could subsequently be applied to African countries' economic systems is that the Asian developmental state model was the product of specific historical circumstances or was developed for different social orders. It can not be replicated or modified to fit African countries socio-political and economic realities. The East Asian development plan needs critical examination before applying it to fit the Ethiopian context. Also, the lessons Ethiopia could have learned from the East Asian development approach is that the chronic poverty and rampant unemployment that it is currently facing can not be tackled in a short period of time. In an era of global economic crisis and still having more than $5 billion external debt, it is a big challenge for Ethiopia to have designed the five-year Growth and Transformation Plan for 2011-2015 by solely relying on external assistance, grants and direct foreign investments from the Ethiopian diaspora.

The African Commission's call for the construction of a democratic governing system, state capacity-building, planning and reinforces state intervention without directly owning productive assets. The economic liberalization, meritocratic recruitment, competency management, and the autonomous functions of government institutions could bring about smooth and speedy transitions from a poverty-ridden country to achieve environmentally sustainable development in Africa. Though the Growth and Transformation Plan designed by the Ethiopian government seems to be audacious, to be successfully implemented, as articulated by Kofi and Desta (2008), Africa's development programs need to be built on existing local knowledge and have to have been agreed upon by the people in order for them to be beneficiaries of the development process. Moreover, for Africa to achieve legitimate and sustainable development, local Africans need to be drivers of change and African governments have to relinquish their direct control over many community organizations. Therefore, to chart environmentally sustainable development for Ethiopia at the grassroots level, the next section: 1) proposes food for democracy, as an alternative development strategy, and 2) outlines how a democratic development-oriented state could foster full employment at stable prices and minimize rent-seeking behavior in Ethiopia.

Food Democracy: An Alternative Development Strategy

The theoretical and practical links between democracy (freedom) and economic development (food prosperity) has preoccupied academics and policymakers alike for several decades. Lipset (1959) argues economic growth first, democracy later. In line with the argument that economic development comes first and then democracy later, the Indonesian government has come to the conclusion that "... economic and political stability with little freedom is much better than starving and being frustrated with full freedom" (Yamin, Aug 3, 2001). Scholars, who support democracy first, development later, indicate that democratic countries consistently outperform non-democracies on social socio-economic indicators. So they argue that promoting democracy should be prior to expanding economic development in developing countries (Weintraub, 2003;and Siegle, Weinstein, and Halperin, 2004). Contrary to the democracy for development argument, the former chancellor of Germany, Helmut Schmidt, persuasively argued that the developing countries of South East Asia (such as China, Singapore, Hong Kong, South Korea, and Taiwan), needed authoritarian governments for the economic development that they achieved over the last four decades (Weintraub, 2003).

Using food and freedom as important variables, Sen (1987) argues that food fosters freedom and freedom may have a causal influence on success in the pursuit of food for all. Assuming that there is mal-distribution of resources in a nation, free political agitation by the masses may result in the bonding of food and freedom. Then, once people have access to food, they can vigorously demand that their government distribute other basic necessities to vulnerable groups. For example, despite its achievement of economic wealth under the late Moammar Gadhafi's dictatorial leadership, the democratic revolution in Libya blew Gadhafi's authoritarian regime to pieces. Thus, the lesson that other African nations could learn for Botswana and Mauritius is that they need to be skillful in the "...grafting of prosperity and democracy if holistic advancement is to take place without recourse to dictatorships" (Akosah-Sarpong, October 2, 2011). In other words, the experience of Botswana and Mauritius clearly shows that if African governments are to develop without dictatorship, democracy and prosperity should be simultaneously connected in the proposition for Africa's sustainable progress (Akosah-Sarpong, October 2, 2011).

Considering the two opposing directions, (i.e. from food to freedom, and from freedom to food,) in order to reduce anti-Americanism, the U.S. State Department's web site subscribes to the idea that poor countries must develop economically before they democratize. Therefore, to renew Africa's agricultural growth to bring about Africa Food Security Program, the United States, Agency for International Development, ran the Africa Food Security Program in May 19, 2012, at the annual summit of the group of Eight (G8) at camp David, in Maryland (Weintraub, 2003;Siegle, Weinstein, and Halperin, 2004). The food security conference and the forthcoming aid might be regarded as worthwhile for Africa because Africa received new funds of $3 Billion. However, it also needs to be understood that the U.S. aid might be considered a plague across the continent because it may take the pressure off African governments and cause them to delay rearranging development priorities that would make their governments more democratic, and instead favor producing agricultural goods for exports to fulfill the needs of global capitalism.

Thus, regarding the causalities between food and freedom or economic development and democracy, a brief review of the literature indicates the connections between the two variables are controversial and inconclusive. Also the argument that freedom is better than food mirrors the ideologies of the well-to-do. Actually, the provision of food for the wretched masses is not based on a utopian slogan but it reflects an entitlement that meets some of the basic human rights components. People can enjoy freedom provided they are entitled to basic necessities. In fact, as argued by Akosah-Sarpong, putting freedom or political democracy before economic development has not particularly made African countries to prosper; instead it has placed them in unimaginable turbulence. Therefore, when we think of promoting the connection between food and freedom, or the linkage between democracy and economic development, we need to refrain and review the literature before we assert any one of them.

If we are concerned about poor people, particularly in Ethiopia, we need to assert for food democracy. Food democracy is a framework for making the food system more responsive to the needs of its citizens in a decentralizing system of control. Food democracy emphasizes social justice in the food system, and food is viewed as the center of the democratic process. That is, citizens need to have tenure to land and be engaged in their food production system (Fischer, 2010). In short, in a food democracy, eaters are not only owners but also producers of a healthy food system because we are what we eat. "Eventually, by creating food democracy by creating in a bottom-up democracy through freedom farms and freedom villages, the consumers and co-producers can be made to actively participate in the political process" (Shiva, V. 2007).

In short, Ethiopia is an agrarian-dominated country where more than 70 percent of the population depends on agricultural and rural off-farm activities. However, it is in Ethiopia where the level of malnourishment has significantly increased in recent years. Though many innovations in agriculture have been introduced, Ethiopia has not benefited from the new agricultural technology. Thus, if agricultural growth is likely to reduce the cycle of poverty, hunger and famine, and eventually achieve food democracy, Ethiopian policy makers need to concentrate on mobilizing the hidden creativity of Ethiopian farm families to rediscover their agrarian heritage and achieve broad-based agricultural growth (Kofi and Desta, 2008).

Environmentally Economic Development for Full Employment

The high unemployment accompanied with rampant inflation persistent in Ethiopia cannot be solved without appropriate adjustments in real income and factors of production. Through the lens of insufficient effective demand, in the Keynesian monetary and fiscal demand management model it is assumed that unemployment could be countered and the economy could be stimulated by an increase in money supply, a reduction in taxes or an increase in government spending. As the Keynesian aggregate demand policies failed to show remarkable results, policy makers attempted to use a combination of the Keynesian and Neo-classical framework to tackle the problem of some stagnating economies. However, a number of countries didn't realize any significant results in their economies as a result of using this new approach. Based on the economic thinking initiated for developed countries by the heterodox economists (that draws from radical, post-Keynesian, and institutional economic theories) and in the last few years, it has been adopted by a number of developing countries to eliminate unemployment and provide price stability (See for example, Kregel, 1991, Kaboub, 2007, and Wary, 1997).

Although, not yet fully conceptualized as a new catch-up model in mainstream development economics, the "Employer of Last Resorts" (ELR) - led model of development is inconsistent with the interests of *laissez-faire* capitalism. In solving cyclical types of unemployment, the Employer of Last resort (ELR) policy focuses on guarantying full employment by governments to those who are ready and willing to work at a basic wage rate (Wary (2007). Though the ELR tolerates the inevitability of frictional and structural types of unemployment, it is not an emergency program or a substitute for private employment, the ELR is a permanent government initiated type of full employment and is complemented with the private sector employment. By increasing the economic incentives for investment and substantially reducing costs of production, the ELR stimulates productivity and reduces unemployment and inflation. The ELR also plays a vital role in stabilizing the economy by minimizing the occurrence of business cycles (economic fluctuations) and is supposed to achieve sustainable development in the long run (Becker (1993). Realizing that productive and full employment shows a respect for fundamental principles of rights at work and serves to attain sustainable development, the United Nations World Submit in 2005 and Economic and Social Council (ECOSOC) of 2006 encouraged to placing productive employment and decent work into economic policy and to utilize the ELR economic model in order to strategize their development plans (Wary (2007).

Adherents of the "Employment of Last Resort" strongly believe that ELR is an automatic stabilizer because a perfectly elastic supply of ELR jobs can be made to accept the demand of ELR vacancies, for which government spending can stimulate private sector demand and expand private sector employment trends. If public investments don't interfere or compete to crowd out the private sectors, workers from the public sector could automatically be drawn off from the ELR rolls and reduce government spending. As narrated by Kaboub (May 2007), though undermined by the rise of neo-liberal political economic models of the 1980s,

> *...ELR literature began to blossom in the 1960s with the work of Hyman Minsky who argued that the government should act as employer of last resort to ensure an infinitely elastic demand for labor, thus creating an automatic stabilizer mechanism through which the size of public sector employment would expand during recessions to absorb unemployment labor, and conversely it would shrink during economic expansion to allow the private sector access to labor power at the a premium above the ELR-wage".*

However, it needs to be noted at this juncture that full re-employment of all those who are affected by increased mechanization can not be fully sustained due to continual structural and technological changes (see for example, Palley, 2001). To counteract this argument Murray suggests that since the unemployed suffer the dual-nature of losing previously acquired skills but also do not develop new skills for new techniques, the ELR program can tackle this problem by offering continual on the job training programs because the government always has the financial capacity (creates or supplies fiat money) to pay for these programs. Also, the public sector employment can forgo automation and be labor intensive, a luxury which is not available for the private sector in capitalist economies to entertain (Murray 2010). Kalecki (1943) also argues that government stimulants can actively pursue full employment to provide for the welfare of its citizens if it undertakes public investments (i.e., build schools, hospitals, and highways) or subsidizes mass consumption by providing family allowances, reduction of indirect taxes, or subsidies to keep down prices of necessities. Such government expenditures increase employment and stimulate the demand for consumer and investment of goods and services from the private sectors resulting in aggregate output and employment in the private sector resulting a fall in output and employment of the government ELR sector. For example, it was estimated that the cost of financing ELR ranges from less than 1% of GDP for the Unites States to about 3.5% of Australia's GDP (Mitchell, W. Watts, M. (1997), but had it taken the multiplier effects of the income earned by ELR workers it would have been insignificant. Since the ELR is a national program, its implementation has to be at the local level. Employees in the ELR program purchase goods and services from other businesses in the region and increase the multiplier effect of the ELR program (See for example, Murray, 2010).

As succinctly argued by Murray (2010), employer of last resort approach can achieve both macro goals of full employment and environmental sustainability. Though estimating the structural, technological, and growth rate in the population is very challenging, given the Ethiopian case, since agriculture is the backbone of its economy and about 80% of the population depends on agriculture, the excess labor that could arise as a result structural and technological changes could easily be solved if the government would concentrate on labor intensive types of activities. Given that Ethiopia is endowed with abundant natural resources, applying the employer of last resort program to full employment could present the greatest potetntial for domestic resources and for resolving the types of unemployment problems that might arise because of economic recessio. Therefore, the public sector jobs generated in Ethiopia under the ELR program should be designed to promote not only economic development but also need to tailored to solve ecological problems (see for example Lieuw-Kie-Song, 2009). The central question of the remaining section of this chapter is: can decentralized community-based employment dynamics funded by Ethiopia's national government be strategized to achieve a dignified and environmentally sustainable development?

Employer of Last Resort (ELR) Approach

As pointed out elsewhere, though halfheartedly implemented, the economic rehabilitation measures in Ethiopia for the last seven years have contributed to strong economic growth which has lifted the economic and social well-being of at least some of the more fortunate Ethiopians. In contrast, however, the majority of Ethiopians have remained at the margin of this process, failing to share the benefits of economic growth. To tackle the chronic poverty and rampant unemployment that the country is facing, policy makers have attempted more recently to retool the country's economic structure to mirror the East Asian Developmental State economic model. Accordingly, the policy makers in Ethiopia have embarked on the five-year Growth and Transformation Plan. To rekindle hope for Ethiopia's economic future, Ethiopia's Developmental State Model has been guided by very strong government intervention in the market, giving power and authority to the government bureaucracy to plan, supervise, and implement the developmental processes of the country.

With the benefit of hindsight, it needs to be pointed out again that over the years the government has attempted to design a number of policies and reforms such as the Sustainable Development and Poverty Reduction program (SDPRP) and Plan for Accelerated and Sustainable Development to End Poverty (PASDEP). Had the intended plans been implemented systematically there is no doubt that they could have achieved their intended goals. However, many of the more fruitful projects were unduly delayed because the governmental functionaries lacked the professionalism and commitment needed to mobilize the limited resources of the nation (See Desta, July 7, 2011). In other words, if the Ethiopian functionaries had been willing to operate efficiently to address the economic challenges of the country and if government intervention had been implemented carefully, there is little doubt that these plans would have generated the greatest welfare for the largest numbers of Ethiopians. However, as pointed out by Fischer (2011) one of the missing preconditions that caused the failure to adopt sound developmental policies in developing countries in Ethiopia was the lack of consideration of the prevalence of rent-seeking behavior.

Other than the standard economic constraints such as resources, technology and unforeseen exogenous shocks, the rent-seeking behavior prevalent in country could have challenged the implementation of reform policies in Ethiopia. Therefore the central purpose of this study is to review rent-seeking conditions or abuses of power by government officials to take into account their possibly formidable impediment to the implementation of various poverty-alleviating programs in Ethiopia. As shown in Chapter 13, since Ethiopia is affected by rent-seeking, could addressing the challenges of rent-seeking serve to create positive opportunities to bring about a positive transformation? Therefore, the first part of the paper reviews the concept and the significant attributes of rent-seeking. The second part compares the difference between the Developmental State and the Employer of the Last Resort (ELR) models in terms of rent-seeking attributes. The third and final part focuses on the effects of ELR in the formation of autonomous communities with little or no government intervention so that they may serve as benchmarks for initiating an environment conducive to the enhancement of output and a reduction of the level of unemployment in rural and urban Ethiopia.

The Attributes of Rent-Seeking Behaviors

The term rent-seeking behavior as it applies to developed countries was first discussed as an abstract concept by Gordon Tullock in 1967. But, the concept was operationalized to be amenable for research by Anne O. Krueger in 1974. In conventional economics, the term is generally used to represent a payment for the use of a resource (land, labor, capital, ideas, etc). In contrast to profit-making, rent-seeking behavior can be operationalized as the ability of individuals or entrepreneurs to extract uncompensated wealth for non-productive activities from others over and above the marginal cost of the product.

As discussed by Fischer (2010), some attributes of rent-seeking in many developing countries "...are characterized by poor policies and weak institutional settings, where corruption and embezzlement are rampant and privileged interest groups manage to capture a large share of the nation's income in a decidedly non-productive way." In other words, since rent-seeking is a means of resistance to reform, it may be seen as a kind of 'legitimized theft' purposely designed by government officials to appropriate rent in order to maximize its utility for embezzling funds and demanding bribes from their clients (See Kaufmann, 1998, p. 524). In addition, rent-seekers may also be powerful interest groups or lobbyists who exert considerable influence and who bribe government bureaucrats to hinder other competitors so that their inefficient companies win governmental tenders. As described by Kornai (1979) rent-seeking behavior is also applicable to soft budget constraints that describe the bailing out of predominantly public companies which receive transfers from the government when revenues do not cover costs. In other words, in a static sense, a rent-seeking payment is any manipulation of the work environment so as not to give wages or render compensation to an entrepreneur as a reward for contributions that approximate his or level of productivity. In a dynamic sense, however, rent-seeking is regarded as inefficient, detracting from social welfare because it strongly encourages entrepreneurs to spend real resources to prevent competitive market outcomes through lobbying action for monopoly power. From an ethical point of view, rent-seeking is an integral part of an ailing economy. It is reprehensible and socially undesirable because it fosters rewards for unproductive agents instead of rewarding those who have contributed to societal welfare (Falchamps, M. 1989).

As mentioned before, based on policy formulation strategies, Ethiopia has introduced well- planned reforms that are meant to address the country's poverty level. However, the policy outcomes of the various projects have not been implemented adequately. Reasons for this are many, either the donor conditionalities were not whole- heartedly endorsed by the ruling party, or the government's decisions to introduce reforms lacked coalition support by policy advisers and technocrats, or perhaps it was due to the lack of technical and capacity-related problems, or to use the former socialist countries economists' phrase, privatization has become "an orgy of sweetheart deals" because many state-owned companies were sold below market prices. There is also the possibility that the existence of various rent-seeking groups took strategic advantage of resisting reforms and implemented rent-seeking delays and setbacks. Given the prominent characteristics of rent-seeking, the question that needs to be addressed is: In order to bring about full employment can rent-seeking interference in Ethiopia be minimized by using the Employer of Last Resort (ELR) rather than the Developmental State Model currently in use?

Briefly, the Developmental State Model assumes that the state in its developmental affairs needs to be managed by a bureaucracy for which highly disciplined professional functionaries and technocrats are recruited based on meritocracy to fulfill the clearly spelled out functional obligations. However, as mentioned before, if Ethiopia desires to use the state as a very important vehicle to tackle its deep-rooted developmental problems, it needs to improve the competence of its public administration sector and to encourage its public employees to remain politically neutral. As it stands now, Ethiopia's developmental state is neither operating in a market-friendly environment nor does it mirror the country's socio-political and economic realities. Moreover, a number of the government-initiated developmental plans are either obstructed or unduly delayed for implementation because the professionalism of some of the government functionaries lacks commitment to mobilizing the limited resources of the nation for development purposes. They appear to be interested in maximizing their utilities by imposing hidden rent-seeking agendas. The Ethiopian political and economic environment seems confounded giving the appearance of operating as a centrally-planned economic system. Rather than adhering to the principles of developmental state, the bureaucracy is not disciplined; its management system manifests extreme forms of inefficiency and endemic corruption. Thus given that the existing Developmental State Model is dysfunctional and has been an obstacle to implementation of the well intentioned poverty-minimizing reforms because it is engulfed by rent-seeking attributes, it needs to look at the Employer of Last Resort (ELR) model as an alternative model for minimizing the rent-seeking behavior in order to empower local citizens and achieve full employment.

Respecting the fundamental right to work, the ELR framework needs to focus on guaranteeing full employment by governments to those who are ready and willing to work at a minimum wage in sustainable activities. The ELR not only stimulates productivity and lowers unemployment and inflation but it plays a vital role in stabilizing the economy by reducing economic fluctuations (Wary 200, and Becker, 1993). Therefore, given that Ethiopia is endowed with abundant natural resources and Article 8 No.1, of the constitution states that nations, nationalities and peoples of Ethiopia are the sole owners of power and have equal rights to benefits from the nation's resources; the implementation of the Employer of Last Resort (ELR) management system could be made to be structurally and financially independent from the centralized bureaucratic system (Selamta, December, 2013)). To achieve locally-based cooperative enterprises, the ELR need not be dependent on benevolent rulers or non-governmental organizations. If the ELR is to be fully implemented, the Ethiopian government needs to be willing to relinquish its direct control and allow self-managed cooperatives at the grass roots level to become actively dependent on labor-intensive projects.

In short, if the ELR type of people-centered cooperative organizations, managed by democratically elected local leaders, were to be implemented in a decentralized way, the empowerment of local communities would present the greatest potential for the development of domestic resources, and end cyclical unemployment. In addition, employing the most vibrant working-age Ethiopians based on the powerhouse development of a full employment program led by the ELR will likely empower the employed to be involved in their own environmentally sensitive projects to reduce poverty and the overall socio-political and economic exclusion of the marginal groups in rural and urban Ethiopia.

Government Initiated, Environmentally Sustainable Projects for Ethiopian Communities

Based on the GDP scoreboard, while Ethiopia has manifested a high growth rate over the years, it has faced a high rate of unemployment and rampant inflationary pressures. Given that the economic growth rate has continued without significant impact on employment, it is therefore very pathetic to see that the poor in Ethiopia have remained at the margin, admiring the life style of the well-to-do from the side. The analysis generated below attempts to forward a tentative design by interweaving environmental and developmental issues to foster Ethiopia's economic development plan that could generate full-employment. However, it needs to be mentioned here that by realizing that natural resources are the foundation of an economy, and although too general because it does not include strategies for rigorous implementation, monitoring and evaluation, Ethiopia has already mandated a comprehensive statement of Environmental Policy for the Federal Democratic Republic of Ethiopia. The goals of the environmental policy approved by the Council of Ministers in April 1997 were to improve and enhance the health, social, and the long run economic development of the Ethiopia (UNEP Training Resource Manual, 2006).

This study using Kaboub's (May 2007) framework tailored for designing the "Employer of Last Resort" (ELR) model for Tunisia, attempts to replicate and modify the Tunisian model to fit the Ethiopian situation. In addition, going one step further than Kaboub's theoretical model, the Ethiopian model attempts to incorporate the concept of environmentally sustainable development into the ELR theoretical model. Also, environmentally sustainable development is operationally defined to include economic sustainability (maintaining the basic needs and livelihoods at full employment in a local community), social sustainability (includes seeing improvements in both individual well-being and the overall social welfare), and environmental sustainability (focuses on maintaining a stable resource base, reducing overexploitation of renewable resources, maintaining the health of living systems, and the management of biodiversity).

As suggested by Kaboub, in order to avoid a shock when implementing the ELR framework in the Ethiopian situation, a gradual strategic approach is used in order to

> *...allow economic agents to adjust their behavior and their expectations 'to new economic conditions, and, more specifically, to the presence of the ELR administration as a major institutional actor in the economy. Inflation expectations (and therefore actual inflation) will be easier to manage when ELR is introduced gradually, since the financial cost will be phased in slowly and the benefits of ELR will be assessed progressively by economic agents, which will help reshape expectations' about the program* (May 1997).

Thus, two programs have been designed. The first strategy is a cooperative long-term program that deals with the unemployed and underemployed (i.e., individuals working but not working at full capability) rural labor force in Ethiopia. Since not efficiently utilizing the labor force in rural Ethiopia is a barrier to economic development, the plan is designed to help the unemployed and underemployed in rural Ethiopia to master techniques in sustainable agriculture and appropriate technology that could be used to add value to their crops by processing them locally rather than selling them as raw materials. It also addresses some of the ways cooperative communities improve their quality of life and preserve the environment on which their future depends. The second phase of this tentative plan addresses how through the ELR program the government could hire those who have been unemployed in urban sectors of the country for less than one year but are now willing and able to work in environmentally sensitive projects at the country's per capita income of about 4500 birr per year. The second phase suggests paying 5000 birr per year by the

ELR program to those urban unemployed for retraining in vocational schools and involving them in developmental internships that deal with urban and rural greening techniques, such as organic farming, recycling, and irrigation systems, school tutoring, and rescue resource degradation schemes.

Possible ELR Programs for Rural Ethiopia

Agriculture accounts for about 45% of gross domestic product, 60% of exports and about 85% of total employment. Though rural Ethiopia is dependent on agriculture, the unemployed in the rural sectors of the Ethiopian economy are heavily dependent on agricultural income for their households. Given that agriculture is the motor of Ethiopia's economy, over the years Ethiopia has attempted to reengineer its agricultural sector through the transformation and expansion of its agricultural capabilities. However, since it has shown insignificant results thus far, instead of perceiving that industrialization is an expedient way of restructuring the Ethiopian economic system as stated in the Growth and Transformation Plan (GTP), a better way of tackling underemployment and achieving full-employment is by making the landholding in rural Ethiopia to be cooperatively owned at the grassroots level rather than leaving it under the monopoly of the state. Currently the government leases fertile land to foreign agri-business investors to produce wheat, rice and corn for consumption back home. This is based on mono-cropping, capital intensive, and contributes to mass unemployment and underemployment instead of fulfilling the promise of building infrastructure with jobs for native residents (Belineh, G. May, 2009). Though the Ethiopian government may have had to give up short term hard currency for leasing land to foreigners, it would have been wiser to think that the leased land would likely be exposed to diminishing biodiversity in the long run.

Therefore, the rural sectors of Ethiopia should instead be labor-intensive and involved in cooperative enterprises so that the rural people who become fully employed are included in controlling and utilizing the natural resources of the leased and rural part of the country to their benefit. Though ambitious, it needs to be stated that the Ethiopian government is currently planning a "... voluntary settlement program that will target Ethiopia's pastoral communities in the Somali region and parts of Gambella in an effort to group its naturally scattered semi-nomadic people into permanent settlements" (Nazret,.com, July 1, 2011). To achieve cooperative enterprise on communal land, the ELR need not be dependent on benevolent rulers or nongovernment organizations. Poor people have strength in their numbers which will help them to press their demands. Thus, the Ethiopian government must relinquish its direct control over much of the rural Ethiopia. The rural community organization needs to be implemented in a decentralized way and funded by the national government (See for example, Kofi and Desta, 2008 and Kaboub, May 2007).

Initially, the ELR government branch could give the average per capita of 5000 birr per year for each farmer as a subsidy for two years to hire unemployed Ethiopian rural people to counter the periodic droughts that may arise until they become self-sufficient. Of course, giving money to the underemployed by the ELR organization until the unemployed are organized to self-sufficiency might contribute to the widening of the already existing national budget deficits. But, we have to take into consideration that employing the most vibrant working-age of the rural population could empower the rural people to be involved in self-created environmental cleanup projects involving reforestation, recycling, sanitation, and anti-desertification projects. These activities to make the environment green are most likely to stimulate the Ethiopian economy and thereby reduce poverty and the socioeconomic exclusion of the poor. In Ethiopia, the rural people are dependent on natural resources, making ecosystem degradation and, resource scarcity challenging to ending poverty. For example, the main cause of soil erosion is the removal of vegetation. Among other things, the method of ploughing, the time of planting, the nature of the crop, and the size of the fields have an influence on the severity of erosion. To combat soil erosion and eventually contribute to sustainable development, the government could use its mandate from the ELR program in rural areas to train the unemployed to be involved in re-vegetation programs in their communities, to stop stream water bank erosion, and be involved in crop management (i.e., crop rotation, reforestation, strip cropping, terracing, installing wind breaks, and the suppression of wind erosion) techniques.

Also, mass education for the rural Ethiopian community could be initiated as a new problem-solving framework for making the community aware that the environment provides their livelihood and that they must change the way they interact with the environment. In other words, both formal and informal education could help create resilient cooperative communities that could readily anticipate and adapt to change through clear decision-making processes. As it is done in Cuba, Ethiopia could utilize its high school and Technical Vocational and Training centers (TVET) to give services and encourage their students to carry out internships in the rural areas. By offering these types of experiential environmental education programs to the rural people, Ethiopian schools can be made to integrate their school curriculum into effective rural development (See Kofi and Desta 2008).

As a result of establishing a successful platform for creating rural self-managed cooperatives at the grass roots level, the rural people would be both consumers and producers providing for themselves the necessary goods and services. Through agricultural extension programs, basic facilities equipment, processing, and marketing services could be provided to the rural cooperative by the ELR management program. Each person in the rural development community cooperatives could also be given a share of the products equivalent to the value of his (her) contribution of land and labor.

In short, though there are rural development programs in Ethiopia, they have not been designed to contribute to full employment because they are ideologically oriented, excessively controlled by central governments with top managements who are insensitive to local conditions. Landownership in rural Ethiopia is controlled by the state. Nowadays, more and more land is falling under lease agreements or formal rental agreements to private owners. However, under the decentralized full-employment development ELR program that is suggested here, by banning land grabs by foreign governments and agri-business firms, land in rural Ethiopia must be owned and managed by the local people so that they can diversify their agricultural sector through horizontal diversification into organic crops. Also, members of the cooperatives, through their transparent and accountable leadership styles, need to be involved in creating social capital and the empowerment of rural areas to reducing the unsustainable trend of rural-urban migration (See for example, UNEP, 2011).

To summarize, the formation of people-oriented cooperative rural development managed by democratically elected local leadership following the ELR program not only would stimulate the formation of cooperative developments to strengthen the capabilities of the citizenry at large to undertake similar cooperative strategies but also to enhance the welfare and empower the marginal groups in Ethiopia (See Kofi and Desta, 2008). Thus, to salvage Ethiopia from heavy unemployment and underemployment in the rural sector of Ethiopia, local communities need to be structured for powerhouse development of full employment programs led by ELR. If properly implemented, the autonomous ELR-led developments are likely to reduce per unit cost, increase the bargaining power of producers and customers, and encourage self-employment based on labor-intensive strategies. Thus if ELR-led development is to operate effectively the Ethiopian government has to relinquish its direct control strategies of development and instead empower local citizens to produce significant assets in a decentralized way. As stated by the ILO Asia – Pacific Working Paper Series, "A considerable degree of decentralization would be absolutely essential for the success of the employment program. Decentralization needs to be established, strengthened at local governments and not treated simply as implementing agents for the national government. In addition, decentralization requires to be transparent and accountable to reduce inefficiency and corruption" (International Labour Organization, 2006).

Possible ELR Programs for Urban Ethiopia

In urban Ethiopia, unemployment, particularly among the youth which constitutes over a third of the population is unbearable and calls for an urgent intervention through ELR programs. As stated by Serneels (2004), "With around 50% of the urban men between age 15-30 unemployed, Ethiopia has one of the highest unemployment rates worldwide....Mean duration of unemployment is close to four years and is (even) higher for those aspiring to public sector jobs." What is astonishing is that almost half of the first-time job seekers have college education. Given that public and private colleges are growing exponentially in Ethiopia, the trend of unemployed college graduates is likely to continue in the future. Based on this trend, though implementing a full employment policy in Ethiopia is very challenging, it is certainly achievable if Ethiopia takes its fate in its own hands by reclaiming sovereignty over its domestic economy instead of pursuing irrelevant economic blueprints and abiding by the rules of international markets that have shown no significant impact on employment (see for example, Kaboub, May 2007).

To tackle unemployment in urban Ethiopia, the autonomous ELR program needs to focus on assigning public jobs to those who recently dropped out or have recently graduated from high schools and post-secondary educational programs. Those who have been out of the labor market for more than one year need to be paid allowances to get further training at the TVET centers in order to be acquainted with new technological developments in the job market. As mentioned before, the now unemployed for less than one year should be willing and able to work at fixed, socially-established market floor wage rates, that is, the average per capita income of 5000 birr per head, in order to participate in the ELR job programs.

Leaving aside the national deficit that could rise as a result of the ELR program; the study assumes that the government has the financial capacity to pay for the ELR program by creating *fiat* money to reduce unproductive government spending. Once having income to meet basic needs, employed individuals after gaining additional skills and wages could buy and contribute their income to the private sector economy thereby raising the output of the private sector enabling more hiring as production of its goods and services increases. The rise in private sector employment in turn draws workers off the rolls of the ELR program, resulting in an automatic reduction of government spending and closing the gap of the national debt, used for generating tax obligations to pay off the budget for the ELR programs (Palley, 2001).

Employer as the Last Resort (ELR) in Ethiopia must therefore introduce new community-based employment dynamics in decentralized public sectors in order to hire "hardcore unemployed" individuals who are willing and able to work at a minimum wage in sustainable activities. The ELR employed workers could be involved in upgrading and expanding infrastructure facilities, improving community health care services (water supply, sewage and sanitation, drainage, solid waste management, helping senior citizens), helping with community recycling projects, building tables, chairs, tutoring in public school, acting as tourist guides, community historians and ethnographers, and also participating in activities to preserve biological diversity.

To conclude then, when compared with Neo-liberalism policies and Development state policies, full employment-led development is within the reach of Ethiopian policy makers through Employer as the Last Resort (ELR) programs with decentralization and high levels of community participation not entrusted to bureaucratic administration at the Central or Regional State levels. ELR entails development for the marginal local people and needs to be administered by democratically elected members of the same socially depressed people. Poverty can be eradicated not by providing the poor with purchasing power alone but by providing employment with dignity to raise a sense of self-esteem for those who are willing and able to work at a reasonable wage rate. Therefore, in the ELR programs, the unemployed workers can be given the vacancies created by ELR. Then, government spending to finance ELR programs will be slowly reduced as the ELR stimulates the private sector to draw off workers from the ELR payrolls.

Therefore, if policy makers want to get out of the existing theoretical framework which has contributed to high rates of unemployment, the ELR-designed programs are within their reach since it costs about 5% of Ethiopia's gross domestic product (GDP). Furthermore, as long as an employment scheme results in environmentally sensitive product activity financed either through government printing of currency, or borrowing from multi-lateral financial organizations the cost could be immaterial because in the final analysis, the created jobs will result in tax revenues that would finance the budget deficits incurred as a result of implementing the ELR programs. In a market-driven economy, the tentative road-map depicted above shows that environmentally-sensitive; productive employment created for the unemployed is the most reasonable and the surest way to lift everyone to a tolerable standard of living and that will enhance the dignity and self-esteem of the now unemployed but potentially productive members of Ethiopian society. (See for example, Bhaduri, 2005).

Conclusion

To conclude then, when we compare the modus operandi of the Developmental State that is being currently practiced in Ethiopia with the Employer of Last Resort paradigm that is proposed, we find that by design or default, the

Developmental State seems to be heavily influenced by a rampant rent-seeking environment as a result of institutional factors. The conspicuous rent-seeking behaviors that have become detrimental to the implementation of reforms in Ethiopia include weak institutional settings, where corruption and embezzlement have become quite obvious. For example, the conversion of the Ethiopian economic system from socialism to a Revolutionary Democratic State that converted state-owned enterprises to privately-owned firms was affected by 'an orgy of sweetheart deals.' Therefore, from an ethical point of view, rent-seeking behavior in Ethiopia is reprehensible because unproductive agents were being rewarded indirectly instead of paying directly those economic agents who accomplished their societal obligations. Thus, if the Ethiopian government wants to see the implementation of its well-designed reform packages, it has to give up the Developmental State paradigm which has become synonymous with rent-seeking. Instead, it has to entertain the Employer as the Last Resort (ELR) model of development.

As discussed before, the ELR approach introduces new community-based employment dynamics in decentralized public sectors in order to hire hardcore unemployed individuals who are willing and able to work at a minimum wage in sustainable activities. More importantly, rather than the complex Developmental State apparatus run by government officials who may have a rent-seeking agenda, the ELR is not affiliated politically. It focuses on creating communities with local level participation that is supervised by watchdogs chosen by the community. Participation, if managed by the representatives of the community, has many advantages. First, it enables the participants to benefit from the experience and insights of each other. Second, participation can ensure that policies and programs are truly responsive to the needs of vulnerable groups. Third, participation empowers the poor and the unemployed, a vital step toward poverty alleviation because lack of power exacerbates poverty. Finally, with the community as stakeholders and working in collaboration with a decentralized ELR, officials can facilitate innovation and create new knowledge (Warner K. and Kirschenmann, F. 2007 and see also, Schutter, O and Vanioqueren, G, August 2011).

However, since rent-seeking practices could change strategies and take countervailing actions, to implement the ELR approach, the supervisors and employees of the decentralized ELR organizations need to be extensively trained and undergo a thorough experiential learning process and be highly encouraged to master their professional ethics. As argued by Fischer (2010, p. 554), a promising strategy and an effective way "to strengthen the civil society is to bring politics closer to the population by decentralization (restructuring and strengthening local government). Communicating responsibilities and making local civil servants and politicians personally accountable for benefits and failures adds (significant) non-monetary value to adopting sound policies and delivering high-quality public services." Rent-seeking behavior is part and parcel of an ailing economy. If Ethiopia has the desire to be out of the deep-rooted rent-seeking environment and achieve full employment, it is worth mentioning that employees of the ELR institutions need to be bestowed with the passion to help the socially marginal to be productively employed and counteract as much as possible the reemergence of hybrid rent-seeking types of behaviors in the country.

References

Introduction

Bowles, S. and Gintis, H. (1976). *Schooling in Capitalist America: Educational Reform and the Contradictions of Economic Life.* New York: Basic Books, Inc.

Carnoy, M. (1974). *Education as Cultural Imperialism.* New York: David McKay, Co., Inc.

Carnoy, M. and Levin, H. (1976) *The Limits of Educational Reform.* New York: David McKay, Co. Inc.

Carter, M. (1976). " Contradiction and Correspondence: analysis of the Relation of Schooling to Work." Martin Carnoy, et al (eds). New York: David McKay Co. Inc.

Grossman, D. (December 1975), "You can't Grow Rice on a blackboard. The Theory of Practice of Education in china." *LACDES Quarterly,* Vol. 5, No.1.

Lange,, O. (1962) *Political Economy,* Vol.1. New York: Macmillan

Chapter 1

Addis, H. (1975). *Ethiopia: From Autocracy to Revolution*, London: Review of African Political Economy.

Bondestam, L. (1975). "Notes on Foreign Investments in Ethiopia." In *Multinational Firms in Africa,* Goesh Widstrand (ed), Uppsala, Stockholm: Scandinavian Institute of African Sturides.

Bondestam, L. (September 1974). "People and Capitalism in the North-Eastern Lowlands of Ethiopia." *The Journal of Modern African Studies,* Vol. 12, No. 3. Brockway, Fenner. *African Socialism.* Chester Springs, Penn Bufour Edition, 1963.

Chole, E. (15-18, January, 1992). " Ethiopia at the Crossroads: Reflections on the Economics of the Transition Period." A paper prepared for the Symposium on the Ethiopian Economy, Organized by the Inter-African Group.

Markakis, J. (1974). *Ethiopia: Anatomy of the Traditional Polity.* London: Claredon Press, Oxford.

Markakis, J. (November 1977). "Class and Revolution in Ethiopia." *A Paper presented to the 20th Annual Meeting of African Studies Association at Houston, Texas.*

Pankhurst, R (1965/66). "Menelik and the Utilization of Foreign Skills in Ethiopia." A paper prepared in Advance of the Faculty of Arts Seminar, Haile Selassie I University. Unpublished paper (mimeograph) Addis Ababa..

______ (1967). "The Textbook of Italian Colonial Africa." *Ethiopia Observer,* Vol. 9, No. 4.

______ *(1968). Economic History of Ethiopia 1850-1935.* Addis Ababa: Haile Selassie I University Press.

______ (1966*). Ethiopia Observer.* Vol. 10, No. 6 (1966).

CHAPTER 2

Del Boca, A. (1965). *The Ethiopian War, 1935-1941.* Chicago: The University of Chicago Press.

Fines, H. (1965). *Mussolini's Italy.* New York: The Universal Library.

Lipsky, G.A. (1962). *Ethiopia: Its People, Its Society, Its Culture.* New Haven: Conn. Kraf Press.

Mesfin, W. (June 1970). "Problems of Urbanization." In the *Proceedings of the Third International Conference of Ethiopian Studies.* Addis Ababa: Institute of Ethiopian Studies, Haile Selassie I University.

Pankhurst, R. (1968). *Economic History of Ethiopia 1950-1935.* Addis Ababa: Haile Selassie University.

Schawb, P. (1972). *Ethiopia and Haile Selassie.* New York: Facts on File, Inc.

Villari, L. (1956). Italian Foreign Policy Under Mussolini. New York: The Devin-Adoi Co.

CHAPTER 3

Abdul Mejid, H. (1976). Hussein, *Rehab: Drought and Famine in Ethiopia,* London: International African Institute.

Admassu, B. (1978). "Balance of Payments, Constraints and Economic Development of Ethiopia: 1960-74." Unpublished doctoral dissertation, University of California, Berkeley.

Addis, H. (1975). *Ethiopia: From Autocracy to Revolution,* London: Review of African Political Economy, 1975.

Ahooja, K (1966). "Foreign Investment and Legal Safeguards for its Protection." *Ethiopian Observer,* Vol. 10, No. 4.

Assefa, B. and Eshetu C. (1969). *A profile of the Ethiopian Economy*: Addis Ababa, Oxford University Press.

Blaug, M. (1973) "Report of the Exploratory Employment Policy Mission in Ethiopia," unpublished paper (mimeograph), Addis Ababa.

Bondestam, L. (1975). "Notes on Foreign Investments in Ethiopia." In *Multinational Firms in Africa*, Goesh Widstrand (ed), Uppsala, Stockholm: Scandinavian Institute of African Studies.

Bondestam, L. (September 1974). "People and Capitalism in the North-Eastern Lowlands of Ethiopia," *The Journal of Modern African Studies*, Vol. 12, No. 3.

Ellis, G. (June 1976). "The Feudal Paradigm as a Hindrance to Understanding Ethiopia." *The Journal of Modern African Studies*, Vol. 14, No. 2.

Ethiopian Government Central Statistics Office, *Statistical Abstract*. Addis Ababa: Central Statistics Office, 1972.

Ethiopian Observer, (December 1958)

Ethiopian Economic Review (1966).

Ethiopian Economic Review, No. 7 (September 1973).

Geiger, T. (April 1959). "TWA'S Service to Ethiopia: Eighth Case Study in an NPA Series on United States Business Performance Abroad".

Getachew, Belayneh. "The Role of United States Economic Assistance in Ethiopia." Unpublished doctoral dissertation, University of Utah, 1971.

Holmberg, J. (1977). *Grain Marketing and Land Reform in Ethiopia: An Analysis of the Marketing and Pricing of Food Grains in 1976 after the Land Reform*. Uppsala. The Scandinavian Institute of African Studies.

Lipsky, George A (1962). *Ethiopia: Its People, Its Society, Its Culture*. New Haven, Conn.: Kraf Press.

Markakis, J. (1974). *Ethiopia: Anatomy of the Traditional Polity*. London: Claredon Press, Oxford.

Newson, D. (1970) quoted in Getachew, Belayneh. "The Role of United States Economic Assistance in Ethiopia." Unpublished doctoral dissertation, University of Utah, 1971.

Schwab, P. (1972). *Ethiopia and Haile Selassie*. New York: Facts on File, Inc.

Spencer, John H. (1977). *Ethiopia, the Horn of Africa and U.S. Policy*. Cambridge, Mass., Institute for Foreign Policy Analyses, Inc.

Stahl, M. (1973). *Contradictions in Agricultural Development: A study of Three Minimum Package Projects in Southern Ethiopia*. Uppsala: The Scandinavian Institute of African Studies.

United Nations, (19754). *1974 Report on the World Social Situation*. New York, Department of Economic and Social Affairs.

United States Senate Committee on Foreign Relations (August 1976). *Ethiopia and the Horn of Africa*. Washington, D.C., U.S. Government Printing Office.

Chapter 4

Abebe, B. and Mohammed, A. (1970). "Historical Development of Ethiopian Secondary Education." HSIU and U.S.A.I.D. Summer Interns, Addis Ababa, USAID.

Addis, H. (1975).. *Ethiopia: From Autocracy to Revolution*, London: Review of African Political Economy.

African Education Commission (1925): *A Study of East Central and South Africa, 1923-24*. London: Edinburgh House Press.

Andargatchew, T (1973). " The Training and Development of Manpower for the social Services in Ethiopia." Unpublished doctoral dissertation, the University of Michigan, Ann Arbor.

Bowen, D. (1976). " Historical Background of Education in Ethiopia." *Language in Ethiopia*. L.M. Bender et al. (eds). London: Oxford University Press.

Carnoy, M.and Levin. H. (1976*). The Limits of Educational Reform*. New York, David McKay Co., Inc.

Del Boca, A. (1965). The Ethiopian War, 1935-1941. Chicago: The University of Chicago Press.

Desta, A. (1971). "A Descriptive Analysis of the Ethiopian Comprehensive Secondary School Curriculum Objectives, Contents and Methods." Unpublished Education Specialist Thesis, Kansas State Teachers College.

Desta, A. (1977). "Student Alienation: A Study of High School Students in Ethiopia," unpublished doctoral dissertation, Stanford University.

Ethiopian Ministry of Education (1971). *Seminar of Junior and Senior Secondary School Directors*, Addis Ababa: Berhane Salem Printing Press..

Ethiopian Ministry of Education, (1955). *A Ten-Year Plan for the Controlled Expansion of Ethiopian Education*. Addis Ababa, Ethiopian- United States Cooperative Education Press.

Ethiopian Ministry of Education, (1972). *Education Challenge to the Nations. Report of the Educational Sector* Review. Part C. Technical Paper.

Ethiopian Ministry of Education, (1974). *School Census of Ethiopia, 1969-70 – 1972/73, Part I* Addis Ababa: Berhane Salem Printing Press.

Ethiopian Ministry of Education,(1964)., *"Junior and Senior Secondary School Curriculum Book II*. Addis Ababa Curriculum and Teaching.

Ethiopian Ministry of Education *(1964). Handbook for Elementary Schools*. Addis Ababa: Department of Elementary and Adult Education.

Foster, P. (1965). *Education and Society change in Ghana*. Chicago: The University of Chicago Press.

Getachew, B. (1971). "The Role of United States Economic Assistance in Ethiopia." Unpublished doctoral dissertation, University of Utah.

Gilkes, P. (1975). *The Dying Lion: Feudalism and Modernization in Ethiopia*, London: Julian Friedman Publishers, Ltd.

Girma, A. (1967)."aims and Purpose of church Education in Ethiopia." *Ethiopian Journal of Education.* Vol.1, No. 1.

Grey, R. (1970). "Education and Politics in Ethiopia." Unpublished dissertation, Yale University.

Hess, R. (1970). *Ethiopia, The Modernization of Autocracy.* Ithaca, N.Y. Cornell University Press.

Haile Gabriel, D. (1974). "Social Foundations of Ethiopian Education." Unpublished paper (mimeograph) Addis Ababa: Faculty of Education, Haile Selassie I University, 1974.

Haile Gabriel, D. (1976). "Non Government Schools in Ethiopia." *In Language in Ethiopia,* L.M. Bender et al. (Eds) London: Oxford University Press, 1976.

Haile, W. (1976). "Government Schools in Ethiopia." In *Language in Ethiopia,* L.M. Bender et al. (Eds) London: Oxford University Press, 1976.

Levine, D. (1965). *Wax and Gold Tradition and Innovation in Ethiopian Culture.* Chicago: The University of Chicago Press.

Lipsky, G. (1962). Ethiopia: Its People, Its Society, Its Culture: New Haven, Conn: Kraf Press.

Markakis, J. (1974). *Ethiopia: Anatomy of the Traditional Polity.* London: Claredon Press, Oxford, 1974.

Markakis, J. (November 1977). "Class and Revolution in Ethiopia." *A Paper presented to the 20th Annual Meeting of African Studies Association at Houston, Texas.*

Mazrui, Ali A. "The African University as a Multinational Corporation. Problems of Penetration and Dependency." *Harvard Educational Review,* (May 1975).

Miaza, B. (1966). "A study of Modern Education in Ethiopia. Its Foundation, Its Development, Its Future, with Emphasis on Primary Education. Unpublished doctoral dissertation, Columbia University.

Pankhurst, R. (1965/66). "Menelik and the Utilization of Foreign Skills in Ethiopia." A paper prepared in Advance of the Faculty of Arts Seminar, Haile Selassie I University. Unpublished paper (mimeograph) Addis Ababa.

______. (1967). The Textbook of Italian Colonial Africa." *Ethiopia Observer,* Vol. 9, No. 4 (1967).

______. (1968). *Economic History of Ethiopia 1850-1935.* Addis Ababa: Haile Selassie I University Press, 1968.

Paulos M. (December 1976). "Traditional Institutions and Traditional Elites. The Role of Education in the Ethiopian Body-Politic." *African Studies Review,* Vol. 19, No. 3..

Perham, M. (1947). *The Government of Ethiopia.* London: Faber and Faber.

Schwab, P. (1972). *Ethiopia and Haile Selassie.* New York: Facts on File, Inc.

ter Weele, A. (1973). " A comparison of Education, Financing in Ethiopia, Kenya and Tanzania." Unpublished paper (mimeograph), Addis Ababa.

Tickher, H. (1975). "Ethiopian Educational Development." *Education in Eastern Africa*. Vol. 5, No. 2.

Ting-yi, lu. (1962). "Education Must be Combined with Productive Labor." *Chinese Education Under Communism*. Chang Tu Hu (ed). Newyork: Bureau of Publications, Teachers' College, Columbia University.

Trudeau, E. (1964). "A survey of Higher Education in Ethiopia, with Implications for Future Planning and Development." Unpublished doctoral dissertation, Columbia University, N.Y.

United States Senate, Committee on Foreign Relations (1976). *Ethiopia and the Horn of Africa*. Washington. D.C. U.S. Government Printing Office.

Youth Action, 1970.

Weiler H. (1972). "Political Socialization and Political System: Consensual and Conflictual linkage Concepts." *State, School and Politics*. Michael W. Kirst (ed). Lexington, Mass.: D.C. Heath.

Chapter 5

Addis, H. (1975). *Ethiopia: From Autocracy to Revolution*, London: Review of African Political Economy.

Alemayehu, G. (2011). "Recent Macroeconomic `Development Ethiopia". A paper presented at International Conference on contemporary Development Issues in Ethiopia, Western Michigan University, Kalamazoo, Michigan, USA , August 16-18.

All Africa.com. http://allafrica.com. Retrived, October 18, 2010.

Association of African Universities (AAU). The African Brain Drain: Using intellectual diaspora to manage the drain: What are the options? Conference of Rectors, Vice Chancellors and Presidents of African universities (COREVIP).

Atanga, et al (2006). Brain Drain in third world universities: perceptions and perspectives among commonwealth schools in British universities. Paper presented at ASAUK Biennial conference, September 2006.

Balsvik, R. R. (1985). *Haile Selassie's Students: The Intellectual and Social Background of Revolution, 1952-1977).* Addis Ababa.

Dzvimbo, K. P. (September 23-25, 2003). The internationalization migration of skilled human

capital from developing countries. A case study prepared for a Regional Training Conference on Improving tertiary education in sub-Saharan Africa: Things that work. Accra, Ghana, 23-25, 2003.

Emeagwali, (2010). Brain drain education in Africa: Interview of Emeagwall. http://emeagwali.com/interviews/brain-drain/education-in-africa-brain-problem-wo. Retrieved , October 26, 2010.

Emerson, W. R. (April 5, 2009). The benefits of dual citizenship to the socio-economic and political development of Ghana. http://www.modernghana.com. Retrieved, October 20, 2010.

Eshetu Chole, (1992). "Ethiopia at the Crossroads: Reflections on the Economics of Transition Period." Paper presented for the Symposium on the Ethiopian Economy, organized by the Inter-Africa Group, Addis Ababa, 15-18 January 1992.

Eshetu, C. and Makonnen Manyazewel (November1991). "The Macroeconomic Performance of the Ethiopian Economy, 1974-90." Paper prepared for the First Annual Conference on the Ethiopian Economy, organized by the Department of Economics of Addis Ababa University, Nazareth, 22-26.

Federal Democratic Republic of Ethiopia (September 2010). Growth and transformation plan (GTP) 2010/11 -2014/15 *(Draft)*. Ministry of Finance and Economic Development (MoFED).

Gada. A.com (2012). "The Oromo Chronology, The Ethiopian Revolution and the Derg Regime." Cited in http://www.gadaa.com/DERG.tml. Decemb 27, 2012.

Getachew, D. (2010). "Peasant Reflections on the Agricultural Development Led Industrialization (ADLI) Programmme." Department of Sociology and Anthropology, Addis Ababa, University).

Grandy, C. (June 1999). Technology, endogenous growth, and public policy." http://www2.hawaii.edu/~grandy/Writins/Endogenous-Growth-and-Technolgy.htm. Retrieved, October 24, 2010.

Groizard L. J. and Llull, J. (November 2004). Brain drain and aid growth. First draft.

Hague, N. and S. Kim (1995). Human Capital Flight: Impact of migration on income and growth, IMF staff papers 42(3):577-607.

Hunger, U. (January 2002). The brain drain hypothesis: Third-World elites in industrialized countries and socioeconomic development in the home country. The Center for Comparative Immigration Studies. San Diego: University of California, working paper 47.

Idehen, K. (2010). Reversing Nigeria's brain drain http://the willnigeria.com/opinion/4705-Reversing Nygeria's brain drain.html. Retrieved, December 3, 2010.

Korner, H. (January/ February , 1996). The brain drain from developing countries - an enduring problem." Intereconomics.

Levine, W. (1965). Wax Gold: Tradition and innovation in Ethiopian culture. Chicago: University of Chicago Press.

Lowell, B.L. (2001). International Migration Papers, 45: Policy responses to the international mobility of skilled labour. Geneva,: International Migration Branch.

Lucas, R. Jr. (January 1988). On the mechanics of economic development, Journal of Monetary Economics, 22, pp. 3-42.

Manby, B. (2010*)*. Citizenship law in Africa: A comparative study. New York: Open Society Foundation, p. 58.

Marchiori, L. Shen, I-Ling, and Docquier (June 2009). Brain drain in globalization: A general equilibrium analysis from the sending countries' perspective. The Institute for the Study of Labor (IZA), Discussion Paper No. 4207.

Markakis, J. (November 1977). "Class and Revolution in Ethiopia." *A Paper presented to the 20th Annual Meeting of African Studies Association at Houston, Texas.*

Mishra, P. (January 2006). Emigration and brain drain: Evidence from the Caribbean. International Monetary Fund Working Paper.

Mohamoud, A.A. (2005). Reversing the brain drain in Africa: Harnessing the intellectual capital; of the diaspora for knowledge development in Africa. Amesterdam: SAHAN Wetenschappelijk Adviesbureau, 2005, p. 7. See also World Bank, 2002.

Mpofu, B. (2010). Zimbabwe: Dual citizenship would boost forex inflows.

Ottaway, M. (September 1976). "Social Classes and Corporate Interests in the Ethiopian Revolution." *The Journal of Modern African Studies,* Vol. 14, No. 3.

Raghuvanhi, A. (2010). Dual citizenship: Impact of overseas of India. http://www.legalserviceindia.com. Retrieved October 20, 2010.

Romer, P. (1994). The origins of endegenous growth, Journal of Economics Perspectives, 3-22.

Sachs, J. (January 17, 2005). Investing in development: A practical plan to achieve the millenium development goals. http://www. unmillenniumproject.org.

Solow,R.M. (1956). A contribution to the theory of economic growth. Quarterly Journal of Economics.70.

Rena, R. (2008). Brain drain and brain gain in Africa. Africa Economic Analysis. http;//www.africaeconomic analysis.org/articles/gen/brain_drain_.html.

Suranovic, S.M. (2006). International trade theory policy: http://International .com/ Trade/Tch60-14.php (Retrieved October 16, 2010.

Tadesse, B. (1995). "Agricultural and Rural Development in Ethiopia" Unpublished doctoral dissertation, Michigan State University, East Lansing.

Tamene, B. (2010). Ethiopia receives $3.2 billion in remittances-World Bank. http:// nazret.com. Retrieved, November 4, 2010.

Terrazas, M. A (June 2007). Beyond regional circularity: The emergence of an Ethiopian diaspora. Migration Information Sources. http://www.migration information.org/Profiles/display.cfm?ID=604. Retrieved, October 18, 2010.

Tettey, J. W. (May 1, 2003). Africa's options: return, retention or diaspora? Science and Development network. May 1, 2003.

Ting-Yi, Lu. (1962*)*. "Education Must be Combined with Productive Labor." Chinese Education Under Communism.*" Chang Tu Hu (ed). New York: Bureau of Publication -Teachers' College, Columbia University.*

University World News, (25 November 2007). United Nations: Losing many of a country's best minds. Issue: 0007.

Wilson, J. D. (September 14-16, 2006). A voluntary brain-drain tax. East Lansing: Michigan State University,

Woldeyensae, Y. (September 2007). Optimizing the African brain drain: Strategies for mobilizing the intellectual diaspora towards brain-gain. A paper submiited at the Conference of Rectors, Vice Chancellors and Presidents of African Universities (COREVIP) in Tripoli, Libya, October 21-25, 2007.

Zar-Zar Bargbhor, E. (August 19, 2005), Dual citizenship and its importance to Liberia's economic development. The Perspective, Atlanta Georgia. http://www.theperspective.org/articles/0819200501.html. Retrieved October 16, 2010.

Chapter 6

Ahluwalia, M.S., N. Cater, and H. Chenery, *"Growth and Poverty in Developing Countries," in Gerald M. Meier, Leading Issues in Economic Development (Fifth Edition).* New York: Oxford University Press, 1989.

Aiga Forum, "Hunger Rates in Eritrea 'are Extremely Alarming http://aigaforum.com/news/hunger_eritrea .php. (retrieved October 13, 2010.)

Atkinson, A.B. and Brandolini, (2009), "On data: a case study of the evolution of income inequality across time and across countries." *Cambridge Journal of Economics,* 2009, 33, 381-404.

Barro, R.J. (2000), " Inequality and Growth in a panel of countries", *Journal of Economic Growth,* vol. 5, iss. 1, pp. 5-32.

Behrman, et al (2000), "Economic Reform and wage differentials in Latin America", Working paper, Inter-American Development Research Department.

Beyer, H. et al (1999), "Trade Liberalization and wage inequality," *Journal of Development Economics,* Vol. 59, pp. 103-123.

Bhatta, S.D. (2002), "Has the increase in world-wide openness to trade worsened global income inequality", *Papers in Regional Science,* vol. 82, iss. 2, pp. 177-196.

Chang, J. y and Ram, R. (2000), "Level of Development , Rate of Economic Growth and Income Inequality", *Economic Development and Cultural Change,* vol. 48,pp 787-800.

Chenery, H. etal., (1974), *Redistribution with Growth.* New York: Oxford University Press.

CIA (2010), *The World Factbook-country Comparison: Distribution of Family Income –Gini.* https://www.cia.gov/library/publications/the -world-factbook/. (Retrieved October 4, 2010.)

Crisis Group, (4 September 2009). "Ethiopia: Ethnic Federalism and Its Discontents" *Africa Report No. 153.*

Deininger, K. and Squire, L. (1998), " New Ways of Looking at Old Issues: Inequality and Growth", *Journal of Development Economics,* vol. 57. Pp. 259-87.

Desta, A (2010), "*Tackling Poverty by Ethiopians or Globalization Wave: A Book Review.*" http://aigaforum.com/artices/bookreview_aklog_birra_on _ poverty.htm

Desta, A. (2012). "Centrally Planned or Developmental-oriented State" A Review of the Ethiopian Economic System." *Journal of Academy of Business and Economics.* Vol. 12, No. 2.

Dixion, PM, Weiner J. Mitchell-Olds T, Woodley Guy, R. (1987), Boot –strapping the Gini coefficient of inequality. Ecology , 68:1548-1551. And also see Word IQ, http://www.wordiq.com/definition/Gini_coefficient (Retrieved October 4, 2010).

Eshetu, C. (1992). "Ethiopia at the Crossroads: Reflections on the Economics of Transition Period." Paper presented for the Symposium on the Ethiopian Economy, Organized by the Inter-Africa Group, 15-18 , January 1992, Addis Ababa.

Federal Democratic Republic of Ethiopia, "Proclamation No. 1/1995" Federal Negasit Gazeta, August 21, 1995, Addis Ababa Ethiopia.

Fielding, D and Torres, S. (2005), " A simultaneous equation model of economic development and income inequality", *Journal of Economic Inequality,* vol. 4, pp. 279-301.

Forum of Federations (October 1999, August 2002, March 2005). *The International Conference on Federalism.*

Frank, C.R and Webb, R.C, (1977), *Income Distribution and Growth in the Less Developed Countries.* Princeton, N.J: Princeton University Press.

Habtu, A. (July 11-12, 2003). Ethnic Federalism in Ethiopia: Background, Present Conditions and Future Prospects." A paper submitted to the second EAF International Symposium on Contemporary Development Issues in Ethiopia. The Ghion Hotel, Addis Ababa, Ethiopia.

Habisso, T. (December 6, 2010). "The Moral and Sentimantal Value of Federalism: A Southerner's View."

Hirbe, T. (August 13, 2010). "Ethnic federalism: Problems or Solution? http://addis-voice.com/2010/08/ethnic -federalism-problem-orsolution/

Jha, S.K. (1996), " The Kuznets curve: A reassessment", *World Development,* vol.24, pp. 773-778.

Kofi ,T. A and A. Desta (2008*). The Saga of African Underdevelopment: A viable Approach for Africa's Sustainable Development in the 21st Century.* Trenton, NJ: Africa World Press.

Kuznets, S (1955), "Economic growth and income inequality" American Economic Review, vol 49, pp. 1-28.

Lisane Masie (March 2012). "Key Findings of Ethiopian Welfare Monitoring Survey 2011". Vol. 16, No. 16.

Lu, X. 2008, "Income distribution, effective factor endowments and trade openness: A Study based on provinces panel data", *The Journal of Quantitative & Technical Economics,* no.4, pp. 53-64.

Meier, G. (1989), *Leading Issues in economic Development* (Fifth Edition). New York: Oxford University Press.

Park, W.G. and Brat, D. A. (1995), " a Global Kuznuts Curve." *Kyklos. Vol. 48, pp. 105-131.*

Ram, R. (1995), " Economic development and income inequality: An Overlooked regression constraint", *Economic Development and Cultural Change,* vol. 43, pp. 425-434.

Randolph, S. M. and Lott, W. F. (1993), "Can the Kuznets effect be relied on to induce equalization growth? *World Development, vol. 21, pp. 829-840.*

Rogers, P. etal. *An Introduction to Sustainable development. London: Earthscan.*

Selamta *(Dec, 2013). Ethiopian Constitution.*

Sen, A. (1999). *Development as Freedom* . New York: Oxford University Press.

Serra-Horguelin, A. (1999). *The Federal Experiment in Ethiopia: A socio-Political Analysis.* Centre d'etude D'Afrique Noire. No. 64-1999.

Silva, J. A (2007), " Trade and Income Inequality in a less developed country: The Case of Mozambique, " *Economic Geography,* vol. 83, iss.2, pp. 111-136.

Solow, R.M. (1956), "A Contribution to the theory of economic growth", *Quarterly Journal of Economics.*70.

Suranovic, S. M. (2006), *International Trade Theory and Policy.* http: //internationalecon.com/Trade/Tch60/T60-14.php (Retrieved October 16, 2010.

Tabor, L. G. and Manlam, B. (Summer 2010). "Globalization –Trends and Perspectives of a new Age." *The Businsess Review, Cambridge,* Hollywood, Vol. 15, Iss. 1; pp 39, 7 pgs.

Todaro, M. (1994), *Economic Development* (Fifth Edition). Reading, Massachusetts: Addison-Wesley, p. 155.

Todaro, M. (1996), *Economic Development* (Sixth Edition). Reading, Massachusetts: Addison-Wesley.

Wikipedia, "Gini Coefficient". http://love.iciba.com/gini+coefficient/ (Retrieved October 4, 2010).

World Bank Group (2010), *Beyond Economic Growth: Meeting the Challenges of Global Development.* http://www.worldbank.org/depweb/beyond/global/chapter 5.html. (Retrieved October 6, 2010.

United Nations, (2010). *United Nations-Gini Coefficient.* http://www.scribd.com/com. (Retrieved October 4, 2010).

United Nations, Article 13.2 (a). International Covenant on Economic, Social and Cultural Rights. Cited in http://www2.ohchr.org/english/law/cescr.htm#art13).

UNESCO (2007). "A Human Rights-Based Approach to Education for all. Cited in http://unesdoc.unesco.org/images/0015'0015486E.pdf. UNESCO and UNICEF, 2007. Pp.7 cited in http://unesdoc.unesco.org/images/0015/001548/154861E.pdf.

World Bank (2005), *Education in Ethiopia: Strengthening the Foundation for Sustainable Progress:* A World Bank Country Study. Washington, D.C.

World Bank (2012). " School Enrollment: Primary; Private (of the total primary) in Ethiopia. Cited in http://www.tradingeconomies.com, Ethiopia/school-enrollment-prime.

Chapter 7

Ageba, Gebrehiwot. "Micro-finance Institutions in Ethiopia: Issues of Portfolio Risk, Institutional Arrangements and Governance." Retrieved September 31, 2007 from http://www.eeaecon.org/eje/v7n2/gebrehiwot/GEBRH-A.htm

Ajit, D, Sunil, R, and Raman, K.R (2006). "Micro-credit and Repayment Rates: A case study of Kudumbashree Micr-Enterprise Program in Kerala."

Al-bagdadi H. and Bruntrup, M. (2002). Microfinance Associations: The Case of the Association of Microfinance Institutions Ethiopia(AEMFI). Division 4, Economic Development and Employment Promotion.

Alson J. and Shepherd A (2008-09). "Escaping Poverty Traps" *The Chronic Poverty Report 2008-09.* Manchester: Chronic Poverty research Centre, 2008-09, p, vii.

Amha, W. et al. (2006). "Business development services (BDS) in Ethiopia; Status, prospects and challenges in the micro and small enterprise sector." *International Journal of Emerging markets.* Vol.1, Iss. 4 and ABI/INFORM Global.

Armendariz, B and Morduch, J. (2007). *The Economics of Microfinance.* Cambridge: Massachusetts Institute of Technology.

Banerjee A. B and Duflo, E. (2006). "The Economic Lives of the Poor," *Journal of Economic Perspectives.*

Becker, G. (1991). *A Treatise on the Family.* Cambridge, Harvard University.

Bradshaw, J. and Finch N. (2003). "Overlaps in Dimensions of Poverty." *Journal of Social Policy.* Oct. 2003;32. Pp. 513-525.

Carney, D. (ed.) 1998. Sustainable *Rural Livelihoods: What Contributes can We Make*? London: Department of International Development (DFID).

Chowdhury, A. Gosh, D. and Wright, R. E. (2005). " The Impact of Microcredit on Poverty: Evidence from Bangladesh." *Progress in Development Studies.* Vol. 5 , No. 4, 298-309.

Desta, A. (1998). *Environmentally Sustainable Economic Development.* Westport, CT: Praeger Publishers.

Doocy, S. et al, "Outcomes of an Ethiopian Microfinance Program and Management Actions to Improve Services." *Journal of Microfinance,* 7.1, Summer 2005.

Duran, J. (2002). "Kenyan Drought: A Community Based Approach With Micro credits." International Federation of Red Cross, Africa Department.

Elahi, Khandakar Q. i and Danopoulos.Constantine P. "Microfinance and Third World Development: A critical Analysis." *Journal of Political and Military Sociology*, Vol. 32, No. 1, summer 2004, pp. 61-77

Ellis, F. 2000. *Rural Livelihoods and Diversity in Developing countries.* Oxford: Oxford University Press.

Fisher , T and Sriram, M.S. ed.(2002). Putting Development Back into Microfinance: New Delhi: Oxfam r Publishing.

Flynn, P. (2007). "The Newest Financial Technology of the Washington Consensus." *Challenge: The Magazine of Economic Affairs. Vol. 50, No. 2.*

Gehlich-Schillabeer, M. (2008). "Poverty alleviation or poverty traps? Microcredits and Vulnerability in Bangladesh." *Disaster Prevention and Management.* Vol.17, Iss.3; p. 396.

Gibson, B. Robert, et al. (2007). *Sustainability Assessment: Criteria and Processes.* London: Earthscan.

Hagenaars, A. (1987). "A Class of Poverty Index". *International Economic Review.* Vol 28, no.3, 583-607.

Hardi, P. and Zdan, T. (1997). *Assessing Sustainable Development: Principles in Practice. International Institute for Sustainable Development.* Winnipeg: Canada.

Harkness, S. (2004). "Social and Political Indicators of Human Well-being." Research Paper No. 2004/33, United Nations University, World Institute for Development Economics Research (WIDER).

Hume, D. and Mosley, P. (1996). Finance Against Poverty (London: Rutledge, 1996.

Hulme, D. and McKay A. (June, 2005). Identifying and Measuring Chronic Poverty: Beyond Monetary Measures, Chronic Poverty Research Centre (CPRC)-IIPA Working Paper 30, Indian Institute of Public Administration.

International Federation of Red Cross and Red Crescent Socities (2009). Case Study: Micro-credit, A Rwandan Experience.

International Institute for Environment and Development (2002). *Development Strategies: A resource Book Sustainable.* London: EARTHSCAN.

Jain, S. (2003). "The Microfinance Revolution: Sustainable Finance for the Poor." *Journal of Economic Literature,* Dec 2003, 41,4; ABI/Inform Global.

Karnani, A. (2007). "Microfinance Misses its Mark." *Stanford Social Innovation Review.* Retrieved July 8, 2009 from http://www.ssireview.org/site/printer/micrifinance_misses_its_mark/

Khandker, S.R. (1998). *Fighting Poverty with Microcredit Experience in Bangladesh.* Washington, D.C.: World Bank

______, (April, 2003). Microfinance and Poverty: Evidence from Bangladesh. *Grameen Dialogue,* no. 54.

Lamarre, J. (2000). From a multidimensional to a socio-political definition of poverty." *Understanding Poverty in Vietnam and the Philippiness: Concepts and Context,* edited by De Koninck et al. Université de Montreal, 2003..

Lamarre, J. and Miller, M. (2003). "An Organizational Approach to Poverty." *Understanding Poverty in Vietnam and the Philippiness: Concepts and Context, edited by De Koninck etal. Université de Montreal*.

Latifee, H. I. (2003). "Micro-credit and Poverty Reduction." A paper presented at the International Conference on 'Poverty Reduction through Micro-credit ' held at Ceylon Inter-Continental Hotel, Taksim-Istanbul, Turkey from June 9-10, 2003.

Macfarlane, A. (2002). "The Dimensions of Famine." Working Paper, Department of Anthropology, Cambridge University.

Microcredit Summit (1997), *Declaration and Plan of Action.* Retrieved July 2, 2009 from http://www.microcreditsummitt.org

Nazret, "Ethiopia-Amhara Credit and Savings Institution and Dedebit Credit and Savings Institution among Top 50 Microfinance Institutions." *Top Microfinance Institutions.* Retrieved December 1, 2009 from http://nazret.com/blog/index.php?title=ethiopia_amhara_and_Dedbit _among _top_50-&mo...

Neff, G. (October 1996). "Microcredit, Micro results." *The Left Business Observer.* No. 74.

Njeru, E.H.N. (2004). "Bridging the Qualitative-Quantitative Methods of Poverty Analysis. " Paper written for workshop on saga qualitative-Quantitative Methods for poverty analysis, March 11, 2004.

Oyen, E. et al. (1996). "Poverty Research Rethought." Poverty, A Global Review. Paris: UNESCO, pp. 3-17.

Parris, M. Thomas and Kates, M. Roberts (2003). "Characterizing and Measuring Sustainable Development." *Annual Review Environmental Resources.* 2003, 28: 13.1-13.28.

Pearce, W. David and Warford, J. Jeremy. *World without End: Economics, Environment and Sustainable Development.* New York: Oxford University Press, 1993.

Prosterman. R. (April 2005). "The U.N.'s empty plan for poverty." *Far Eastern Economic Review,* Vol. 168, No. 4, pp. 43-45.

Scoones, I. 1998 " Sustainable Rural Livelihoods: A framework for Analysis", IDS Working Paper 72, Institute of Development Studies, University of Sussex.

Sen, A. (1983)."Poor Relatively Speaking." Oxford Economic Papers, 35, 153-169.

Sen, A. (1985). *Commodities and Capabilities,* Amesterdam: North Holland.

Sen ,A. (1992). *Inequality Reexamined.* Oxford: Oxford University Press.

Sen, A. (1999). *Development as Freedom.* New York: Alfred Knopf.

Shannon Doocy, et al., (2005). "Outcomes of an Ethiopian Microfinance Program and Management Actions to Improve Services." *Journal of Microfinance;* Summer 2005; 7, 1. Pp.79-94.

Sharma, M. (2005). "Emerging Contours of Micro Finance: Where do we go from Here?" *The Business Review,* Cambridge: Summer 2005; 4,1.

Shimeles, A and Thoenen, R. (2005). "Poverty Profiles: A Methodological note on measuring poverty", Poverty and Social Policy Team, Economic and Social Policy Division, United Nations Economic Commission for Africa, ESPD/NRP/04/05.

Somilleda, A. (2010). "Sustainability-Focused Microcredits: A Temporary Movement or Lasting Solution?" Dominican University of California.

Stiglitz, J.E (1990). "Peer Monitoring and Credit Markets." *World Bank Economic Review.* 4, pp. 351-366.

Thinkquest.org , "A Dollar a Day: Poverty Overview: Measuring Poverty." Retrieved June 28,2009 from http:// library_thinkquest.org/05aug/00282/over measure1.htm

Thirlwall, A.P. (1995). *Growth and Development* (Fifth Edition). Boulder, Colorado: Lynne Rienner, p. 12.

Tsogbe, Y. Edem (2002). "Microcredit, Agricultural Output, and Food Security" *Africa Advocacy Forum II, Microcredit – A solution for Africa?* New York: United Nations, 14 November, 2002.

UNDP (2003). ***World Population Prospect: The 2002 Revision – Highlights,*** www.un.org/esa/population/puplications /wpp2002/WPP2002-HIGHLIGHT-Srev1.PDF.

United Nations, (14 November 2002). Africa Advocacy Forum II: Microcredit—A solution for Africa? New York: United Nations.

United Nations Environmental Programme (UNEP), (1995). *Poverty and the Environment. Nairobi, Kenya, p.10.*

United Nations World Commissions on Environment and Development, (1987), Our Common Future. New York: Oxford University Press.

Vargas, C. M. (Feb. 2008). "Community development and micro-enterprises: fostering sustainable development." *Sustainable Development.* Vol. 8, No. 1; ABI/INFORM Global.

Varian, H. (1990). "Monitoring Agents with Other Agents." Journal of Institutional and Theoretical Economics. 146, pp. 153-174.

Vilei, S. and Chisholm, N. (2002). "Impact of credit as perceived by resource-poor Ethiopian households." Department of Food Business and Development, National University of Ireland, Cork.

Wikipedia, the free encyclopedia, "Measuring Poverty." Retrieved June 28, 2009 from http://en-wikipedia.org/wiki/Measuring_poverty

World Bank, *World Development Report. "Development and the Environment."* New York: Oxford University Press, 1992.

United Nations World Summit on Social development, the Copenhagen Declaration........

Yunus, M. (2003). "Halving Poverty by 2015-We can actually make it happen." Commonwealth Lecture, Commonwealth Institute, London, March 11, 2003.

Zamperetti, F. and Franca Dalla Costa, G. (2008). *Sharing Trust: Women and Microcredit in Eritrea.* Trenton, NJ: The Red Sea Press, Inc.

Chapter 8

Assefa, B. (2010). "Examination of some Western versus Japanese Management Techniques in the Context of Ethiopia."

Anh , P. et al. (2011). "Empirical study on Transferability of Kaizen Practices." *The 11th International DSI and the 16th APDSI Jint Meeting, Taipei, Taiwan, July 12-16, 2011.*

Aoki, K. (2008). "Transferring Japanese kaizen activities to overseas plants in China." *International Journal of Operations and Production Management.* 28(6), 518-539.

Assefa, B. (2010*).* "Examination of some Western versus Japanese Management Techniques in the Context of Ethiopia."

Becker, Kurt H and Snow, James (1997). "American KAIZEN: A Perspective on American Management Theories. " *Journal of Industrial Technology.* Winter, 1997.

Beer, S. (1966). *Decision and Control.* Chichester: Wiley.

Berihu Assefa (2010). "Examination of Some Western versus Japanese Management Techniques in the Context of Ethiopia."

Brunet, A.P & New, S. (2003). " Kaizen in Japan: An Empirical Study", *International Journal of Operation & Production Management,* vol. 3, no. 12, pp. 1426-1446.

Choudhury, S.R. ((November 2005). " TheSpillover Effect of Japanese Foreign Direct Investment in Human Resource Management: A case Study of Honda Siel." *Centre for Studies in International Relations and Development (CSIRD),* India.

Choy, C.L and Jain, H.C. (1987). "Japanese Management in Singapore: Convergence of human resources management practices," *Asia Pacific Journal of Management.* 4(2), 73-89.

Chow, C etal., (1991). "The effects of Management Controls and National Culture on Manufacturing Performance: An Experimental Investigation." *Accounting Organizations and Society.* Vol. 16, No. 3, pp. 209-226.

Dobi, Sandor (2006). "The KAIZEN and the Japanese Company Culture"

Ethiopian Ministry of Industry, (Mar. 10, 2011). *Ethiopia's KAIZEN has Now a Manual.*

Fukuda, K.J. (1988). *Japanese style Management Transferred: The Experience of East Asia.* New York: Rutledge.

Gebrehiwot, B. A. (2010). "Comparative analysis of some Western versus Japanese management techniques in the context of Ethiopia."

Genobz (July 15, 2010). " Understanding kaizen and 5S: Japan's widely acclaimed key to competitive success." http://genobz.wordpress.com/2010/07/15. Retrieved, March 30, 2011.

Hayashi, S. (1988). *Culture and management in Japan.* Tokyo: University of Tokyo Press.

Hosono, A. (October 2009). "Kaizen: Quality, Productivity and Beyond." *Introuction Kaizen In Africa.* GRIPS Development Forum.

Ihara, H. (2004). "Reexamination of Japanese Management System." *Management Japan,* Vol. 36.

Imai, M. (1986). *Kaizen: the Key to Japanese Competitiveness Success:* New York: Random House Business Division.

Ishiwata, A. (October 2009) "Needs for kaizen Activities by African Manufactures." *Introuction Kaizen In Africa.* GRIPS Development Forum.

Kaplinsky, R. and Posthuma (1994). "Easternisations: The Spread of Japanese Management Techniques to the Developing Countries."

Lillrank, P. (1995). *"The Transfer of Management Innovation from Japan." Organization Studies.* Vol. 16, No. 6, Pp 971-989.

Malhotra, Y. 2003). "Is Knowledge the Ultimate Competitive Advantage?", Businees Management Asia, 3Q, No. 4, 66-69.

Mandel, (February 20, 2011). "How the Japanese "Kaizen" Method Can Change Your Life" *Stress Management Site* . http://www.bellaonline .com. Retrieved February 25, 2011.

Ohno, K. (October 2010). "Industrial Policy in Africa: Learning Mindset and Methods from East Asia." National Graduate Institute for Policy Studies (GRIPS), Tokyo,

Ohno, I. Hhno, K and Uesu, S. (October 2009). "Introducing Kaizen in Africa." *GRIPS Development Forum Tokyo:* Roppongi, Minato-ku.

Recht, R. (December 1, 1998). "Kaizen and Culture: On the transferability of Japanese suggestion systems" http://www.science direct.com/science? Retrieved, March 30, 2011.

Shaari, Jamal Abdul Nassir and Nariai, O. (May 2006). *International Review of Business Research Papers.* Vol. 2. No. 1, May 2006. Pp. 100-114.

Shaari, J. A.N (November 2010). " *Barriers to Implement TQM in Japanese Way: A study of Companies in Malaysian." International Review of Business Papers.* Vol. 6, Number 5, Pp. 400-410.

Sonobe, T. (2009). "Kaizen, skill Development, and Industrial Clusters". Foundation for advanced Studies on International Development (FASID) and National Graduate Institute for Policy Studies (GRIPS), Japan.

Tasie, G. (May, 2009). *"Can Japanese management styles be applied to Africa? African Journal of Business Management.* Vol. 3 (4), pp. 233-239.

The IMD World Competitiveness Yearbook (2011). " Overall Ranking and Competitiveness Factors." http://www.imd.org/research /publications/wcy/wcy/__book.cfm. Retrieved March 28, 2011.

Weldemariam, H. (2010). Ethiopia applying thee Japanese management philosophy that promises big rewards through continuous incremental change: "kaizen". http://hiwoteethiopia.blogspot.com/2010/09. Retrieved March 30, 2011.

Yokozama, K. et al (2010). " The influence of national culture on Kaizen transfer: An exploratory study of Japanese subsidiaries in the Netherlands."

Yokozama, K. et al (2010). "Recent Experience with transferring Japanese Management Systems Abroad," *Journal of Strategic management Studies,* 2 (1).

Yong, AKB (1996). "Malaysian Human Resources management." Kuala Lumpur: Malyasian Institute of Management.

Zimmerman, W. (1991). " kaizen: the Search for Quality." *The Journal of Continuing Higher Education.* Vol. 39, No. 3, pp. 7-10.

Chapter 9

Alden, C., "China in Africa." *Survival*, 47 93, 2005, 147-164.

Alden, C. and Davis, M., "A Profile of the Operations of Chinese Multinationals in Africa." *South African Journal of International Affairs*. Vol. 13, (1), Summer/ Autumn 2006, 83-96.

Alves, A., "China's Preferential Trade Policy as a Foreign Policy Tool." *Centre for Chinese Studies (CCS)*, Stellenbosch University, South Africa, 2008.

Asche, H., "China's Engagement in Africa- Opportunities and Risks for Development." Hamburg: Africa Department, Economics Affairs, 2008, 3.

Akkurt, A. D. and Ratha, D., "South-South FDI Flows: How Big Are They?" In Transnational Corporations, Vol.13, (1), 2004.

BBC News, "China to Double its aid to Africa." November 4, 2006.

Bosshard, P., "China's Environmental Footprints in Africa." China in Africa Policy. China in Africa Project of the SA Institute of International Affairs (SAIIA), No. 3, April 2008.

Broker., "China and Africa, How will the Beijing Consensus Benefit Africa?" April, 2007. *www.thebrokeronline.eu/en/articles/How-will-the-Beijing-Consensus-benefit-Africa*. Retrieved May 19, 2009.

Chau, Donovan C., "Political Warfare in Sub-Saharan Africa: U.S. Capabilities and Chinese Operations in Ethiopia, Kenya, Nigeria, and South Africa." March 2007.

Corkin, L. and Burke, C. "Constructive Engagement: An Overview of China's Role in Africa's Construction Industries." *Centre for Chinese Studies (CCS)*, Stellenbosch University, South Africa, 2008.

Doha., "The Need for a South Platform." Prepared by the South Centre on the Occasion of the Second South Summit. 2005.

ECOWAS-SWAC/OECD "Africa and China Economic Series of the Atlas on Regional Integration in West Africa," 2006. *www.atlas.estafrica.org*. Retrieved May 19, 2009,

Ellis, Linden J. "China EXIM Bank in Africa." China Environmental Forum, March 22, 2007. Woodrow Wilson Center for Scholars, www.wilsoncenter.org. Retrieved May 19, 2009.

Ezekwesili, O. K., "World Bank: China Helps Africa Grow." *www.nowpublic.com/ world/world-bank-china-helps-africa-grow* Retrieved July 11, 2008,

GebreEgziabher, T., "The Developmental Impact of China and India on Ethiopia with Emphasis on Small Scale Footwear Producers." Development Policy Research Unit, Johannesburg, South Africa, October 18-20, 2006.

Gelb, S., "South-South Investment: The Case of Africa." Africa in the World Ecnomy- The National, Regional and International Challenges. December, 2005.

Gill, B., et al., "Assessing China's Growing Influence in Africa." *China Security*, Vol. 3 (3), 2007, 3-21.

Gu, J., and Humphrey, J., "The Impact of Africa on China." African Economic Research Consortium Working Paper No. ADWP-05. 2007. *www.jcer.or.jp/eng/research / assia.html* Retrieved October 31, 2008.

Habib, A., "Seeing the New African Scramble for what it really is: Reflections on the United States and China." *Centre for Chinese Studies (CCS)*, Stellenbosch University, South Africa, 2008.

Hamrin, C. L., "*Domestic Components and China's Evolving Three World Theory.*" Auburn House Publishing Company, Dover, MA, 1986.

Hanson, S., "China, Africa, and Oil." Council on Foreign Relations. June 6, 2006. www.cfr.org/publication/9557/. Retrieved July 12, 2008,

Harris, L. C. and Worden, Robert L., *China and the Third World: Champion and Challenger?* Auburn House Publishing Company, Dover, MA. 1986.

Holslag, J., "China's New Mercantilism in Central Africa." *African and Asian Studies,* Vol. 5 (2), 2006. 15-16.

JETRO. "Africapractice: The Impact of the Chinese Presence in Africa". Isaac Idun-Arkhurst and James Laing (eds). *Africapractice*, London, 2007.

Jian-Ye, W., "What Drives China's Growing Role in Africa?" International Monetary Fund Working Paper, 07/211. Washington D.C., 2007.

Kennan, J., and Stevens, C., *Opening the Package: The Asian Drivers and Poor-Country Trade*. Sussex University: Institute of Development Studies, 2005.

Lake, A. and Whitman, C. T., "More Than Humanitarianism: A Strategic U.S. Approach Toward Africa." New York: Council of Foreign Relations Independent Task Force Report No. 56, 2006.

Large, D. "Beyond Dragon in the Bush: The Study of Chin-Africa Relations." *African Affairs*, 107/426, 2008, 45-61.

Le Pere, G., "Prospects for a Coherent African Policy Response: Engaging China." New Impulses from the South: China's Engagement of Africa. Hannah Edinger, et al., [eds.], *Centre for Chinese Studies (CCS)*, Stellenbosch University, South Africa, 2008, 14.

Looney, R., *New International Economic Order*, 1999. http://web.nps.navy.mil/~relooney/routledge_15b.htm. Retrieved October 10, 2008.

Lumumba-Kasongo, T., "China-Africa Relations in the Post-Cold War Era: Dialectics of Rethinking South-South Dialogue." CODESRIA Bulletin, No. 1 & 2, 2007, 8-16.

Muekalia, D. J.,. "Africa and China's Strategic Partnership." *African Security Review*, 13, No.1:5-1, 2004.

Naidu, S., "Introduction." Africa Day Conference: New Impulses from the South: China's Engagement with Africa. *Centre for Chinese Studies (CCS)*, Stellenbosch University, South Africa, 2008..

Ohiorhenuan, J. F. E. and Rathe, A.. "The History & Urgency of South-South Cooperation in Science & Technology." Cooperation South, No 1, 2000.

Okonjo-Iweala, N., "Viewpoint: China Becomes Africa's Suitor." October 24, 2006. *http://news.bbc.co.uk/2/hi/business/6079838.stm*. Retrieved July 12, 2008.

Rocha, J. "China and African Natural Resources: Developmental Opportunity or Deepening the Resource Curse?" *Centre for Chinese Studies (CCS*), Stellenbosch University, South Africa, 2008.

Sebastian, S. "China–Africa Investments: An Analysis of China's Investments in Africa." CHINAVES, 2. September 17, 2008.

UNESCO "Note on South-South Cooperation." United Nations Educational, Scientific and Cultural Organization, ED/EFA?2006/ME/7. June, 2006.

United Nations, UNDP. "*Asian Foreign Direct Investment in Africa: Towards a New Era of Cooperation Among Developing Countries*". United Nations, New York, 2007.

Worden, R.L., "International Organization: China's Third World Policy in Practice." *China and the Third World :Champion and Challenger?* Auburn House Publishing Company, Dover, MA, 1986.

World Economic Forum, Africa Competitiveness Report, 2007. World Bank, Washington, *www.weforum.org/africacompetritiveness.* Retrieved on May 19, 2009, from

Zhaoxi, L., "China's Outward Foreign Direct Investment." *Chinese Multinationals,* Jean-Paul Larcon [ed], Singapore: World Scientific Publishing, Co. Pte. Ltd., 49. 2009.

Chapter 10

Alves, A. (2008). "China's Preferential Trade Policy as a Foreign Policy Tool." A publication of the Centre for Chinese Studies (CCS). Chinese Studies at Stellenbosch University, South Africa.

Antkiewicz, A. and Whalley, J. (2006). "Recent Chinese Buyout Activities and the Implications for Global Architecture." National Bureau of Economic Research (NBER). Working Paper 12072, NBER, Cambridge, MA.

Bosshard, P. (2008). "China's Environmental Footprints in Africa." China in Africa Policy. China in Africa Project of the SA Institute of International Affairs (SAIIA), No. 3, April 2008.

Chau, Donovan C. (March 2007). Political Warfare in Sub-Saharan Africa: U.S. Capabilities and Chinese Operations in Ethiopia, Kenya, Nigeria, and South Africa.

Committee of Ethiopian Eastern Industrial Zone, (2009). The Ethiopian Eastern Industrial Zone Project Supplementary Document to the Ministry of Trade and Industry, prepared and submitted by the Ethiopian Eastern Industrial Zone.

Desta, A. (1993). *International Political Risk Assessment for Foreign Direct Investment and International Lending Decisions.* Needham Height, MA: Ginn Press, 1993.

Desta, A. (1998). *Environmentally Sustainable Economic Development.* Westport, Connecticut: Praeger, 1998.

Donghong, L. (2009). "Innovation & Knowledge Transfer in Chinese Multinationals." *Chinese Multinationals.* Jean-Paul Larcon [ed], New Jersey: World Scientific, 163.

Elmawazini, K., Saadi, S., and Ngouhouo, I. (2005). "Does FDI Imply Productivity Growth for the Host Economy?" Journal of American Academy of Business, Vol. 6, Issue 2.

Fan, Emma Xiaoqin (December 2002). "Technological Spillovers from Foreign Direct Investment: A Survey." Asian Development Bank, ERD Working Paper Series, No. 33, 1.

Gebeyehu, Worku (2004). "FDI in Ethiopia: Size, Nature and Performance." Ethiopian Economic Policy Research Institute, Working Paper No. 2/2004.

GebreEgziabher, T. "The Developmental Impact of China and India on Ethiopia with Emphasis on Small Scale Footwear Producers." Development Policy Research Unit, Johannesburg, South Africa (October 18-20, 2006).

Habib, A. (2008). "Seeing the New African Scramble for what it really is: Reflections on the United States and China." A publication of the Centre for Chinese Studies (CCS), Chinese Studies at Stellenbosch University, South Africa.

Hamrin, C. L. (1986). *Domestic Components and China's Evolving Three World Theory.* Dover, MA: Auburn House Publishing Company.

Holslag, J. (2006). "China's New Mercantilism in Central Africa." African and Asian Studies, Vol. 5, No. 2, 15-16.

Japan Bank for International Cooperation (June 2002). "Foreign Direct Investment and Development: Where Do We Stand?" JBICI Research Paper No. 15.

Lake, A. and Whitman, C. T. (2006). "More Than Humanitarianism: A Strategic U.S. Approach Toward Africa." New York: Council of Foreign Relations Independent Task Force Report No. 56.

Large, D. (2008). "Beyond Dragon in the Bush: The Study of China-Africa Relations." African Affairs, 107/426, 45-61.

Leggett, K. (March 29, 2005). China's Influence in Ethiopia. Retrieved August 1, 2008, from http://www.nazret.com/blog/index

Lumumba-Kasongo, T. (2007). "China-Africa Relations in the Post-Cold War Era: Dialectics of Rethinking South-South Dialogue." CODESRIA Bulletin, No. 1 & 2, 8-16.

Mesfin, M. "China, Africa Stand on Firm Foundation of Trust." Nazret. Retrieved August 1, 2008, from http://www.nazret.com/blog/index.php?title=ethiopia_f_m_seyoum_mesfin_china_africa&more

Mo, P. "Addis Ababa Ring Road Project: A Case Study of a Chinese Construction Project in Ethiopia." Chinese Contractors in Africa: Insights from a Survey. Shanghai, 16 May 2007.

Naidu, S. (2008). "Introduction." Africa Day Conference: New Impulses from the South: China's Engagement with Africa. Centre for Chinese Studies, University of Stellenbosch.

Rhee, Y. W. and Belot, T. (1990). "Export Catalysts in Low-income Countries." World Bank Discussion Papers, 72, Washington, D.C.: World Bank.

Rongping, K. (2009). "The Internationalization Process of Chinese Multinationals." *Chinese Multinationals*, Jean-Paul Larcon [ed], Singapore: World Scientific Publishing, Co. Pte. Ltd.

Tamene, B. (March 19, 2008). "Ethiopia: Country, China to Construct First Private Industrial Zone." Retrieved April 29, 2009, from http://allafrica.com/stories/200803190827.html

Waltainfo.com, 2009

Warner, M., Hong, N. S. and Xu, X. (2004). "Late Development Experience and the Evolution of Transnational Firms in the People's Republic of China." Asia Pacific Business Review, (10(e/4).

Waterpower Magazine. (May 11, 2009). "Hydro Power in Ethiopia—the Staged Construction of Takeze Arch Dam. Retrieved May 11, 2009, from http://www.waterpowermagazine.com/story.asp?sectioncode=46&storyCode=2052913

World Economic Forum (2007). Africa Competitiveness Report 2007. Washington: World Bank. Retrieved on May 19, 2009, from http://www.weforum.org/africa-competritiveness

Xiaojie, G. (August 19, 2008). "China Never Imposes its Will on Ethiopia by the Way of its Assistance." Walta Information Center. Retrieved April 6, 2009, from http://www.waltainf.com

Xinhua News Agency (November 11, 2008). "China Offers Three-point Proposal to Boost Ties with Ethiopia." Retrieved November 11, 2008, from http://english.sina.com/china/2008/1111/197776.html

Zenawi, M. (October 17, 2006). "Ethiopia Calls for New Africa Chinese Strategic Partnership." in CHINAGATE. Retrieved November 12, 2008, from http://en.chinagate.com.cn/english/wb/49017.htm

Zhaoxi, L. (2009). "China's Outward Foreign Direct Investment." *Chinese Multinationals*, Jean-Paul Larcon [ed], Singapore: World Scientific Publishing, Co. Pte. Ltd., 49.

Chapter 11

AfDB/OECD (2007). African economic outlook: Ethiopia.

Barro, Robert (1996, May/June). Inflation and growth. Federal Reserve Bank of Saint Louis Review.

Canzoneri, M. M., Cumby, R., & Dibba, B. (1998). Is price level determined by the needs of fiscal solvency? CEPR Discussion Papers, No. 1772.

Demissie, M. (2008, January 19). IMF's assessment on the Ethiopian economic growth. The Ethiopian Reporter. Retrieved April 8, 2008, from http:/www.theafricmonitor.com/news/ethiopian/april2008/030408/wpf.htm

Desta, A. (1993). International political risk assessment for foreign direct investment and international lending decisions. Needham Heights, MA: Ginn Press.

Desta, A. (1998). Environmentally sustainable economic development. Westport, Connecticut.

Desta, A. & Kofi, T. (2008). The saga of African underdevelopment: A viable approach for Africa's sustainable development in the 21st century. Trenton, NJ: Africa World Press.

Edwards, S. (n.d.). Greening Ethiopia for self-sufficiency. Institute of Science in Society. Retrieved June 23, 2004, from http://www.i-sis.org.uk/GreeningEthiopia.php

ESSGA (2006, November). Food and agriculture indicators: Country Ethiopia.

Friedman, M. (1959). A program for monetary stability. New York: Fordham University Press.

Gebremedhin, H. E. (2007). Constraints and opportunities of horticulture production and marketing in eastern Ethiopia. Drylands Coordination Group (DCG), Norway.

Girma, B. (2008). World food program lauds government measures to stabilize grain market.

Goodo, S. (n.d.). Ethiopia: Soaring inflation deepens economic crisis. Retrieved April 9, 2008, from ***http://www.americanchronicle.com/articles?55196***

Hassan, S. "The causes of the current Ethiopian soaring inflation rate". Sudan Tribune Retrieved May 22, 2008, from

http://www.sudantribune.com/spip.php?article 27050

Hossain A. & Chowdhurry A. (1996), Monetary and financial policies in developing countries. London: Routledge.

International Monetary Fund, "IMF urges 'forceful' policy tightening in Ethiopia." Retrieved July 24, 2008 from ***http://nazret.com/blog/index.php***

Johnson, H. G. (1966, April). Is inflation the inevitable price of rapid development or a retarding factor in economic growth? Malayan Economic Review, Vol. 11, No. 1.

Jung, S. W. & Marshall, J. P. (1996). Inflation and economic growth: Some international evidence on structural and distortionist positions. Journal of Money, Credit, and Banking, Vol. 18, No. 2.

Kassahun, R. (2002, August). Structural adjustment and macroeconomic reforms in Ethiopia.

Meier, G. M. (1995). Leading issues in economic development (6th ed.). New York: Oxford University Press.

Tadesse, T. (n.d.). Ethiopia keeps 10.8% GDP growth forecast for 2008. Retrieved May 15, 2008, from http://Africa.reuters.com/business/news/usnBAN5321131.html

Teshome, A. (2008, May 14). Response to Dr. Said Hassan: On the cause of the current soaring inflation rate. Retrieved May 29, 2008, from http://www.waltainfo.com/Analysis/2008/May/41111.htm

USAID (2005). Global Horticulture Assessment. California: University of California, Davis.

Worku, Z. (2008). Is sustainable food security possible in Ethiopia? Retrieved April 9, 2008, from http://www.etiopians.com/foodsecurity/Zemrdeworku_foodsecurity.htm

Chapter 12

Adedeji, A. (1985). "The Monrovia Strategy and the Lagos Plan of Action: Five Years After." In *Economic Crisis in Africa: African Perspectives and Development Problems and Potentials. Boulder: Lynne Rienner Publishers, 15.*

Berry, S. (1995). "Economic Change in Contemporary Africa, " in *Africa,* 3rd ed. P.M. Martin and P. O' Meara, eds. Bloomington: Indiana University Press, 363.

Deng, L. A. (1998). *Rethinking African Development.* Trenton, NJ: African World Press, Pp. 44-45.

Edigheji, O. (May 2005). " A Democratic Developmental State in Africa: A Concept Paper.?" *Research Report 105.* Centre for Policy Studies, Johannesburg. South Africa.

Economic Commission for Africa (2011), *Economic Report on Africa 201: Governing development in Africa – the role of the state in economic transformation, Addis Ababa, Ethiopia.*

Fingleton, E. (1996). Blindside: Why Japan is Still on Track to Overtake the U.S, by the year 2000. New York: Buttonwood.

Hyun –chin L and Jin-Ho, J. (June 2006). "Between Neo liberalism and Democracy: The Transformation of the Developmental State in South Korea". *Development and Society. Vol. 35, No. 1, pp. 1-28*

Johnson, C. (1982). *MITI and the Japanese Miracle: The Growth of Industrial Policy, 1982-1975.* Stanford,: Stanford University Press.

Kofi, T. and Desta, A. (2008). *The Saga of African Underdevelopment: A viable Approach for Africa's Sustainable Development in the 21st Century.* Trenton, N.J: Africa World Press.

Laakso, L. & Olukoshi, A. O. 1996). " The crisis of the Post-Colonial Nation-State Project in Africa," Challenges to the Nation-State in Africa. Uppsala: The Nordic Africa institute.

Maphunye, K. (April 2009). "Public Administration for a Democratic Developmental State in Africa: Prospects and Possibilities." *Research Report 114.* Centre for Policy Studies, Johannesburg, South Africa.

Meles, Z. (2006). "Africa's Development: Dead Ends and New Beginnings." Cited in http://cgt.columbia.edu/files/conference/Zenawi-Dead Ends and New Beginnings.pdf. Retrieved, June, 2012.

Mohamad, M. (1994). Speech by Mohamad at Rethinking Human Rights, December 5, 1994. Cited in Lee H. P., Constitutional Values in a Turbulent Asia, 14th LAW ASIA Biennial Conference, August 16-20, 1995, Beijing.

Pang, E. (December 2000). "The Financial Crisis of 1997-98 and the End of the Asian Developmental State." *Contemporary Southeast Asia*. 22, 3, pp. 570-593.

Teshome, A. (May 2012). "Meles' Development Paradigm and its Impact on Economic Transformation in Ethiopia."

World Bank, (2009). World Development Report. Retrieved from www.worldbank.org/wdr.

Zalanga, S. (2011). " Ruling Elite coalition and State Bureaucratic capacity: Accounting for Developmental and Predatory State in Malaysia and Nigeria."

Chapter 13

Adedeji, A. (1985). "The Monrovia Strategy and the Lagos Plan of Action: Five Years After." In *Economic Crisis in Africa: African Perspectives and Development Problems and Potentials. Boulder: Lynne Rienner Publishers, 15.*

Ahmad Sarji bin Abdul Hmid, (1994). *The Civil Service of Malaysia: A paradigm Shift.* Kula Lumpur: Percetakan Nasional Malaysia Berhad.

BBC News Africa (May 25, 2010). "EU observers say Ethiopia election 'falls short'.

Berry, S. (1995). "Economic Change in Contemporary Africa, " in *Africa,* 3rd ed. P.M. Martin and P. O' Meara, eds. Bloomington: Indiana University Press, 363.

Bolesta, A. (June 27, 2007). "China as a Developmental State." Preliminary Communications.

Castellis, M. (2000). *End of Millennium* (2nd Edition). Oxford: Blackwell.

Dadize, Richard, B. (2012). "Developmental State and Economic Development: Prospects for Sub-Saharan Africa." *Journal of Sustainable Development.* 5.9: 14-26.

Deng, L. A. (1998). *Rethinking African Development.* Trenton, NJ: African World Press, Pp. 44-45.

Desta,A. (Jan 4,2010). "Industrialization by Invitation: Will it Work in Ethiopia" http://farmlandgrap.org.

Desta, A. (2012). "Centrally Planned or Developmental-Oriented State: A review of the Ethiopian Economic System." *Journal of Academy of Business and Economics (JABE).* Vol. 12, Number 2, 2012.

Desta, A. (2012). "The Effects of Rent-Seeking in Dissipating Developmental Efforts: The Ethiopian Experience." *International Journal of Business and Management Tomorrow.* Vol. 2, No. 1.

Desta, A. (July 7, 2011). " Employer as the Last Resort (ELR)-Led Environmentally Sustainable Development for Full employment in Rural and Urban Ethiopia: A Working Paper."

Edigheji, O. (May 2005). " A Democratic Developmental State in Africa: A Concept Paper.?" *Research Report 105.* Centre for Policy Studies, Johannesburg. South Africa.

Economic Commission for Africa (2011), *Economic Report on Africa 201: Governing development in Africa – the role of the state in economic transformation, Addis Ababa, Ethiopia.*

Evans, P. (1994). "Predatory, Developmental and other Apparatus: A Comparative Political Economy Perspective on Third World State in " Comparative National Development, edited by Douglas Kincaid and Alejandro Portes. Chapel Hill,: University of North Carolina, pp. 84-111.

Evans, p. (1995). *Embedded Autonomy: State and Industrial Transformation.* Princeton: Princeton University Press.

Ezema. B. and Ogujiuba K. (2012). The Development State Debate: Where is Nigeria? *Journal of Sustainable Development,* 5, (1) 100-113.

Fingleton, E. (1996). Blindside: Why Japan is Still on Track to Overtake the U.S, by the year 2000. New York: Buttonwood.

Fischer, P. (2010). *Rent-Seeking, Institutions, and Reforms in Africa: Theory and Empirical Evidence for Tanzania.* Springer: Zurich, Switzerland: NADEL ETH.

Hyun –chin L and Jin-Ho, J. (June 2006). "Between Neo liberalism and Democracy: The Transformation of the Developmental State in South Korea". *Development and Society. Vol. 35, No. 1, pp. 1-28*

Johnson, C. (1982). MITI and the Japanese Miracle: The Growth of Industrial Policy, 1982-1975. Stanford,: Stanford University Press.

Kaufmann, D. (1998. "Corruption in Transition Economics." Peter Newman (ed) : The new Palgrave. Dictionary of Economics and the Law, Vol. 1, pp. 522-30.

Khoo, Su-ming (Dec. 9-11, 2007). " A Tale of Two Tigers? Growth, public policy and regional models in Ireland and Malaysia." Annual Conference on Development and Change Mission: Promoting Development in a Globalized World. Cape Town, South Africa.

Kofi, T. and Desta, A. (2008). The Saga of African Underdevelopment: A viable Approach for Africa's Sustainable Development in the 21st Century. Trenton, N.J: Africa World Press.

Kunama, *G.(May 12, 2011). "Ethiopia Heads towards Building A Green Economy".*

Laakso, L. & Olukoshi, A. O. 1996). " The crisis of the Post-Colonial Nation-State Project in Africa," Challenges to the Nation-State in Africa. Uppsala: The Nordic Africa institute.

Leftwich, A. (Feb. 1995). "Bringing Politics back in: Towards a model of the developmental state " The Journal of Development studies. 31.3.

Maphunye, K. (April 2009). "Public Administration for a Democratic Developmental State in Africa: Prospects and Possibilities." Research Report 114. Centre for Policy Studies, Johannesburg, South Africa.

Marsha, G. (August 12, 2009). "Experts worry about negative consequences: International Agricultural Land Deals Award Ethiopian Virgin Lands of foreign Companies," Retrieved December 15, 2009 from www.ethiomedia.com.

Mohamad, M. (1994). Speech by Mohamad at Rethinking Human Rights, December 5, 1994. Cited in Lee H. P., Constitutional Values in a Turbulent Asia, 14th LAW ASIA Biennial Conference, August 16-20, 1995, Beijing.

New Strait Times, Malaysia (July 16, 1982).

Meles, Z. (2006). "Africa's Development: Dead Ends and New Beginnings." Cited in http://cgt.columbia.edu/files/conference/Zenawi-Dead Ends and New Beginnings.pdf. Retrieved, June, 2012.

Nordlinger, E.A. (1987). "Taking the State Seriously". In M. Weiner and S.P. Huntington (eds.), *Understanding Political Development,* Boston, Ma: Little Brown Co.

Ohashi, K.(June 9, 2011). "Is Ethiopia's five Year economic Plan based on Voodoo Economics?" *Nazret.com, (6/9/2011).* http://nazret.com/blog/index.php/

Pang, E. (December 2000). "The Financial Crisis of 1997-98 and the End of the Asian Developmental State." *Contemporary Southeast Asia.* 22, 3, Pp. 570-593.

Raquib, Md Abdur (Jan 2010). " Empowerment Practices and performances in Malyasia – An Empirical Study." *International Journal of Business and management.* 5.1, Pp. 123-149.

Schutter, O. and Vanioqueren, G. (Aug. 2011). " *The New Green Revolution: How Twenty-First Century Science can Feed The World." Solutions for a Sustainable and Desirable future.* Vol. 2, Issue. 4.

Shah, R. (2013). "Ethiopia's Major Maternal Health Partners". Washington, D.C: U.S. Agency for International Development (USAID).

Tegenu, T.(June 6, 2011). "Speeding up Industrialization In Ethiopia: What works and what does not"

Teshome, A. (May 2012). "Meles' Development Paradigm and its Impact on Economic Transformation in Ethiopia."

Tolina, T.E. (October 2007). " Agricultural Development Led Industrialization (ADLI) Strategy of Ethiopia".

Wade, R. (1989). "What can economics learn from East Asian success?" *The Annals of the American Academy of Political and Social Science.* 505: 77-8.

World Bank, (1993). *The World Debt Tables, 1980-1993.*

World Bank, (2012). "School Enrollment: Primary; Private (of the total primary) in Ethiopia. Cited in http://www.radingeconomics.com, Ethiopia/school-enrollment

World Bank, (2009). *World Development Report.* Retrieved from www.worldbank.org/wdr.

Zalanga, S. (2011). " Ruling Elite coalition and State Bureaucratic capacity: Accounting for Developmental and Predatory State in Malaysia and Nigeria."

Chapter 14

Abe.M. (2006). "Research Note: The Developmental State and Educational Advance in East Asia." *Educate.* Vol 6, No. 1, 2006, pp 6-12.

Akosah-Sarpong, K. (October 2, 2011). "Democracy or Prosperity, Which Comes First ." http://www.ghanaweb.com/. Cited, May 24, 2012.

BBC News Africa (May 25, 2010). "EU observers say Ethiopia election 'falls short'.

Becker, A. (1993). "Full Employment Without Inflation". http://www.coopperativeindividualism'org/ Retrieved May, 9, 2011.

Becker, A. (1993). "Full Employment Without Inflation" http://www.cooperativeindividualism.org/becker-full_employment.html. Retrieved May 9, 2011.

Baiman, R. (Winter, 2006). Unequal exchange without a labor theory of prices: On the need for global Marshall Plan and a solidarity trading regime. *Review of Radical Political Economics.* 38, pp.71-89.

Belaineh, G. May, 2009). "Environment and Economic Development in Ethiopia." http://*Nazret.com/ blog/index.php/2009/05/27.*

Bhaduri Anik (2005), 'Political altruism of Transboundary water sharing' in PhD, Dissertation , Transboundary water sharing between an upstream and downstream country University of Wyoming August 2005.

Bolesta, A. (June 27, 2007). "China as a Developmental State". Preliminary Communications."

CIA World Factbook, The Library of Congress Country Studies (1991). "Ethiopia Unemployment". http://www.photius.com/countries/ethiopia/economy/economy/ethiopia_economy_unemployment.html. *Retrieved, June 18, 2011.*

CIAWorldFactbook,2011.*Populationbelowpovertyline(%)2011CountryRanks,ByRank* http://www.photius.com/rankings/economy/population_below_poverty_line_2011_0.html. Retrieved June 18, 2011.

Castells, M. (2000). *End of Millennium (2nd Edition).* Oxford: Blackwell.

Davison, W. (May 31, 2011). "Ethiopian Economy May Expand 7.5% This Fiscal Year, Slow in 2012, IMF Says." http://www.bloomberg.com/news/2011-05-31/ethiopian -economy-ma.. Retrieved , May, 31, 2011.

Desta, A. (2009). Economic Growth for Inflation: The Ethiopian Dilemma. *International Journal of Global Business and Economics,* 2(1).

Desta, A. (Jan. 4, 2010). "Industrialization by Invitation: Will it work in Ethiopia." http://farmlandgrap.org.

Desta, A. (July 7, 2011). " Employer as the Last Resort (ELR)-Led Environmentally Sustainable Development for Full employment in Rural and Urban Ethiopia: A Working Paper."

Economic Commission for Africa (2005), *Economic Report on Africa 2005: Meeting the Challenges of Unemployment and Poverty in Africa,* Addis Ababa.Ethiopia.

Economic Commission for Africa (2011), *Economic Report on Africa 201: Governing development in Africa – the role of the state in economic transformation, Addis Ababa, Ethiopia.*

Falchhamps, M. (1989). "Microeconomic Theory: Lecture 8, Imperfect Competition and Rent Seeking" in Hal Varian (ed) *Intermediate Microeconomics: A Modern Approach. Berkeley: University of California.*

Edigheji, O. (May 2005). A Democratic Developmental State in Africa: A concept Paper. Centre for Policy Studies, Research Report 105.

Fischer, P. (2010). *Rent-Seeking, Institutions, and Reforms in Africa: Theory and Empirical Evidence for Tanzania.* Springer: Zurich, Switzerland: NADEL ETH.

Fischer. A. (April 7th , 2010). *What is Food Democracy ?Food FirstInstitute.*

Ethiopia, Central Statistical Agency, (2011). Ethiopia: Food prices pushes inflation to nearly 30 percent. http://africa.ibtimes.com/articles/143517/20110510/ Retrieved, May, 23, 2011.

Gada. A.com (2012). "The Oromo Chronology, The Ethiopian Revolution and the Derg Regime." Cited in http://www.gadaa.com/DERG.tml. Decemb 27, 2012.

Getachew, D. (2010). "Peasant Reflections on the Agricultural Development Led Industrialization (ADLI) Programmme." Department of Sociology and Anthropology, Addis Ababa, University).

Habisso, T. (2010). "The Challenges of Implanting and Building Multi_Party Democracy in Multi-Ethnic Socities" http://aigaforum.com/articles/. Retrieved February 13, 2010.

Hassan, A. (Sep. 13, 2010). "The Growth and Transformation Plan: A long time Coming!" http://www.waltainfo.com/index.php? Retrieved, June, 23, 2011.

Hassan. S. ((2011). The Cause of the Current Ethiopian Soaring Inflation Rate: A Non-Technical Analysis. http://www.sudantribunecom/ Retrieved, May, 23, 2011.

Huntington, S. 1991. The third Wave: Democratization in the late Twentieth Century. Norman and London: University of Oklahoma Press.

International Labour Organization,(2006). *Integrated Labour Inspection Training system (ILITI).*

IRIN (2013). "Tackling Ethiopia's Maternal Deaths". http://nazret.com.

Johnson, C. (1982). *MITI and The Japanese Miracle: The Growth of Industry Policy, 1925-1975.* California: Stanford University Press.

Kaboub, F. (Summer 2008). "Elements of a Radical Counter-movement to Neo-liberalism: Employment-led Development." *Review of Radical Political Economics,* Vol. 40. No. 3. pp220-227.

Kaboub, F. (June 2007). *Institutional adjustment planning for full employment. Journal of Economics Issues* 41, 495-502.

Kaboub, F. (May 2007). ELR-led economic development: A plan for Tunisia. Working Paper 499. Annandale-on-Hudson, NY, The Jerome Levy Economic Institute.

Kalecki , M. (1943). *"Political aspects of full employment." Political Quarterly* 14 (4), 322-331.

Kaufmann, D. (1998. "Corruption in Transition Economics." Peter Newman (ed) : The new Palgrave. Dictionary of Economics and the Law, Vol. 1, pp. 522-30.

Kofi T. and Desta A. (2008) The Saga of African Underdevelopment: a Viable Approach for Africa's Sustainable Development in the 21st Century. Trenton, NJ: Africa World Press.

Kornai, J. (July 1979). "Resource-Constrained Versus Demand-constrained Systems. *Econometrica.* Vol. 47, No. 4, Iss.4, pp. 801-18.

Kregel, J. A. (1991). Is Keynesian full employment policy for 'for countries' only? In *The art of full employment : Unemployment policy in open countries,* ed. C. de Neubourg, Amsterdam: North-Holland.

Kregel, J. A. (summer 2004). Can we create a stable international financial environment that ensures net resource transfer to developing countries? *Journal of Post Keynesian Economics.* 26, pp. 573-590.

Kunama, G. (May 12, 2011*).* "Ethiopia Heads towards Building a Green Economy".

Krueger, A. (June 1974). "*The Political Economy of the Rent-Seeking Society.* " *American Economic Review.* Vol. 64, No. 3, pp. 294-303.

Lieuw-Kie-Song, M. (April 2009). "Green jobs for he poor. "*Technical Report*", UNDP Poverty Reduction Discussion Paper PG/2009/002.

Lipset. M. (1963). *Political Man.* New York: Anchor Books.

Lipset, S. (1959). "Some Social Requisites of Democracy: Economic development and Political Legitimacy ."*American Political Science Review.*53(1) 69-105.

Marsha, G. (August 12, 2009). "Experts worry about negative consequences : International Agricultural Land Deals Award Ethiopian Virgin lands of foreign Companies." RetrievedDecember 15, 2009 from www.ethiomedia.com.

Mitchell, William F. and Watts, Martin J. (1997). " The Path to Full Employment" *Australian Economic Review* , 30(4): 433-435.

Mohamad , M. (1994). Speech by Dr. Mohamad at Rethinking Human Rights, 5 December 1994, Cited in Lee H.P., Constitutional Values in a Turulent Asia, 14th LAW ASIA Biennial Conference, August 16-20, 1995, Beijing.

Murakami, Y. (1992). *Anticlassical Political-economic Analysis.* Tokyo: Chuokoronshinsha.

Murray, j. M. (2010). An *Instrumental Approach to Full employment: With Policy Implications.* Unpublished doctoral dissertation, University of Missouri-Kansas, City.

Nazret.com (June 9, 2011). "Is Ethiopia's five year economic plan based on Voodoo Economics? http://nazret.com/blog/index.php/

Nkurunziza , J. D. (2006). "Generating Rural Employment in Africa to Fight Poverty." Paper presented at ECOSOC's High-Level Segment, New York, 9 May 2006.

Ozawa, T. (June 6, 20110. "The role of multinational in sparking industrialization: From " Infant industry protection" to FDI-led industrial Take-off." *Columbia FDI Perspectives": Perspectives on topical foreign direct investment issues by the Vale Columbia Center on Sustainable International Investment.* No. 39.

Palley, T. (2001). "*Government as Employer of Last Resort: Can it Work." Industrial Relations Research Association,* 53rd Annual Proceedings, pp. 269-274.

Prabhakar, A.C. (2010). "Political Economy of Poverty, Backwardness and Food Insecurity in Ethiopia: An Overview of Agricultural Development-Led Industrialization Strategy." Gondar, Ethiopia: University of Gondar.

Selamta, (January 27, 2013). Ethiopian Constitution.

Serneels (2004). "*The Added Worker Effect and Intrahousehold Aspects of Unemployment,*"

Schutter, O. and Vanioqueren, G. (Aug. 2011). " *The New Green Revolution: How Twenty-First Century Science can Feed The World." Solutions for a Sustainable and Desirable future.* Vol. 2, Issue. 4.

Sen, A. (October 29, 1987). "Food and Freedom". Sir John Crawford Memorial Lecture, Washington, D.C.

Siegle, J. Weinstein, M. Halperin, M. (October, 2004). "*Why* Democracies Excel". *Forein Affairs.*57-71.

Shiva, Vandana, ed. (2007) *Manifestos on the Future of Food and Seed.South End Press.*

Solvason, B. (2011). "Ordered Anarchy, State, and Rent-seeking: The Icelandic Commonwealth, 930-126. http://notendur.hi.is/bthru/kafli6.htm. Retrieved August 16, 2011.

Tegenu, T. (June 6, 2011). "speeding up Industrialization in Ethiopia: what works and what does not"

Tolina T. E. (October 2007). "Agricultural Development Led Industrialization" (ADLI) Strategy of Ethiopia.

Tullock, G. (June 1967). "*The welfare costs of Tariffs, Monopolies, and Theft" Western Economic Journal,* Vol. 5, Iss.3, pp. 224-32.

UNEP, (2011). UNEP YEAR BOOK 2011: EMERGING ISSUES IN OUR GLOBAL ENVIRONMENT.

United Nations News Centre (2006). "Full employment key to sustainable development, ministers declares at UN meeting. http;//www.un.org/apps/news/story.asp?News ID. Retrieved April 30, 2011.

United Nations, (2010). *United Nations-Gini Coefficient.* http://www.scribd.com/com. (Retrieved October 4, 2010).

Warner, K. & Kirshenmann, F (2007). *Agroecology in Action: Extending Alternative Agriculture through Social Networks.* Cambridge, MA: MIT Press.

Wary. L. R. (1997). "Government as Employer of Last Resort: Full Employment without Inflation." *Economics Working Paper Archive.* Levy Economic Institute.

Weintraub, S. (November 2003, #47) "Democracy and Development" ISSUES IN INTERNATIONAL POLITICAL ECONOMY.

Wray, L. R (August 2007). "The Employer of Last Resort Programme: Could It Work for Developing Countries?" *Economic and Labour Market Papers.* Geneva: International Labour Office, Economic and Labour Market Analysis Department.

Wray, L. R. (1997). " Government as Employer of Last Resort: Full Employment without Inflation ." *Economics Working Paper Archive.* Levy Economic Institute.

Yacob. T. (October 1, 2010). "Part 2,: Follow the debate on "Growth and Transformation Plan of Ethiopia." http://www. cop-mfdr-africa.org/. Retrieved May 12, 2011.

Yamin, K. (JAKARTA, Aug 3, 2001) "After Wahid, Many Want Food First, Democracy Later" Inter Press Service (IPS). http://www.ipsnews.net/

Index